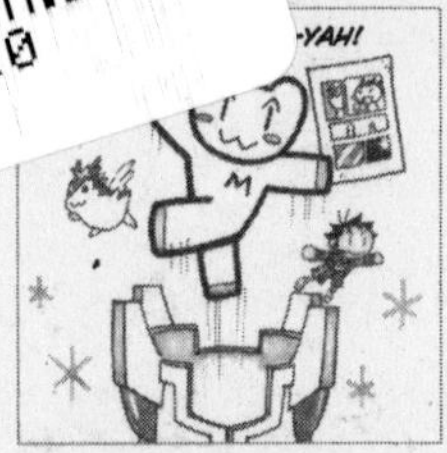
-YAH!

春野まこと

Makoto Haruno

Hello, I'm Makoto Haruno. Many strange things happen in this world and in life, and the fact that I'm drawing comics is one of them. So... Please support this comic about the legendary creatures called "Legendz"!!

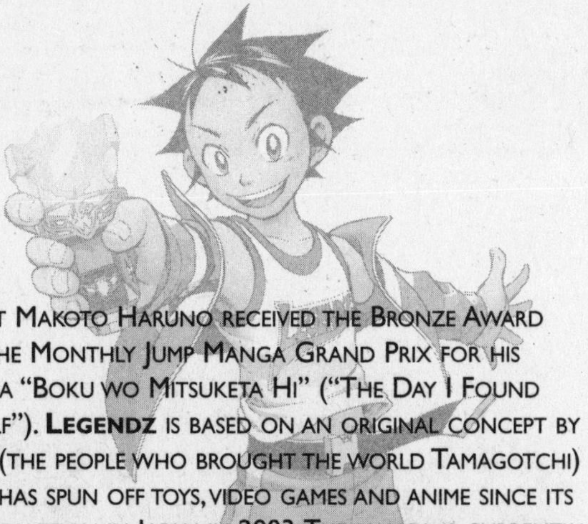

Artist Makoto Haruno received the Bronze Award for the Monthly Jump Manga Grand Prix for his manga "Boku wo Mitsuketa Hi" ("The Day I Found Myself"). **Legendz** is based on an original concept by WiZ (the people who brought the world Tamagotchi) that has spun off toys, video games and anime since its introduction in Japan in 2003. The manga is currently serialized in Japan's **Monthly Shonen Jump.**

LEGENDZ VOL. 2
The SHONEN JUMP Graphic Novel Edition

ART BY MAKOTO HARUNO
STORY BY RIN HIRAI

English Adaptation/Shaenon K. Garrity
Translation/Akira Watanabe
Touch-up Art & Lettering/Mark Griffin
Cover Design & Graphics/Sean Lee
Editor/Yuki Takagaki

Managing Editor/Elizabeth Kawasaki
Director of Production/Noboru Watanabe
Vice President of Publishing/Alvin Lu
Executive Vice President & Editor in Chief/ Yumi Hoashi
Sr. Director of Acquisitions/Rika Inouye
Vice President of Sales & Marketing/Liza Coppola
Publisher/Hyoe Narita

Printed in the U.S.A.

Published by VIZ, LLC
P.O. Box 77010
San Francisco, CA 94107

SHONEN JUMP Graphic Novel Edition
10 9 8 7 6 5 4 3 2 1
First printing, May 2005

LEGENDZ™

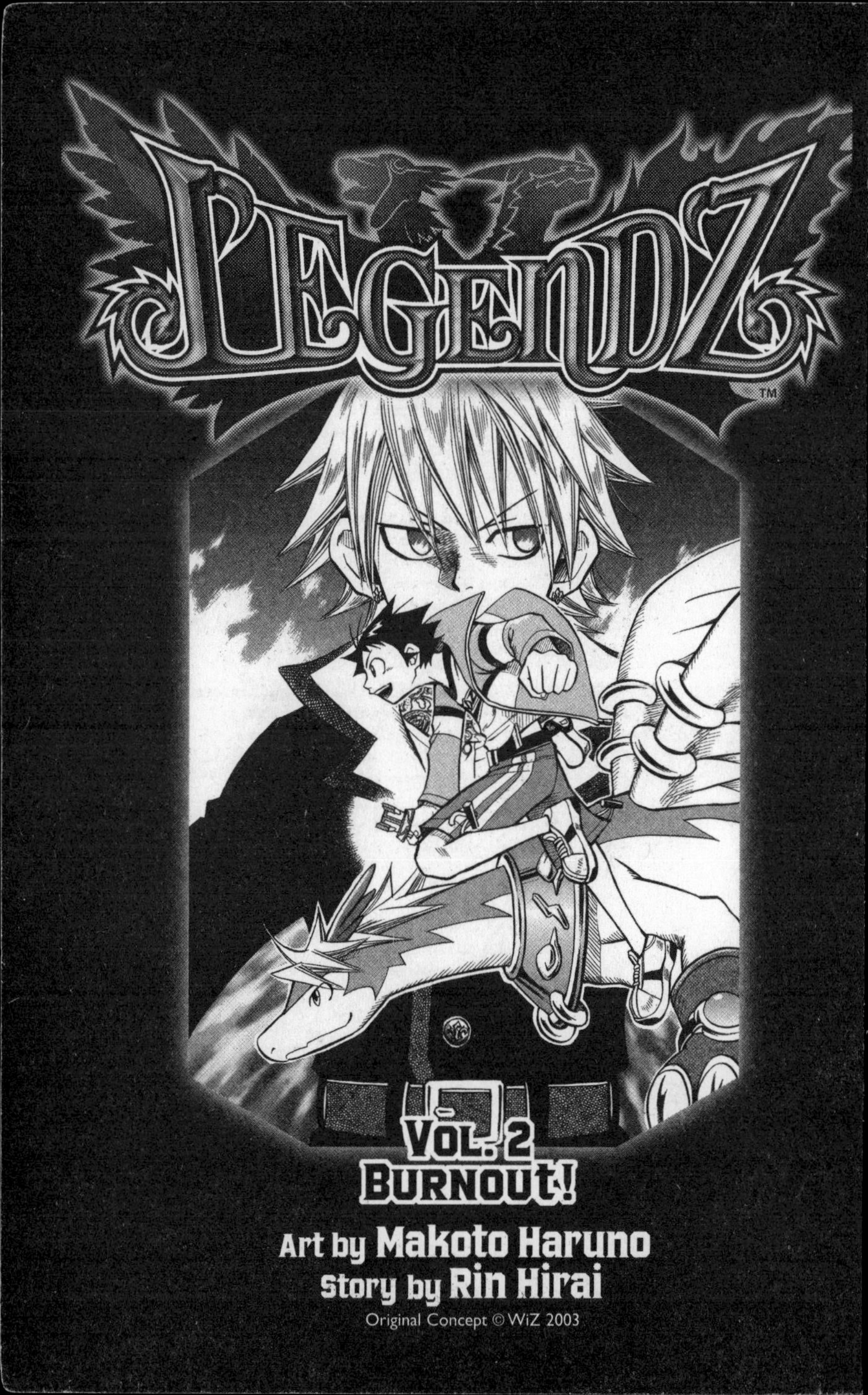

VOL. 2
BURNOUT!

Art by **Makoto Haruno**
Story by **Rin Hirai**

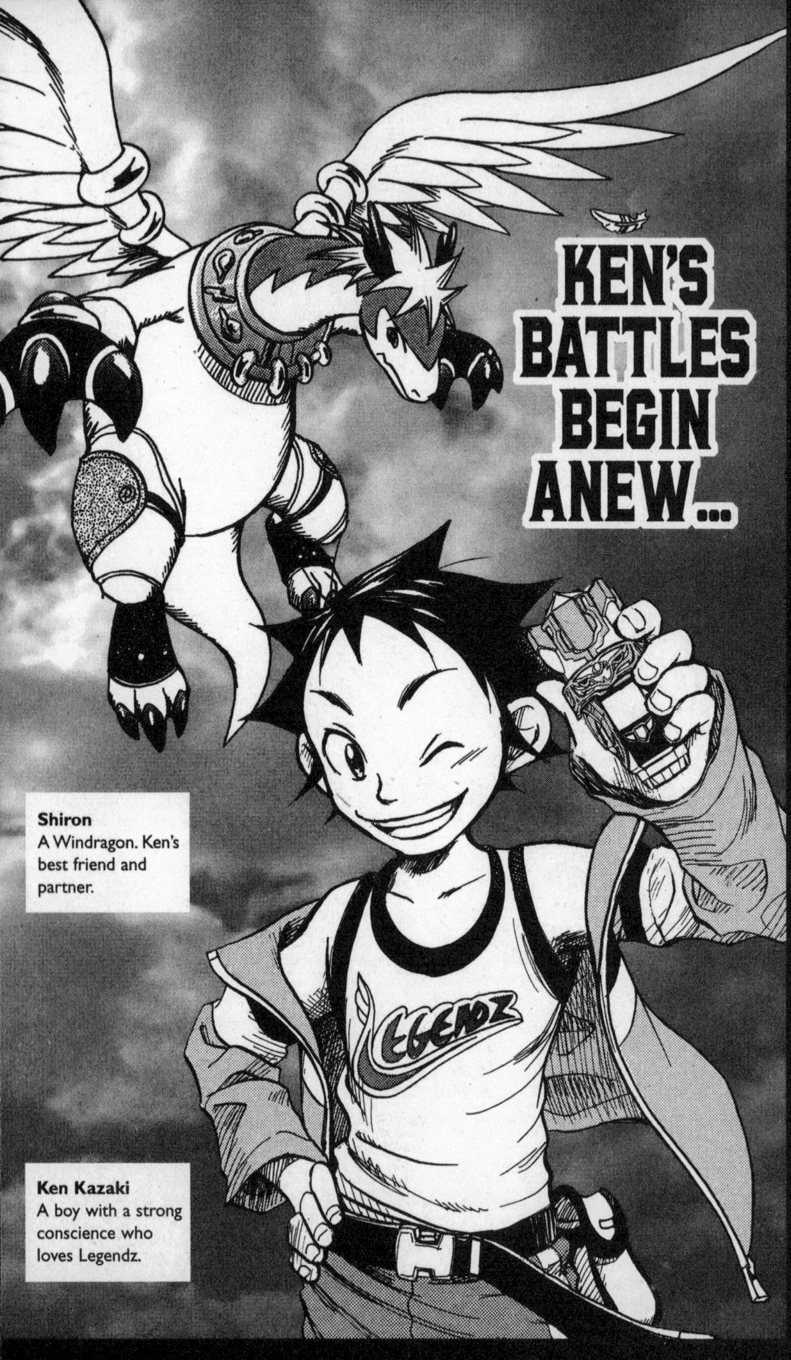
KEN'S BATTLES BEGIN ANEW...
LEGENDZ
Shiron
A Windragon. Ken's best friend and partner.
Ken Kazaki
A boy with a strong conscience who loves Legendz.

LEGENDZ 2

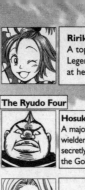

The Story Thus Far

"Legendz" is a computerized game in which legendary monsters are reborn and raised for battle. Ken Kazaki, whose best friend is his Legendz, a Windragon named Shiron, loves the game. On his first day at Ryudo Elementary, Ken proves his ability by beating Hosuke Dekai, a member of the skilled Ryudo Four. Ken soon finds himself caught in a series of heated Legendz battles.

At Ryudo, the Golden Soul Figure holding an unknown Legendz is the symbol of the school's Legendz champion. Right now, it belongs to Yuki Amagi, leader of the Ryudo Four. To find the rightful heir to the Golden Soul Figure, the Ryudo Four organize a school-wide Legendz tournament. Against great odds, Ken manages a stunning victory thanks to his close bond with Shiron. While watching the battles, Yuki decides that Ken is the one to receive the Golden Soul Figure. But Ken has no intention of raising any Legendz other than Shiron. He explains that he learned from Eiji Yashiro, the winner of a past Legendz Carnival, that the secret to being good at Legendz is caring for one's own Legendz and growing stronger along with it. In the midst of this discussion, Ken's friend Ririko is kidnapped by students of rival Kokuryu Elementary who are after the Golden Soul Figure. Agreeing to hold on to the Golden Soul Figure for now, Ken rushes to Ririko's rescue…

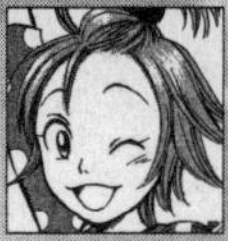

Ririko Yasuhara
A top-notch Legendz wielder at her school.

The Ryudo Four

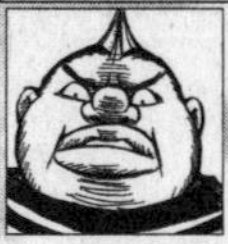

Hosuke Dekai
A major Legendz wielder at Ryudo. He secretly plans to steal the Golden Soul Figure.

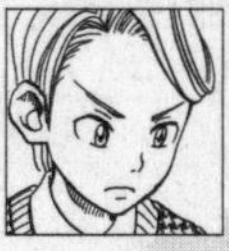

Yuki Amagi
The leader of the Ryudo Four.

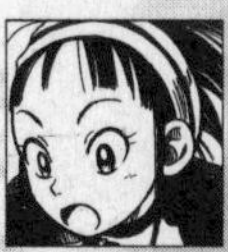

Maki Mitsui
Outgoing and energetic, she's the only female member of the Ryudo Four.

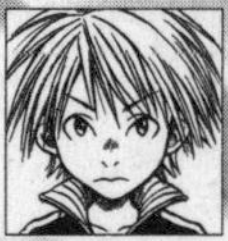

Mitsuru Aoi
The last member of the Ryudo Four. He doesn't talk much.

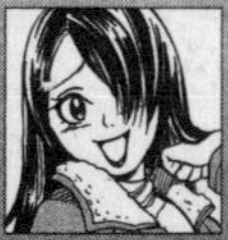

Meiko Kajiwara
A sixth-grader at Kokuryu Elementary. She loves Hosuke Dekai.

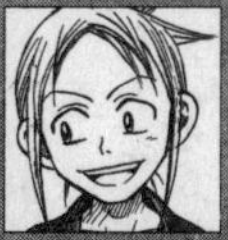

Eiji Yashiro
A champion of the Legendz Carnival.

LEGENDZ

Vol. 2

CONTENTS

LEGENDZ 5
Pool of Radiance

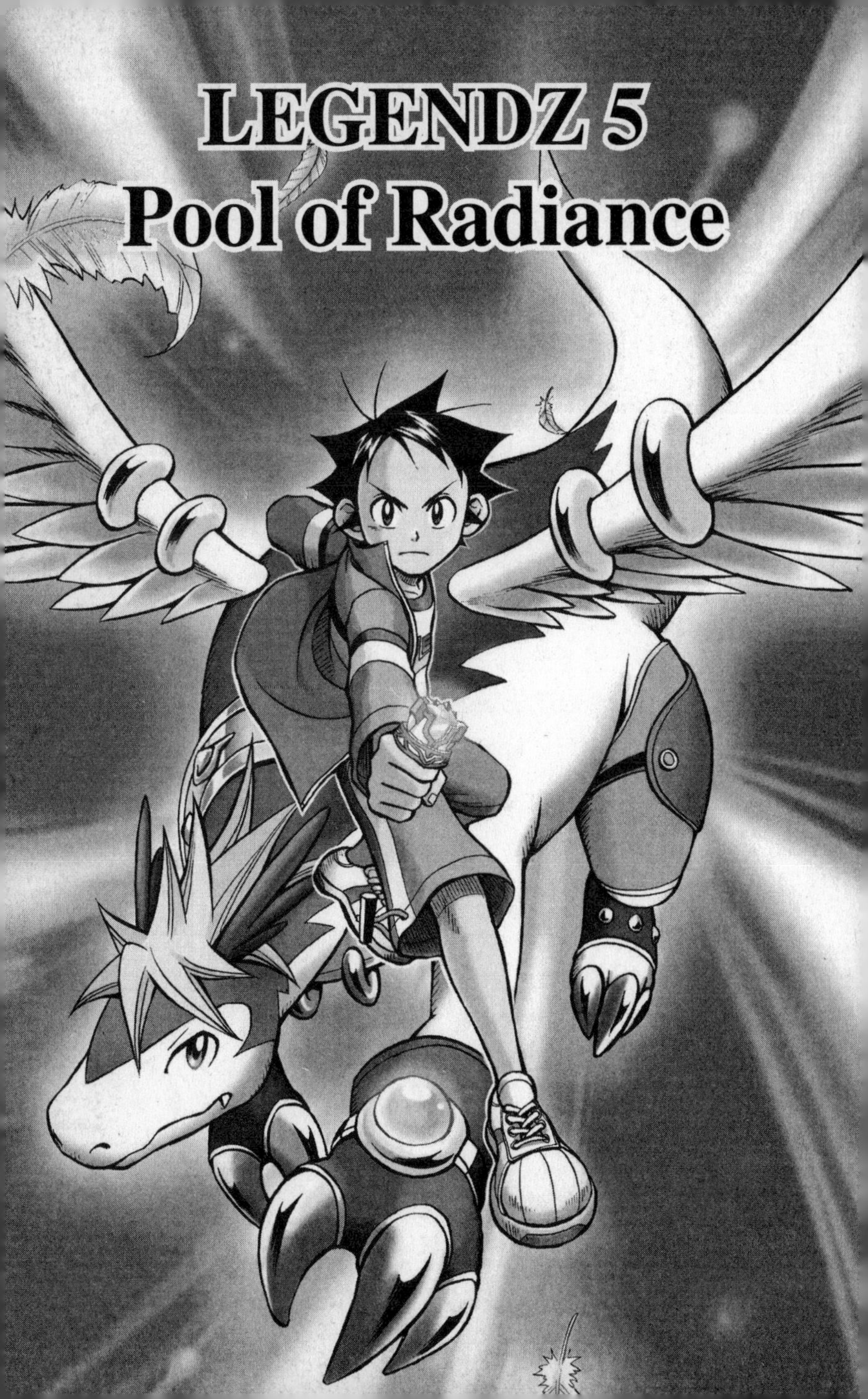

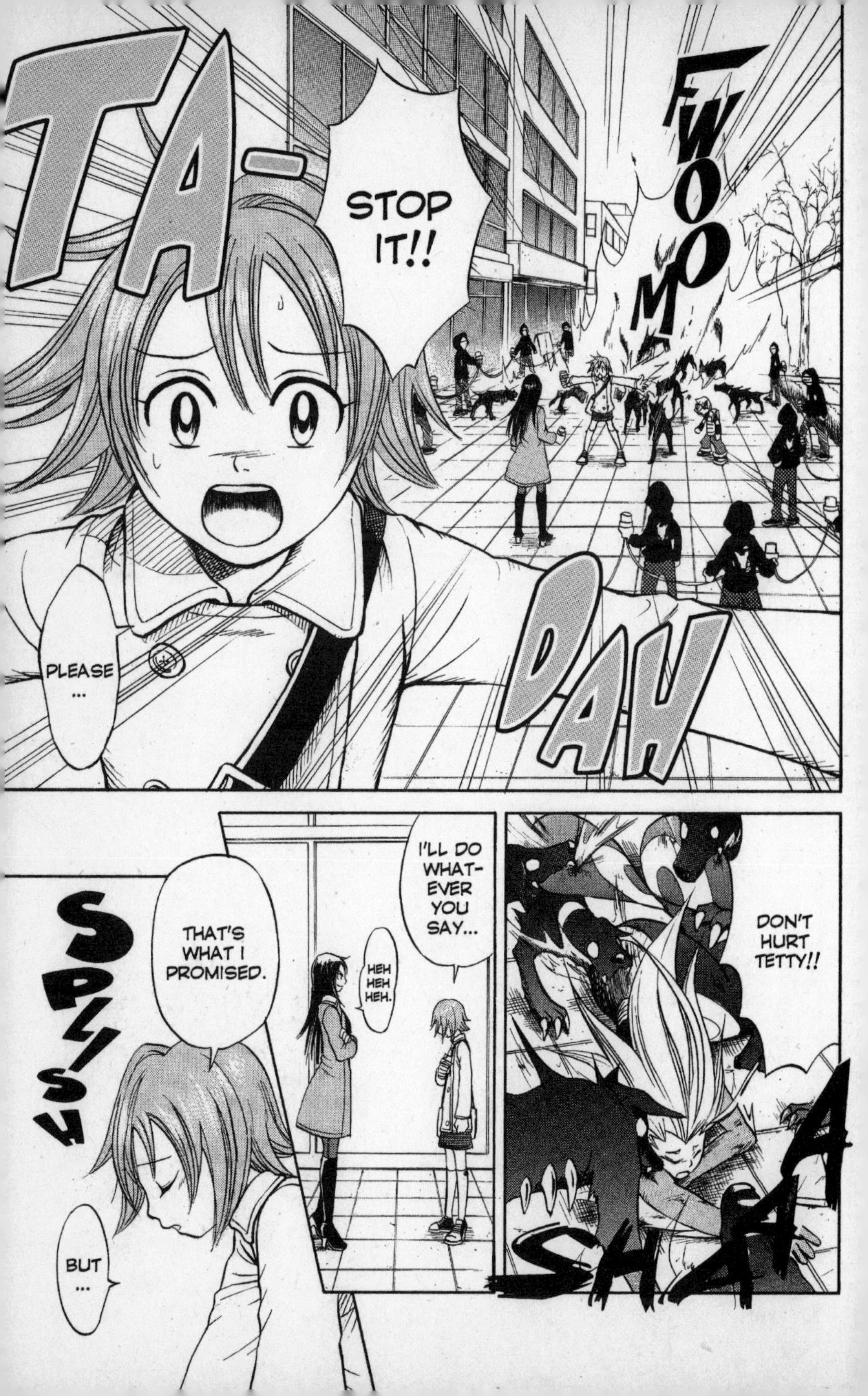
FWOOM
STOP IT!!
TA-
DAH
PLEASE ...
DON'T HURT TETTY!!
SHAA
I'LL DO WHAT-EVER YOU SAY...
HEH HEH HEH.
THAT'S WHAT I PROMISED.
SPLISH
BUT ...

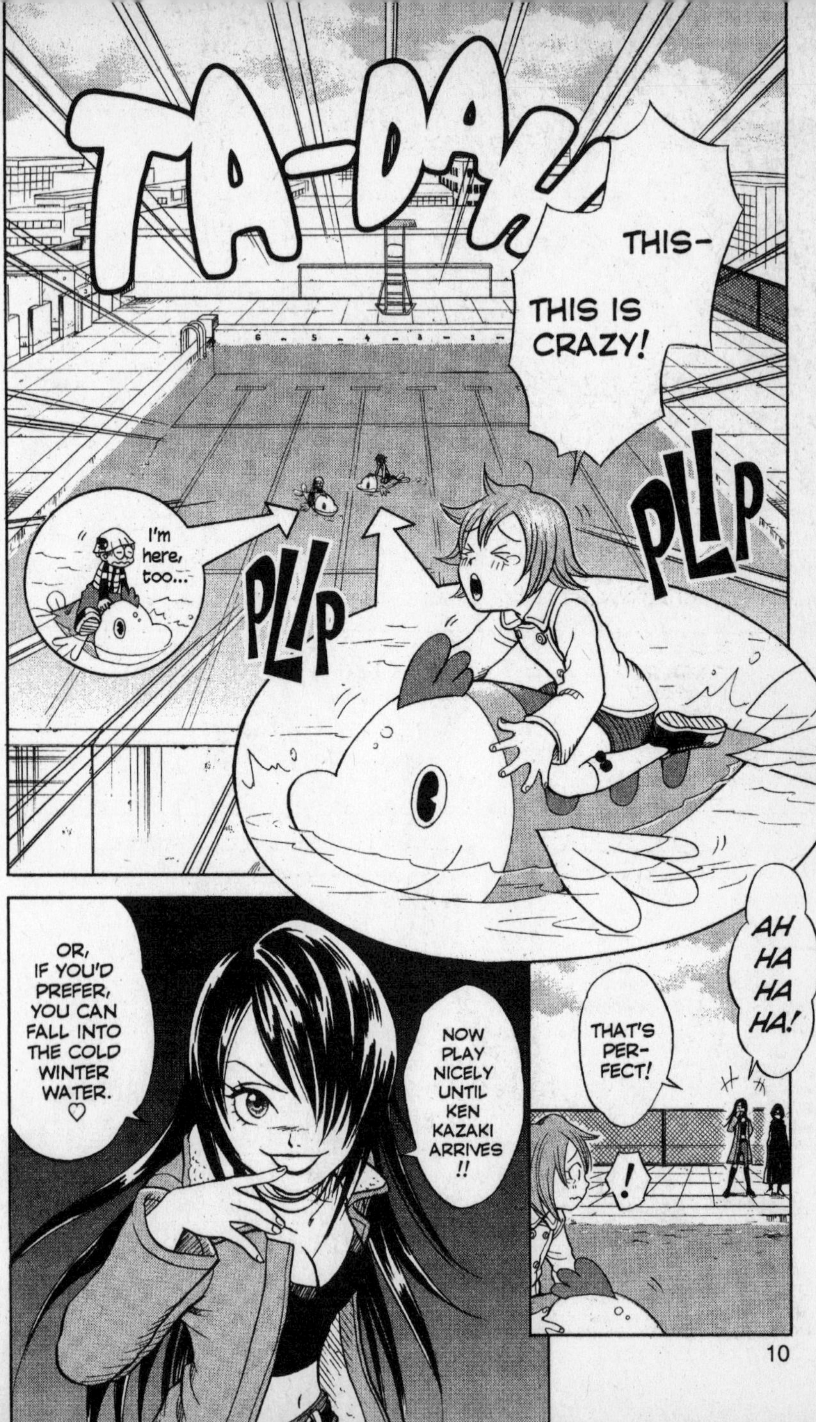
TA-DAH
THIS-
THIS IS CRAZY!
PLIP
PLIP
I'm here, too...
AH HA HA HA!
THAT'S PER-FECT!
!
NOW PLAY NICELY UNTIL KEN KAZAKI ARRIVES!!
OR, IF YOU'D PREFER, YOU CAN FALL INTO THE COLD WINTER WATER. ♡

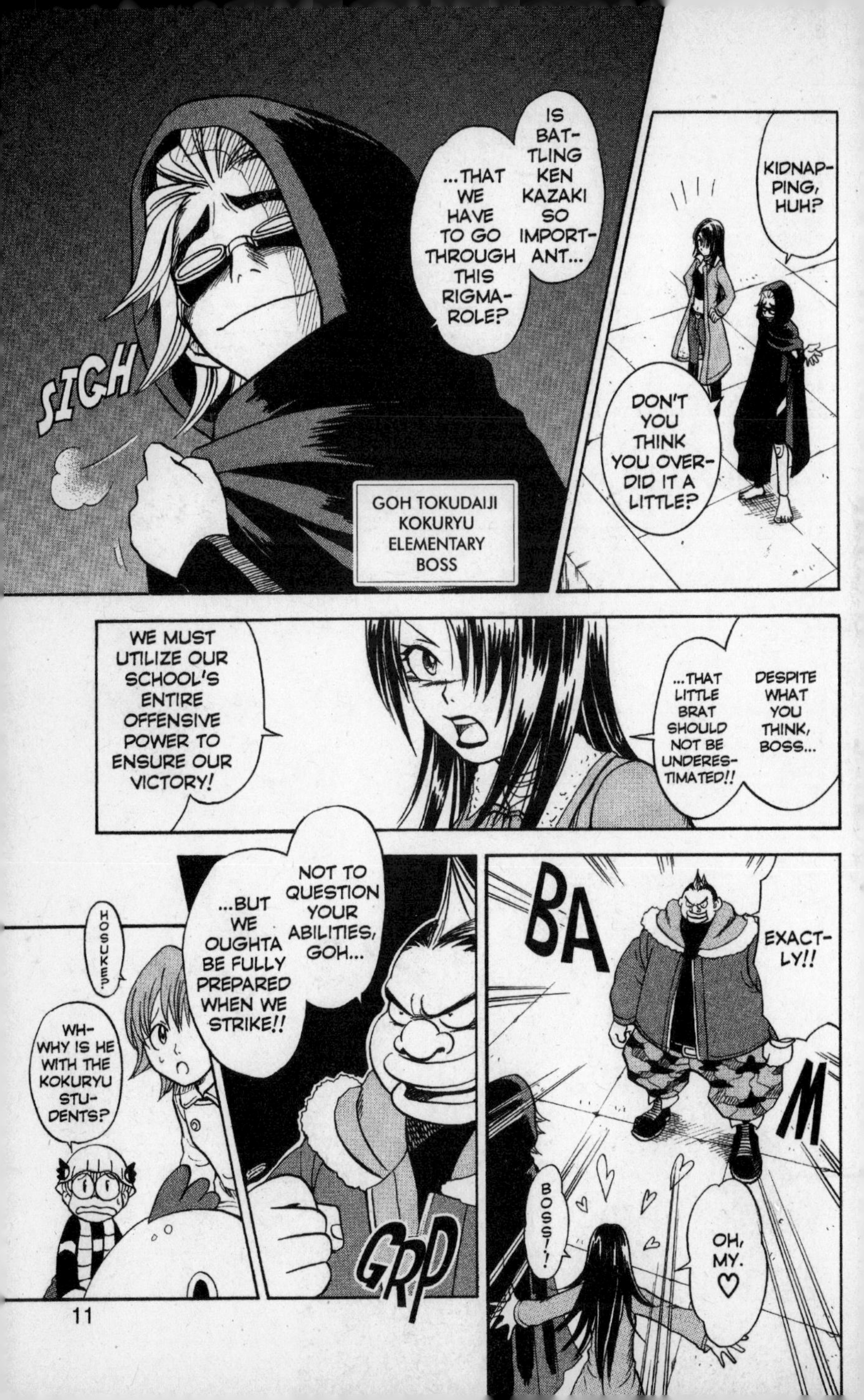
KIDNAPPING, HUH?
DON'T YOU THINK YOU OVERDID IT A LITTLE?
IS BATTLING KEN KAZAKI SO IMPORTANT...
...THAT WE HAVE TO GO THROUGH THIS RIGMAROLE?
SIGH
GOH TOKUDAIJI
KOKURYU ELEMENTARY BOSS
DESPITE WHAT YOU THINK, BOSS...
...THAT LITTLE BRAT SHOULD NOT BE UNDERESTIMATED!!
WE MUST UTILIZE OUR SCHOOL'S ENTIRE OFFENSIVE POWER TO ENSURE OUR VICTORY!
BAM
EXACTLY!!
BOSS!?!
OH, MY. ♡
NOT TO QUESTION YOUR ABILITIES, GOH...
...BUT WE OUGHTA BE FULLY PREPARED WHEN WE STRIKE!!
GRP
HOSUKE!?
WH-WHY IS HE WITH THE KOKURYU STUDENTS?

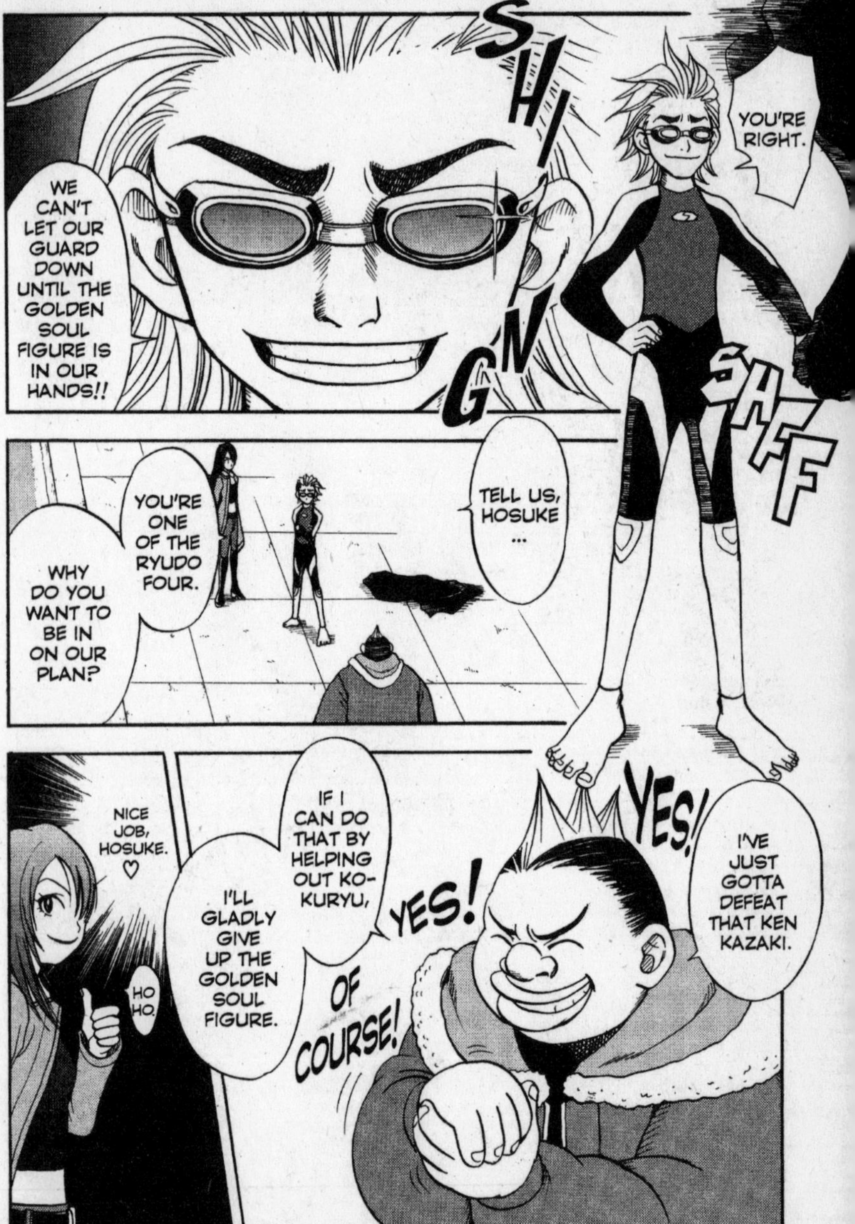
YOU'RE RIGHT.
SHAFF
SHING
WE CAN'T LET OUR GUARD DOWN UNTIL THE GOLDEN SOUL FIGURE IS IN OUR HANDS!!
TELL US, HOSUKE ...
YOU'RE ONE OF THE RYUDO FOUR.
WHY DO YOU WANT TO BE IN ON OUR PLAN?
YES!
I'VE JUST GOTTA DEFEAT THAT KEN KAZAKI.
YES!
IF I CAN DO THAT BY HELPING OUT KO-KURYU,
I'LL GLADLY GIVE UP THE GOLDEN SOUL FIGURE.
OF COURSE!
NICE JOB, HOSUKE. ♡
HO HO.

READ THIS WAY

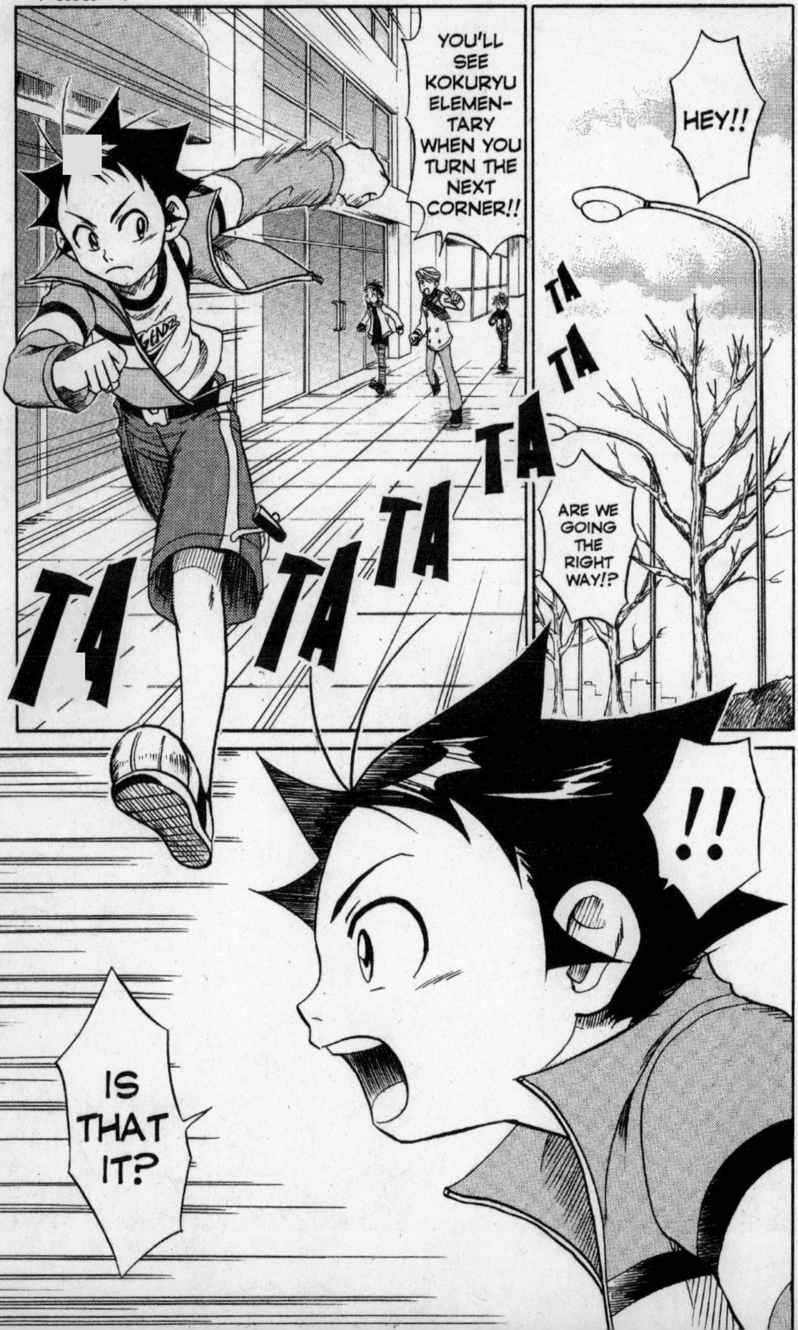
HEY!!
ARE WE GOING THE RIGHT WAY!?
YOU'LL SEE KOKURYU ELEMENTARY WHEN YOU TURN THE NEXT CORNER!!
TA TA TA TA TA TA
!!
IS THAT IT?

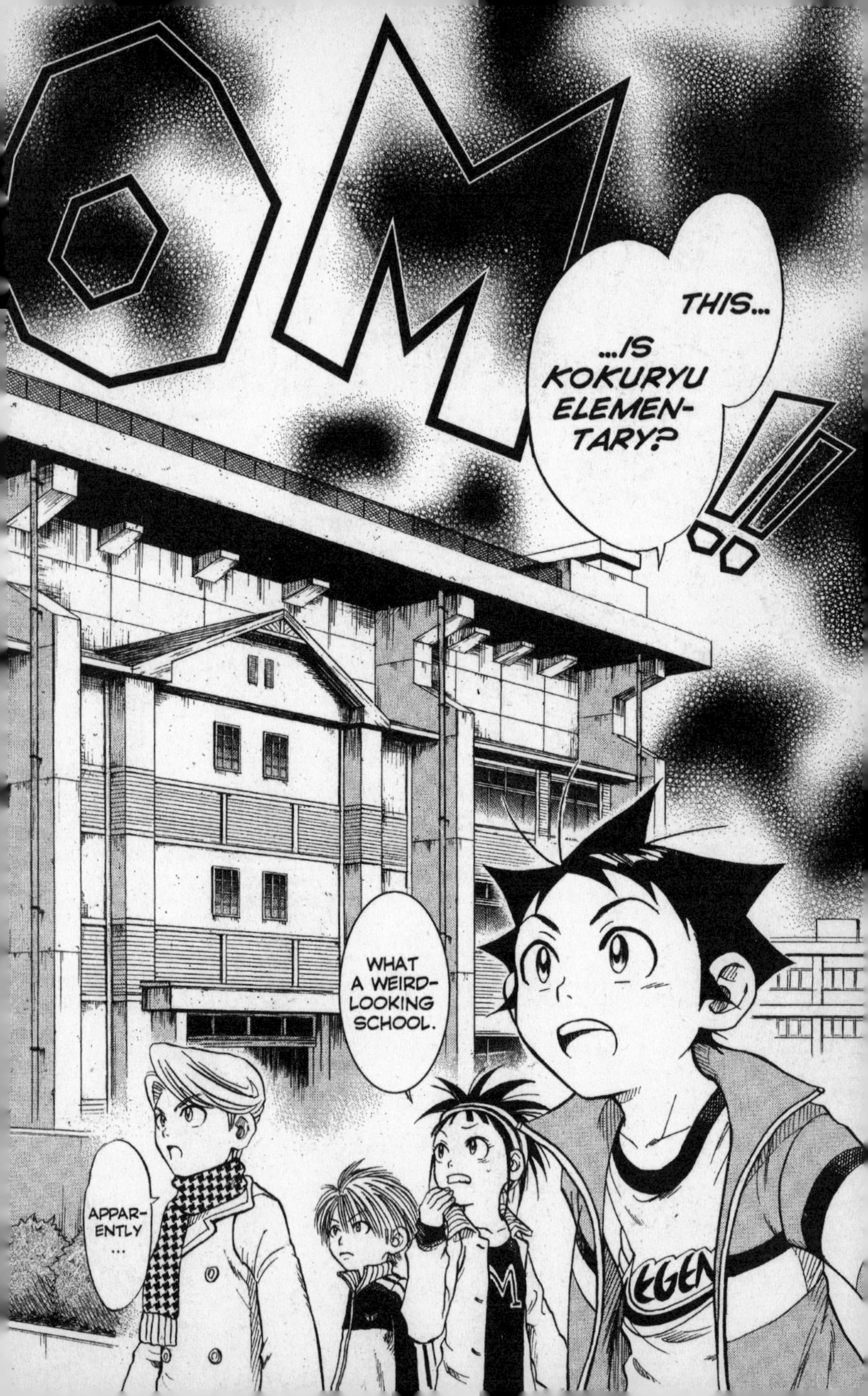
OM!!
THIS...
...IS KOKURYU ELEMENTARY?
WHAT A WEIRD-LOOKING SCHOOL.
APPARENTLY...
LEGEN

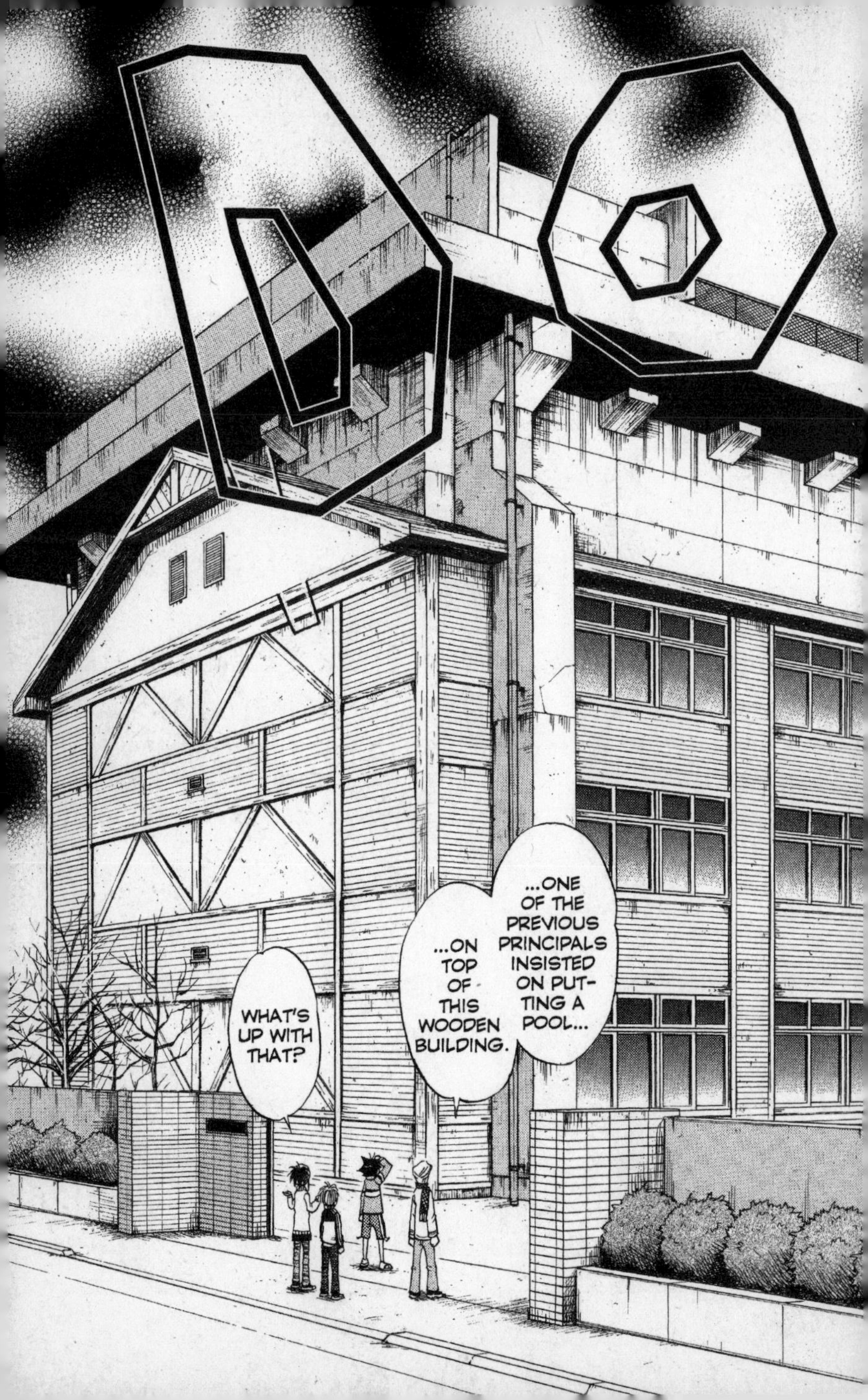
DO
...ONE OF THE PREVIOUS PRINCIPALS INSISTED ON PUT-TING A POOL...
...ON TOP OF THIS WOODEN BUILDING.
WHAT'S UP WITH THAT?

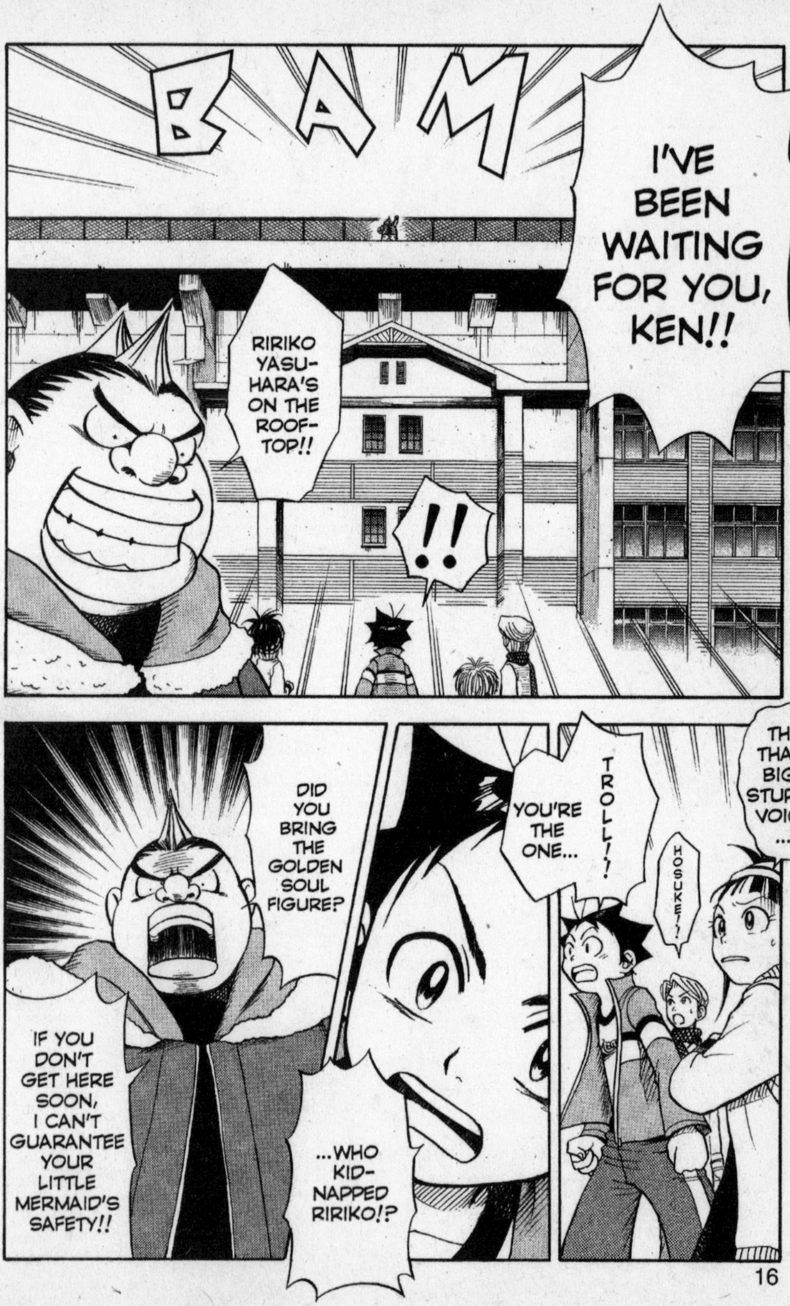
I'VE BEEN WAITING FOR YOU, KEN!!
BAM
RIRIKO YASU-HARA'S ON THE ROOF-TOP!!
!!
TH-THAT BIG STUPID VOICE...
HOSUKE!?
TROLL!?
YOU'RE THE ONE...
...WHO KID-NAPPED RIRIKO!?
DID YOU BRING THE GOLDEN SOUL FIGURE?
IF YOU DON'T GET HERE SOON, I CAN'T GUARANTEE YOUR LITTLE MERMAID'S SAFETY!!

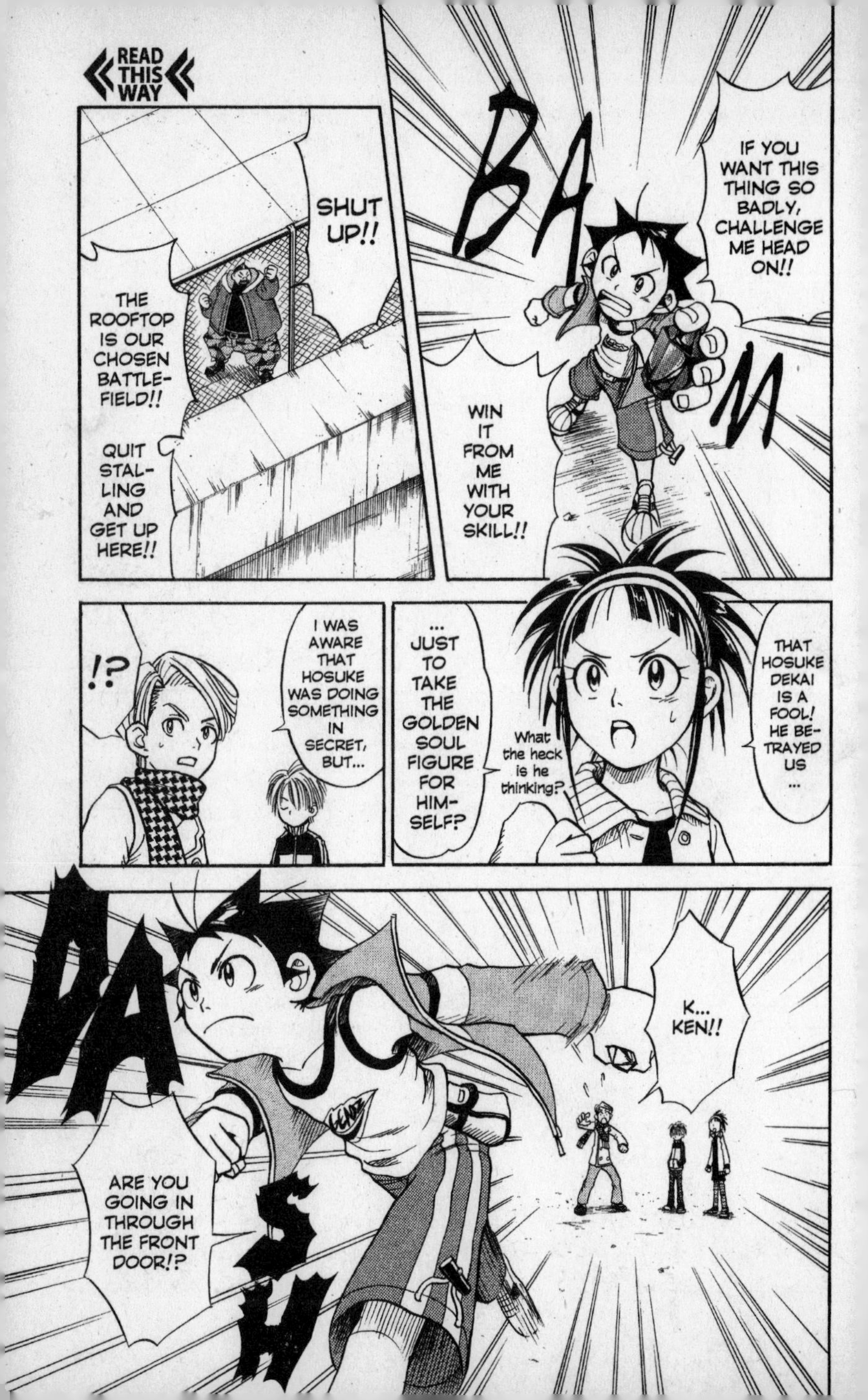
READ THIS WAY
BAM
IF YOU WANT THIS THING SO BADLY, CHALLENGE ME HEAD ON!!
WIN IT FROM ME WITH YOUR SKILL!!
SHUT UP!!
THE ROOFTOP IS OUR CHOSEN BATTLE-FIELD!!
QUIT STAL-LING AND GET UP HERE!!
THAT HOSUKE DEKAI IS A FOOL! HE BE-TRAYED US ...
What the heck is he thinking?
... JUST TO TAKE THE GOLDEN SOUL FIGURE FOR HIM-SELF?
I WAS AWARE THAT HOSUKE WAS DOING SOMETHING IN SECRET, BUT...
!?
K... KEN!!
DASH
ARE YOU GOING IN THROUGH THE FRONT DOOR!?

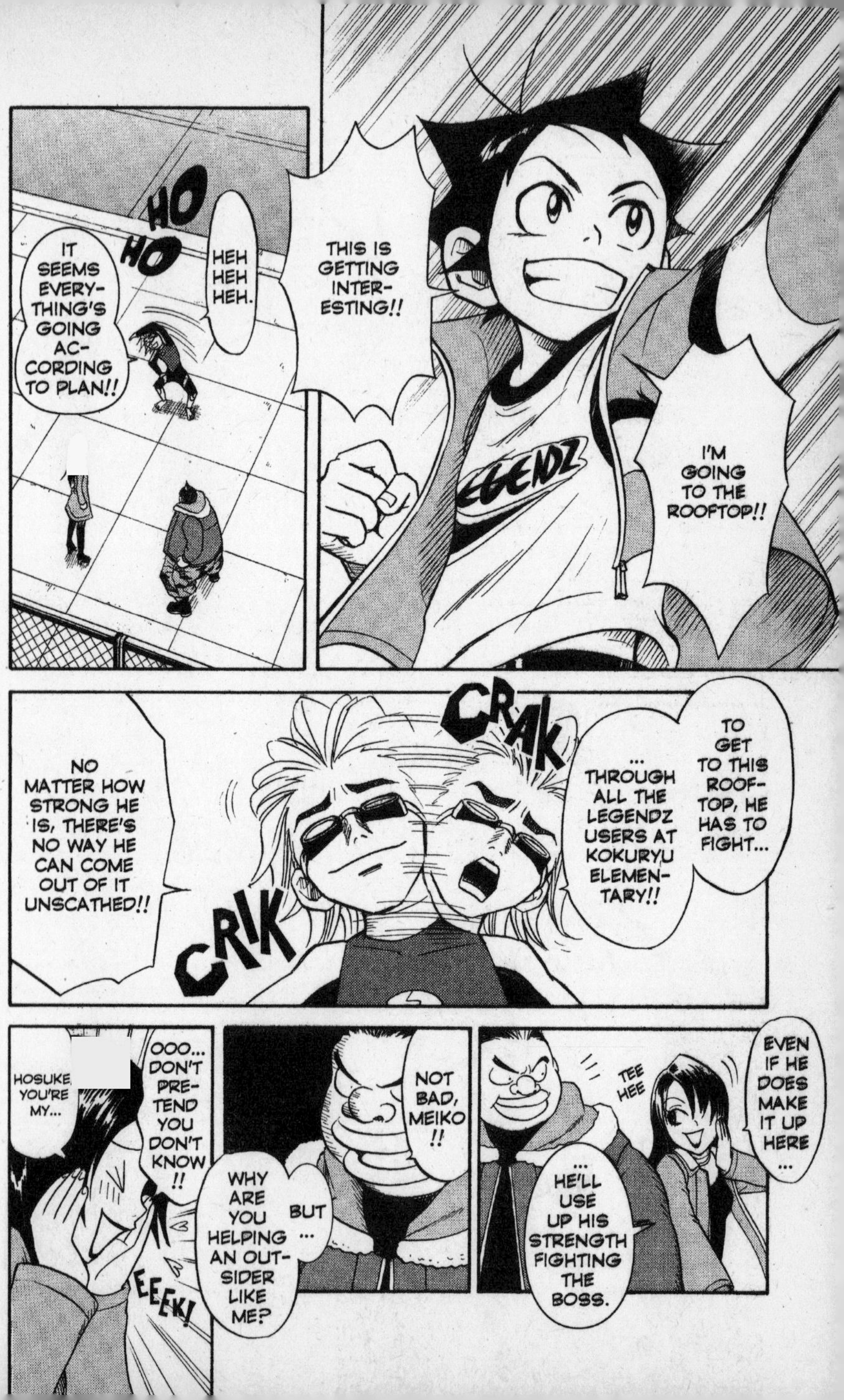
THIS IS GETTING INTER-ESTING!!
I'M GOING TO THE ROOFTOP!!
HEH HEH HEH.
HO HO
IT SEEMS EVERY-THING'S GOING AC-CORDING TO PLAN!!
TO GET TO THIS ROOF-TOP, HE HAS TO FIGHT...
...THROUGH ALL THE LEGENDZ USERS AT KOKURYU ELEMEN-TARY!!
CRAK
CRIK
NO MATTER HOW STRONG HE IS, THERE'S NO WAY HE CAN COME OUT OF IT UNSCATHED!!
EVEN IF HE DOES MAKE IT UP HERE...
TEE HEE
...HE'LL USE UP HIS STRENGTH FIGHTING THE BOSS.
NOT BAD, MEIKO!!
BUT...
WHY ARE YOU HELPING AN OUT-SIDER LIKE ME?
OOO... DON'T PRE-TEND YOU DON'T KNOW!!
HOSUKE, YOU'RE MY...
EEEK!

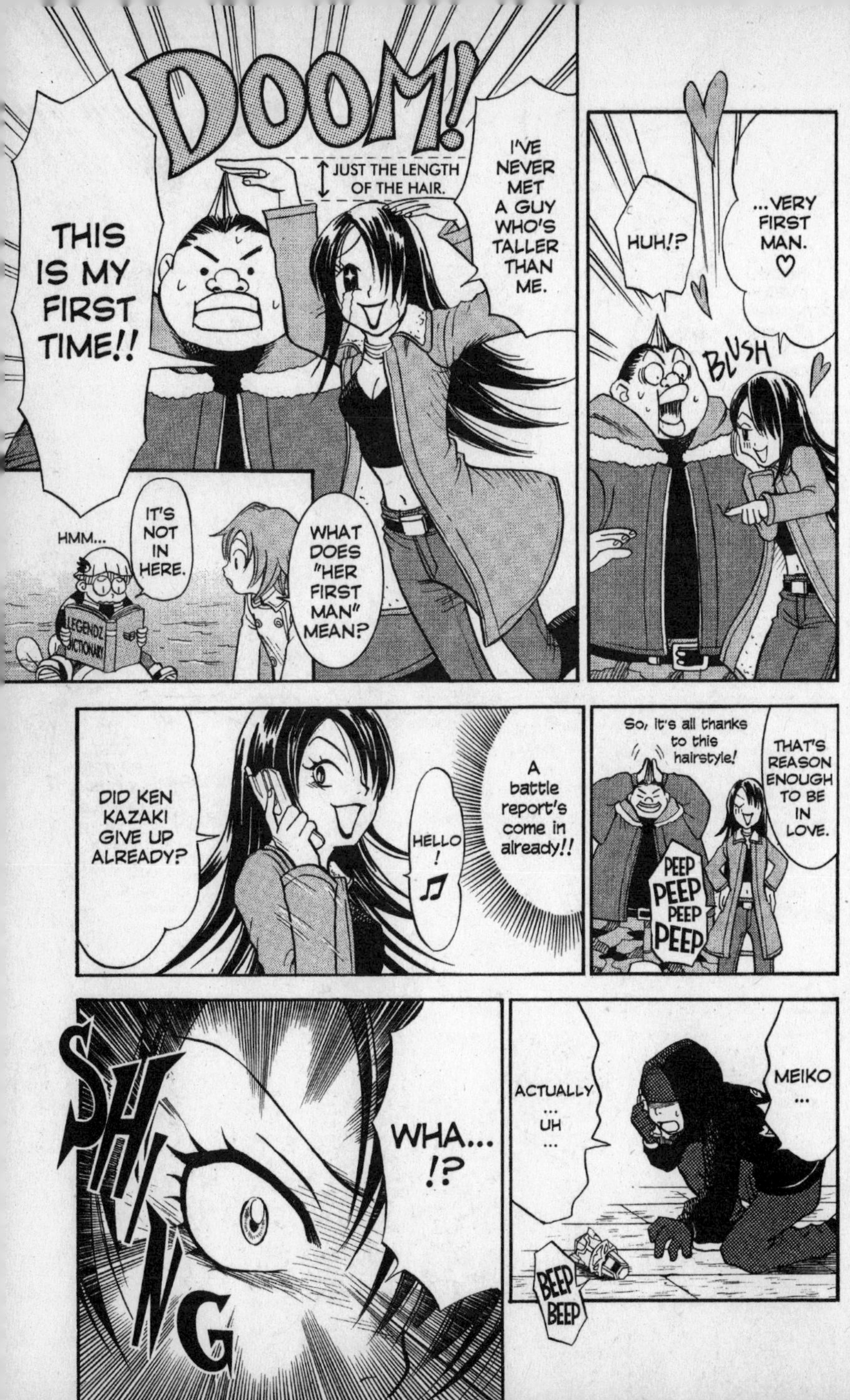
...VERY FIRST MAN. ♡
HUH!?
BLUSH
DOOM!
I'VE NEVER MET A GUY WHO'S TALLER THAN ME.
JUST THE LENGTH OF THE HAIR.
THIS IS MY FIRST TIME!!
WHAT DOES "HER FIRST MAN" MEAN?
IT'S NOT IN HERE.
HMM...
LEGENDZ DICTIONARY
THAT'S REASON ENOUGH TO BE IN LOVE.
So, it's all thanks to this hairstyle!
PEEP PEEP PEEP PEEP
A battle report's come in already!!
HELLO! ♫
DID KEN KAZAKI GIVE UP ALREADY?
MEIKO...
ACTUALLY... UH...
BEEP BEEP
WHA...!?
SHING

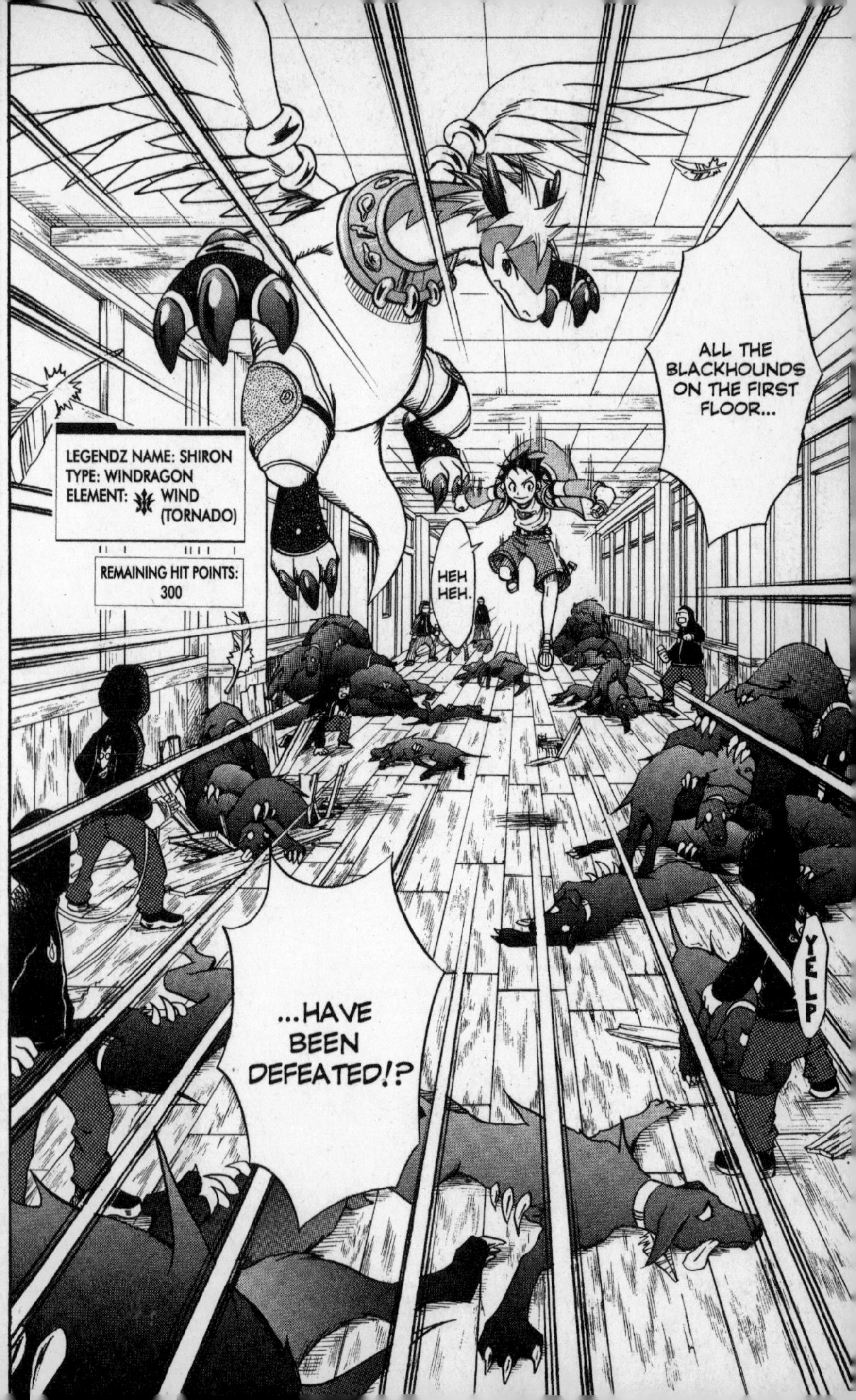
ALL THE BLACKHOUNDS ON THE FIRST FLOOR...
HEH HEH.
LEGENDZ NAME: SHIRON
TYPE: WINDRAGON
ELEMENT: WIND (TORNADO)
REMAINING HIT POINTS: 300
YELP
...HAVE BEEN DEFEATED!?

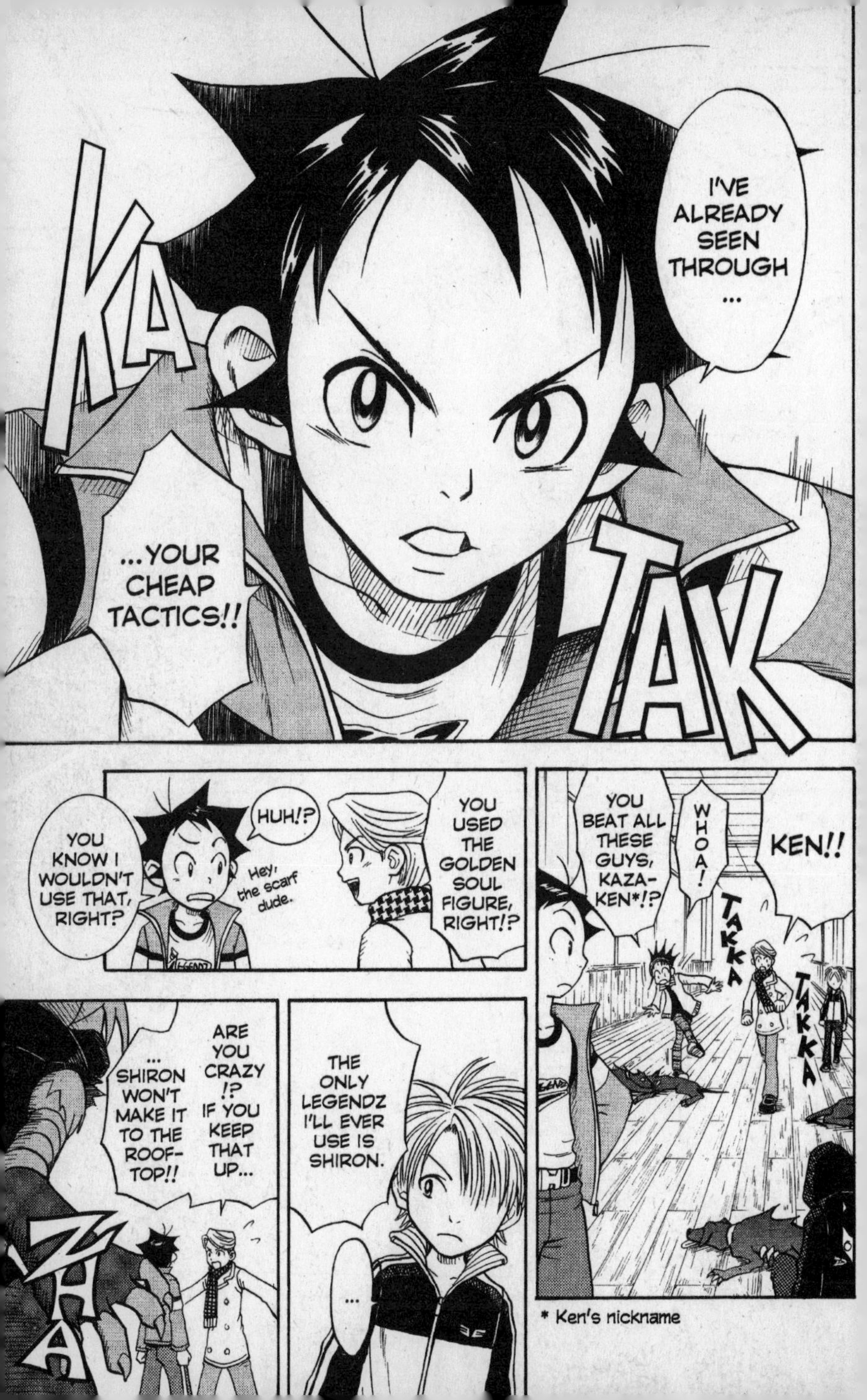
I'VE ALREADY SEEN THROUGH ...
KA
TAK
...YOUR CHEAP TACTICS!!
KEN!!
WHOA!
YOU BEAT ALL THESE GUYS, KAZA-KEN*!?
TAKKA
TAKKA
YOU USED THE GOLDEN SOUL FIGURE, RIGHT!?
Hey, the scarf dude.
HUH!?
YOU KNOW I WOULDN'T USE THAT, RIGHT?
THE ONLY LEGENDZ I'LL EVER USE IS SHIRON.
...
ARE YOU CRAZY!? IF YOU KEEP THAT UP...
...SHIRON WON'T MAKE IT TO THE ROOF-TOP!!
ZHA
* Ken's nickname

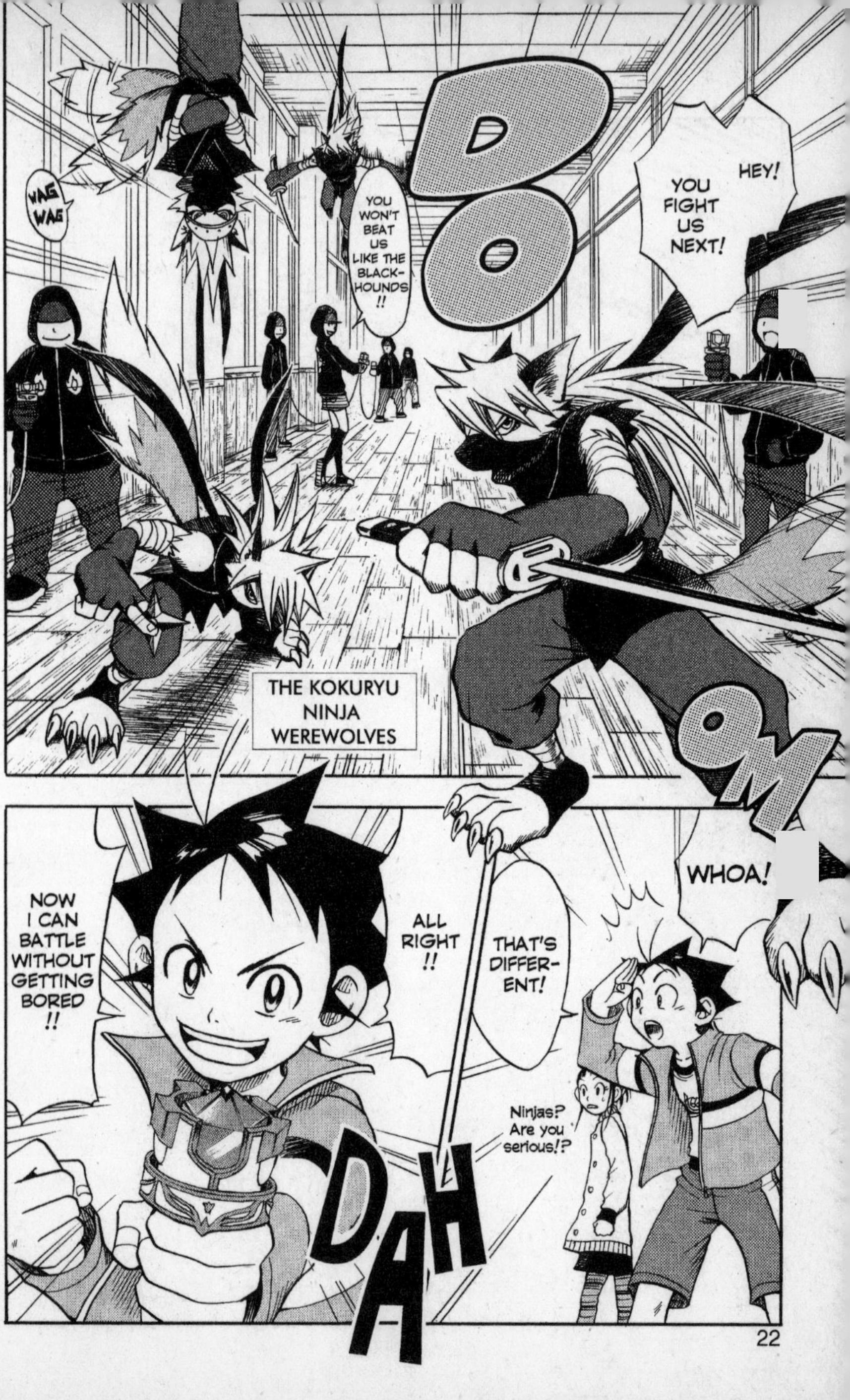
HEY! YOU FIGHT US NEXT!
DO
YOU WON'T BEAT US LIKE THE BLACK-HOUNDS!!
WAG WAG
THE KOKURYU NINJA WEREWOLVES
OM
WHOA!
THAT'S DIFFER-ENT!
Ninjas? Are you serious!?
ALL RIGHT!!
NOW I CAN BATTLE WITHOUT GETTING BORED!!
DAH

READ THIS WAY

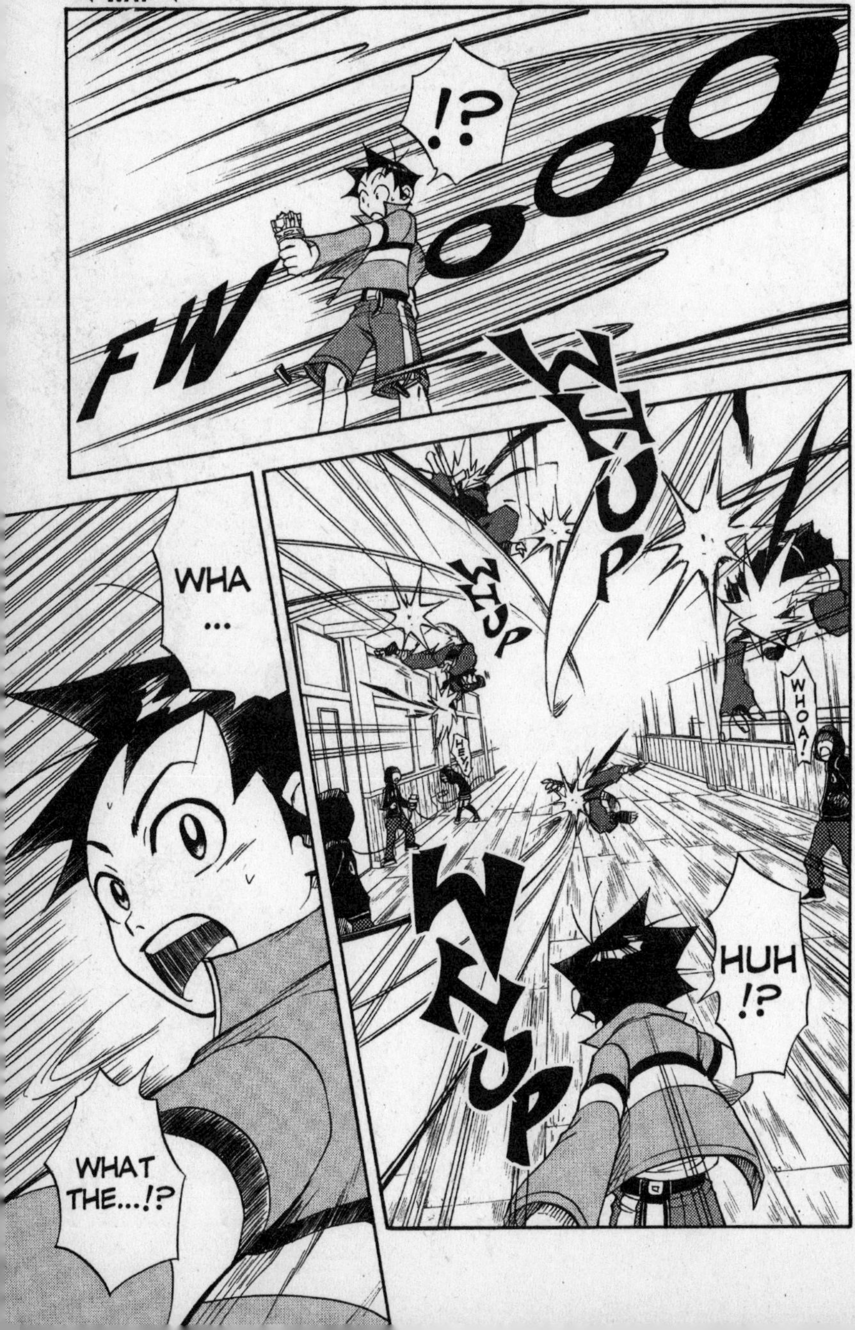
!?
FWOOOOO
WHUP
WHUP
WHOA!
HEY!
WHUP
HUH!?
WHA...
WHAT THE...!?

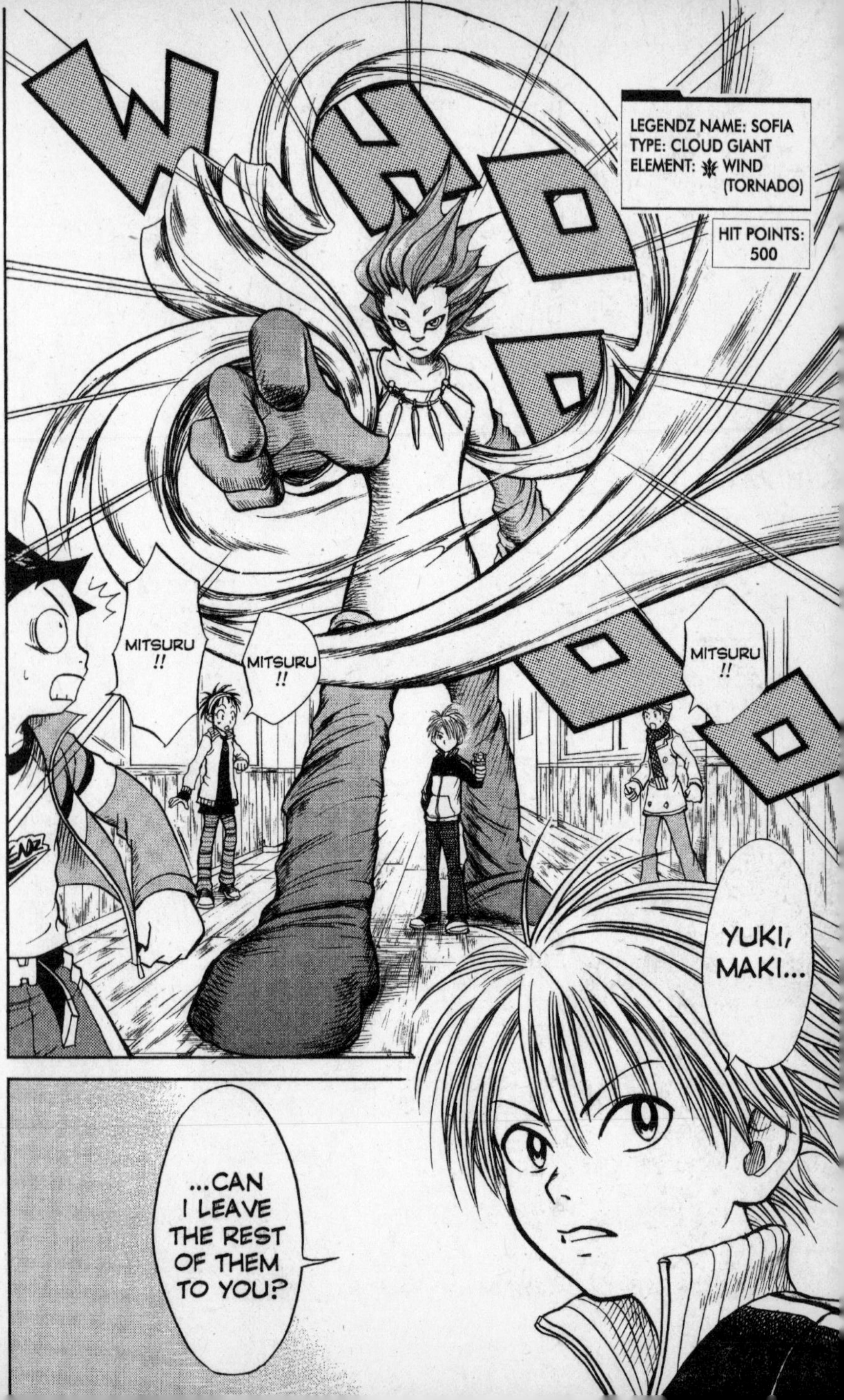
LEGENDZ NAME: SOFIA
TYPE: CLOUD GIANT
ELEMENT: WIND (TORNADO)
HIT POINTS: 500
WHOOOO
MITSURU !!
MITSURU !!
MITSURU !!
YUKI, MAKI...
...CAN I LEAVE THE REST OF THEM TO YOU?

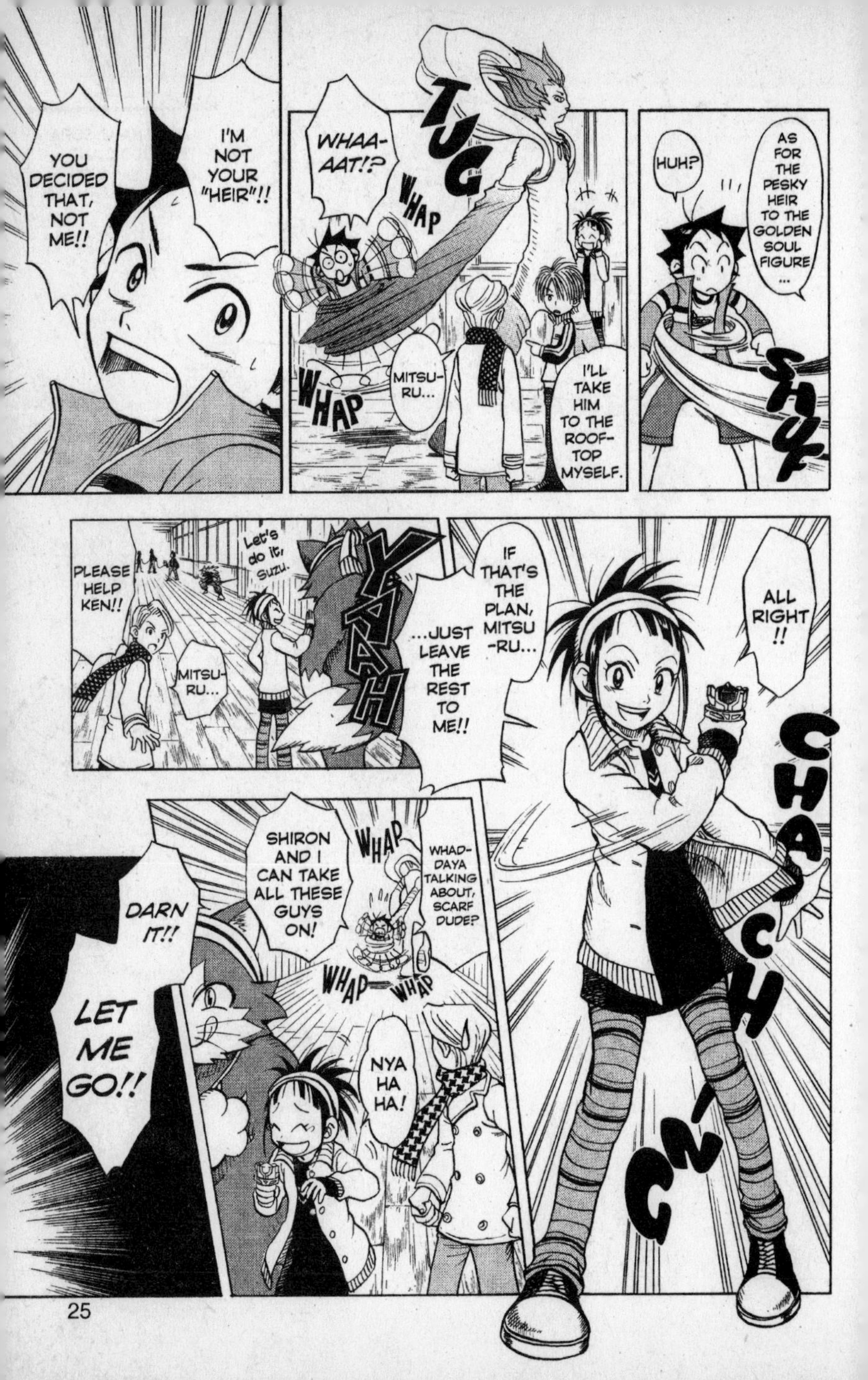
AS FOR THE PESKY HEIR TO THE GOLDEN SOUL FIGURE ...
HUH?
SHUF
I'LL TAKE HIM TO THE ROOF-TOP MYSELF.
TUG
WHAA-AAT!?
WHAP
MITSU-RU...
WHAP
I'M NOT YOUR "HEIR"!!
YOU DECIDED THAT, NOT ME!!
ALL RIGHT!!
IF THAT's THE PLAN, MITSU-RU...
...JUST LEAVE THE REST TO ME!!
CHA
CH
GN'
YAAAH
Let's do it, Suzu.
MITSU-RU...
PLEASE HELP KEN!!
SHIRON AND I CAN TAKE ALL THESE GUYS ON!
WHAP
WHAD-DAYA TALKING ABOUT, SCARF DUDE?
WHAP-WHAP
NYA HA HA!
DARN IT!!
LET ME GO!!

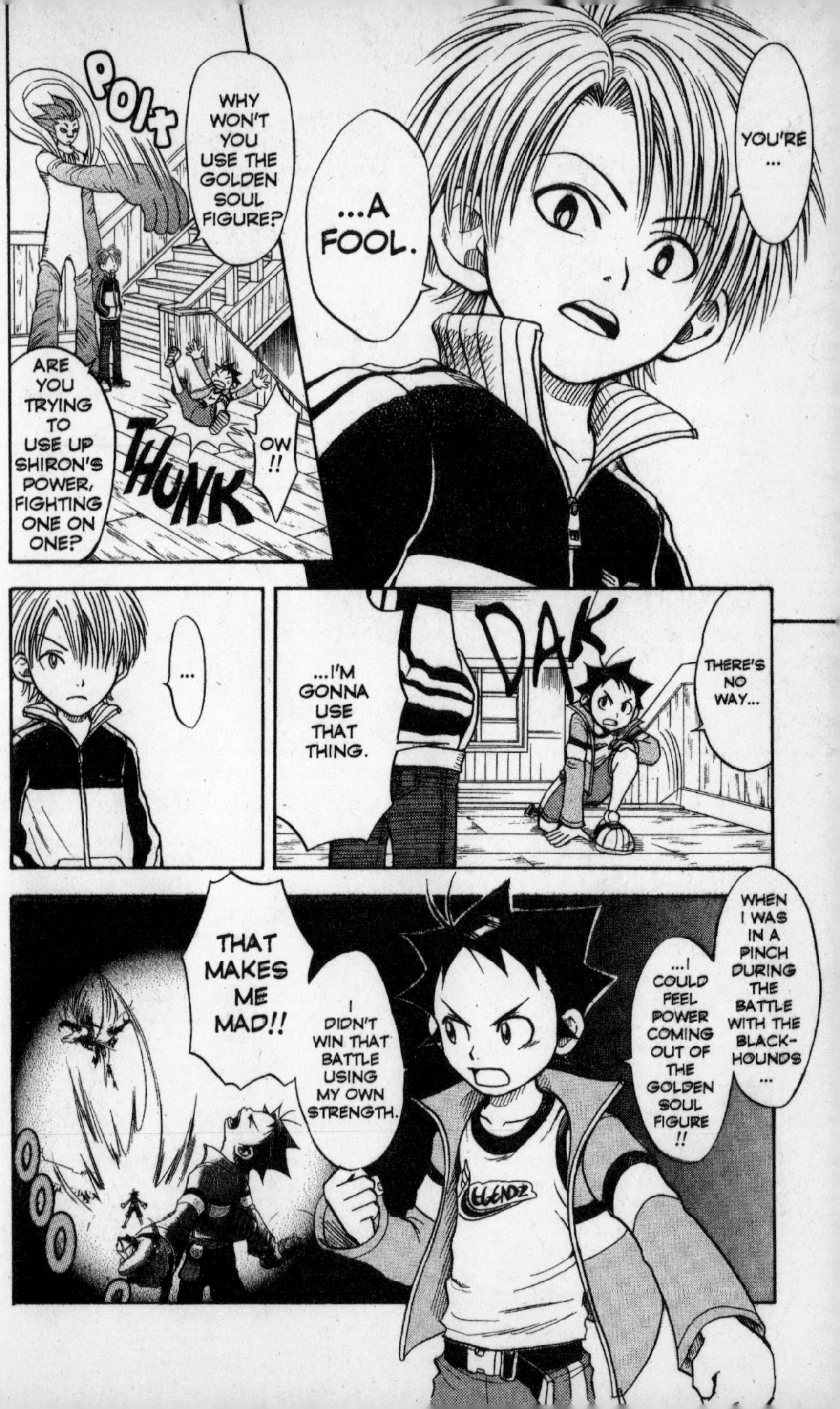
YOU'RE ...
...A FOOL.
WHY WON'T YOU USE THE GOLDEN SOUL FIGURE?
POIT
OW !!
THUNK
ARE YOU TRYING TO USE UP SHIRON'S POWER, FIGHTING ONE ON ONE?
THERE'S NO WAY...
DAK
...I'M GONNA USE THAT THING.
...
WHEN I WAS IN A PINCH DURING THE BATTLE WITH THE BLACK-HOUNDS ...
...I COULD FEEL POWER COMING OUT OF THE GOLDEN SOUL FIGURE !!
I DIDN'T WIN THAT BATTLE USING MY OWN STRENGTH.
THAT MAKES ME MAD!!

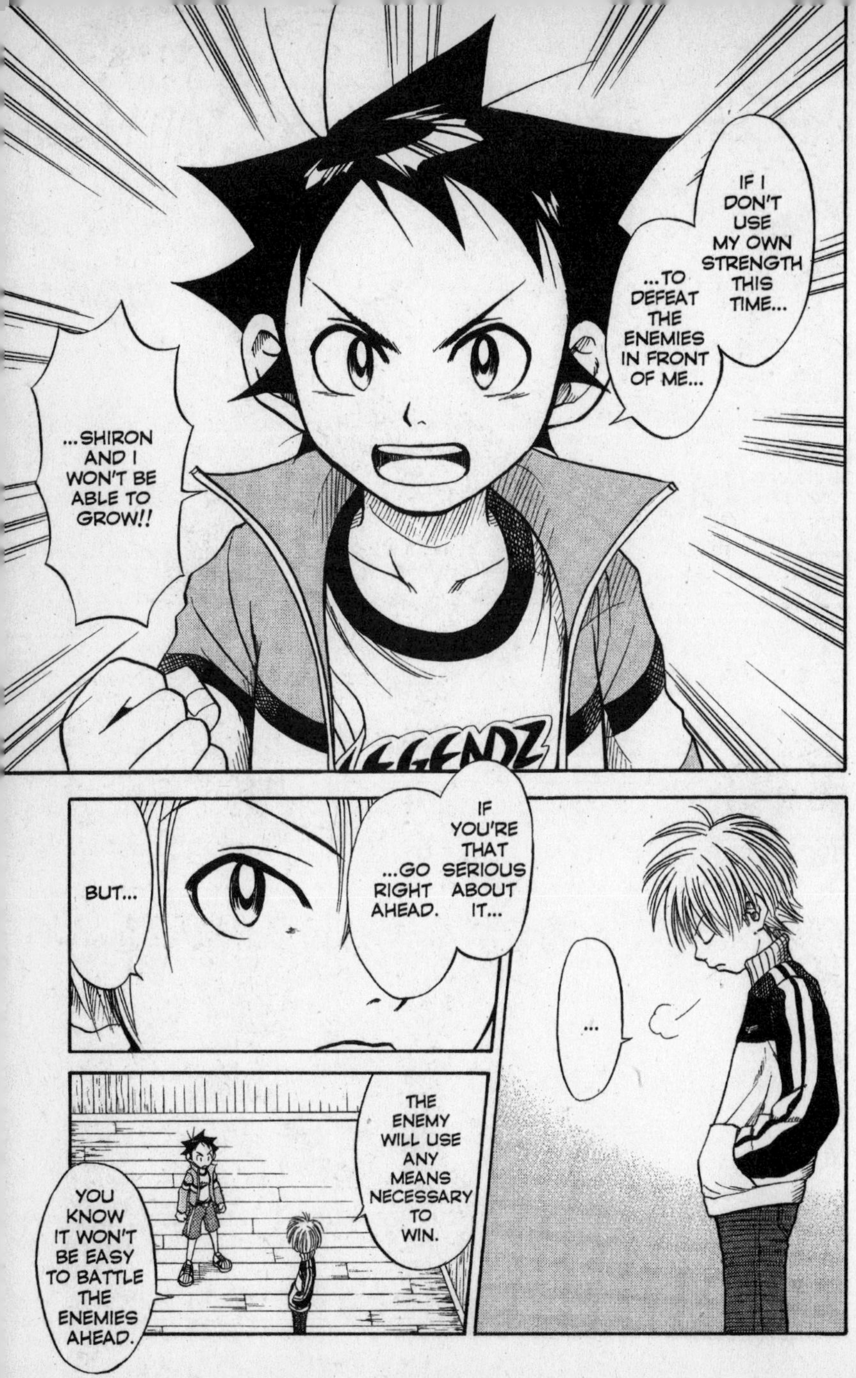
IF I DON'T USE MY OWN STRENGTH THIS TIME...
...TO DEFEAT THE ENEMIES IN FRONT OF ME...
...SHIRON AND I WON'T BE ABLE TO GROW!!
...
IF YOU'RE THAT SERIOUS ABOUT IT...
...GO RIGHT AHEAD.
BUT...
THE ENEMY WILL USE ANY MEANS NECESSARY TO WIN.
YOU KNOW IT WON'T BE EASY TO BATTLE THE ENEMIES AHEAD.

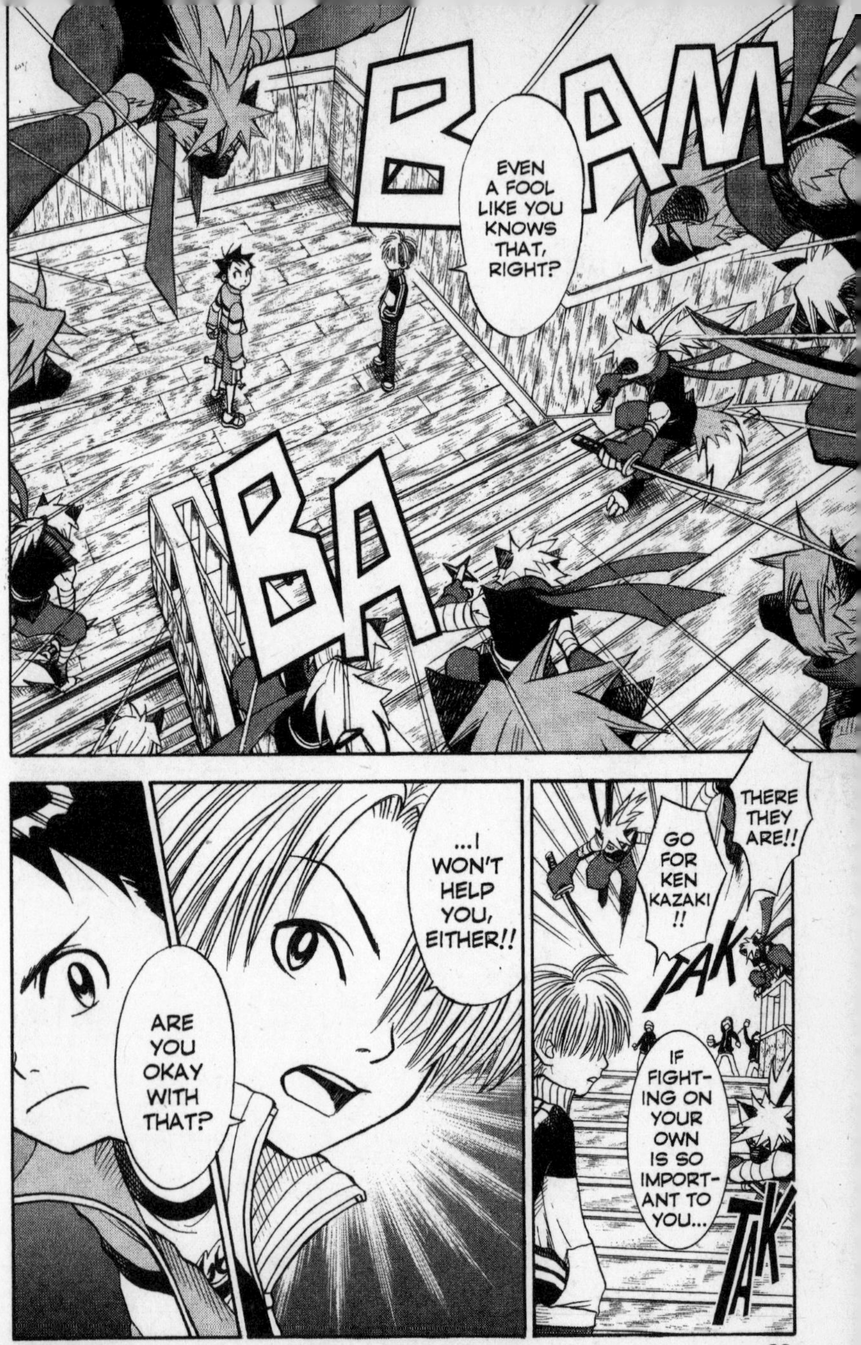
BAM
EVEN A FOOL LIKE YOU KNOWS THAT, RIGHT?
BA
THERE THEY ARE!!
GO FOR KEN KAZAKI!!
TAK
IF FIGHTING ON YOUR OWN IS SO IMPORTANT TO YOU...
TAK
...I WON'T HELP YOU, EITHER!!
ARE YOU OKAY WITH THAT?

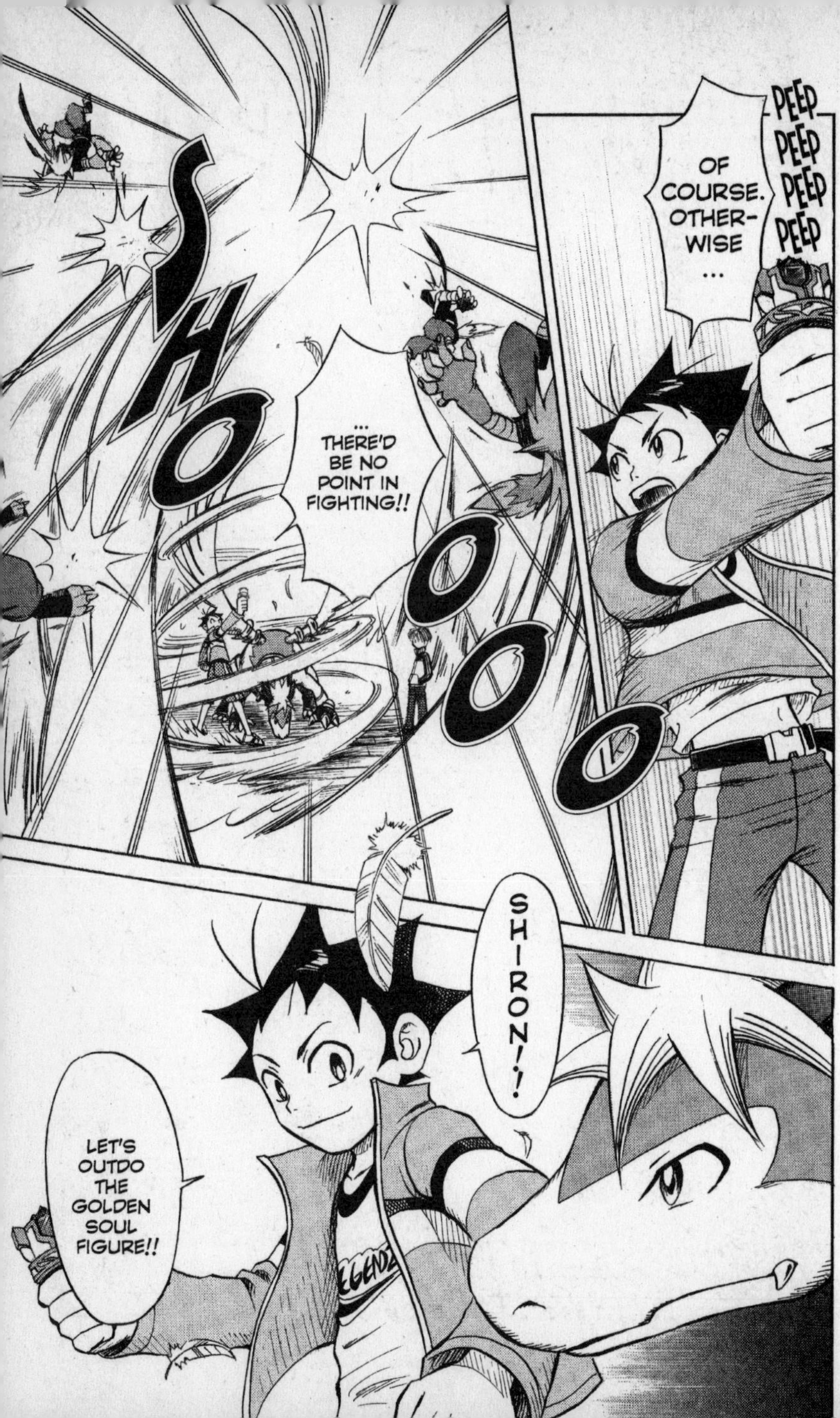
OF COURSE. OTHER-WISE ...
PEEP PEEP PEEP PEEP
SHOOOOOO
... THERE'D BE NO POINT IN FIGHTING!!
SHIRON!!
LET'S OUTDO THE GOLDEN SOUL FIGURE!!

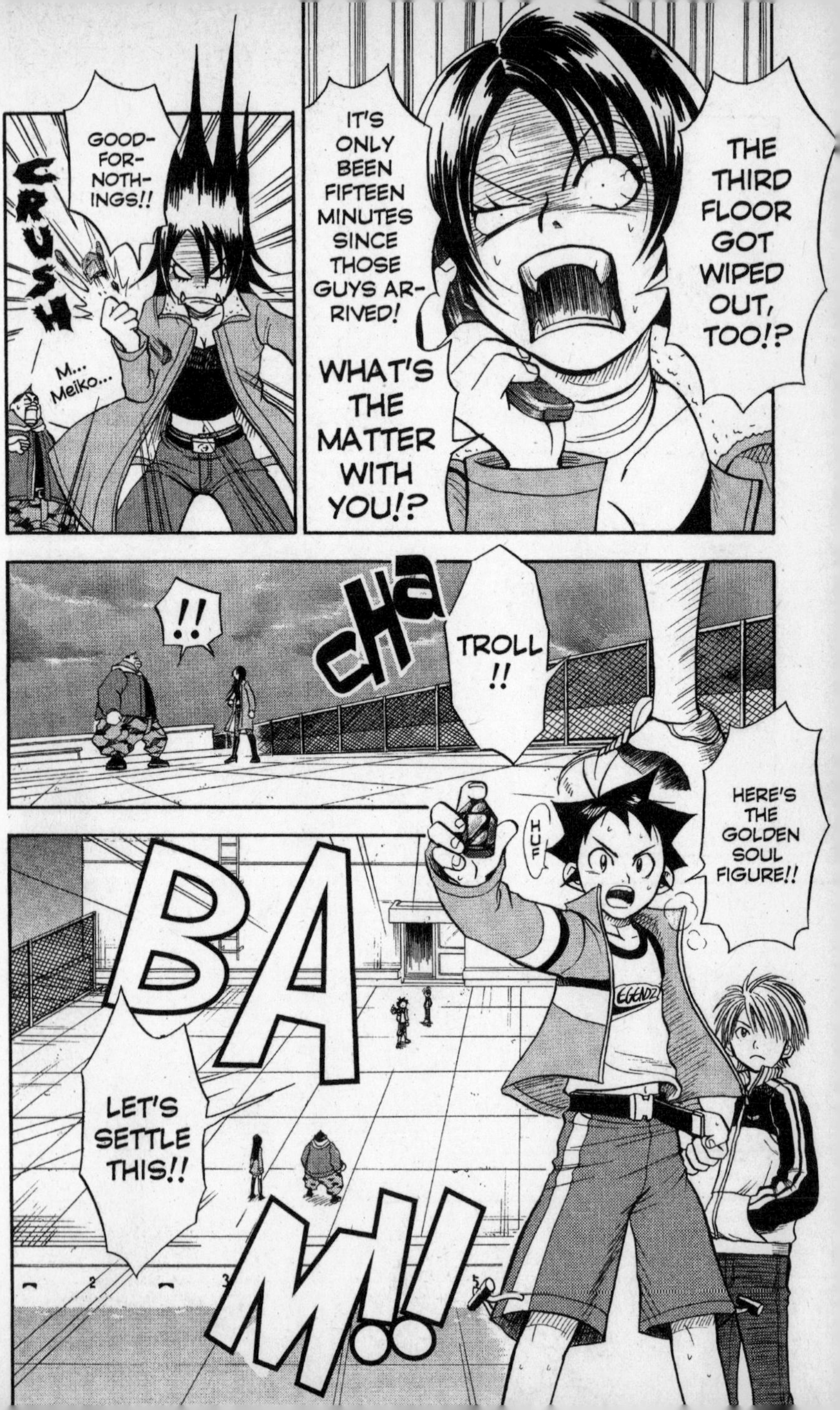
THE THIRD FLOOR GOT WIPED OUT, TOO!?
IT'S ONLY BEEN FIFTEEN MINUTES SINCE THOSE GUYS ARRIVED!
WHAT'S THE MATTER WITH YOU!?
GOOD-FOR-NOTHINGS!!
CRUSH
M... Meiko...
TROLL!!
CHA
!!
HERE'S THE GOLDEN SOUL FIGURE!!
HUF
BAM!!
LET'S SETTLE THIS!!

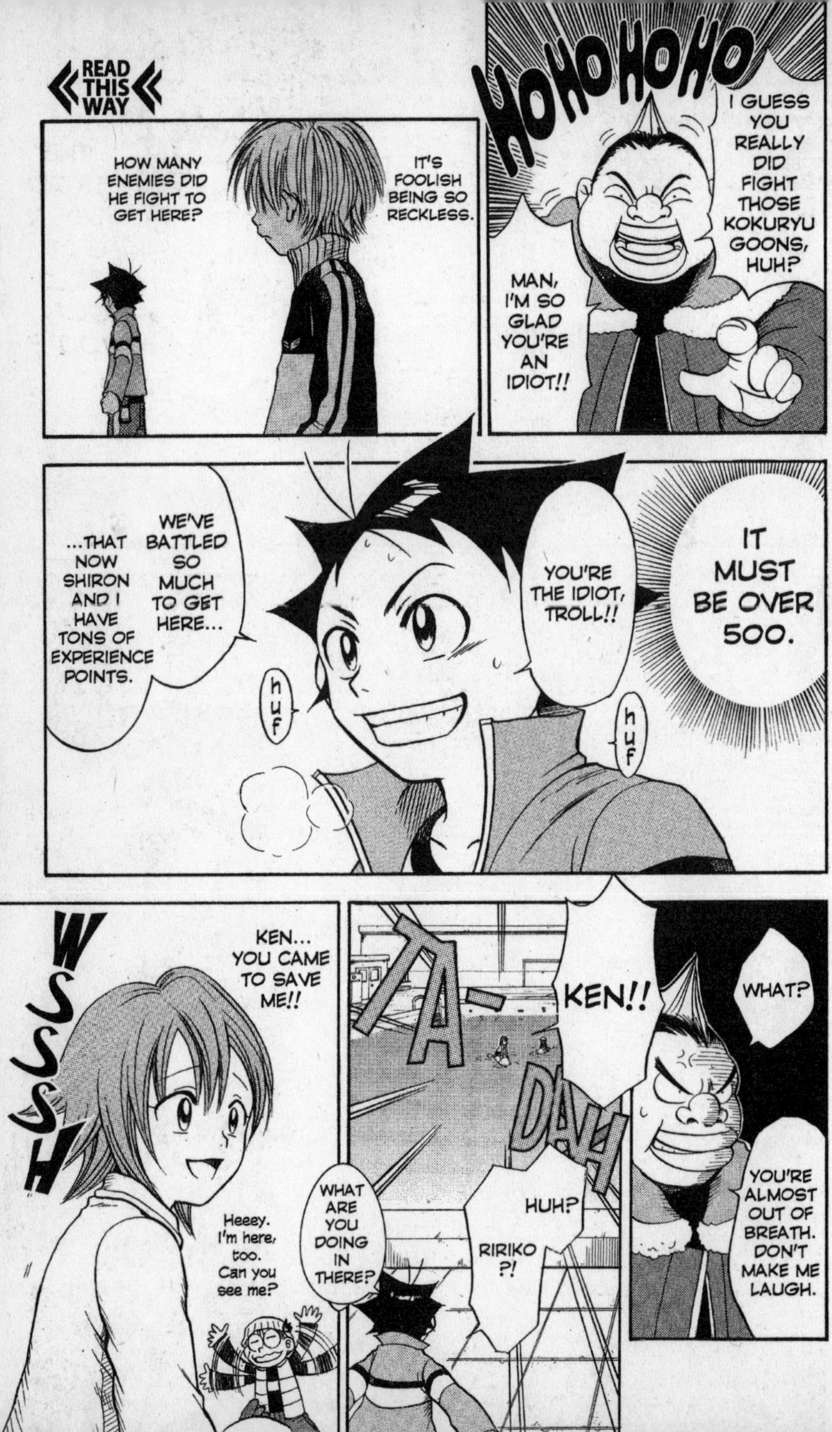
READ THIS WAY
HOHOHOHOHO
I GUESS YOU REALLY DID FIGHT THOSE KOKURYU GOONS, HUH?
MAN, I'M SO GLAD YOU'RE AN IDIOT!!
IT'S FOOLISH BEING SO RECKLESS.
HOW MANY ENEMIES DID HE FIGHT TO GET HERE?
IT MUST BE OVER 500.
YOU'RE THE IDIOT, TROLL!!
huf
huf
WE'VE BATTLED SO MUCH TO GET HERE...
...THAT NOW SHIRON AND I HAVE TONS OF EXPERIENCE POINTS.
WHAT?
YOU'RE ALMOST OUT OF BREATH. DON'T MAKE ME LAUGH.
KEN!!
TA-
DAH
HUH?
RIRIKO ?!
WHAT ARE YOU DOING IN THERE?
WSSSSH
KEN... YOU CAME TO SAVE ME!!
Heeey. I'm here, too. Can you see me?

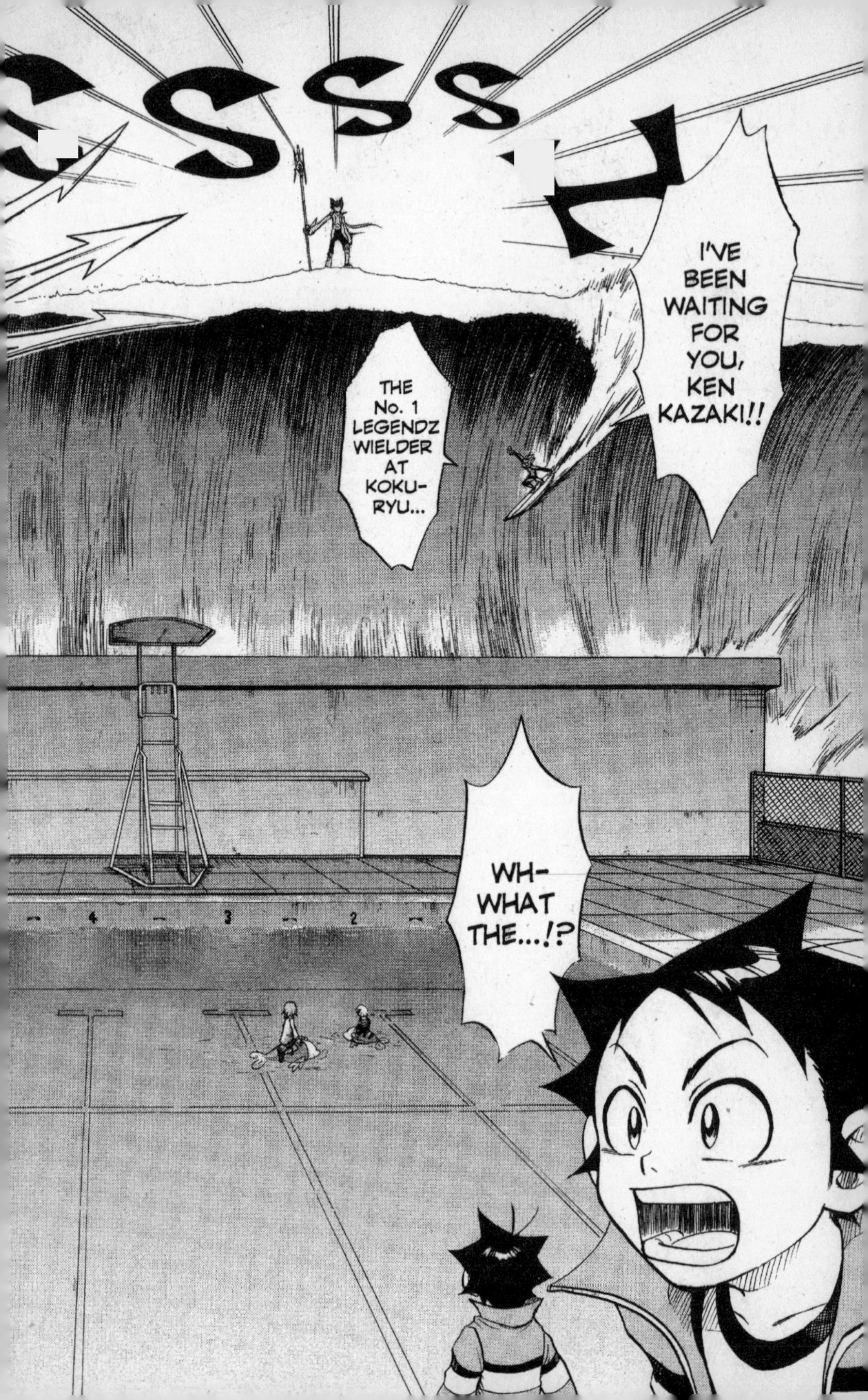
SSSSH
I'VE BEEN WAITING FOR YOU, KEN KAZAKI!!
THE No. 1 LEGENDZ WIELDER AT KOKU-RYU...
WH-WHAT THE...!?

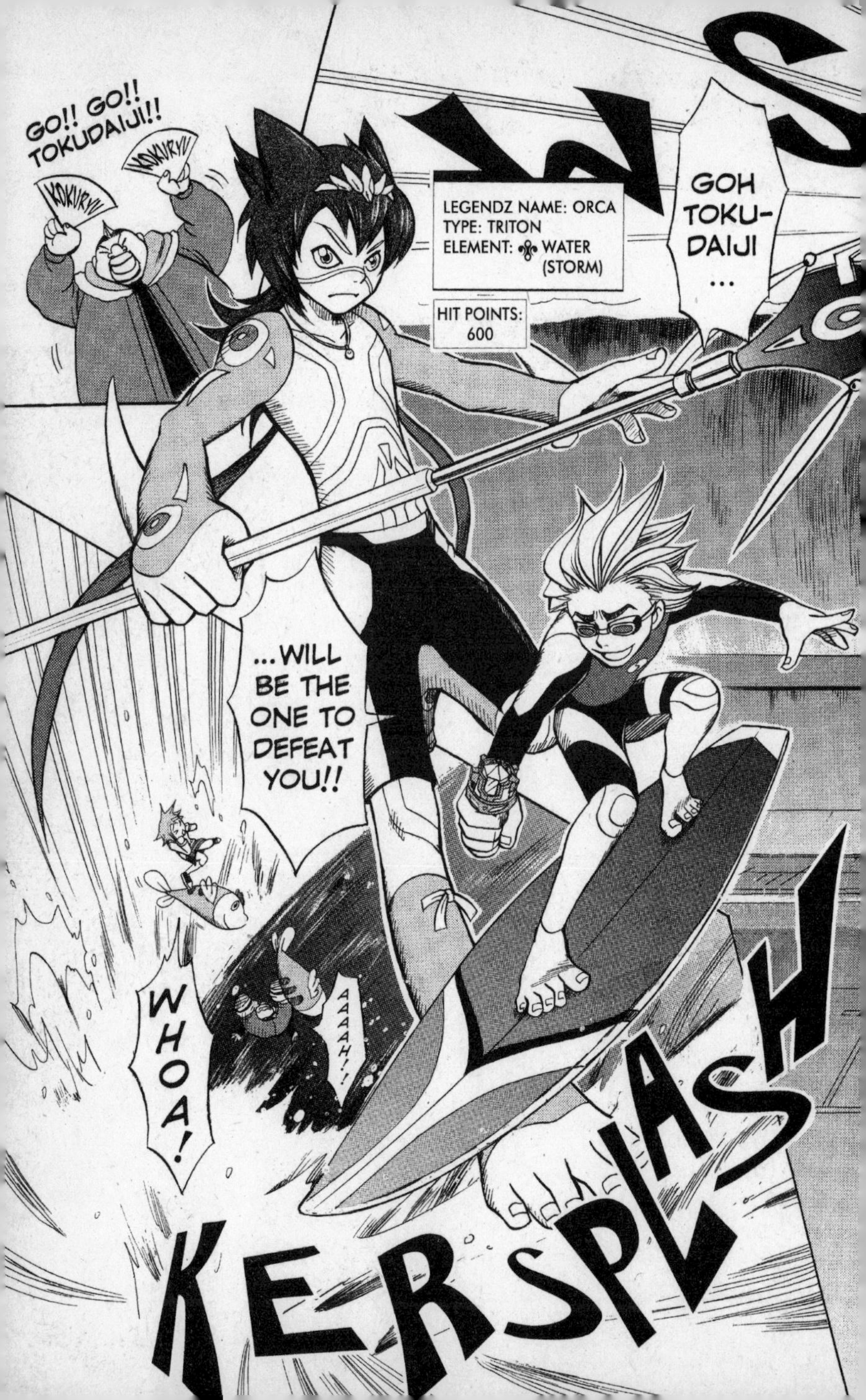
GOH TOKU-DAIJI ...
LEGENDZ NAME: ORCA
TYPE: TRITON
ELEMENT: WATER (STORM)
HIT POINTS: 600
GO!! GO!! TOKUDAIJI!!
KOKURYU
KOKURYU
...WILL BE THE ONE TO DEFEAT YOU!!
AAAAH!!
WHOA!
KERSPLASH

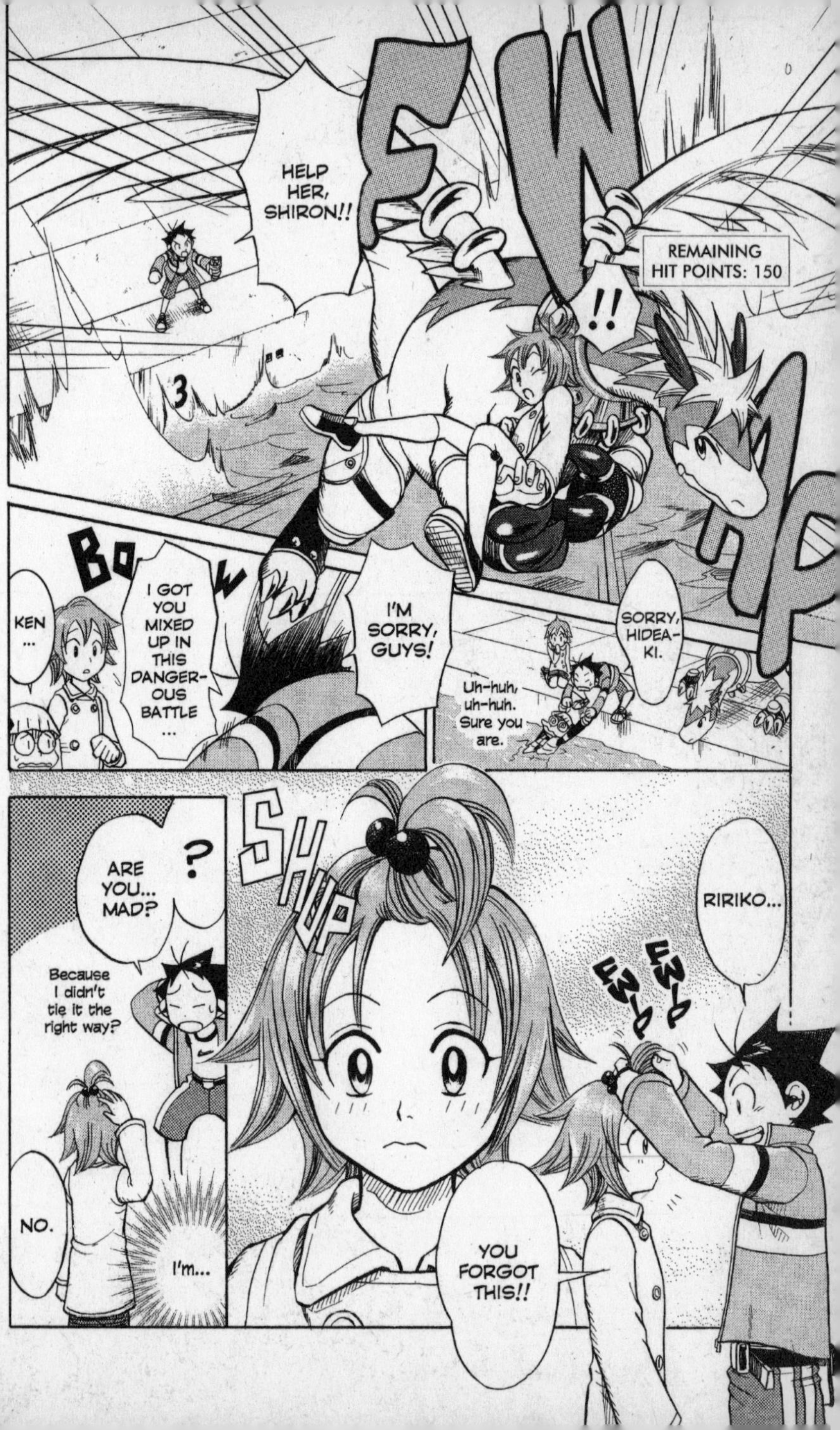
FWAP
REMAINING HIT POINTS: 150
!!
HELP HER, SHIRON!!
3
SORRY, HIDEAKI.
Uh-huh, uh-huh. Sure you are.
I'M SORRY, GUYS!
I GOT YOU MIXED UP IN THIS DANGEROUS BATTLE ...
BOW
KEN ...
RIRIKO...
FWIP FWIP
YOU FORGOT THIS!!
SHUP
ARE YOU... MAD?
?
Because I didn't tie it the right way?
NO.
I'm...

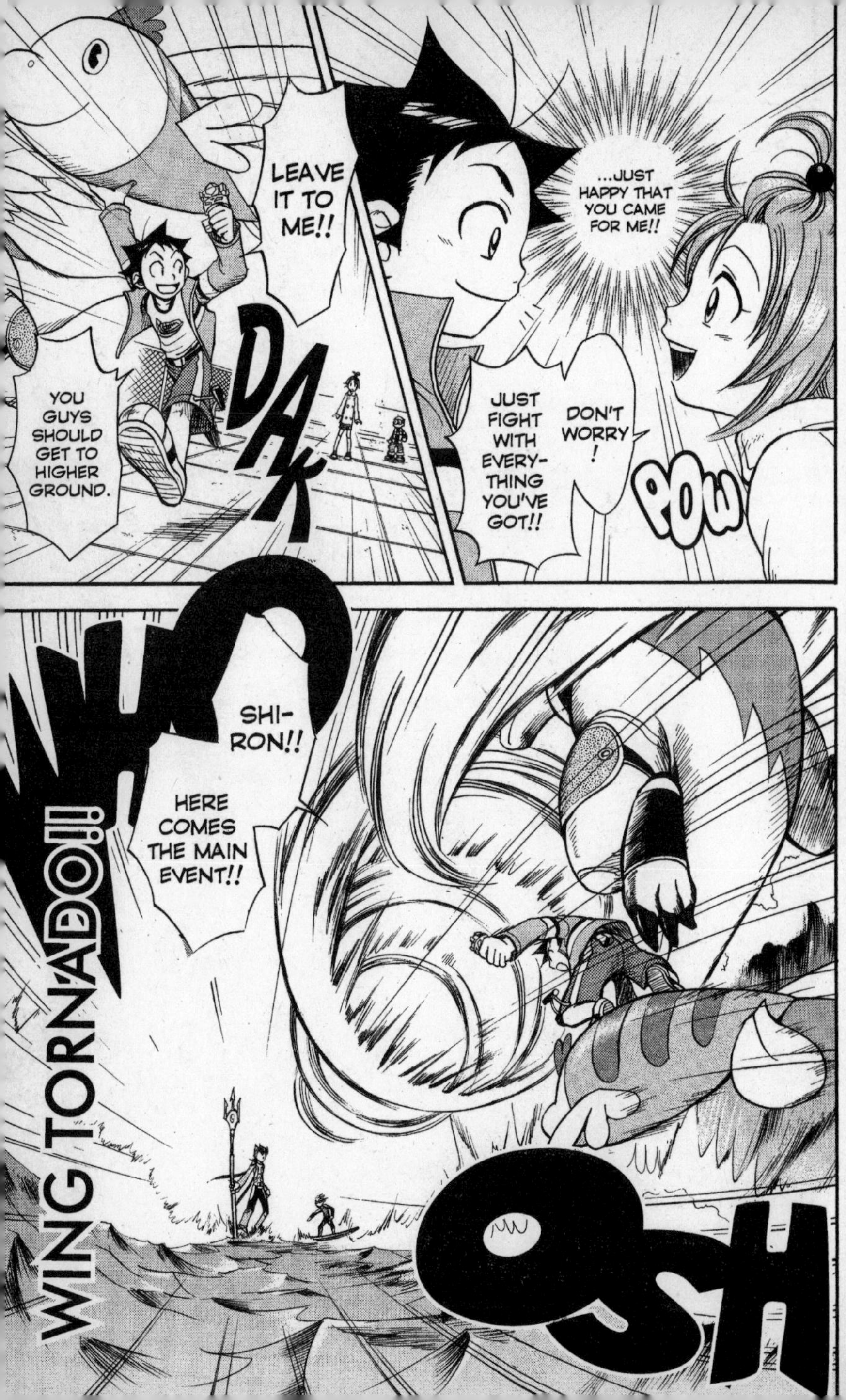
...JUST HAPPY THAT YOU CAME FOR ME!!
POW
DON'T WORRY!
JUST FIGHT WITH EVERY-THING YOU'VE GOT!!
LEAVE IT TO ME!!
DAK
YOU GUYS SHOULD GET TO HIGHER GROUND.
WHO
SHI-RON!!
HERE COMES THE MAIN EVENT!!
WING TORNADO!!!
OSH

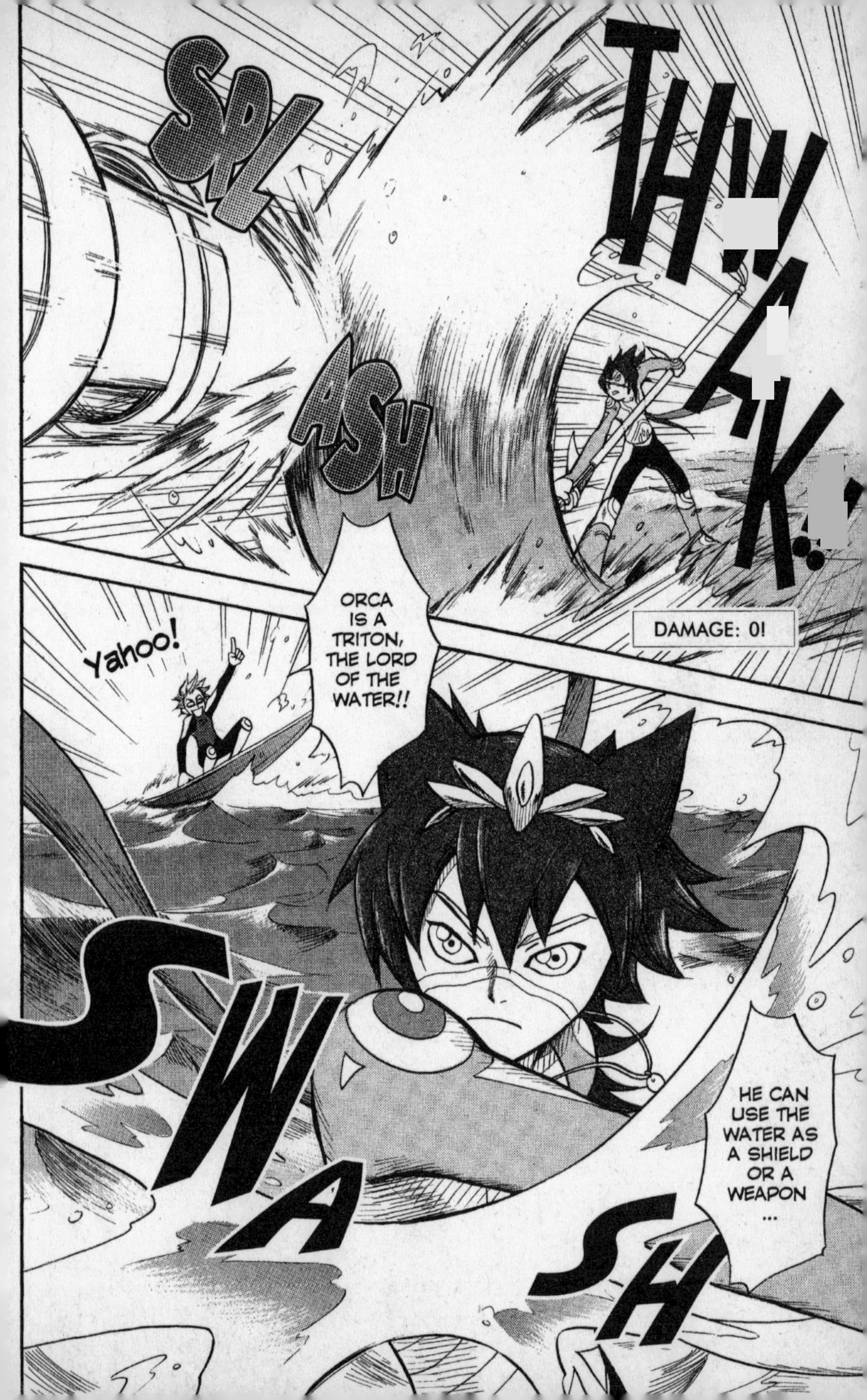
THWAK!!
SPLASH
DAMAGE: 0!
ORCA IS A TRITON, THE LORD OF THE WATER!!
Yahoo!
HE CAN USE THE WATER AS A SHIELD OR A WEAPON ...
SWASH

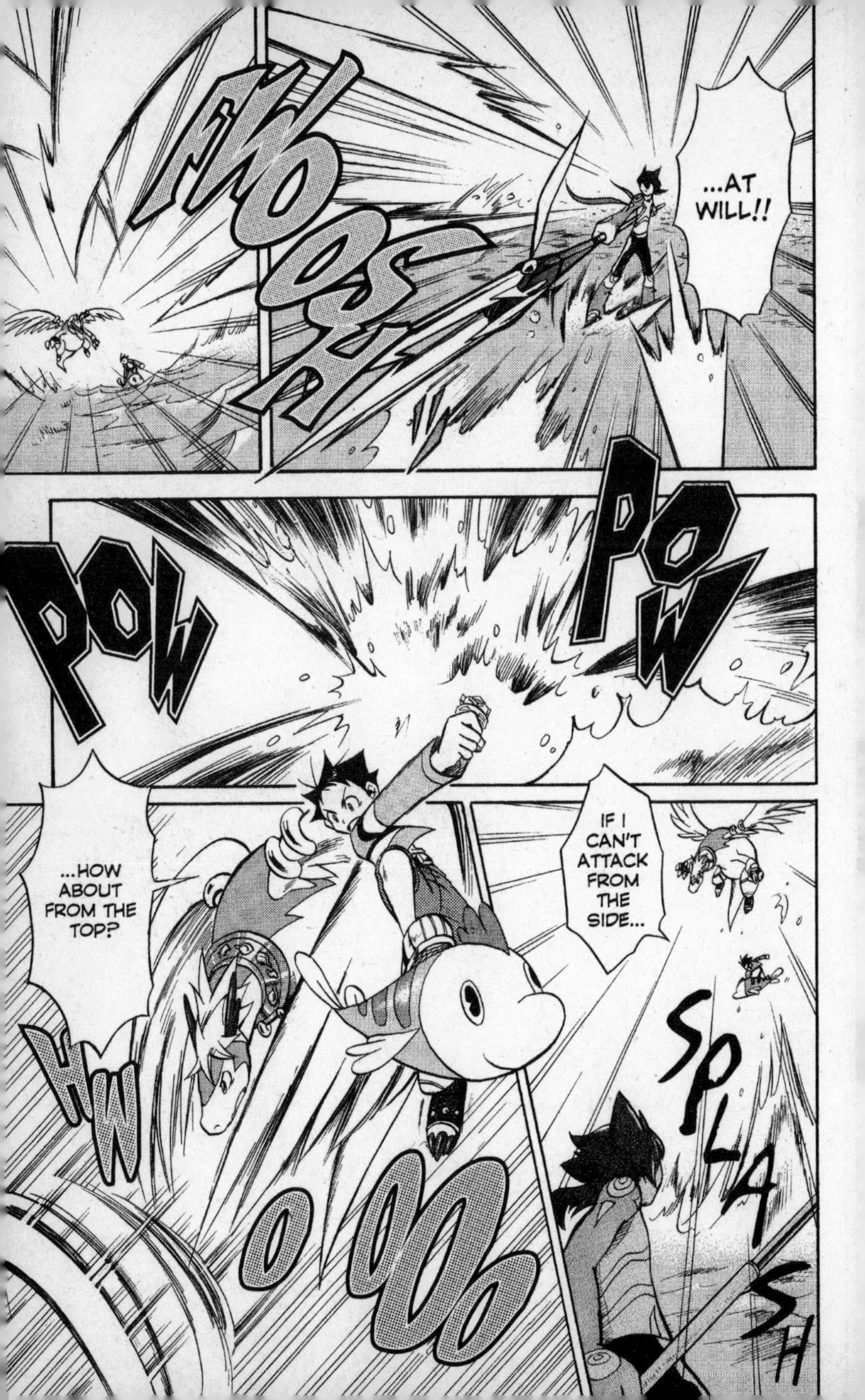

...AT WILL!!
WHOOSH!
POW
POW
IF I CAN'T ATTACK FROM THE SIDE...
SPLASH
...HOW ABOUT FROM THE TOP?
WHOOOO

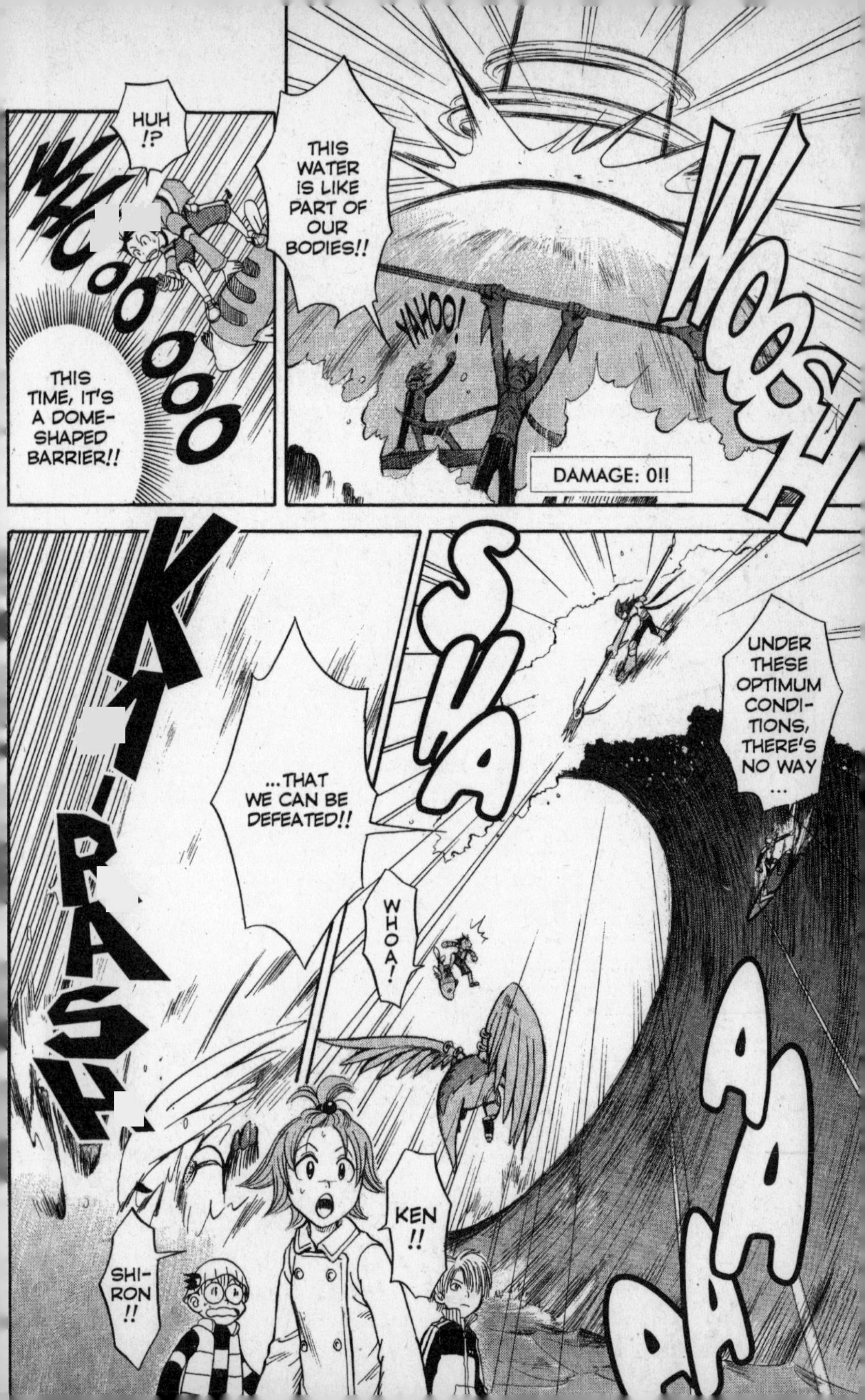
THIS WATER IS LIKE PART OF OUR BODIES!!
YAHOO!
WOOOSH
DAMAGE: 0!!
HUH !?
THIS TIME, IT'S A DOME-SHAPED BARRIER!!
UNDER THESE OPTIMUM CONDITIONS, THERE'S NO WAY ...
...THAT WE CAN BE DEFEATED!!
WHOA!
KEN !!
SHI-RON !!

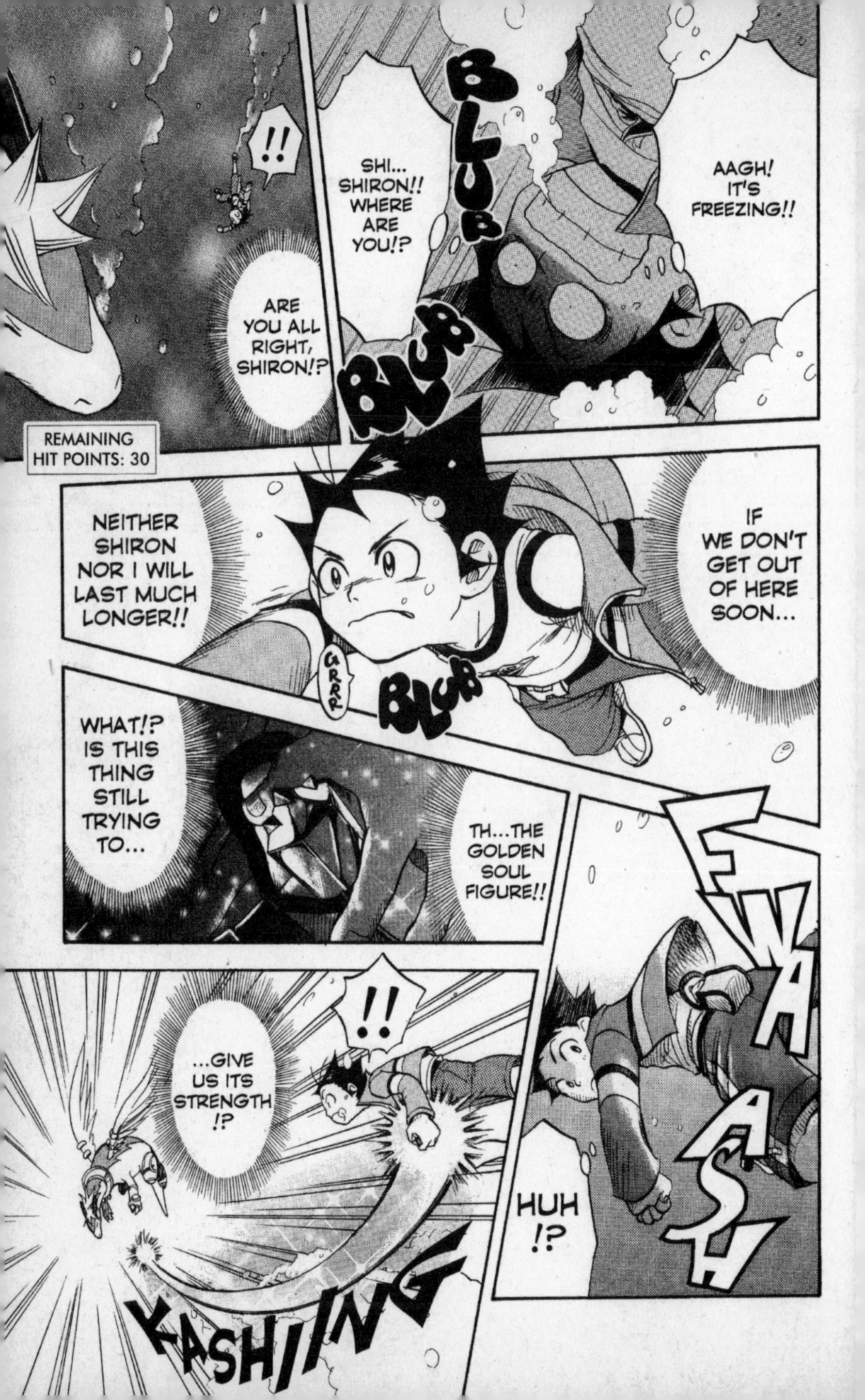
BLUB
AAGH! IT'S FREEZING!!
SHI... SHIRON!! WHERE ARE YOU!?
BLUB
!!
ARE YOU ALL RIGHT, SHIRON!?
REMAINING HIT POINTS: 30
IF WE DON'T GET OUT OF HERE SOON...
NEITHER SHIRON NOR I WILL LAST MUCH LONGER!!
GRRR
BLUB
FWAASH
HUH !?
TH...THE GOLDEN SOUL FIGURE!!
WHAT!? IS THIS THING STILL TRYING TO...
!!
...GIVE US ITS STRENGTH !?
KASHIING

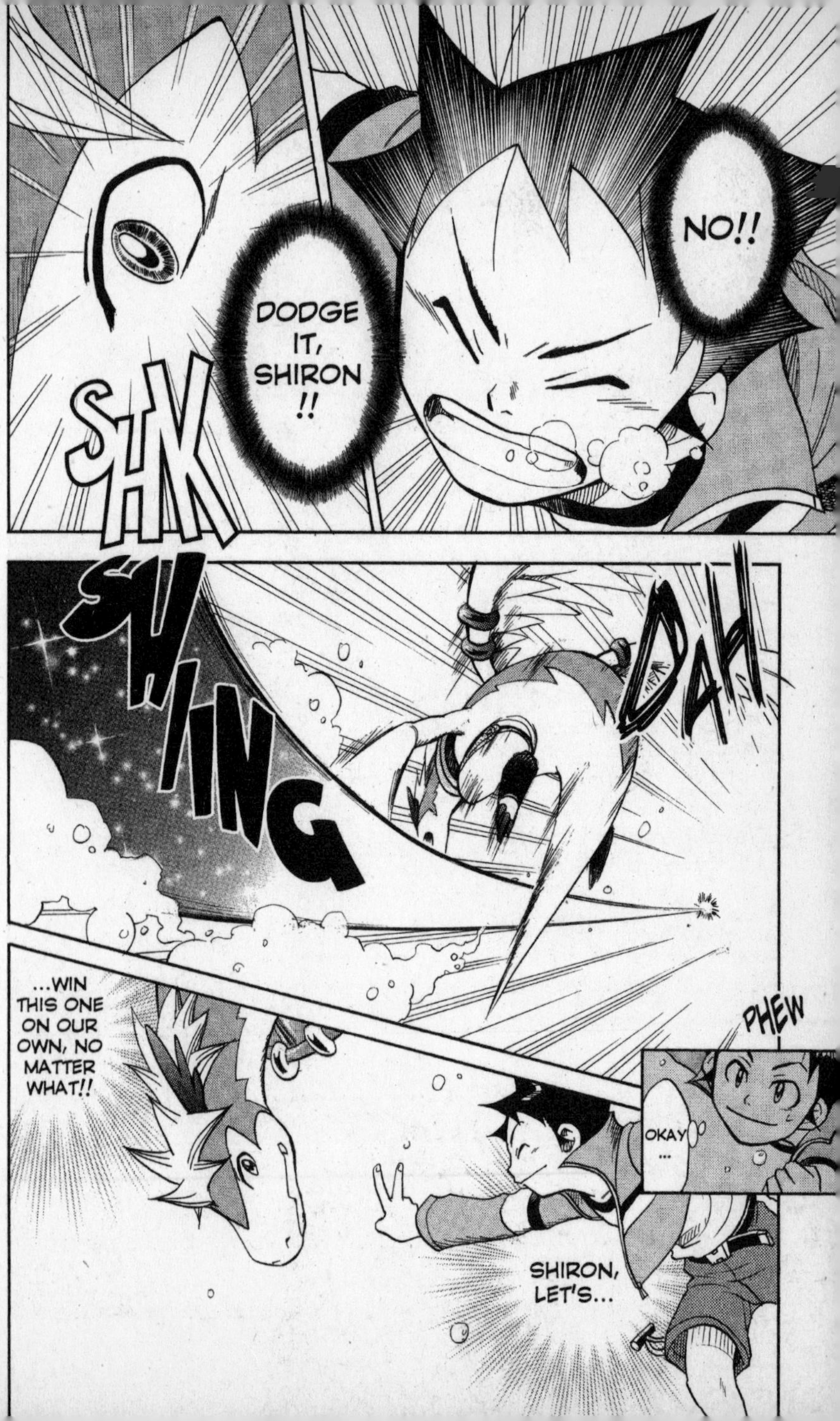
NO!!
DODGE IT, SHIRON!!
SHK
DAH
SHHING
PHEW
OKAY...
SHIRON, LET'S...
...WIN THIS ONE ON OUR OWN, NO MATTER WHAT!!

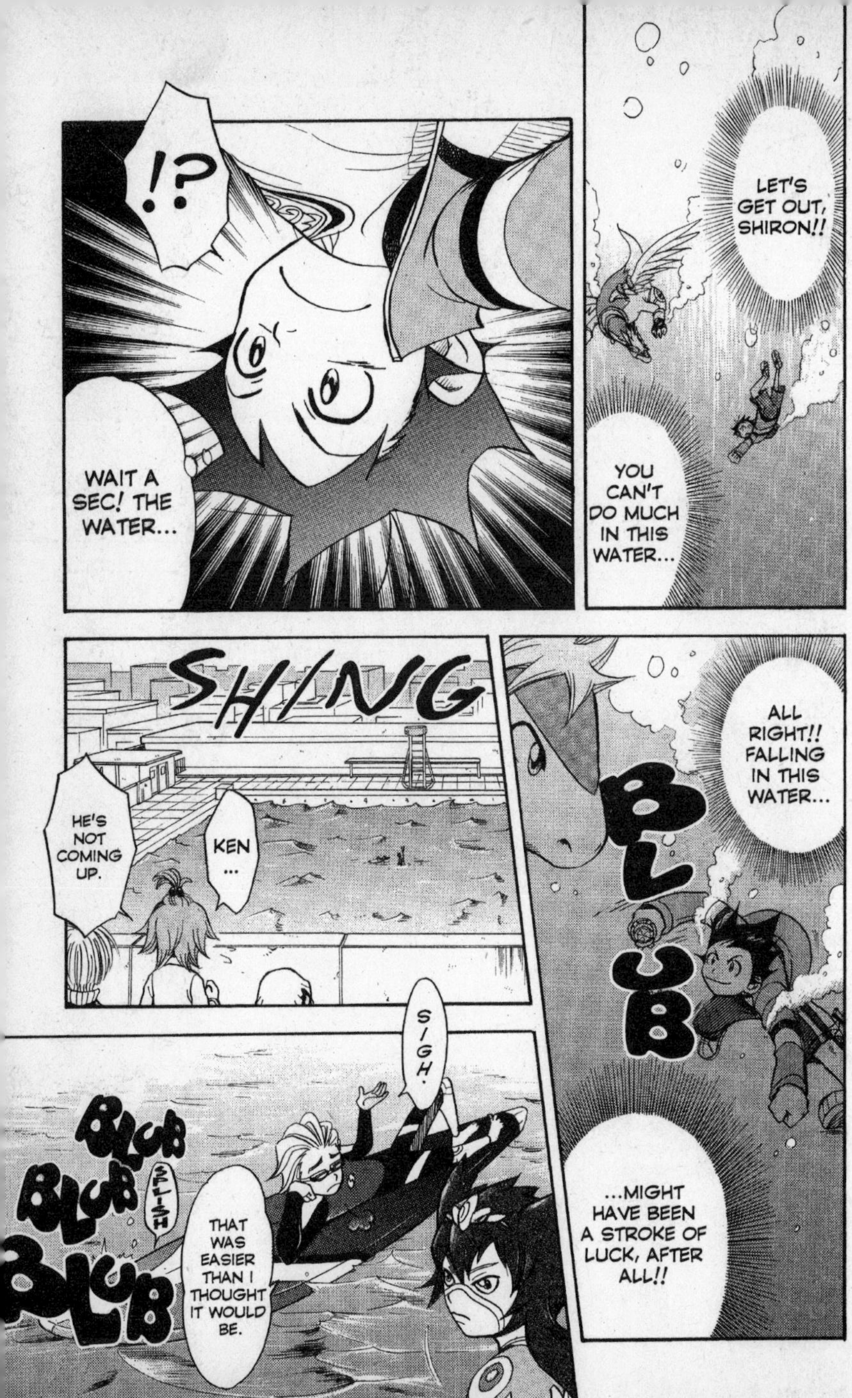
LET'S GET OUT, SHIRON!!
YOU CAN'T DO MUCH IN THIS WATER...
!?
WAIT A SEC! THE WATER...
ALL RIGHT!! FALLING IN THIS WATER...
BLUB
...MIGHT HAVE BEEN A STROKE OF LUCK, AFTER ALL!!
SHING
KEN...
HE'S NOT COMING UP.
SIGH.
THAT WAS EASIER THAN I THOUGHT IT WOULD BE.
SPLISH
BLUB
BLUB
BLUB

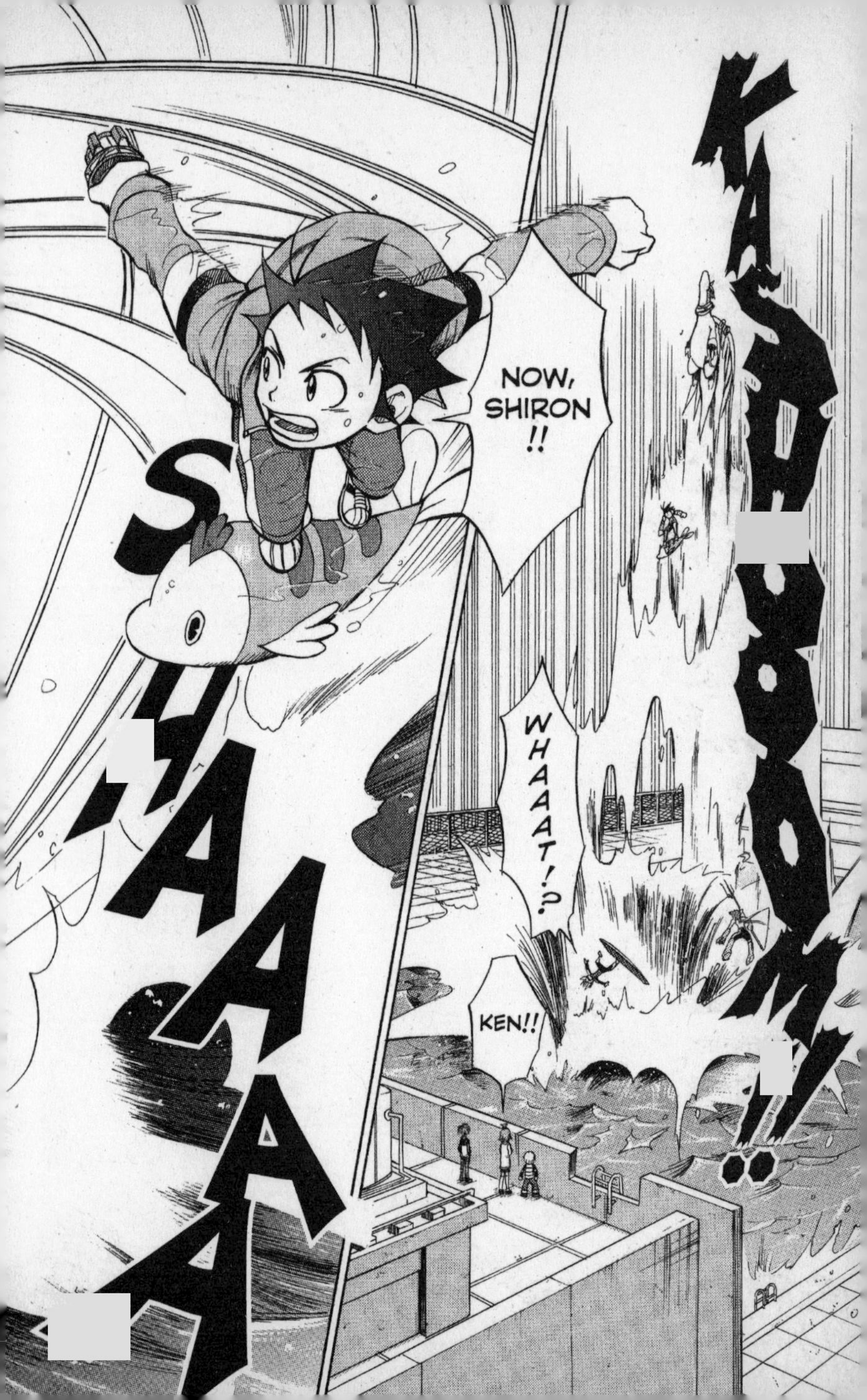
KABOOM!!
NOW, SHIRON!!
WHAAAT!?
KEN!!
SHAAAA

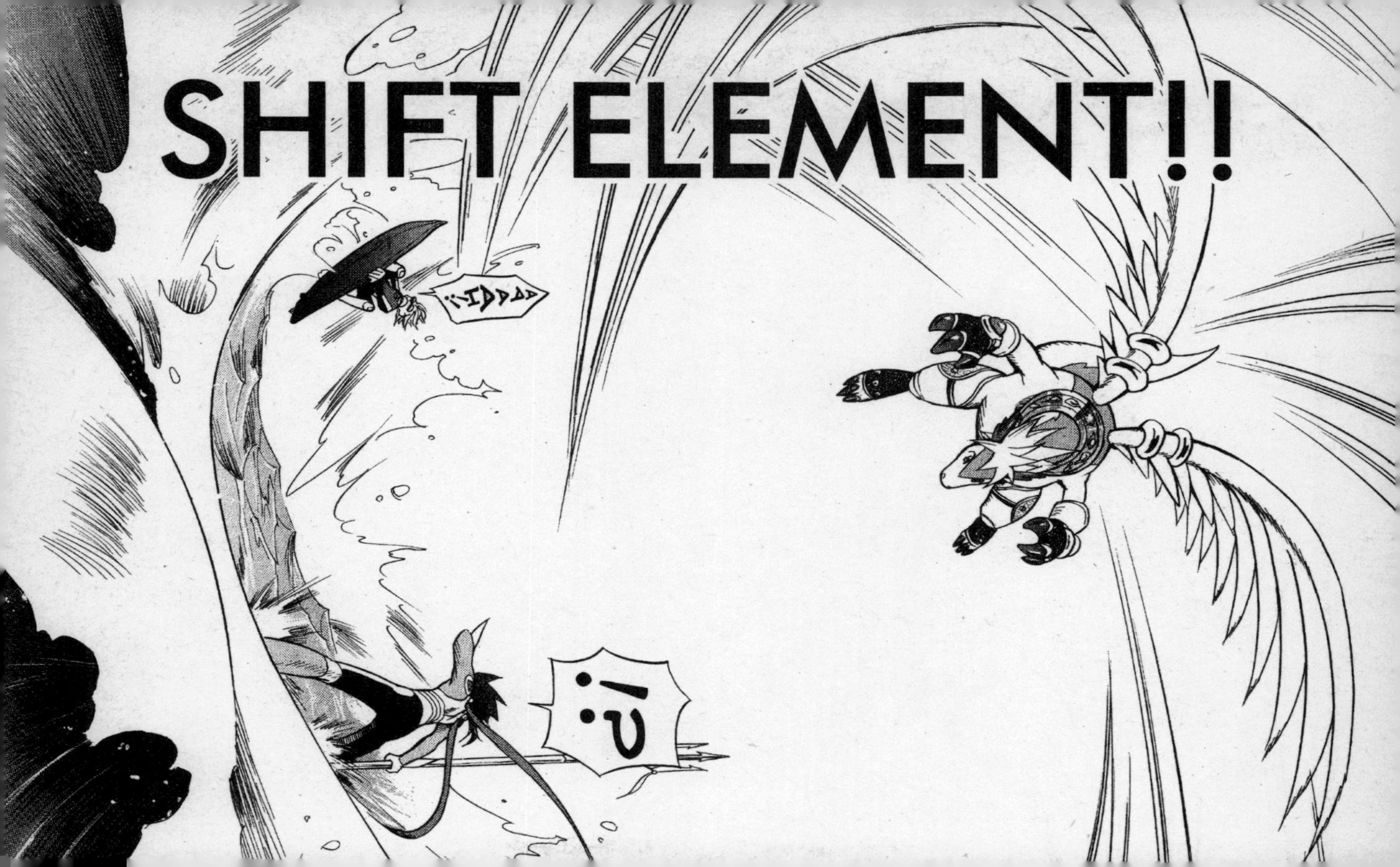
SHIFT ELEMENT!!
!?
AAAAH!!

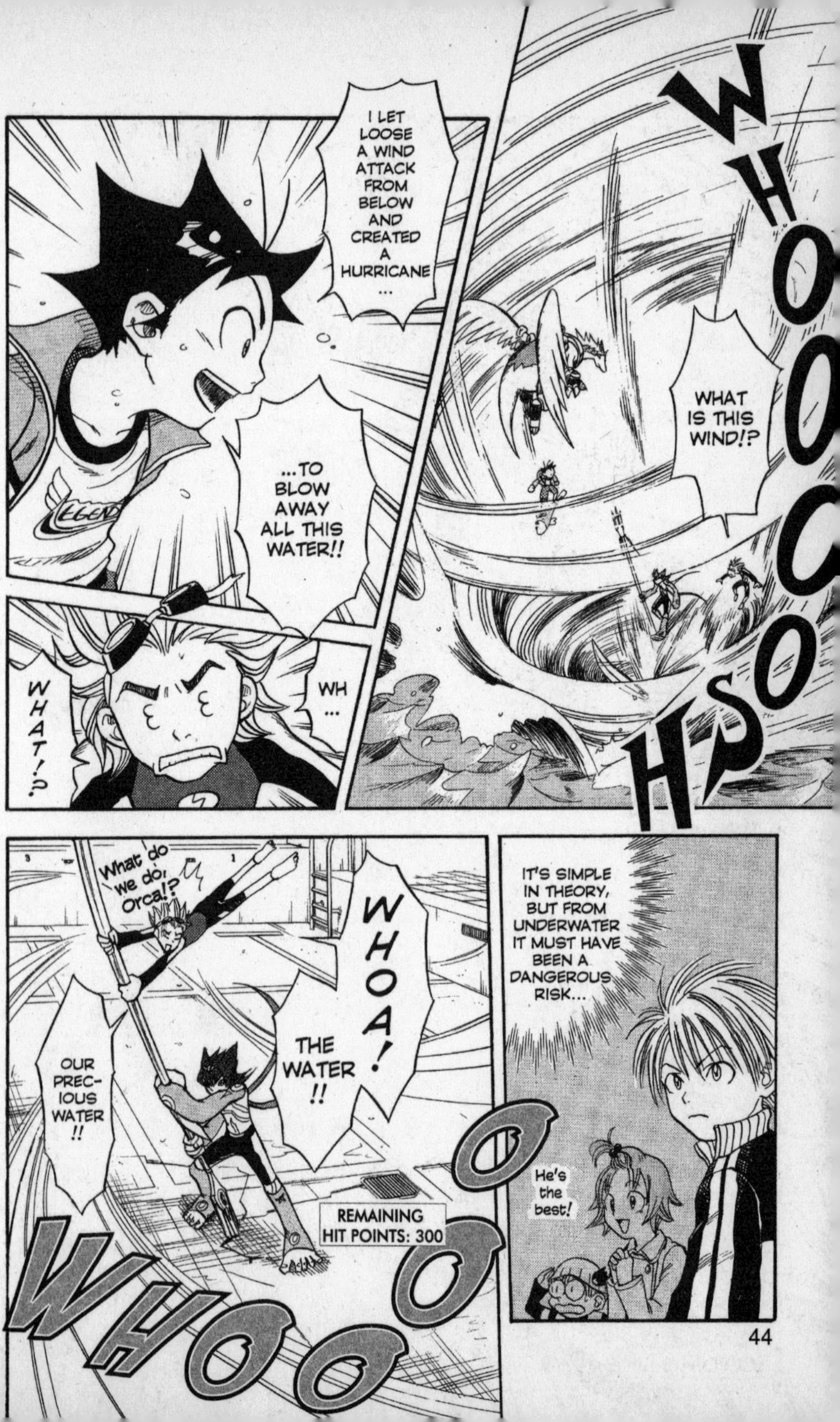
WHOOOOOOSH
WHAT IS THIS WIND!?
I LET LOOSE A WIND ATTACK FROM BELOW AND CREATED A HURRICANE ...
...TO BLOW AWAY ALL THIS WATER!!
WH ...
WHAT!!?
IT'S SIMPLE IN THEORY, BUT FROM UNDERWATER IT MUST HAVE BEEN A DANGEROUS RISK...
He's the best!
What do we do, Orca!?
WHOA!
THE WATER !!
OUR PRECIOUS WATER !!
REMAINING HIT POINTS: 300
WHOOOOO

READ THIS WAY

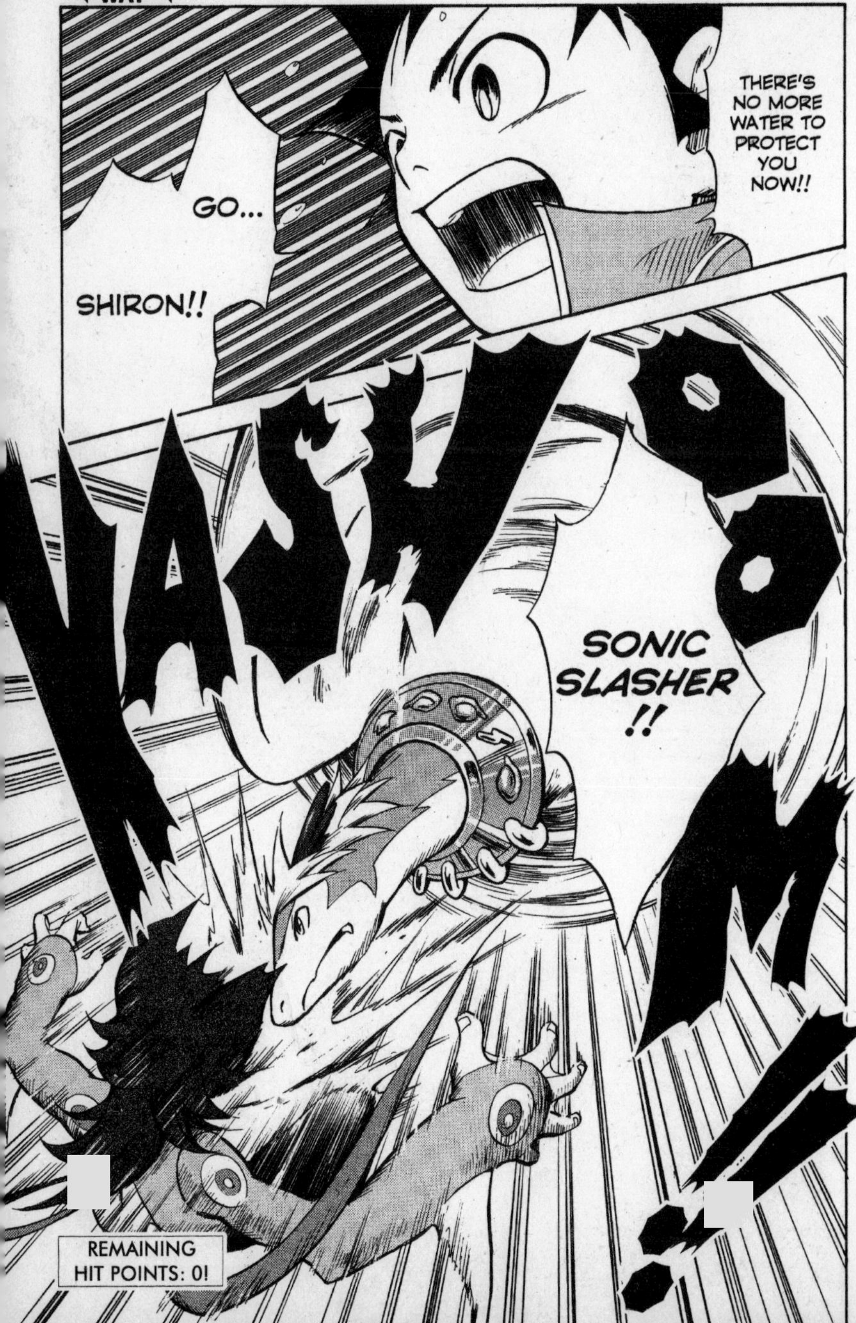
THERE'S NO MORE WATER TO PROTECT YOU NOW!!
GO...
SHIRON!!
SONIC SLASHER !!
REMAINING HIT POINTS: 0!

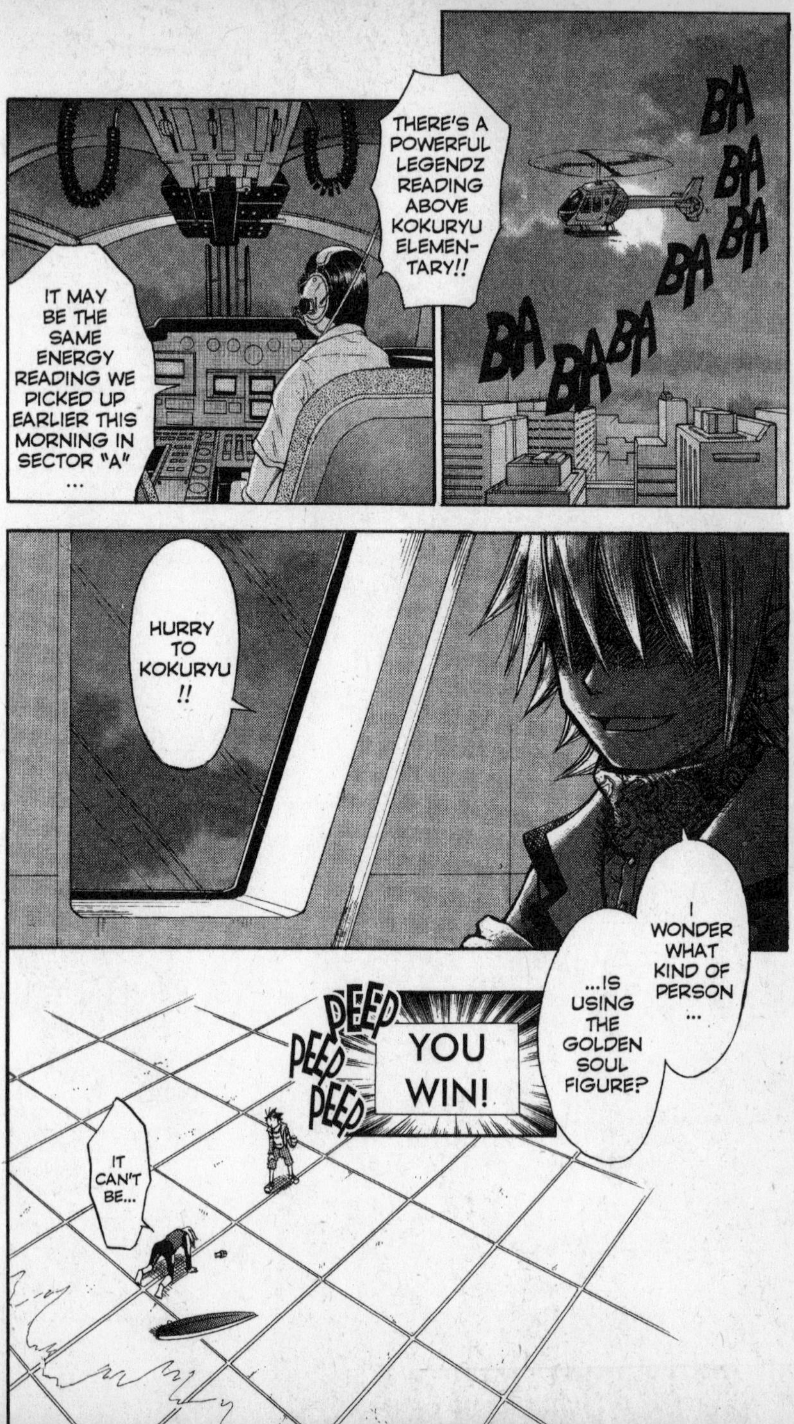
BA BA BA BA BA BA BA BA
THERE'S A POWERFUL LEGENDZ READING ABOVE KOKURYU ELEMENTARY!!
IT MAY BE THE SAME ENERGY READING WE PICKED UP EARLIER THIS MORNING IN SECTOR "A"...
HURRY TO KOKURYU!!
I WONDER WHAT KIND OF PERSON...
...IS USING THE GOLDEN SOUL FIGURE?
PEEP PEEP PEEP
YOU WIN!
IT CAN'T BE...

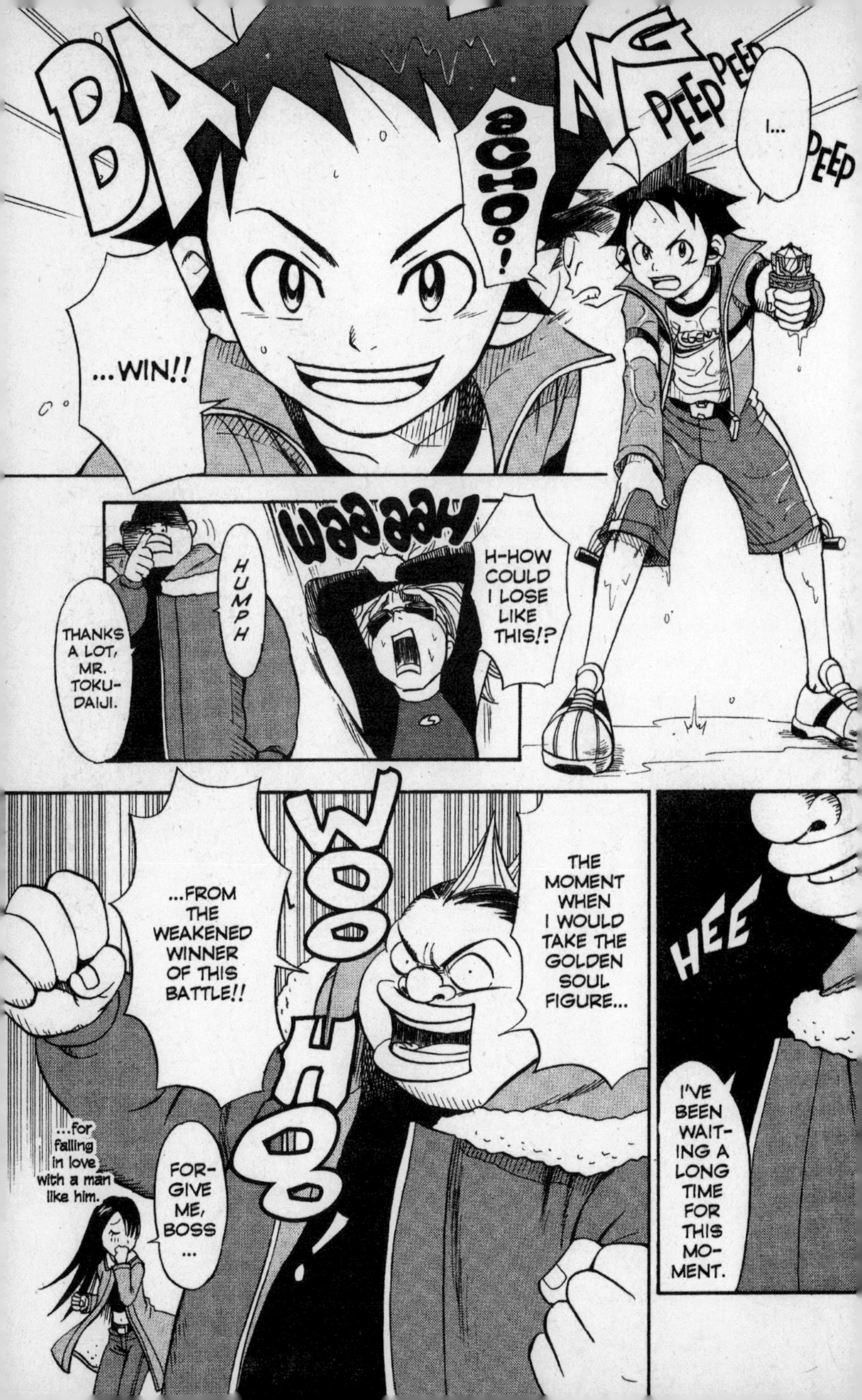
I...
PEEP PEEP PEEP PEEP
BANG
ACHOO!
...WIN!!
H-HOW COULD I LOSE LIKE THIS!?
WAAAAH
HUMPH
THANKS A LOT, MR. TOKU-DAIJI.
HEE
I'VE BEEN WAIT-ING A LONG TIME FOR THIS MO-MENT.
THE MOMENT WHEN I WOULD TAKE THE GOLDEN SOUL FIGURE...
WOOHHO!
...FROM THE WEAKENED WINNER OF THIS BATTLE!!
FOR-GIVE ME, BOSS...
...for falling in love with a man like him.

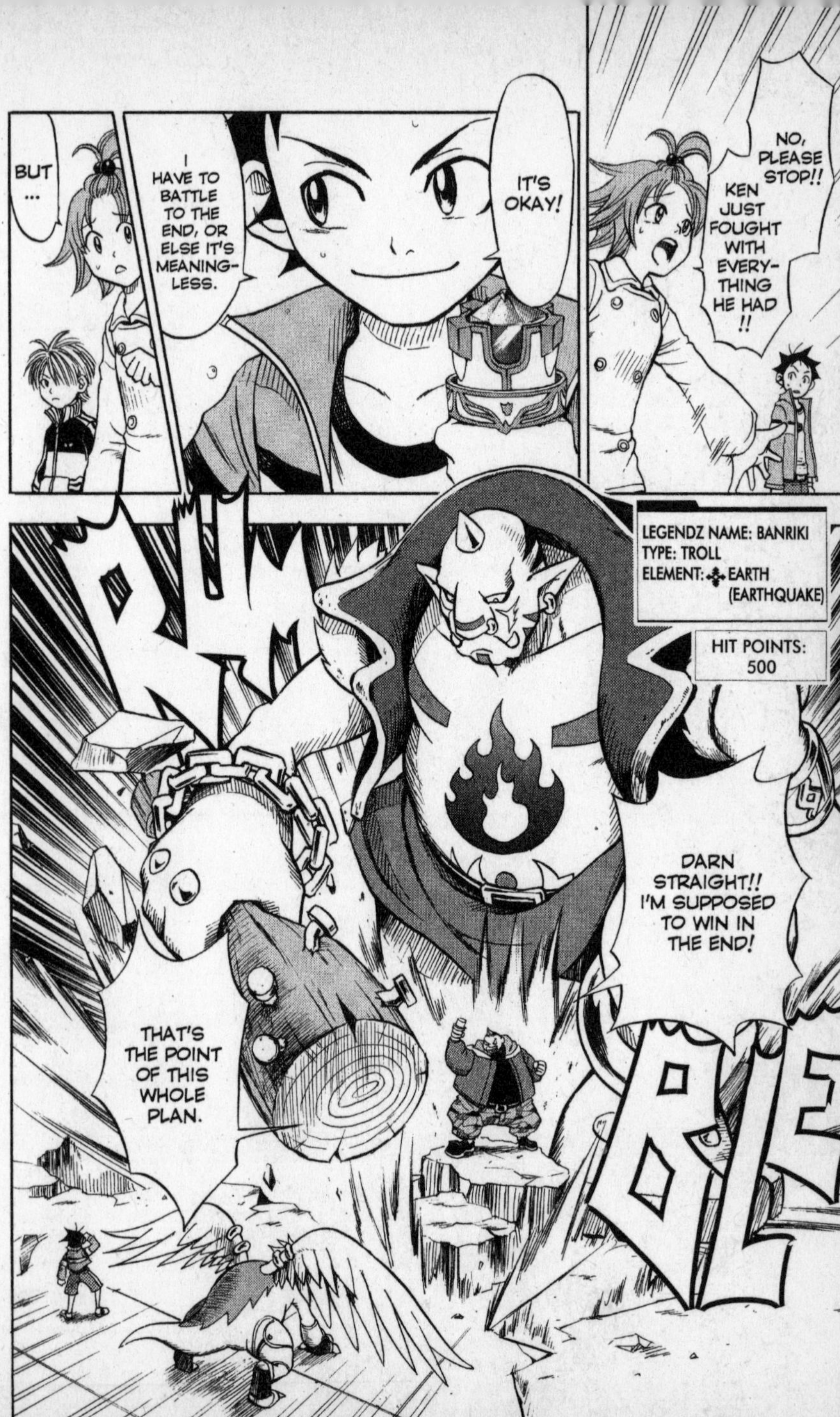
NO, PLEASE STOP!!
KEN JUST FOUGHT WITH EVERY-THING HE HAD!!
IT'S OKAY!
I HAVE TO BATTLE TO THE END, OR ELSE IT'S MEANING-LESS.
BUT ...
LEGENDZ NAME: BANRIKI
TYPE: TROLL
ELEMENT: EARTH (EARTHQUAKE)
HIT POINTS: 500
DARN STRAIGHT!! I'M SUPPOSED TO WIN IN THE END!
THAT'S THE POINT OF THIS WHOLE PLAN.

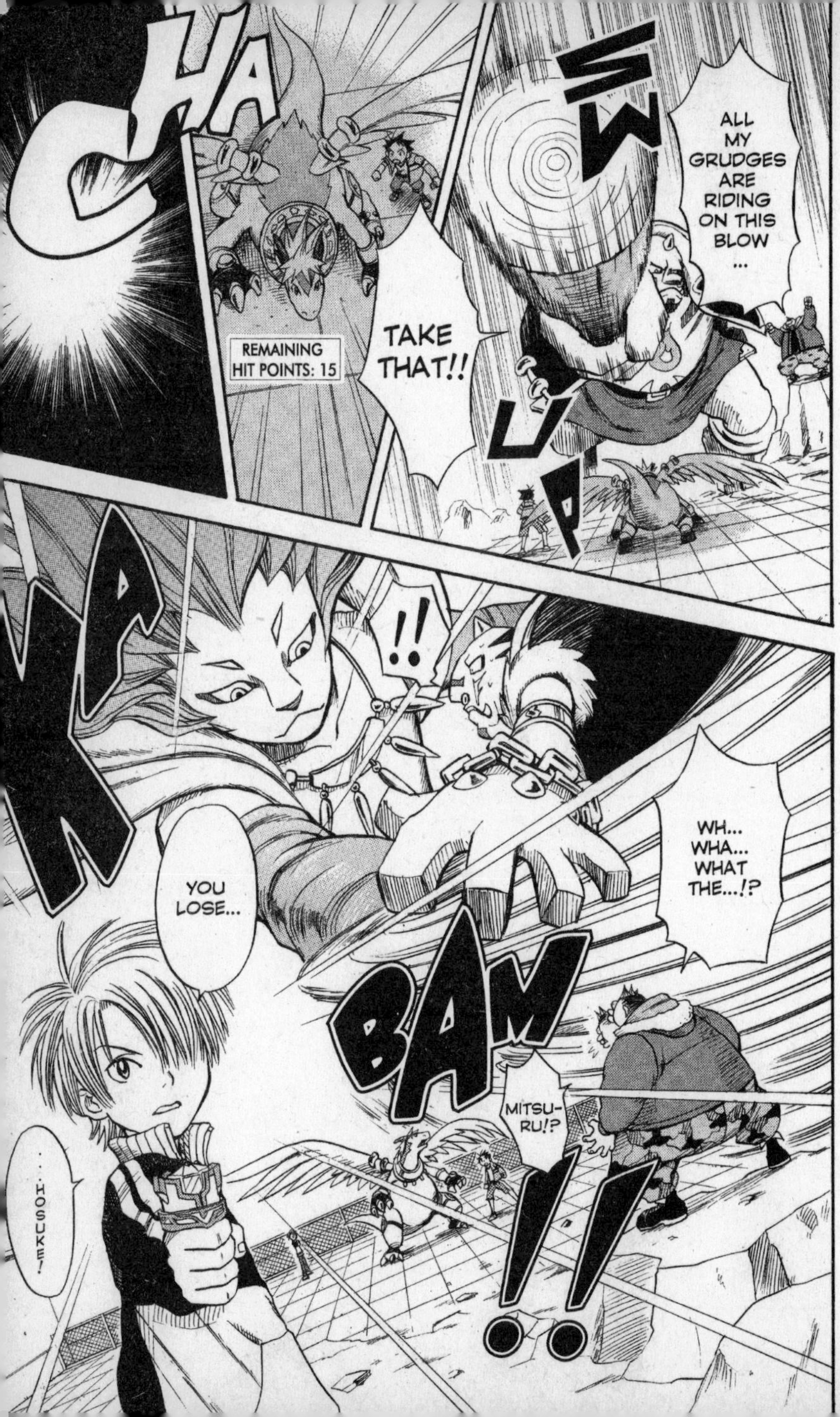
SWUP
ALL MY GRUDGES ARE RIDING ON THIS BLOW ...
TAKE THAT!!
REMAINING HIT POINTS: 15
CHA
!!
WH... WHA... WHAT THE...!?
BAM!!
MITSU-RU!?
YOU LOSE...
...HOSUKE!

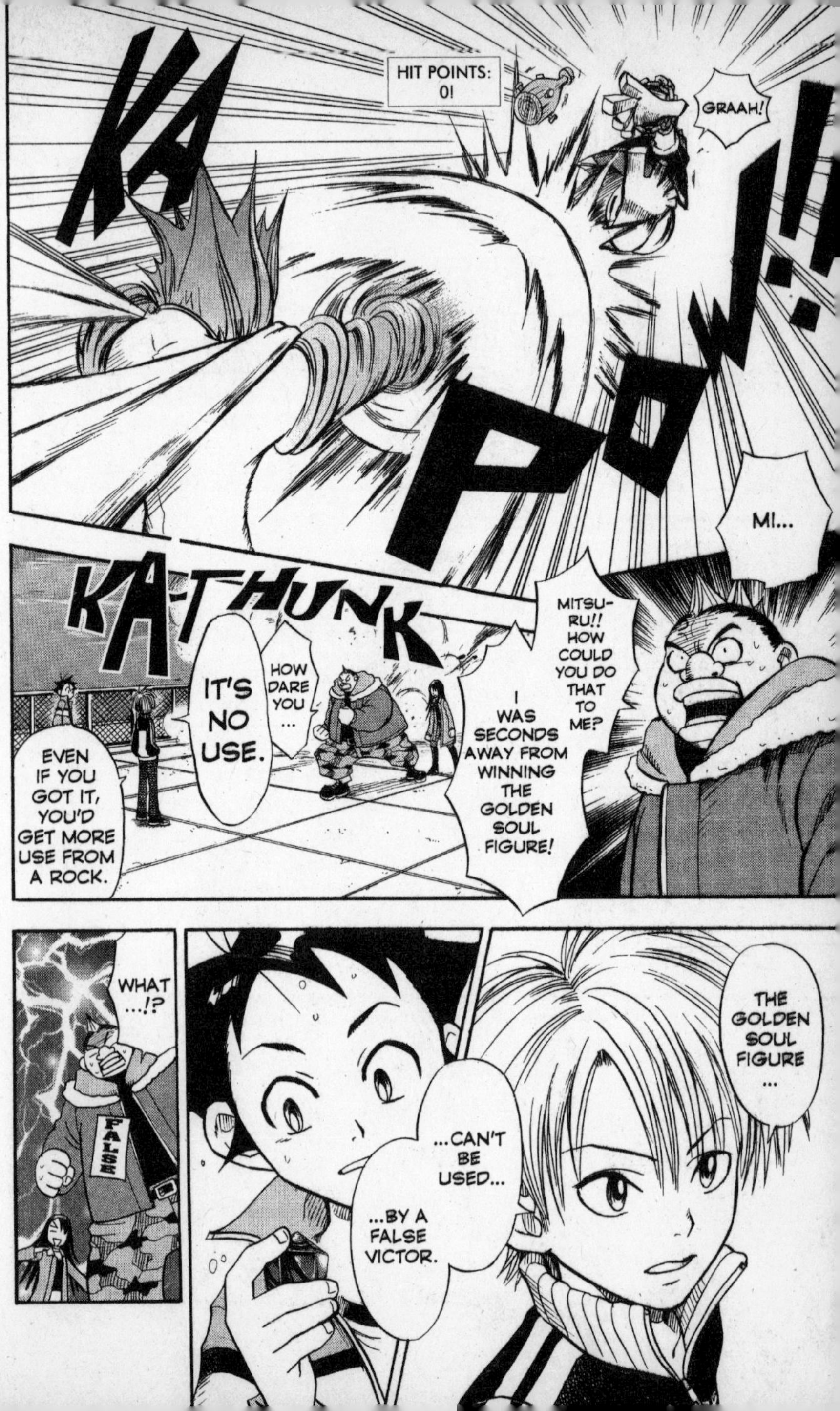
GRAAH!
HIT POINTS: 0!
KA
POW!!
MI...
MITSU-RU!! HOW COULD YOU DO THAT TO ME?
I WAS SECONDS AWAY FROM WINNING THE GOLDEN SOUL FIGURE!
KA-THUNK
HOW DARE YOU ...
IT'S NO USE.
EVEN IF YOU GOT IT, YOU'D GET MORE USE FROM A ROCK.
THE GOLDEN SOUL FIGURE ...
...CAN'T BE USED...
...BY A FALSE VICTOR.
WHAT ...!?
FALSE

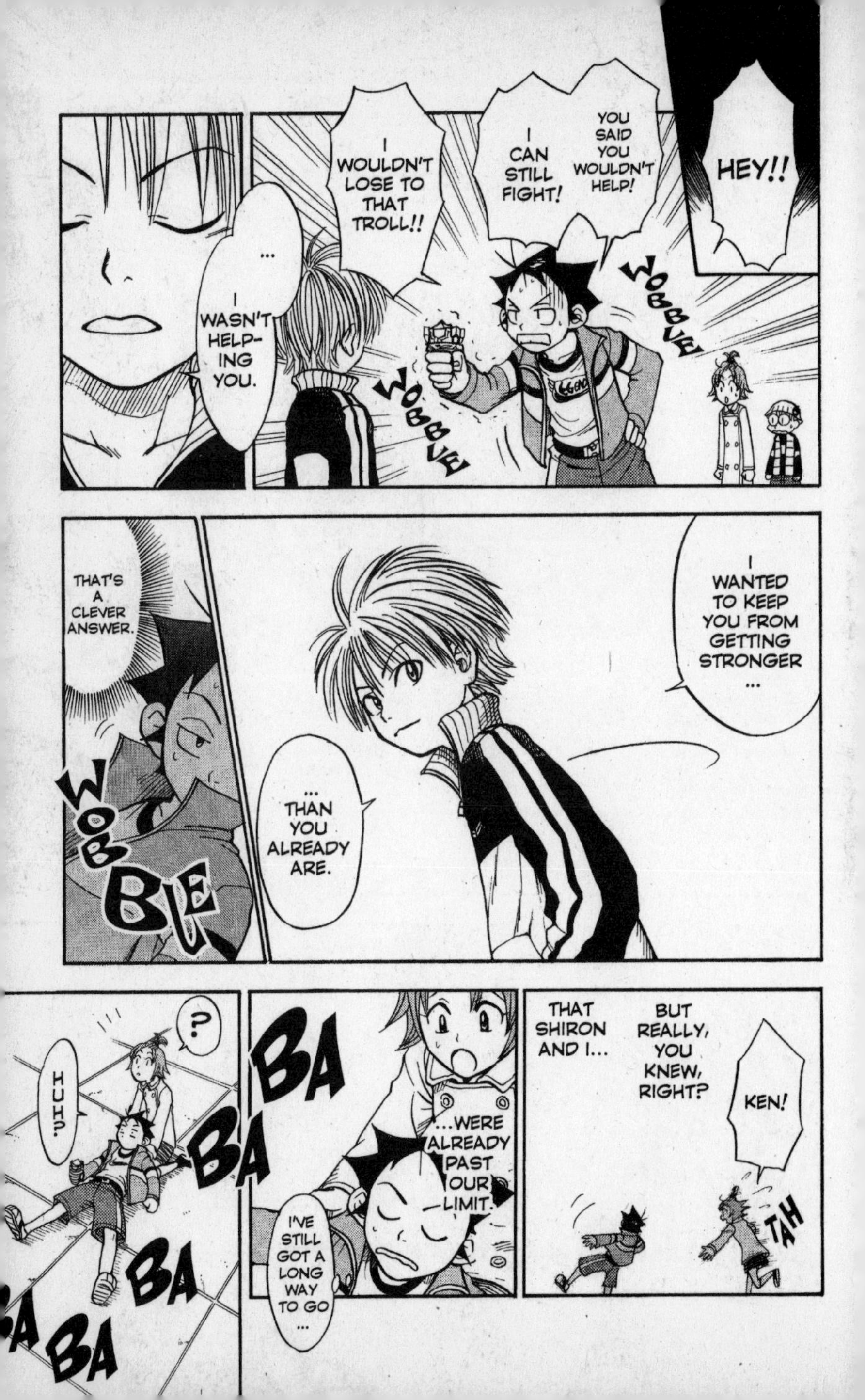
HEY!!
YOU SAID YOU WOULDN'T HELP!
I CAN STILL FIGHT!
I WOULDN'T LOSE TO THAT TROLL!!
WOBBLE
WOBBLE
... I WASN'T HELPING YOU.
I WANTED TO KEEP YOU FROM GETTING STRONGER ...
... THAN YOU ALREADY ARE.
THAT'S A CLEVER ANSWER.
WOBBLE
KEN!
TAH
BUT REALLY, YOU KNEW, RIGHT?
THAT SHIRON AND I...
...WERE ALREADY PAST OUR LIMIT.
I'VE STILL GOT A LONG WAY TO GO ...
BA BA
BA BA
?
HUH?
BA BA BA BA

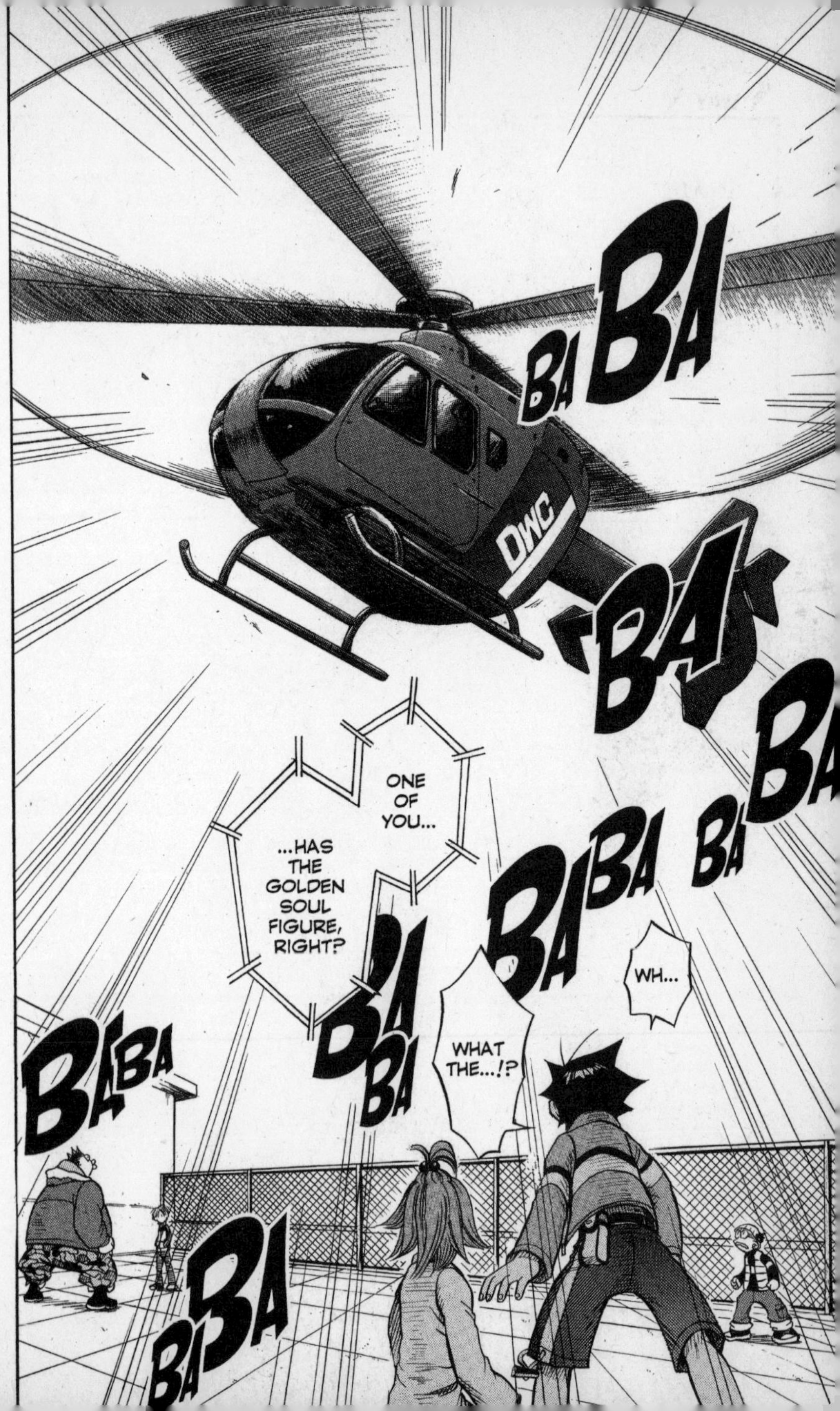
BA BA
BA
BA BA
ONE OF YOU...
...HAS THE GOLDEN SOUL FIGURE, RIGHT?
BA BA
BA BA
WH...
WHAT THE...!?
BA BA
BA BA
BA BA

READ THIS WAY

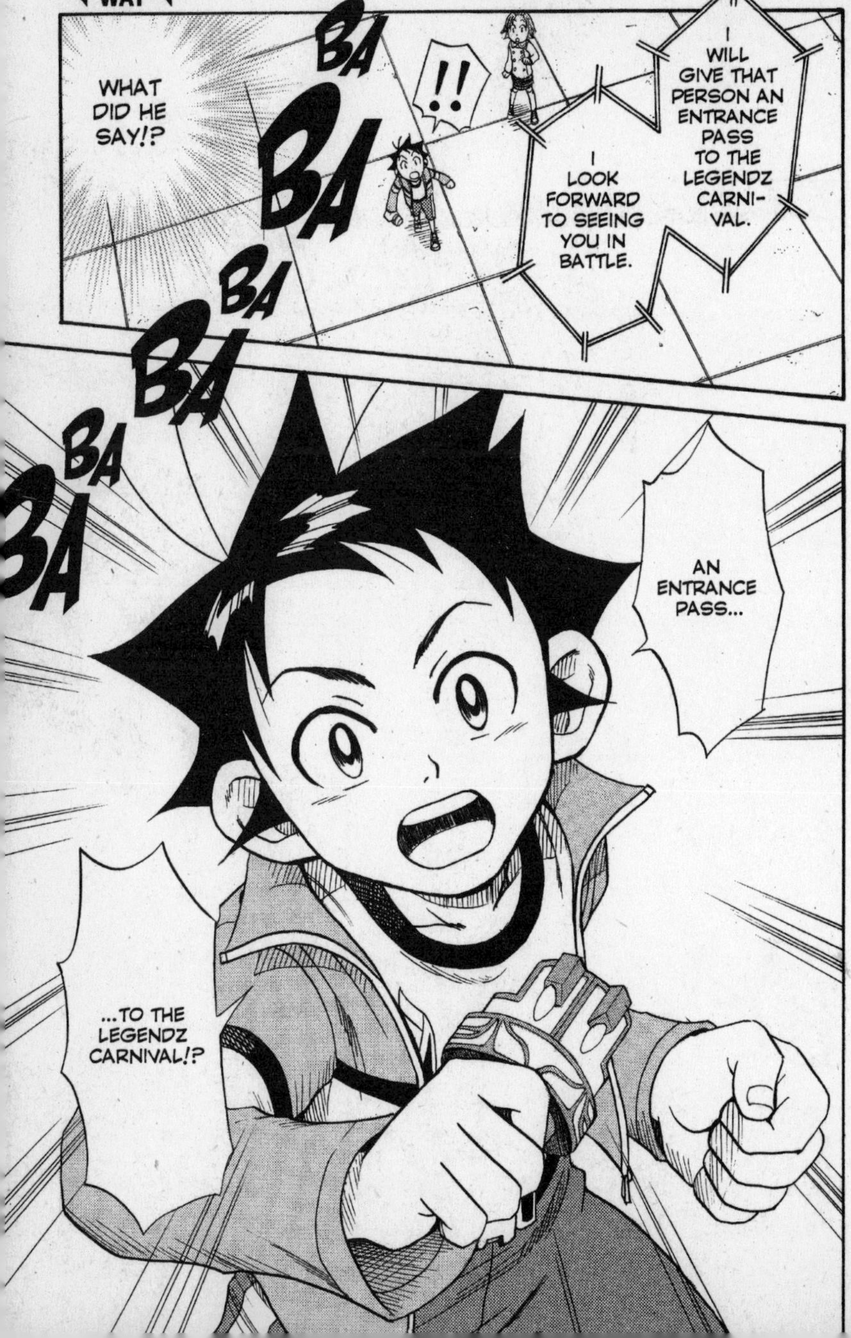

I WILL GIVE THAT PERSON AN ENTRANCE PASS TO THE LEGENDZ CARNIVAL.
I LOOK FORWARD TO SEEING YOU IN BATTLE.
!!
BA BA BA BA BA BA
WHAT DID HE SAY!?
AN ENTRANCE PASS...
...TO THE LEGENDZ CARNIVAL!?

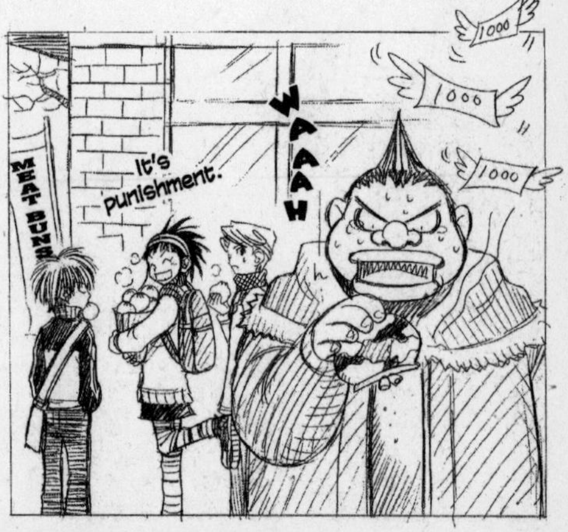
1000
1000
1000
WAAAH
It's punishment.
MEAT BUNS

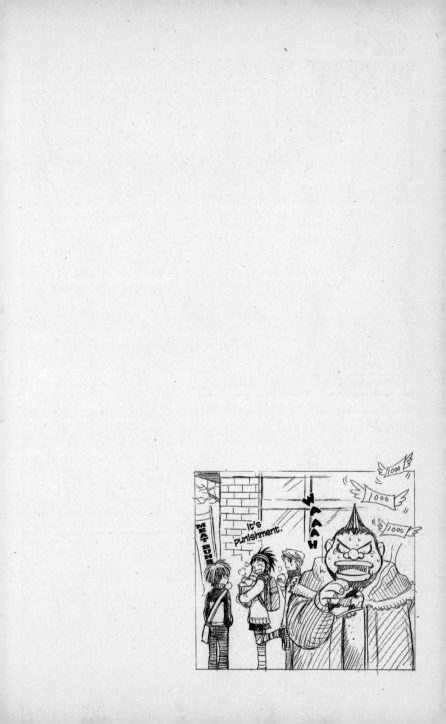

READ THIS WAY

LEGENDZ 6 Burnout!!

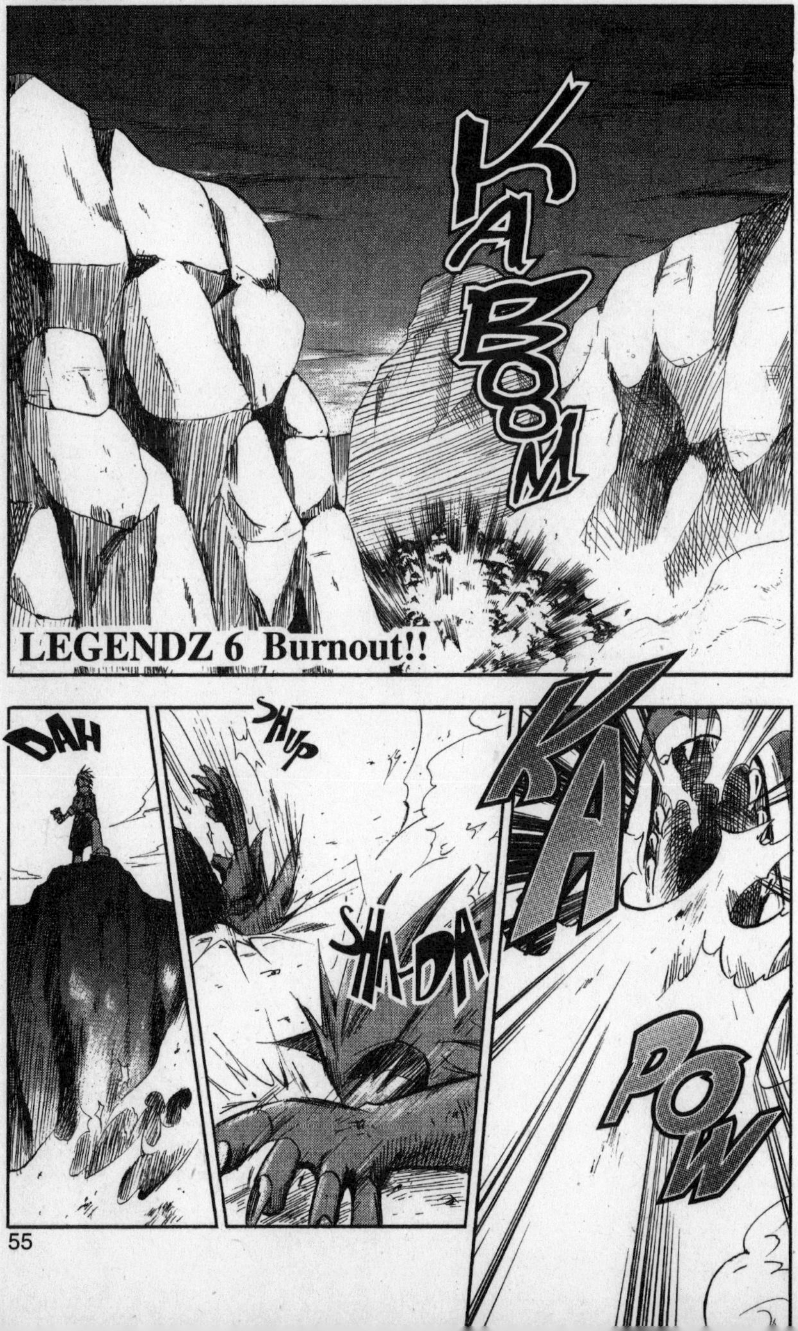
KABOOM
KA
POW
SHUP
SHA-DA
DAH

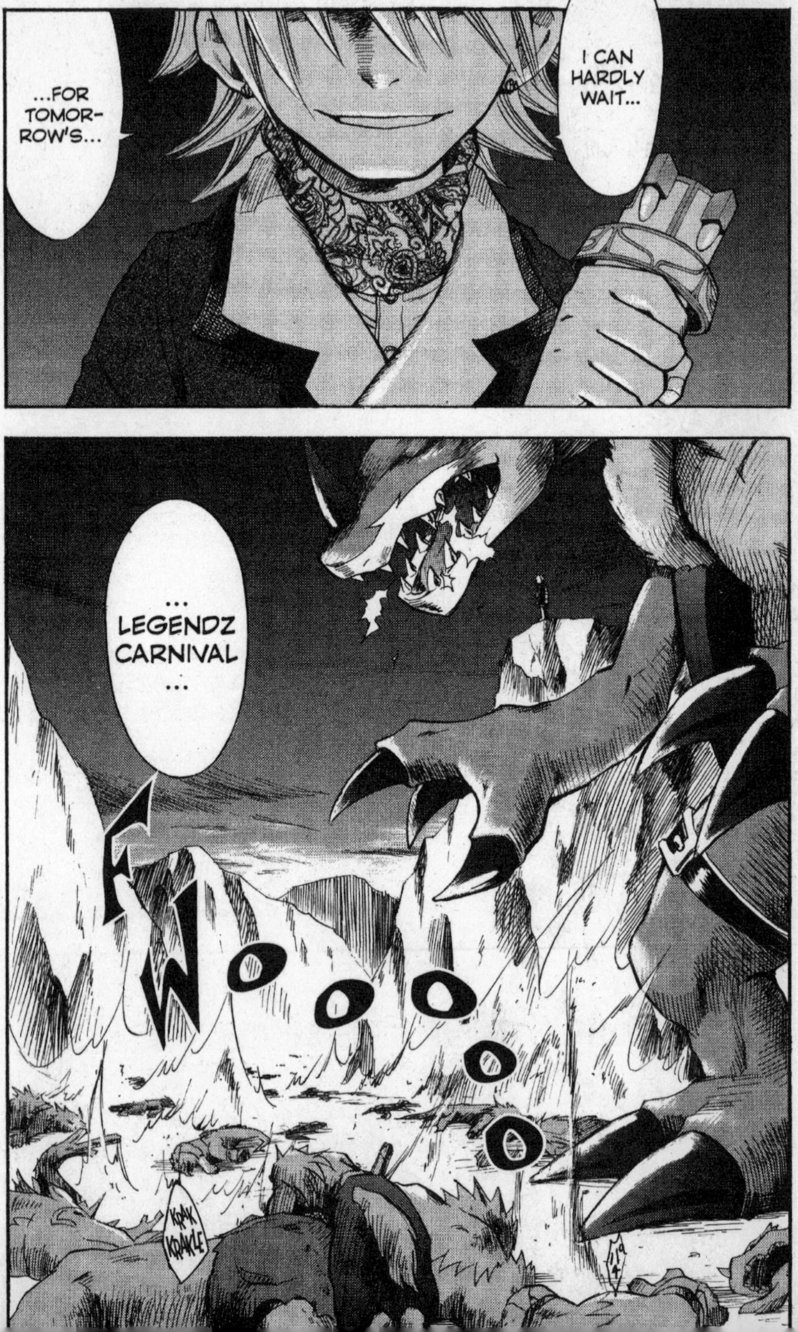
I CAN HARDLY WAIT...
...FOR TOMORROW'S...
... LEGENDZ CARNIVAL ...
FWOOOOOO
KRAK KRAKLE

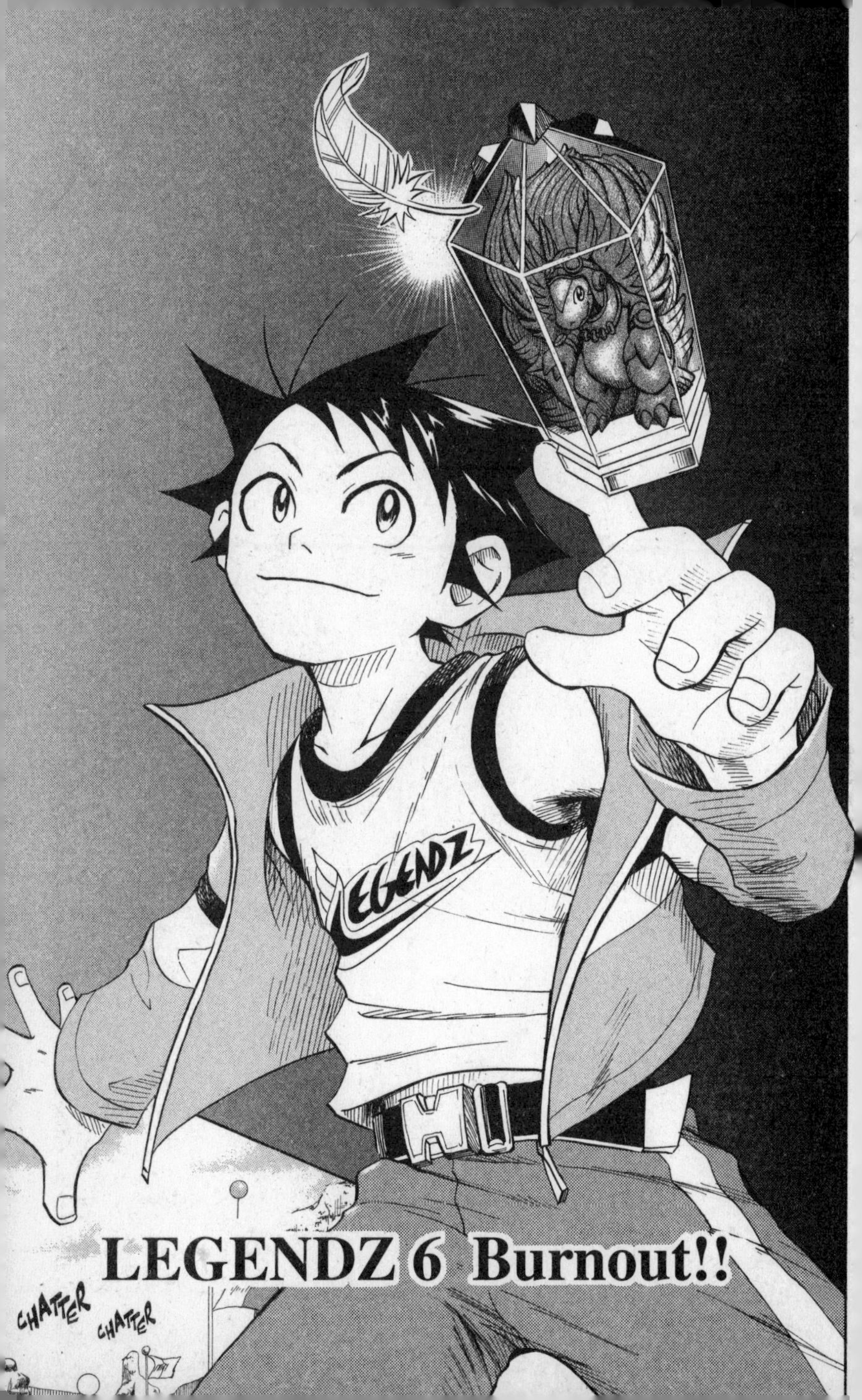
LEGENDZ
LEGENDZ 6 Burnout!!
CHATTER
CHATTER

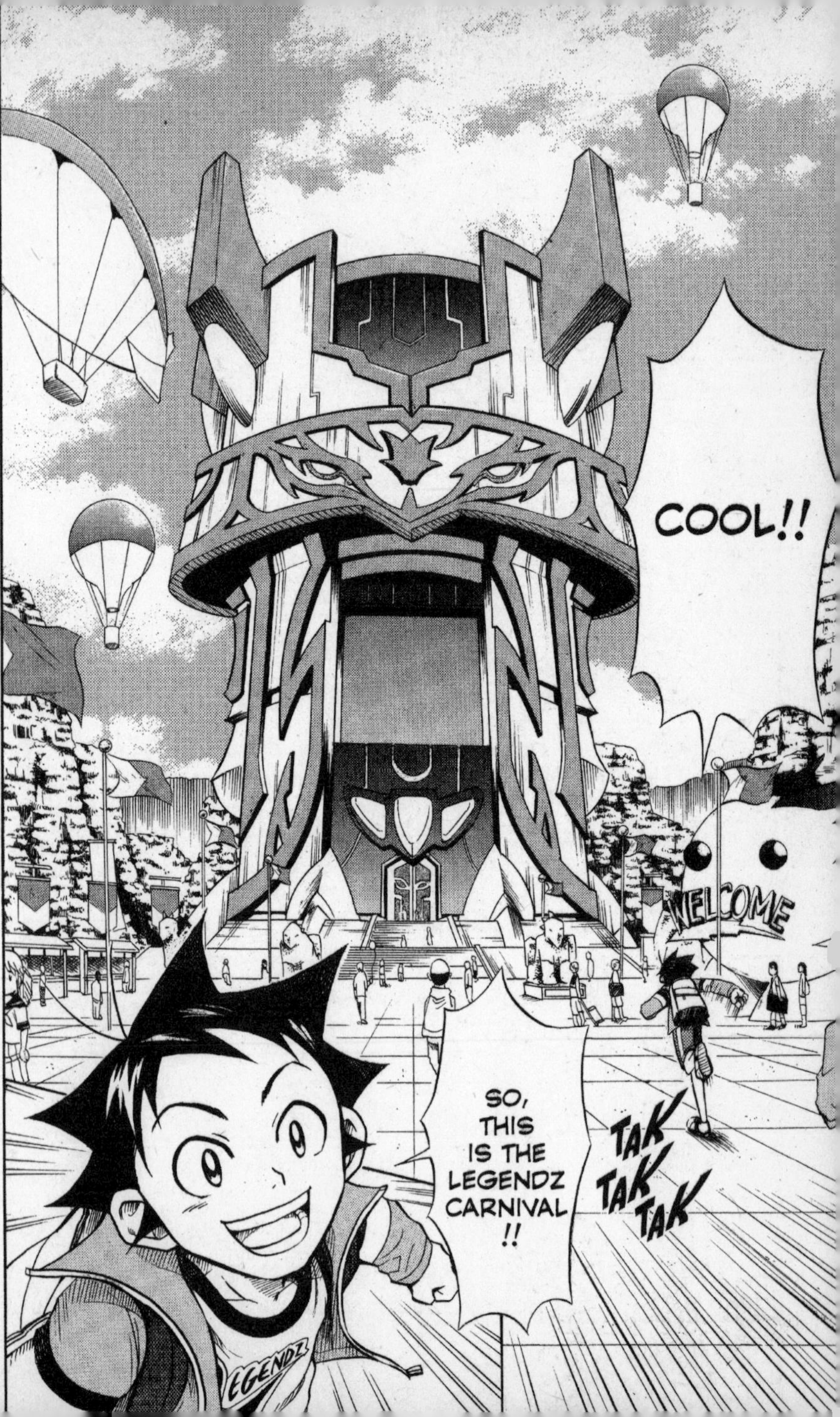
COOL!!
WELCOME
SO, THIS IS THE LEGENDZ CARNIVAL!!
TAK TAK TAK
LEGENDZ

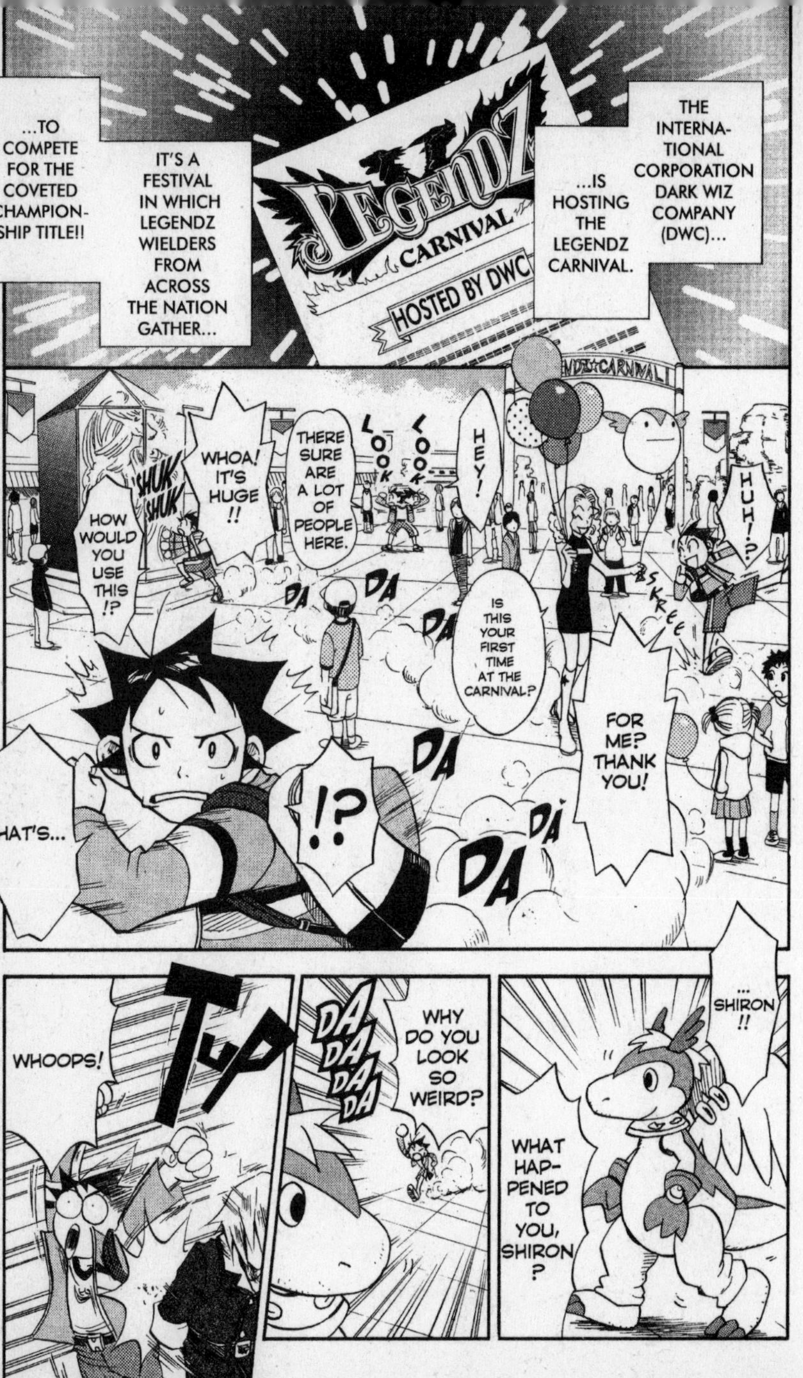

THE INTERNATIONAL CORPORATION DARK WIZ COMPANY (DWC)...
...IS HOSTING THE LEGENDZ CARNIVAL.
LEGENDZ CARNIVAL
HOSTED BY DWC
IT'S A FESTIVAL IN WHICH LEGENDZ WIELDERS FROM ACROSS THE NATION GATHER...
...TO COMPETE FOR THE COVETED CHAMPIONSHIP TITLE!!
HUH!?
SKREE
HEY!
IS THIS YOUR FIRST TIME AT THE CARNIVAL?
FOR ME? THANK YOU!
LOOK LOOK
THERE SURE ARE A LOT OF PEOPLE HERE.
WHOA! IT'S HUGE!!
SHUK SHUK
HOW WOULD YOU USE THIS!?
DA DA DA DA DA DA
!?
THAT'S...
...SHIRON!!
WHAT HAPPENED TO YOU, SHIRON?
WHY DO YOU LOOK SO WEIRD?
DA DA DA DA DA
TUP
WHOOPS!

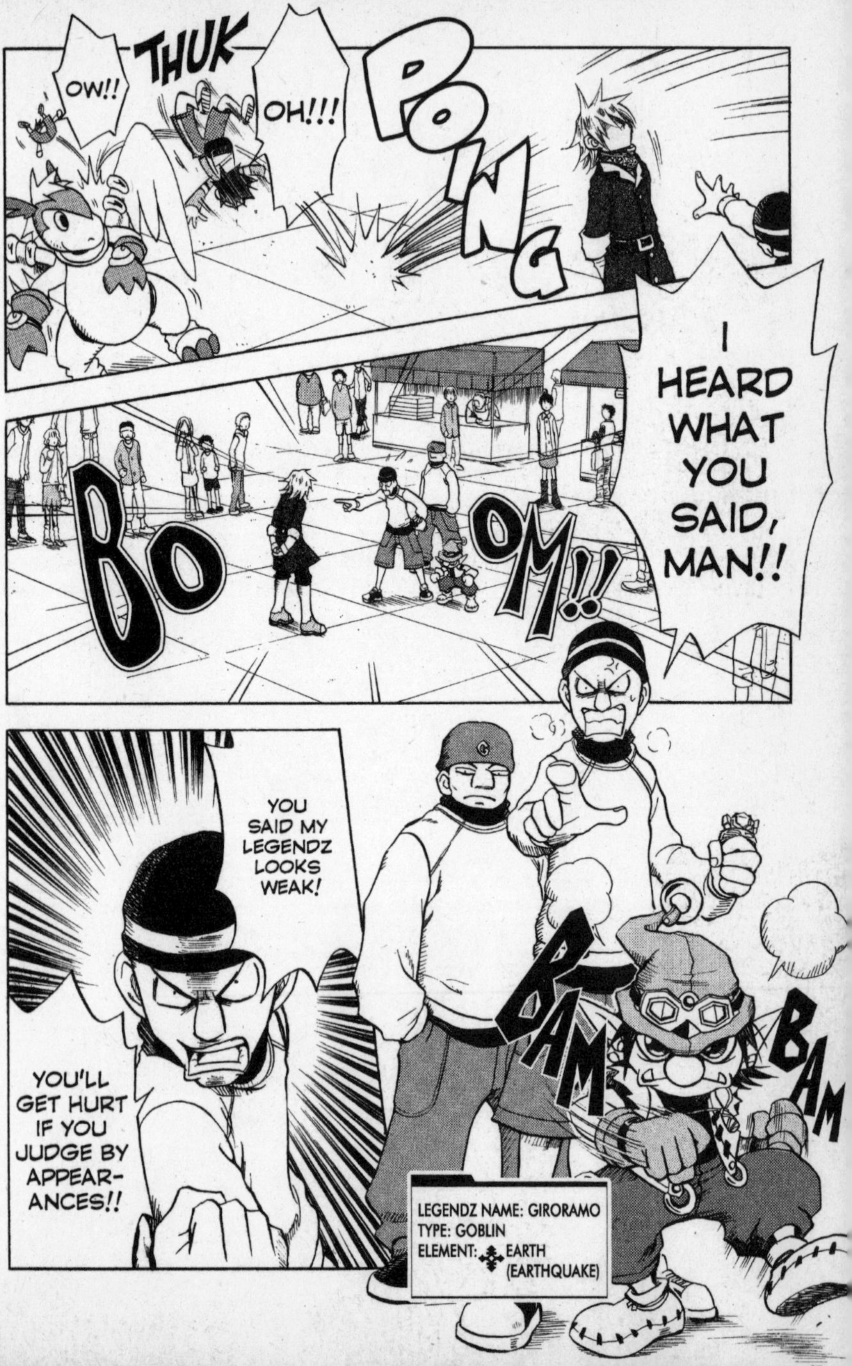

POING
OH!!!
THUK
OW!!
I HEARD WHAT YOU SAID, MAN!!
BOOM!!
BAM
BAM
LEGENDZ NAME: GIRORAMO
TYPE: GOBLIN
ELEMENT: EARTH (EARTHQUAKE)
YOU SAID MY LEGENDZ LOOKS WEAK!
YOU'LL GET HURT IF YOU JUDGE BY APPEAR-ANCES!!

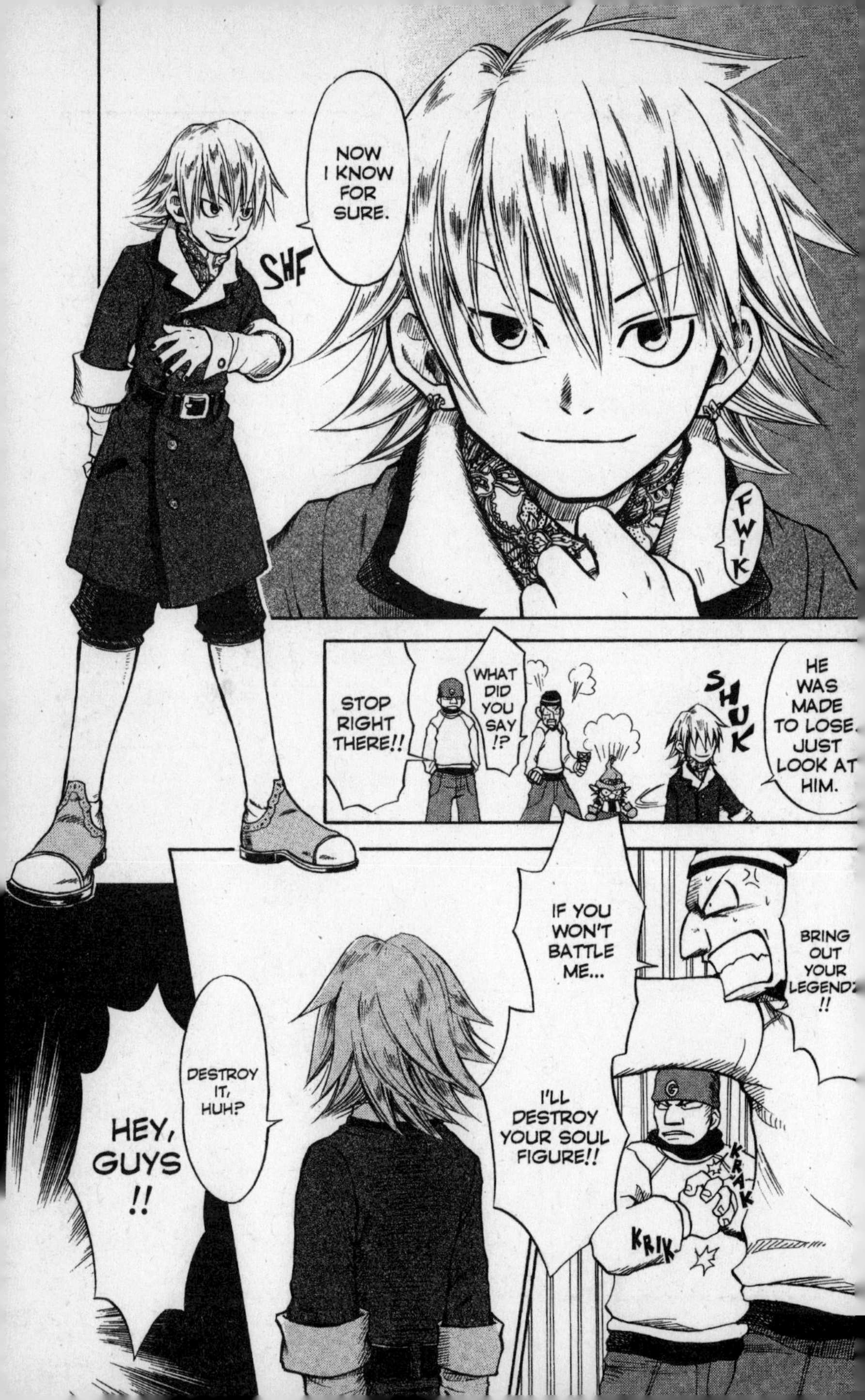
NOW I KNOW FOR SURE.
FWIK
HE WAS MADE TO LOSE. JUST LOOK AT HIM.
SHUK
WHAT DID YOU SAY!?
STOP RIGHT THERE!!
SHF
BRING OUT YOUR LEGENDZ!!
IF YOU WON'T BATTLE ME...
I'LL DESTROY YOUR SOUL FIGURE!!
KRAK
KRIK
DESTROY IT, HUH?
HEY, GUYS!!

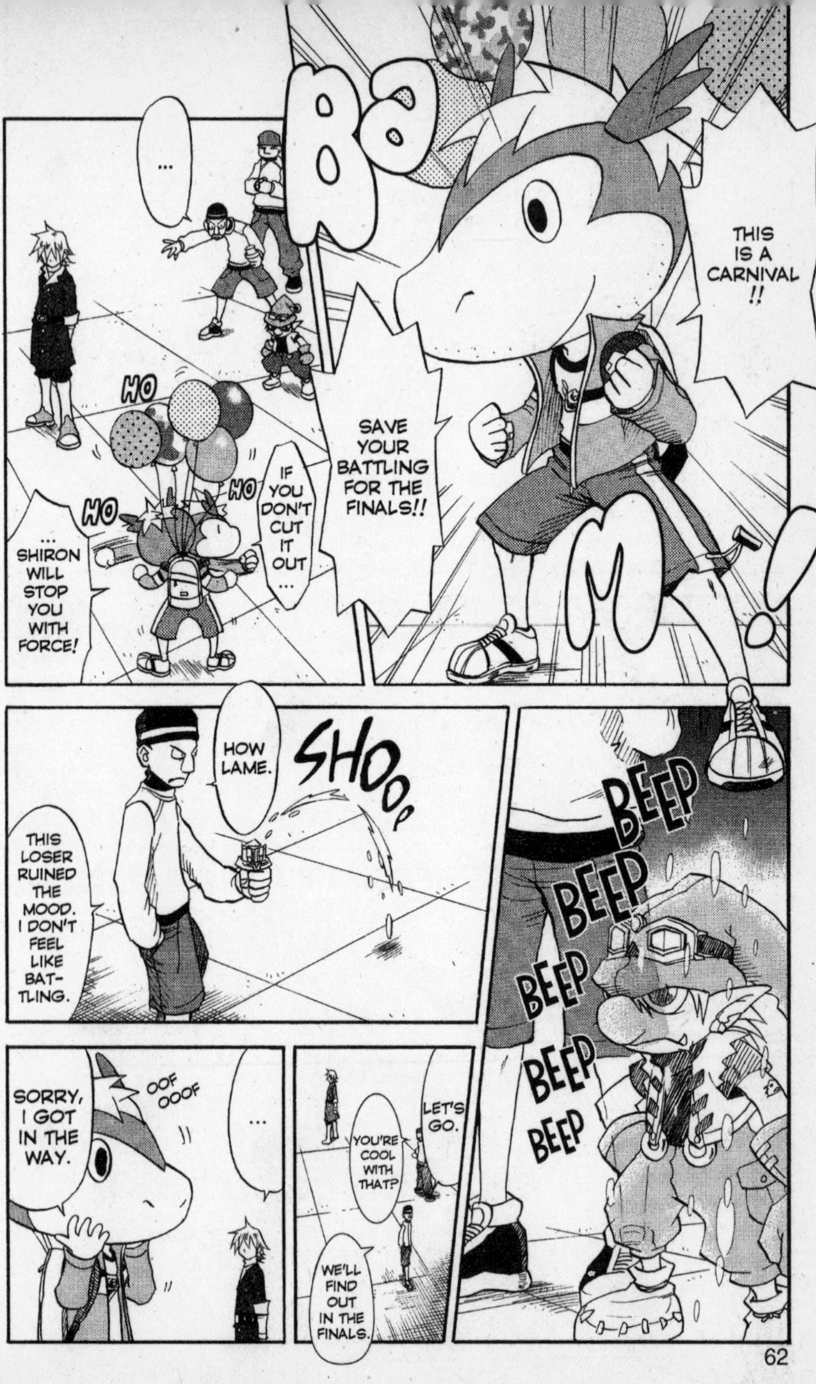
BA
THIS IS A CARNIVAL!!
SAVE YOUR BATTLING FOR THE FINALS!!
M!
...
HO
HO
HO
IF YOU DON'T CUT IT OUT...
...SHIRON WILL STOP YOU WITH FORCE!
BEEP BEEP BEEP BEEP BEEP
HOW LAME.
SHOOP
THIS LOSER RUINED THE MOOD. I DON'T FEEL LIKE BAT-TLING.
LET'S GO.
YOU'RE COOL WITH THAT?
WE'LL FIND OUT IN THE FINALS.
...
OOF OOOF
SORRY, I GOT IN THE WAY.

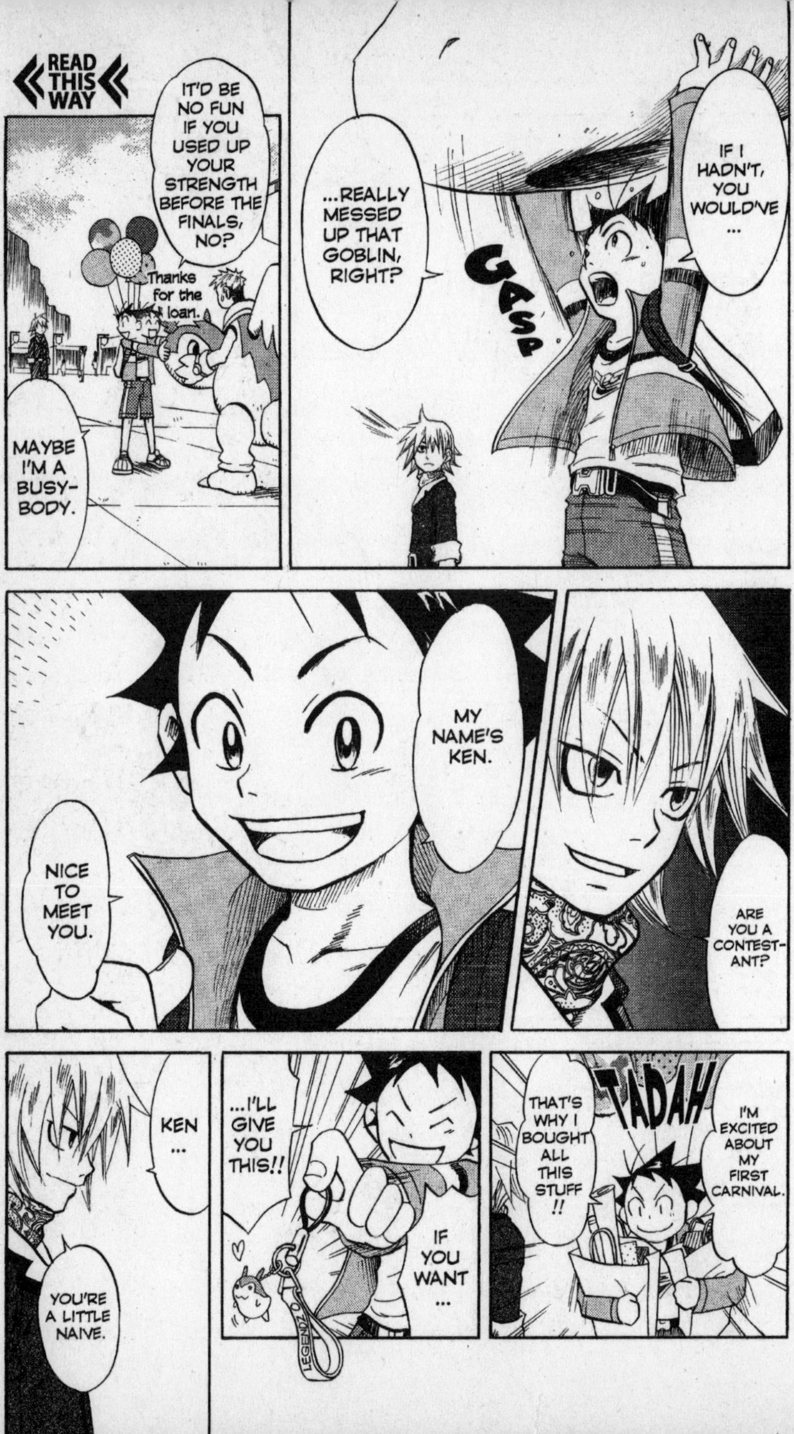
READ THIS WAY
IF I HADN'T, YOU WOULD'VE ...
GASP
...REALLY MESSED UP THAT GOBLIN, RIGHT?
IT'D BE NO FUN IF YOU USED UP YOUR STRENGTH BEFORE THE FINALS, NO?
Thanks for the loan.
MAYBE I'M A BUSY-BODY.
ARE YOU A CONTEST-ANT?
MY NAME'S KEN.
NICE TO MEET YOU.
I'M EXCITED ABOUT MY FIRST CARNIVAL.
TADAH
THAT'S WHY I BOUGHT ALL THIS STUFF !!
...I'LL GIVE YOU THIS!!
IF YOU WANT ...
LEGENDZ
KEN ...
YOU'RE A LITTLE NAIVE.

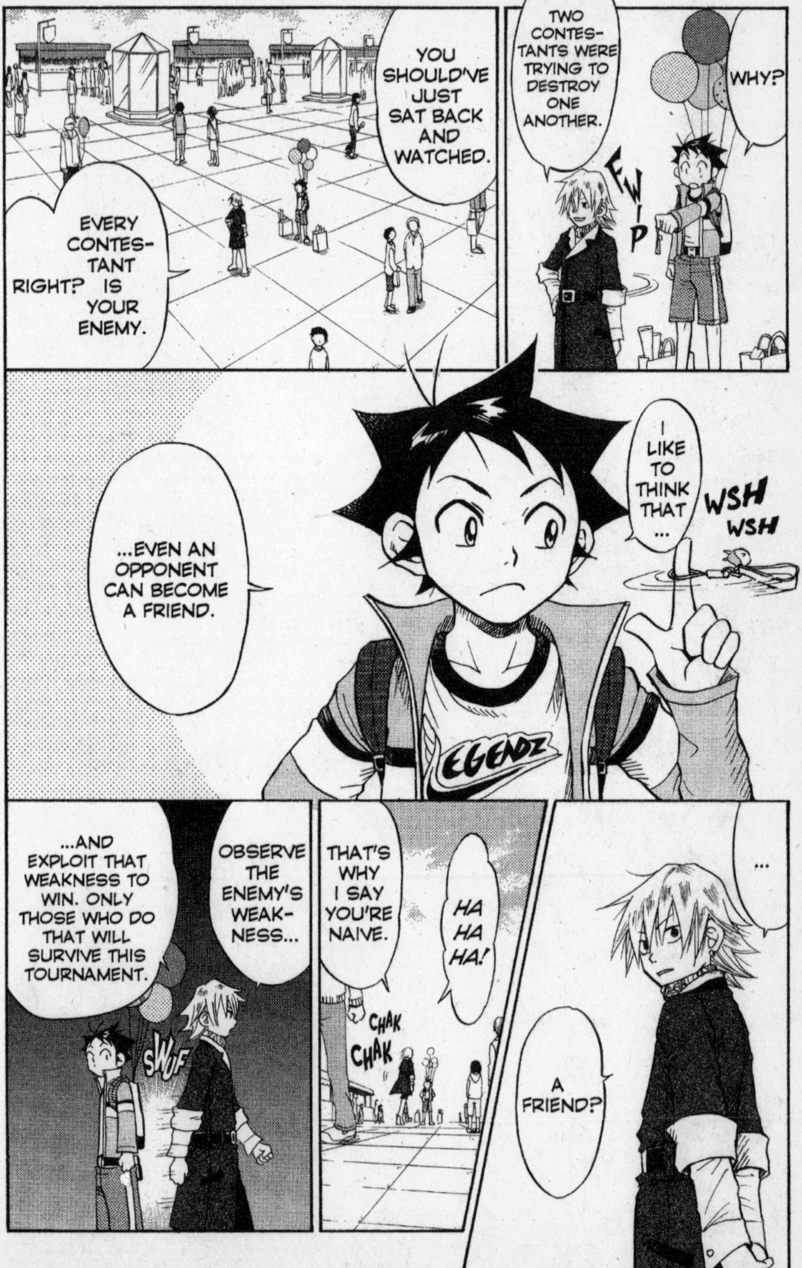
WHY?
TWO CONTES-TANTS WERE TRYING TO DESTROY ONE ANOTHER.
FWIP
YOU SHOULD'VE JUST SAT BACK AND WATCHED.
EVERY CONTES-TANT IS YOUR ENEMY.
RIGHT?
I LIKE TO THINK THAT ...
WSH WSH
...EVEN AN OPPONENT CAN BECOME A FRIEND.
...
A FRIEND?
HA HA HA!
THAT'S WHY I SAY YOU'RE NAIVE.
CHAK CHAK
OBSERVE THE ENEMY'S WEAK-NESS...
...AND EXPLOIT THAT WEAKNESS TO WIN. ONLY THOSE WHO DO THAT WILL SURVIVE THIS TOURNAMENT.
SWUF

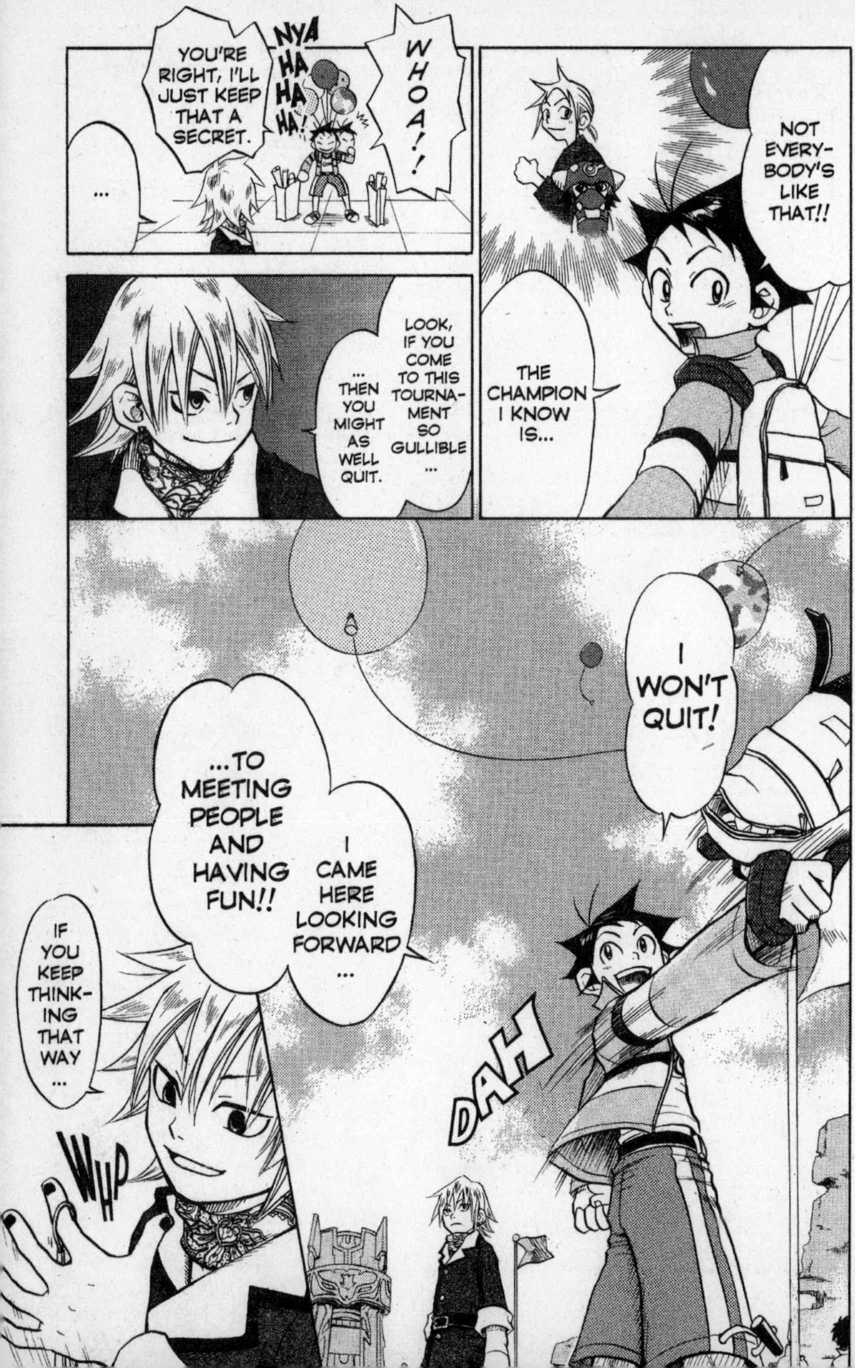
NOT EVERYBODY'S LIKE THAT!!
THE CHAMPION I KNOW IS...
WHOA!!
NYA HA HA HA!
YOU'RE RIGHT, I'LL JUST KEEP THAT A SECRET.
...
LOOK, IF YOU COME TO THIS TOURNAMENT SO GULLIBLE...
...THEN YOU MIGHT AS WELL QUIT.
I WON'T QUIT!
I CAME HERE LOOKING FORWARD...
...TO MEETING PEOPLE AND HAVING FUN!!
DAH
IF YOU KEEP THINKING THAT WAY...
WHP

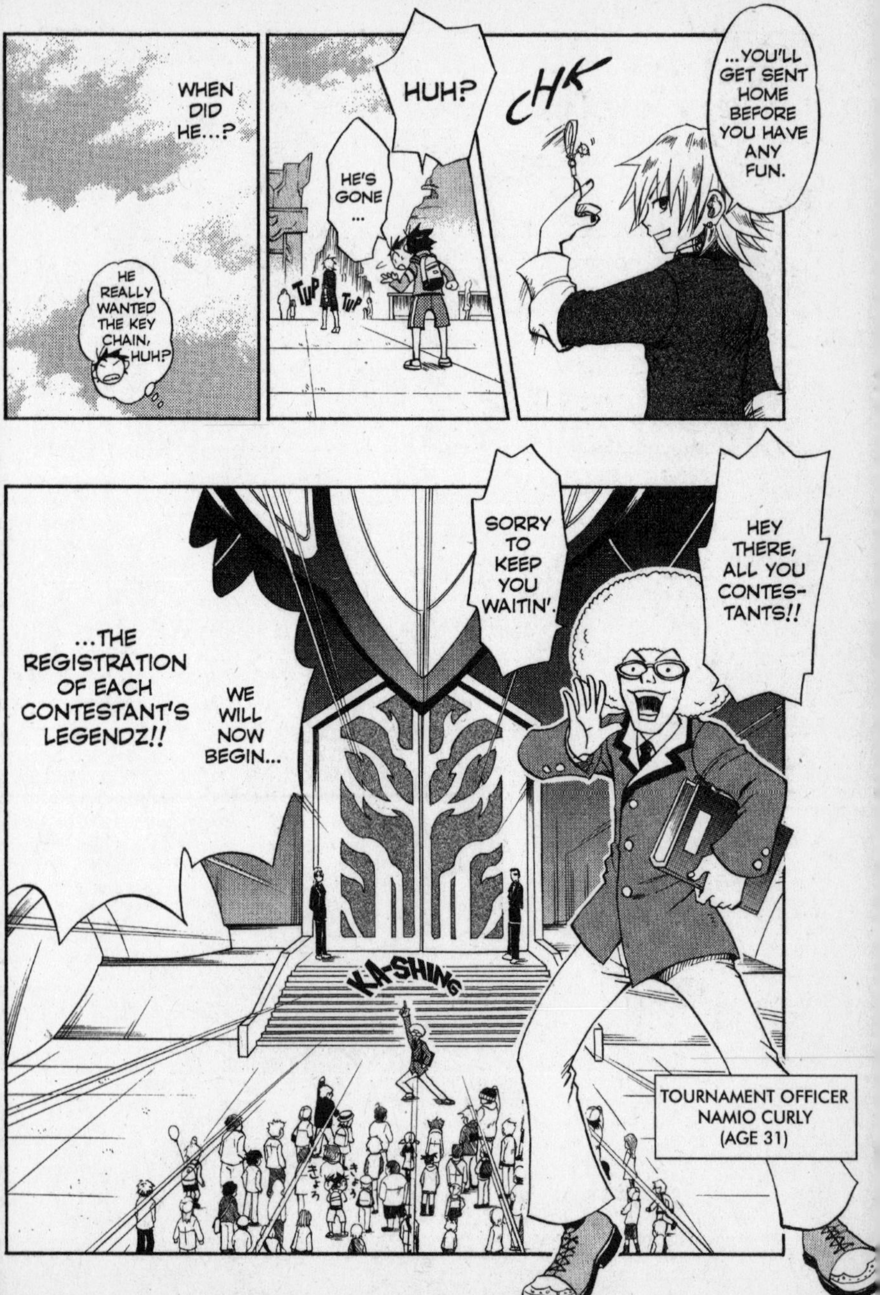
...YOU'LL GET SENT HOME BEFORE YOU HAVE ANY FUN.
CHK
HUH?
HE'S GONE ...
TUP TUP
WHEN DID HE...?
HE REALLY WANTED THE KEY CHAIN, HUH?
HEY THERE, ALL YOU CONTES-TANTS!!
SORRY TO KEEP YOU WAITIN'.
WE WILL NOW BEGIN...
...THE REGISTRATION OF EACH CONTESTANT'S LEGENDZ!!
KA-SHING
TOURNAMENT OFFICER NAMIO CURLY (AGE 31)

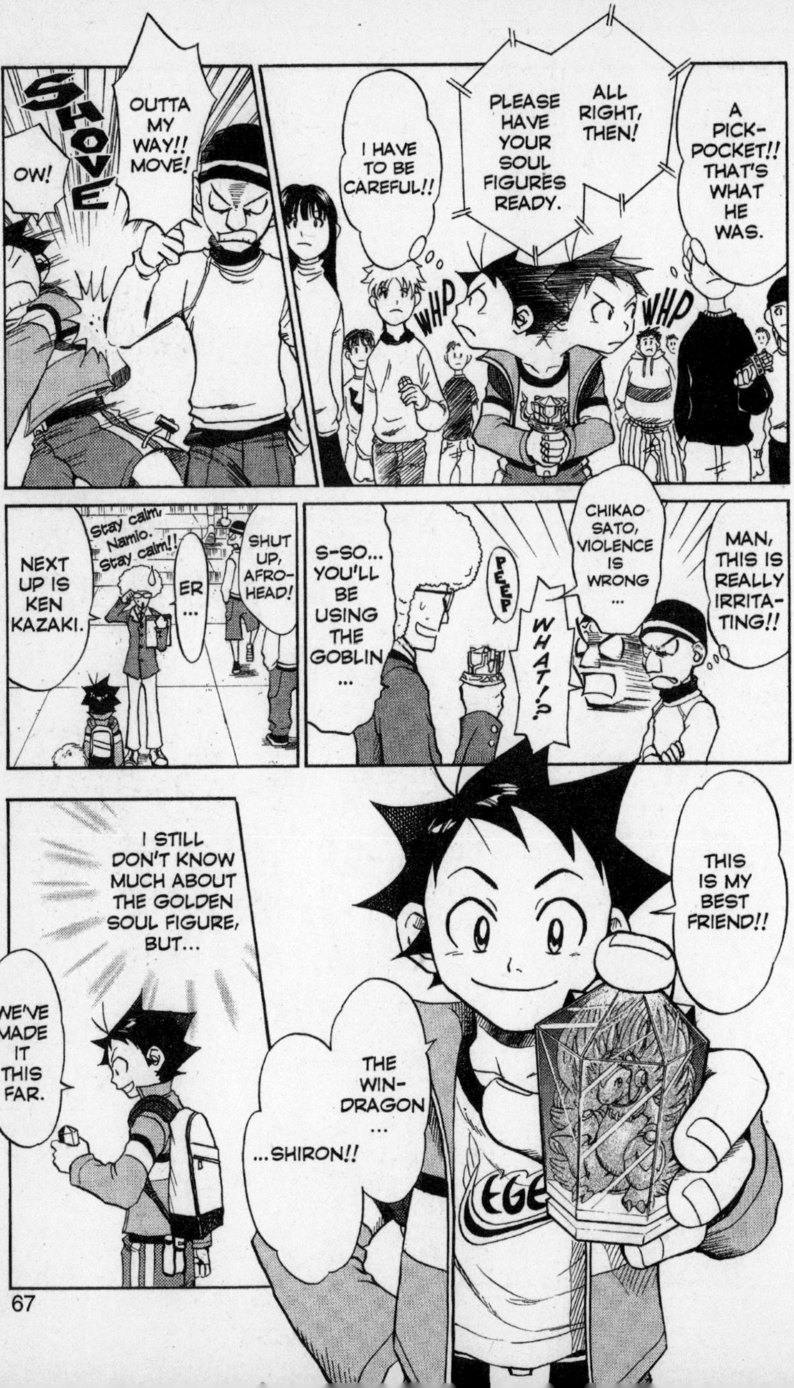
A PICKPOCKET!! THAT'S WHAT HE WAS.
ALL RIGHT, THEN!
PLEASE HAVE YOUR SOUL FIGURES READY.
WHP
WHP
I HAVE TO BE CAREFUL!!
OUTTA MY WAY!! MOVE!
SHOVE
OW!
MAN, THIS IS REALLY IRRITATING!!
CHIKAO SATO, VIOLENCE IS WRONG ...
PEEP
WHAT!?
S-SO... YOU'LL BE USING THE GOBLIN ...
SHUT UP, AFRO-HEAD!
Stay calm, Namio. Stay calm!!
ER ...
NEXT UP IS KEN KAZAKI.
THIS IS MY BEST FRIEND!!
THE WIN-DRAGON ...
...SHIRON!!
I STILL DON'T KNOW MUCH ABOUT THE GOLDEN SOUL FIGURE, BUT...
WE'VE MADE IT THIS FAR.

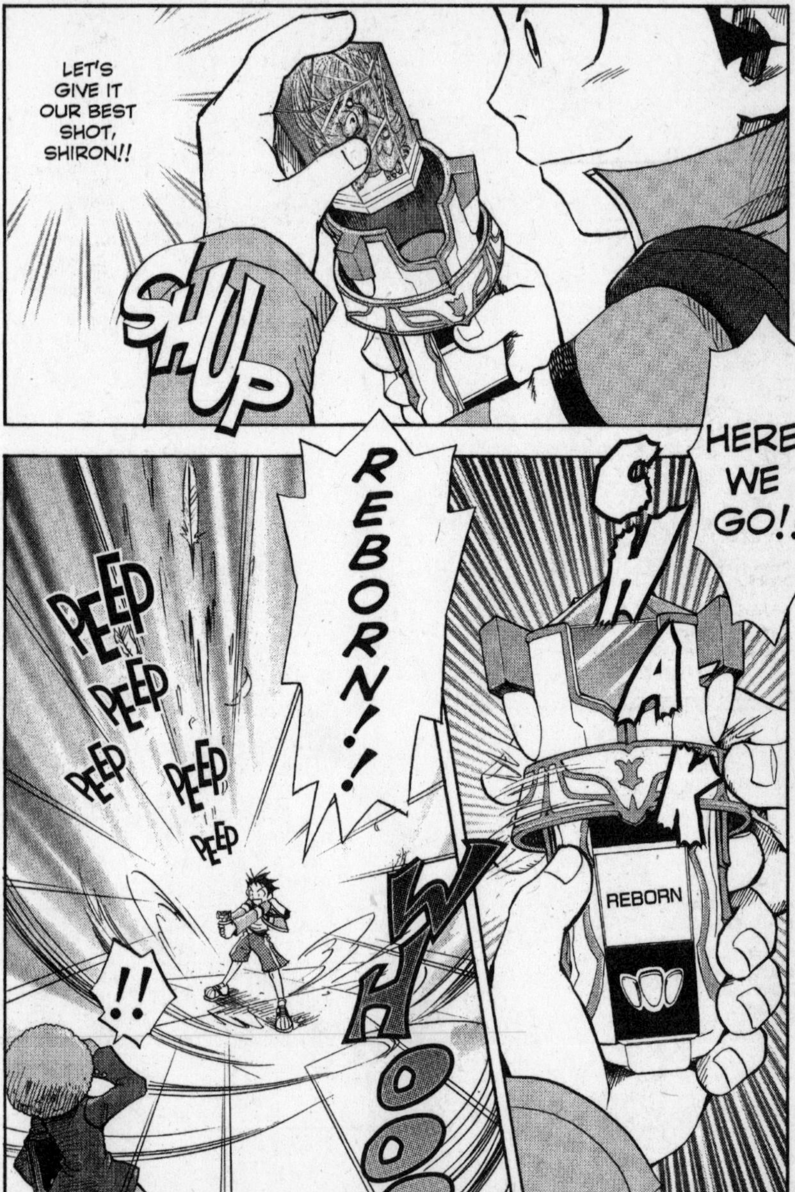
LET'S GIVE IT OUR BEST SHOT, SHIRON!!
SHUP
HERE WE GO!!
CHAK
REBORN
REBORN!!
WHOOOO
PEEP PEEP PEEP PEEP PEEP
!!

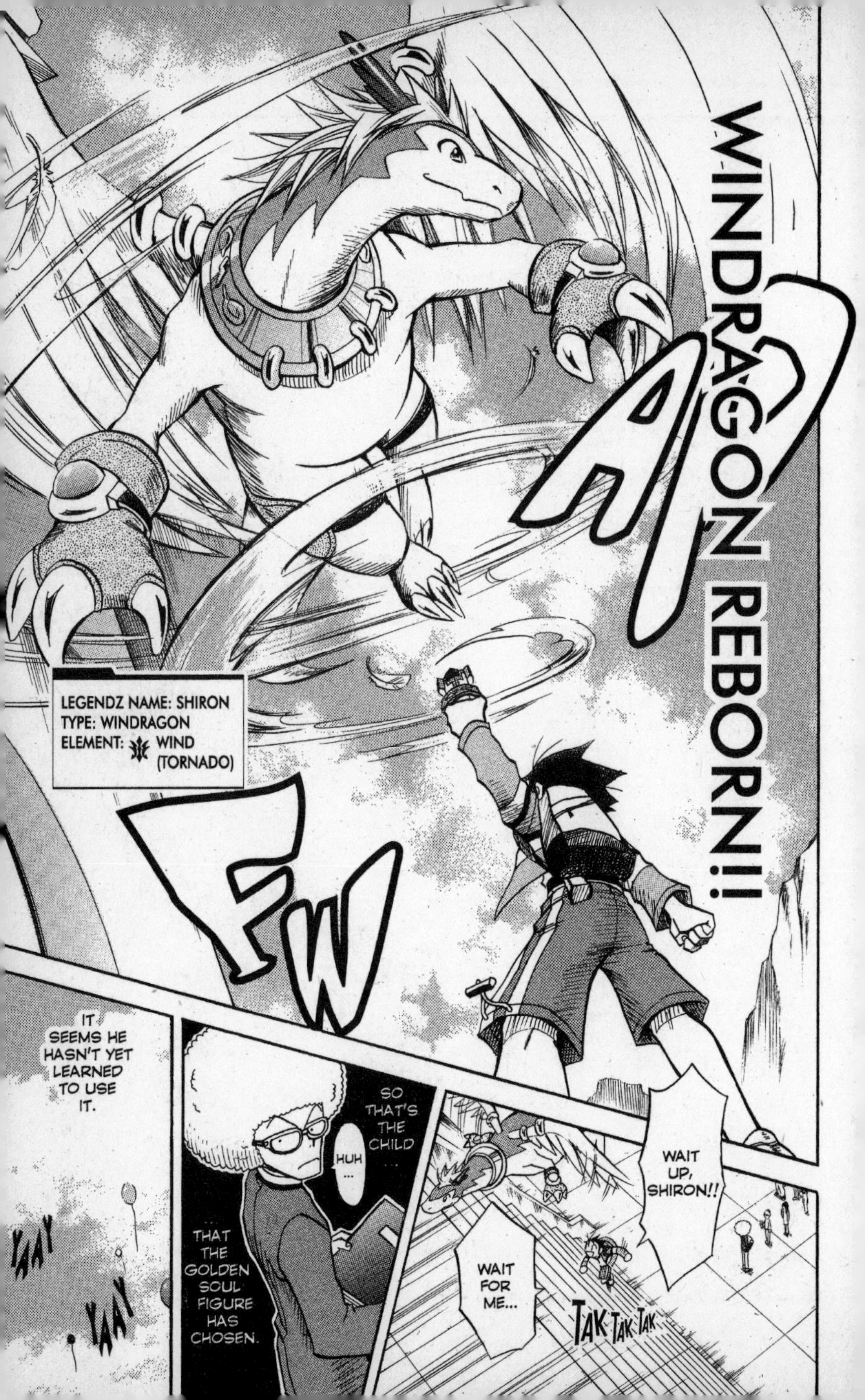
WINDRAGON REBORN!!
LEGENDZ NAME: SHIRON
TYPE: WINDRAGON
ELEMENT: WIND (TORNADO)
FW
WAIT UP, SHIRON!!
WAIT FOR ME...
TAK TAK TAK
SO THAT'S THE CHILD...
HUH...
THAT THE GOLDEN SOUL FIGURE HAS CHOSEN.
IT SEEMS HE HASN'T YET LEARNED TO USE IT.
YAAY
YAAY

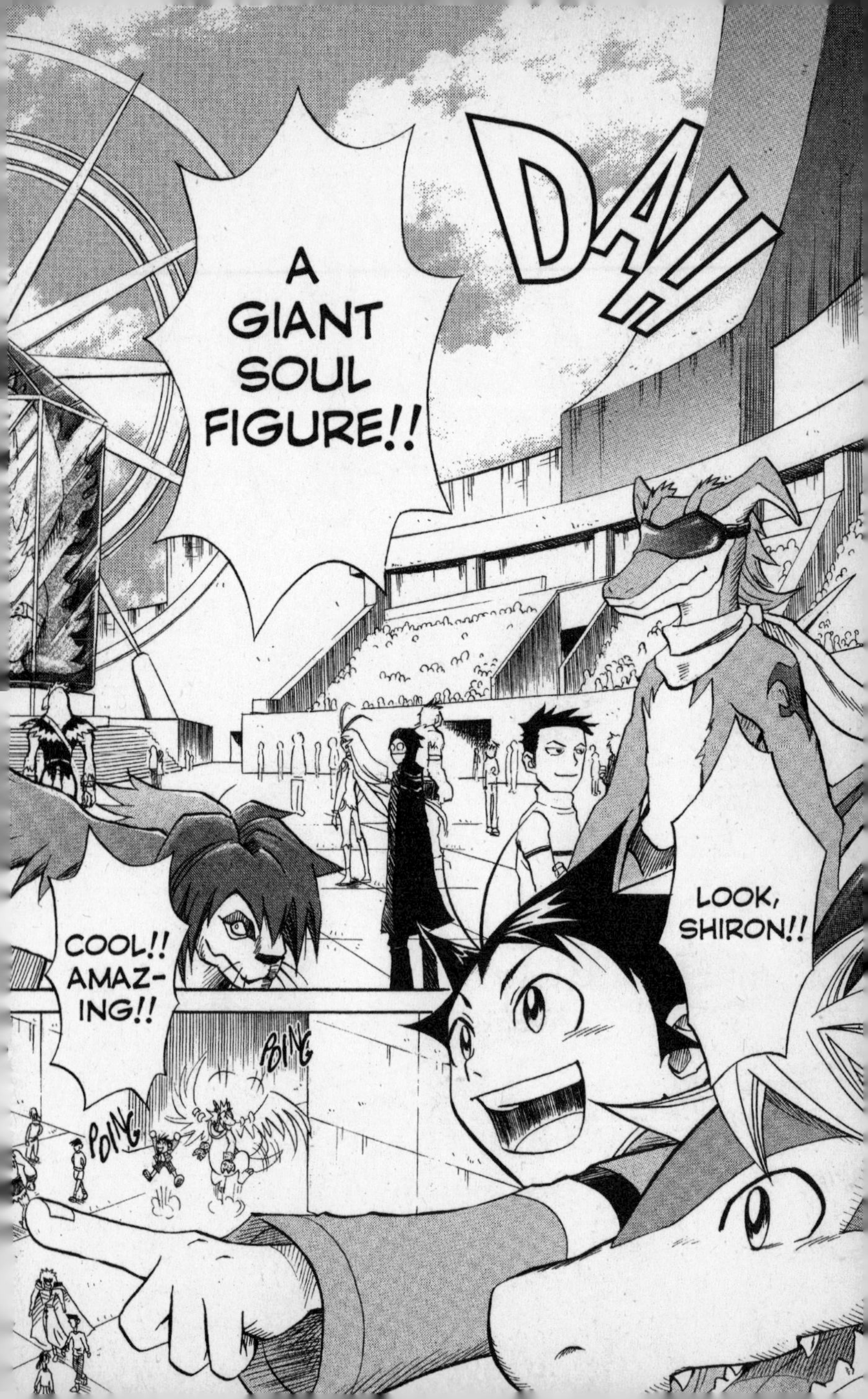
DA!!
A GIANT SOUL FIGURE!!
LOOK, SHIRON!!
COOL!! AMAZ-ING!!
POING
POING

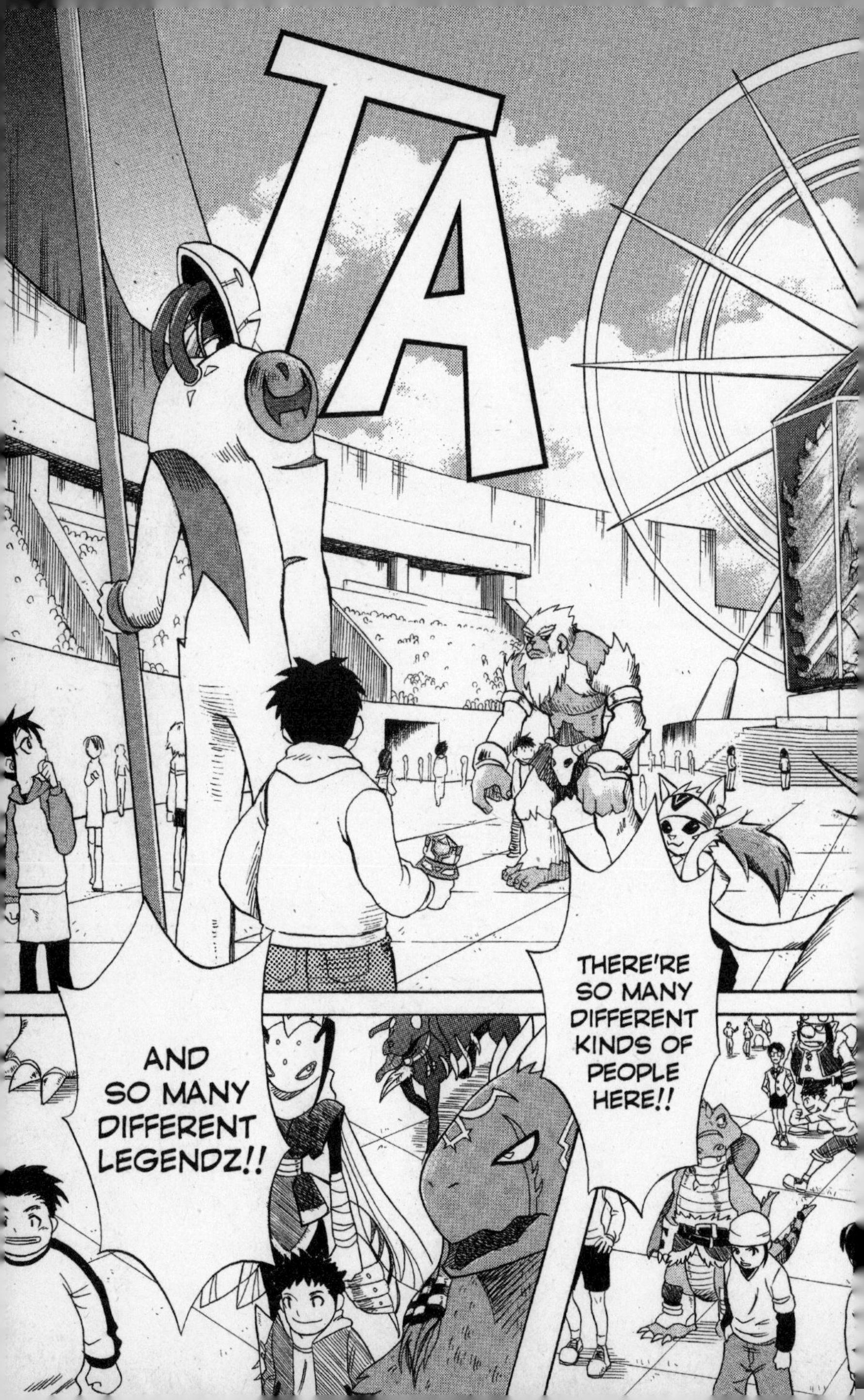
TA
THERE'RE SO MANY DIFFERENT KINDS OF PEOPLE HERE!!
AND SO MANY DIFFERENT LEGENDZ!!

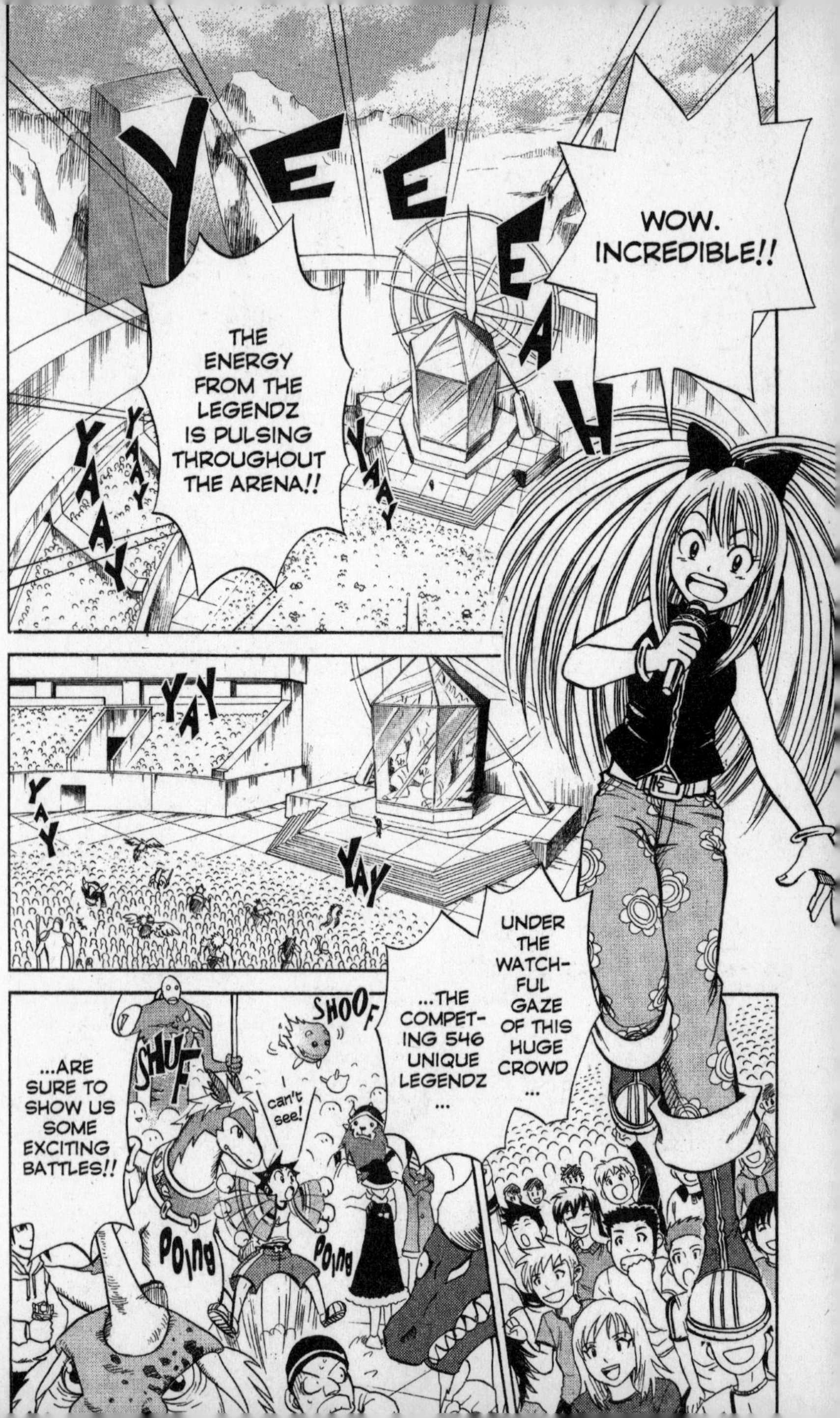
YEEEEAH
WOW. INCREDIBLE!!
THE ENERGY FROM THE LEGENDZ IS PULSING THROUGHOUT THE ARENA!!
YAAAY
YAAAY
YAAAY
YAY
YAY
YAY
UNDER THE WATCHFUL GAZE OF THIS HUGE CROWD...
...THE COMPETING 546 UNIQUE LEGENDZ...
SHOOF
I can't see!
...ARE SURE TO SHOW US SOME EXCITING BATTLES!!
SHUF
POING
POING

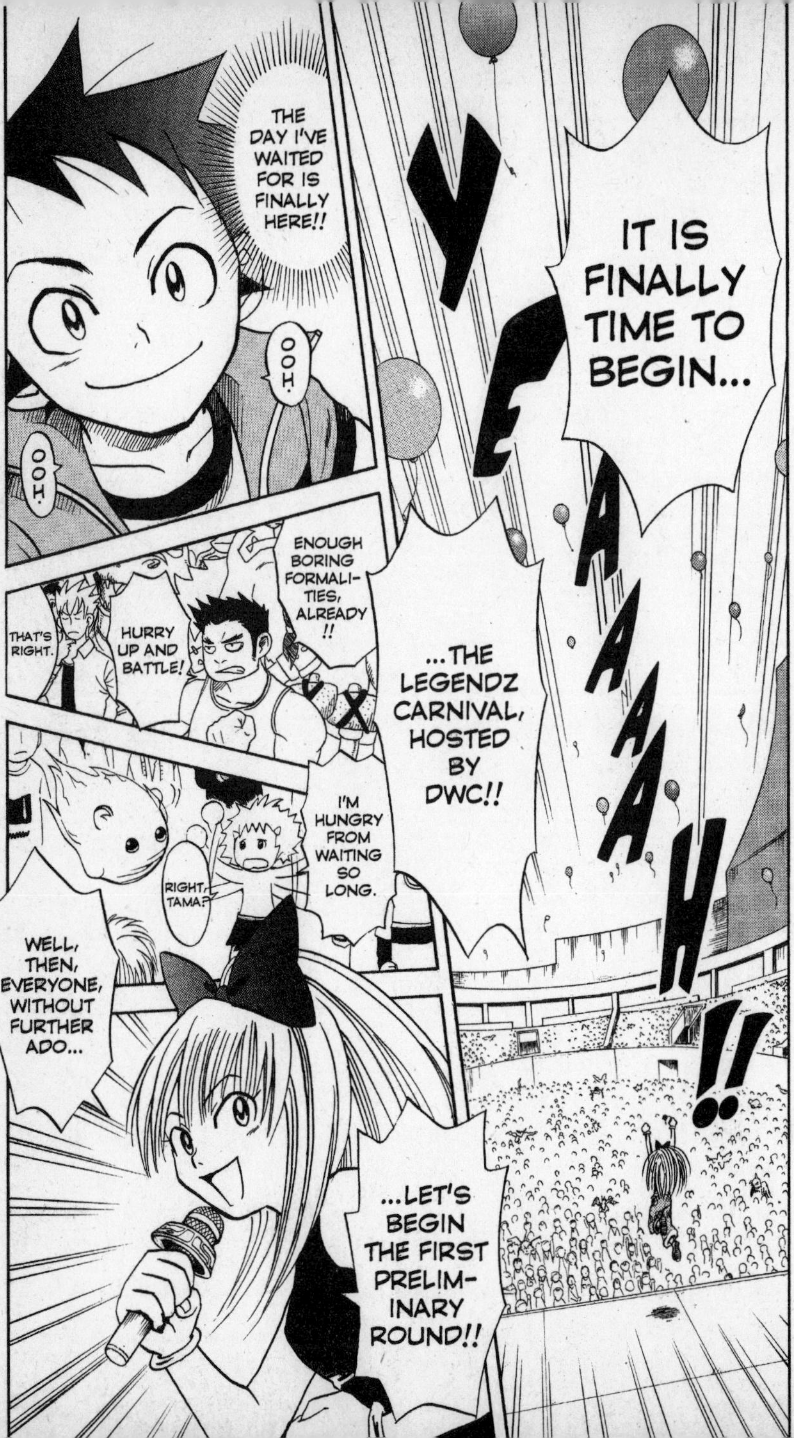
IT IS FINALLY TIME TO BEGIN...
YEAAAAAH!!
...THE LEGENDZ CARNIVAL, HOSTED BY DWC!!
THE DAY I'VE WAITED FOR IS FINALLY HERE!!
OOH.
OOH.
ENOUGH BORING FORMALITIES, ALREADY!!
HURRY UP AND BATTLE!
THAT'S RIGHT.
I'M HUNGRY FROM WAITING SO LONG.
RIGHT, TAMA?
WELL, THEN, EVERYONE, WITHOUT FURTHER ADO...
...LET'S BEGIN THE FIRST PRELIMINARY ROUND!!

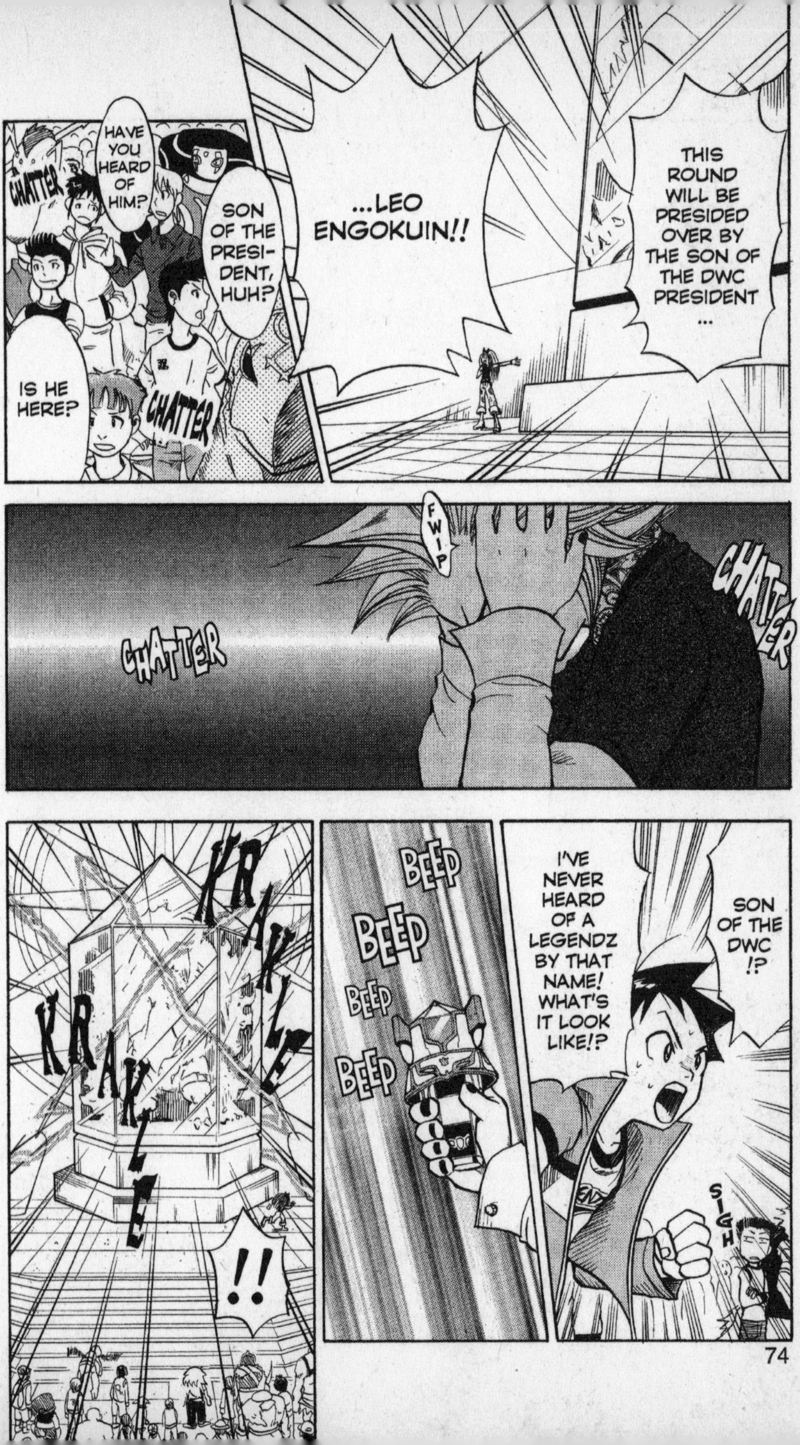
THIS ROUND WILL BE PRESIDED OVER BY THE SON OF THE DWC PRESIDENT ...
...LEO ENGOKUIN!!
SON OF THE PRESIDENT, HUH?
HAVE YOU HEARD OF HIM?
CHATTER
CHATTER
IS HE HERE?
FWIP
CHATTER
CHATTER
SON OF THE DWC !?
I'VE NEVER HEARD OF A LEGENDZ BY THAT NAME! WHAT'S IT LOOK LIKE!?
SIGH
BEEP
BEEP
BEEP
BEEP
KRAKLE
KRAKLE
!!

READ THIS WAY

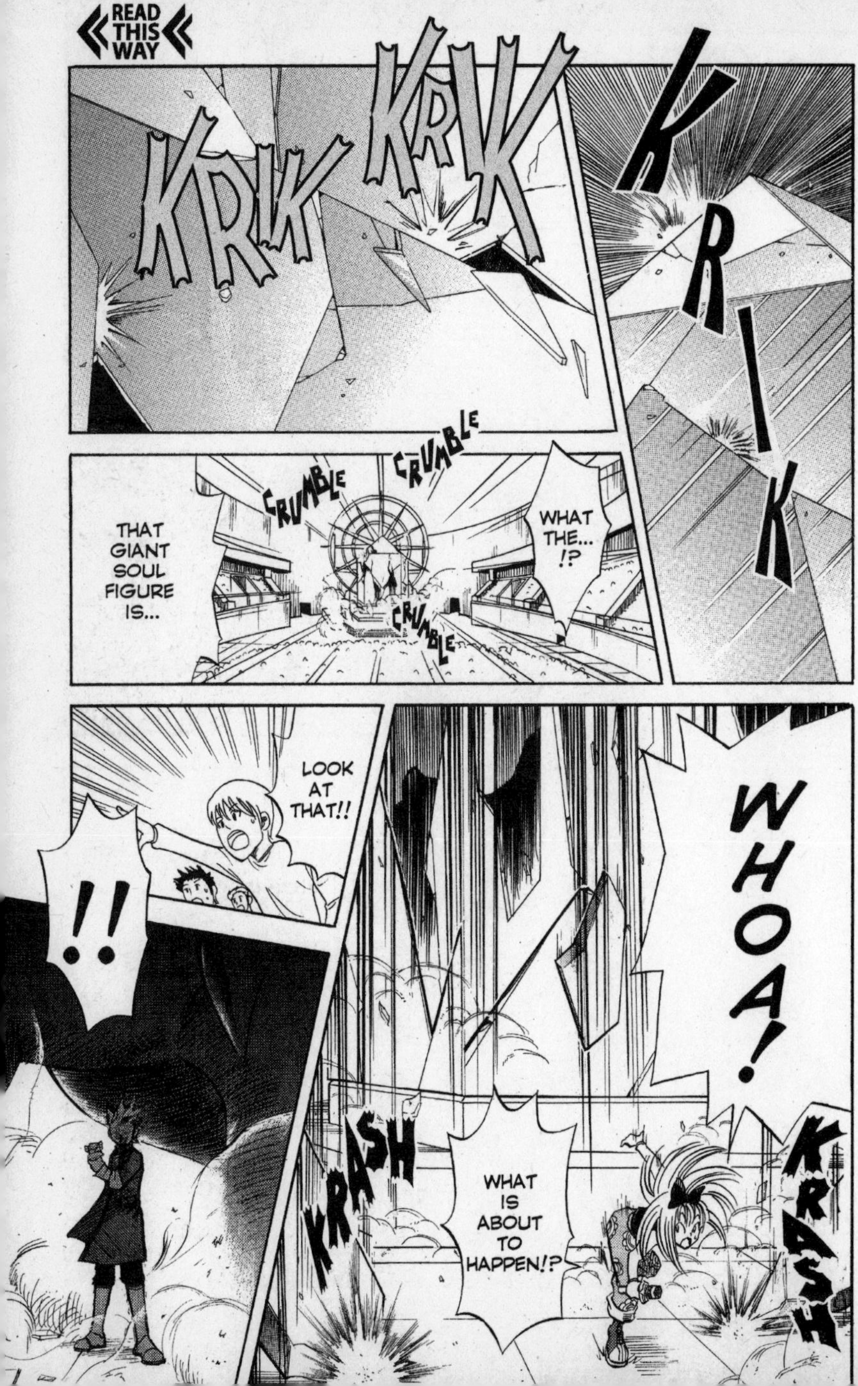
KRIK
KRK
KRIK
CRUMBLE
WHAT THE...!?
CRUMBLE
THAT GIANT SOUL FIGURE IS...
CRUMBLE
WHOA!
KRASH
WHAT IS ABOUT TO HAPPEN!?
KRASH
LOOK AT THAT!!
!!

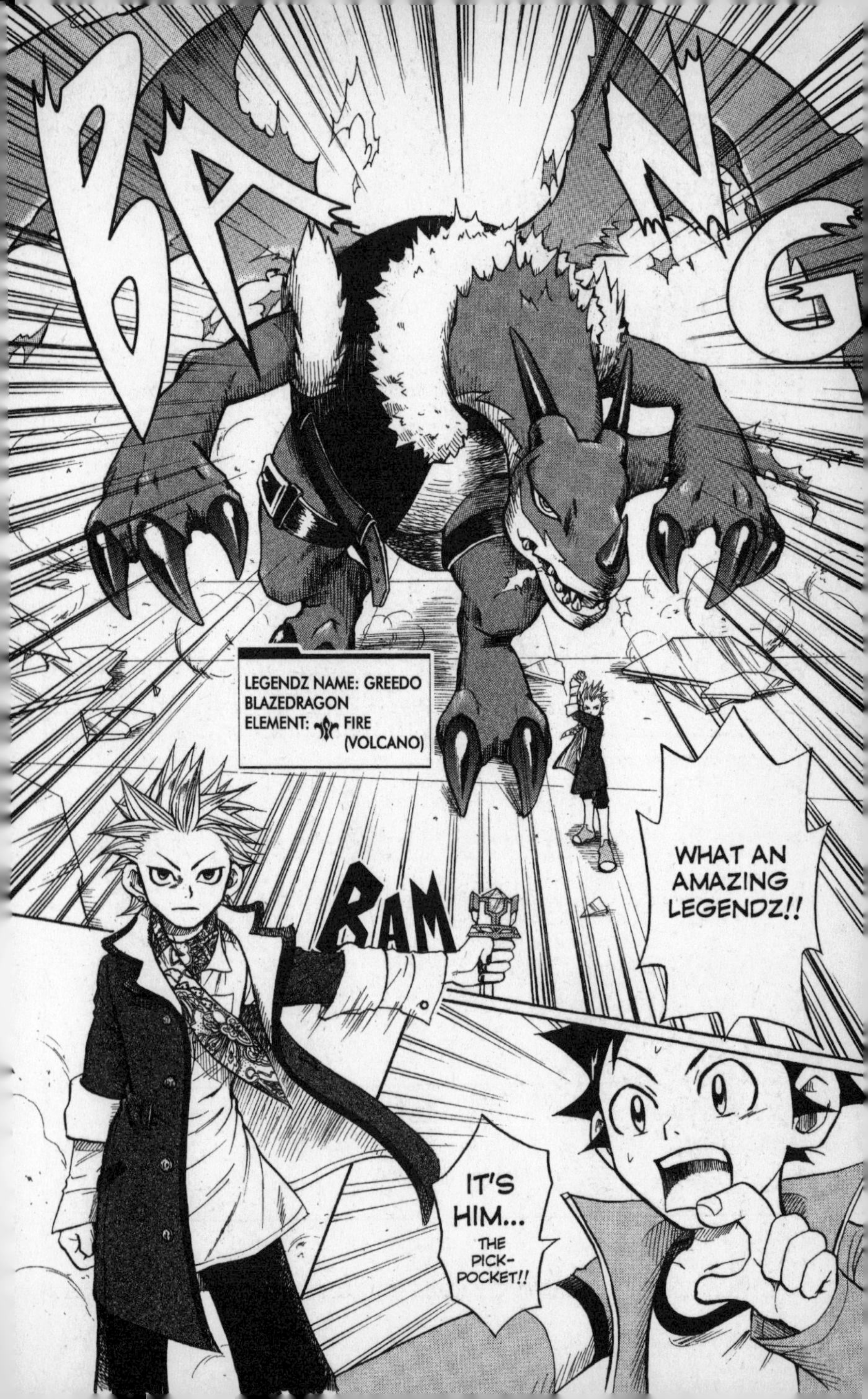
BANG
LEGENDZ NAME: GREEDO
BLAZEDRAGON
ELEMENT: FIRE
(VOLCANO)
WHAT AN AMAZING LEGENDZ!!
BAM
IT'S HIM... THE PICK-POCKET!!

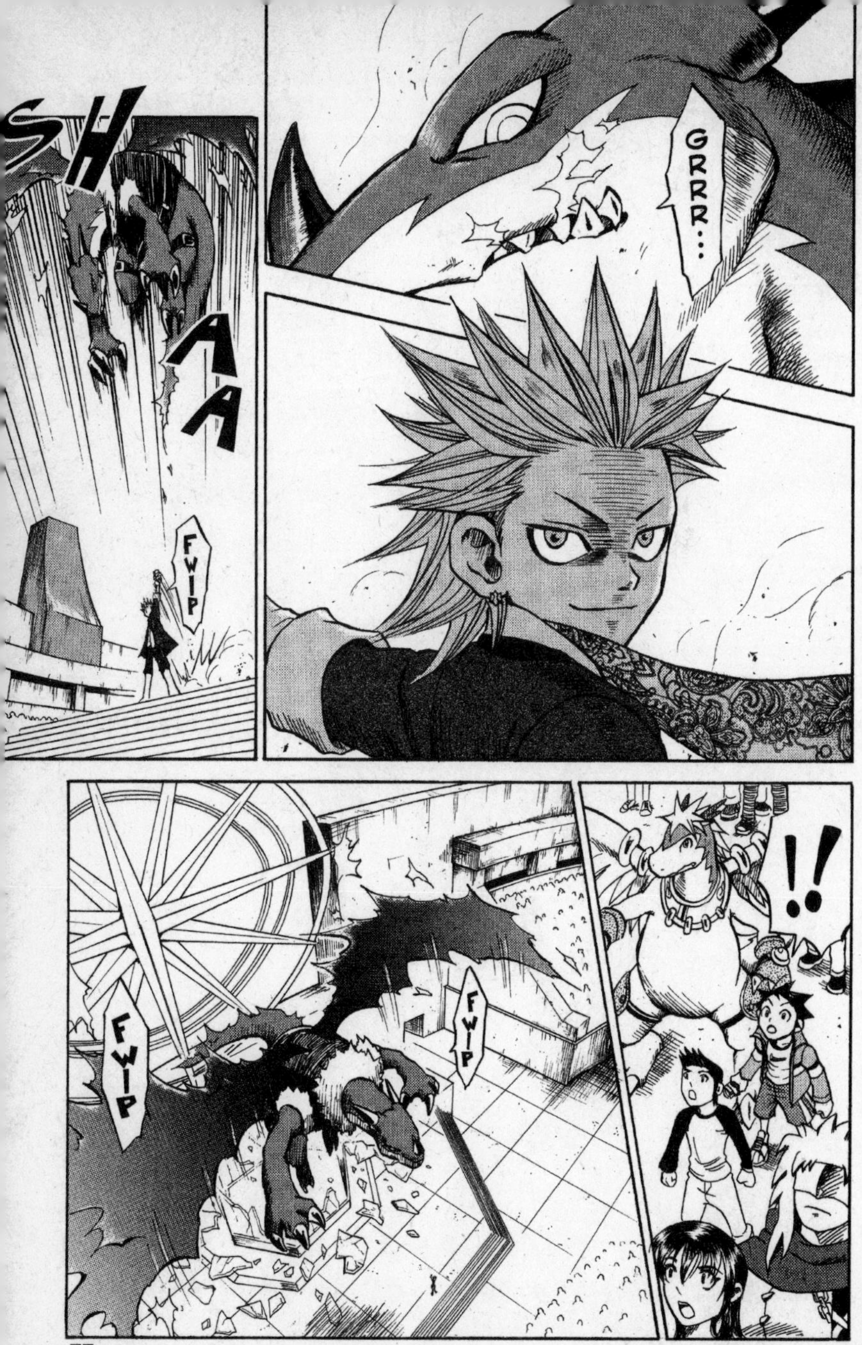
GRRR...
SHAA
FWIP
!!
FWIP
FWIP

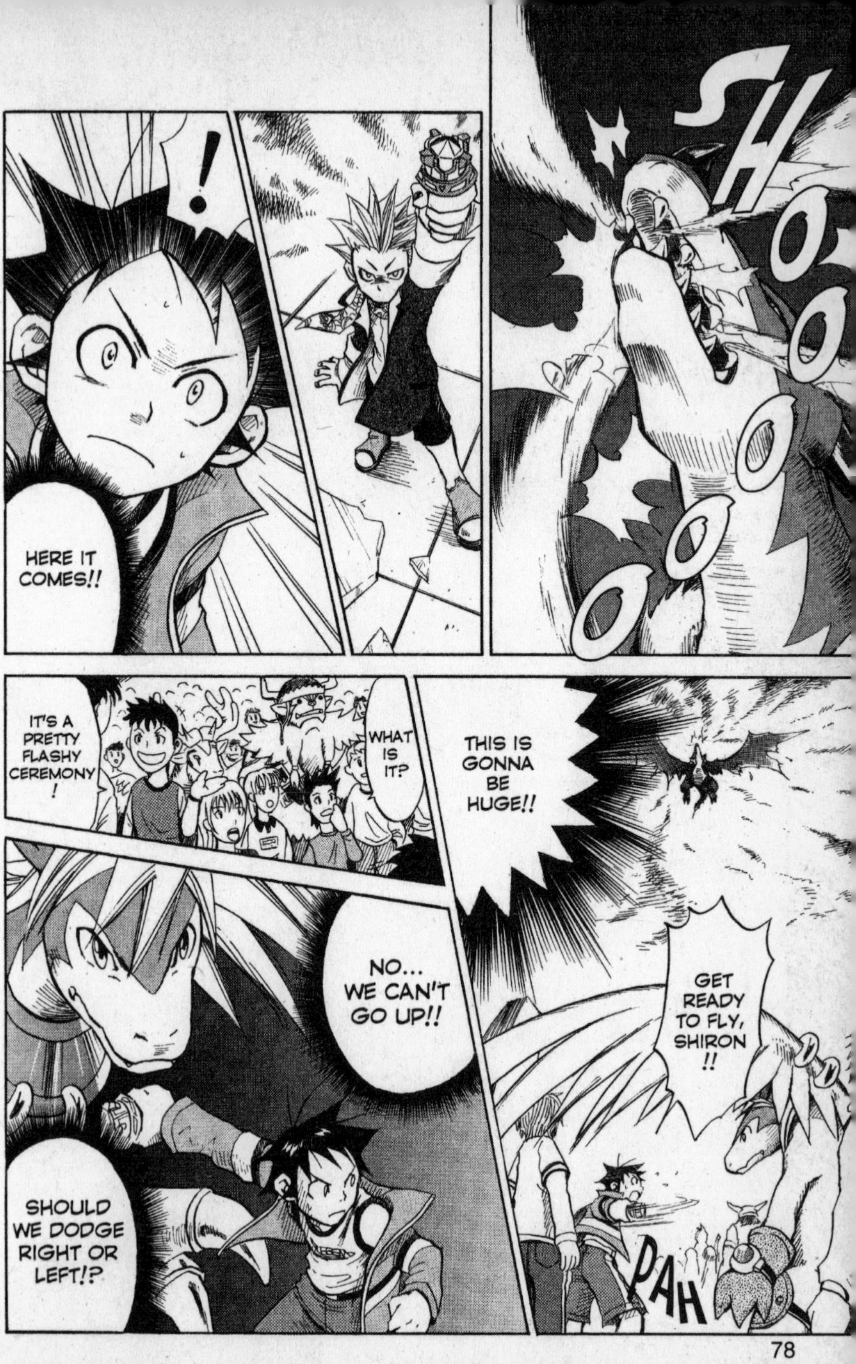
SHOOOOOO
!
HERE IT COMES!!
THIS IS GONNA BE HUGE!!
GET READY TO FLY, SHIRON!!
PAH
WHAT IS IT?
IT'S A PRETTY FLASHY CEREMONY!
NO... WE CAN'T GO UP!!
SHOULD WE DODGE RIGHT OR LEFT!?

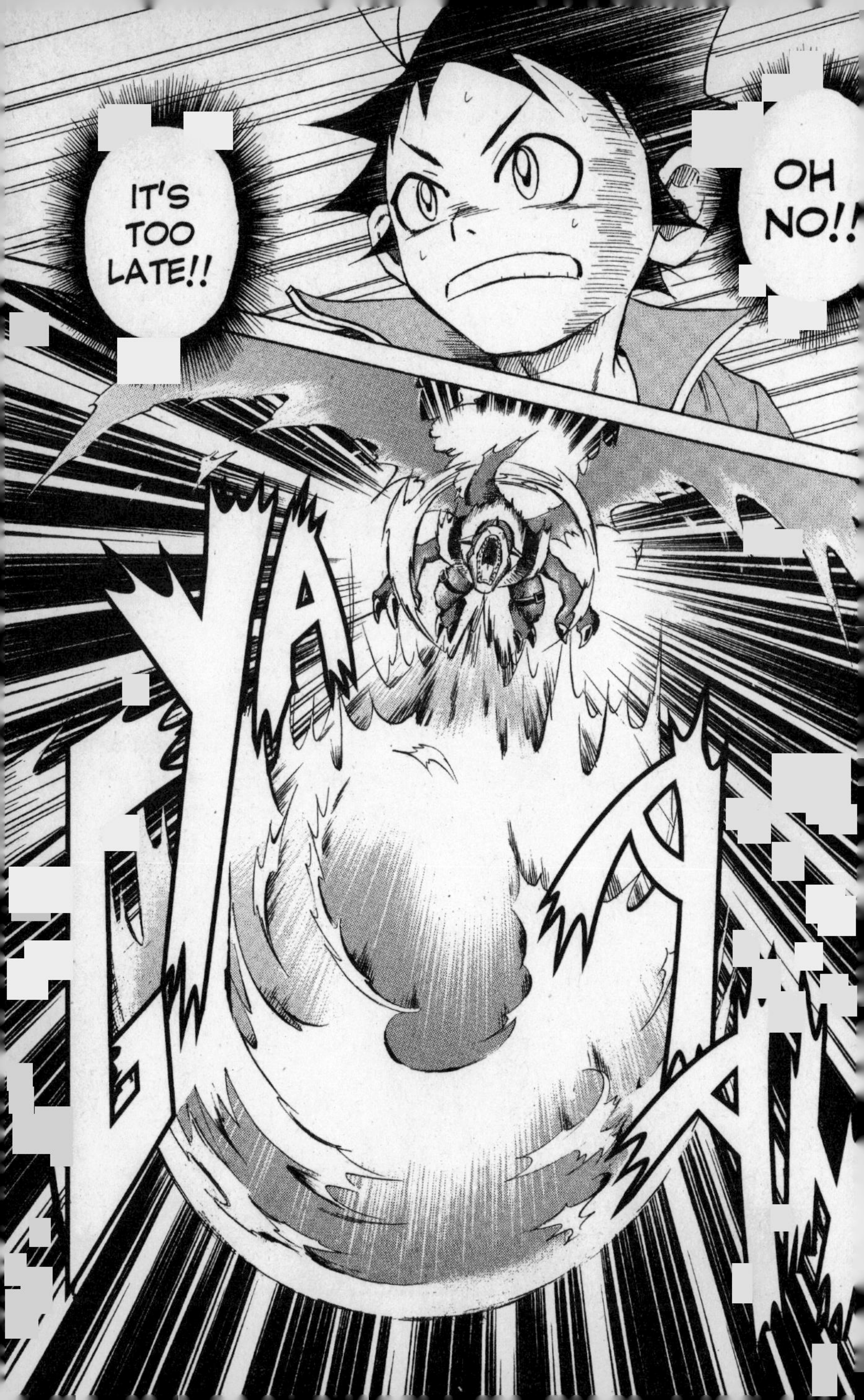
OH NO!!
IT'S TOO LATE!!

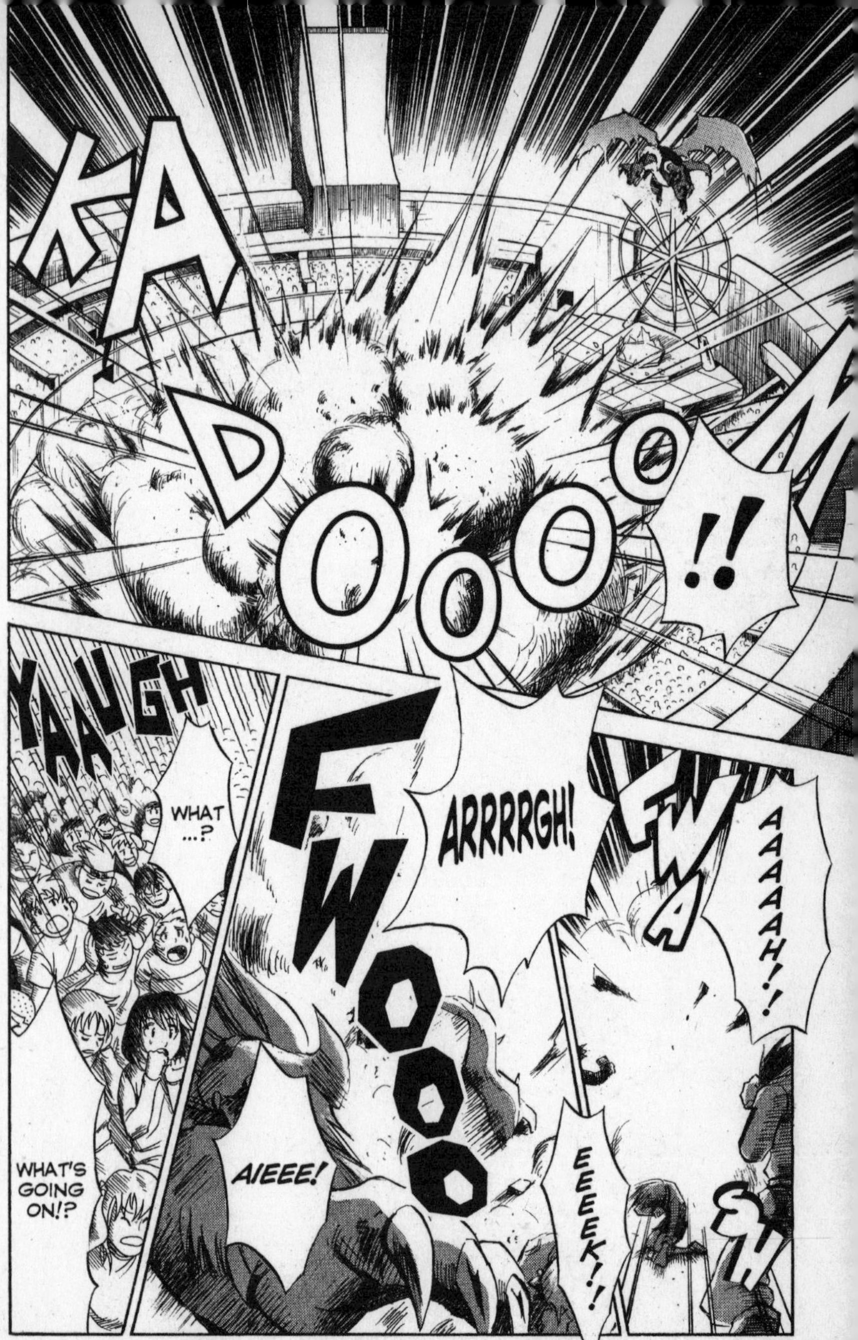
KADOOOOOM!!
FWA
AAAAAH!!
EEEEK!!
SWH
FWOOOOO
ARRRRGH!
AIEEE!
YAAUGH
WHAT ...?
WHAT'S GOING ON!?

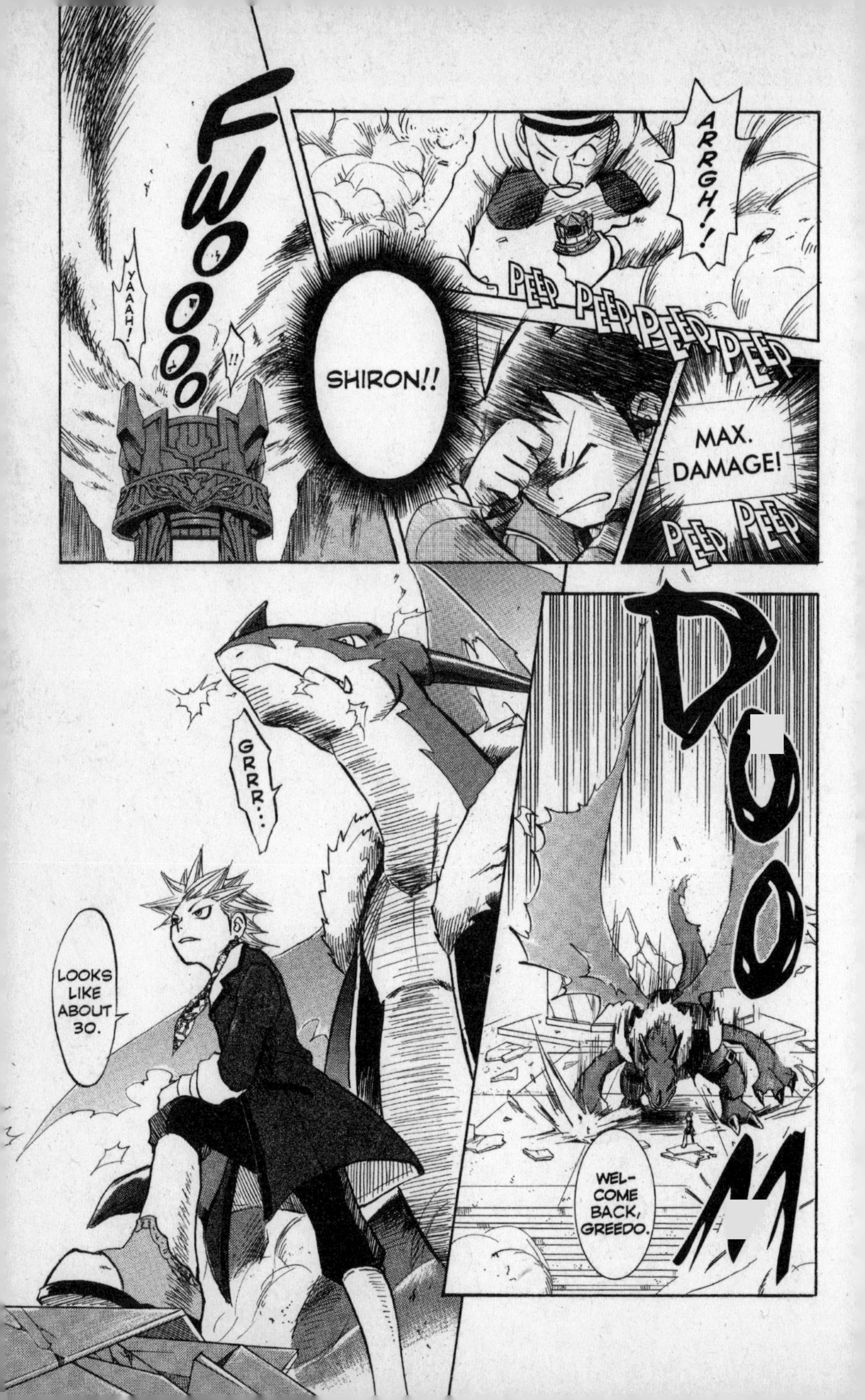
ARRGH!!
PEEP PEEP PEEP PEEP PEEP
SHIRON!!
MAX. DAMAGE!
PEEP PEEP
FWOOOO
!!
YAAAH!
DOOOM
WEL-COME BACK, GREEDO.
GRRR...
LOOKS LIKE ABOUT 30.

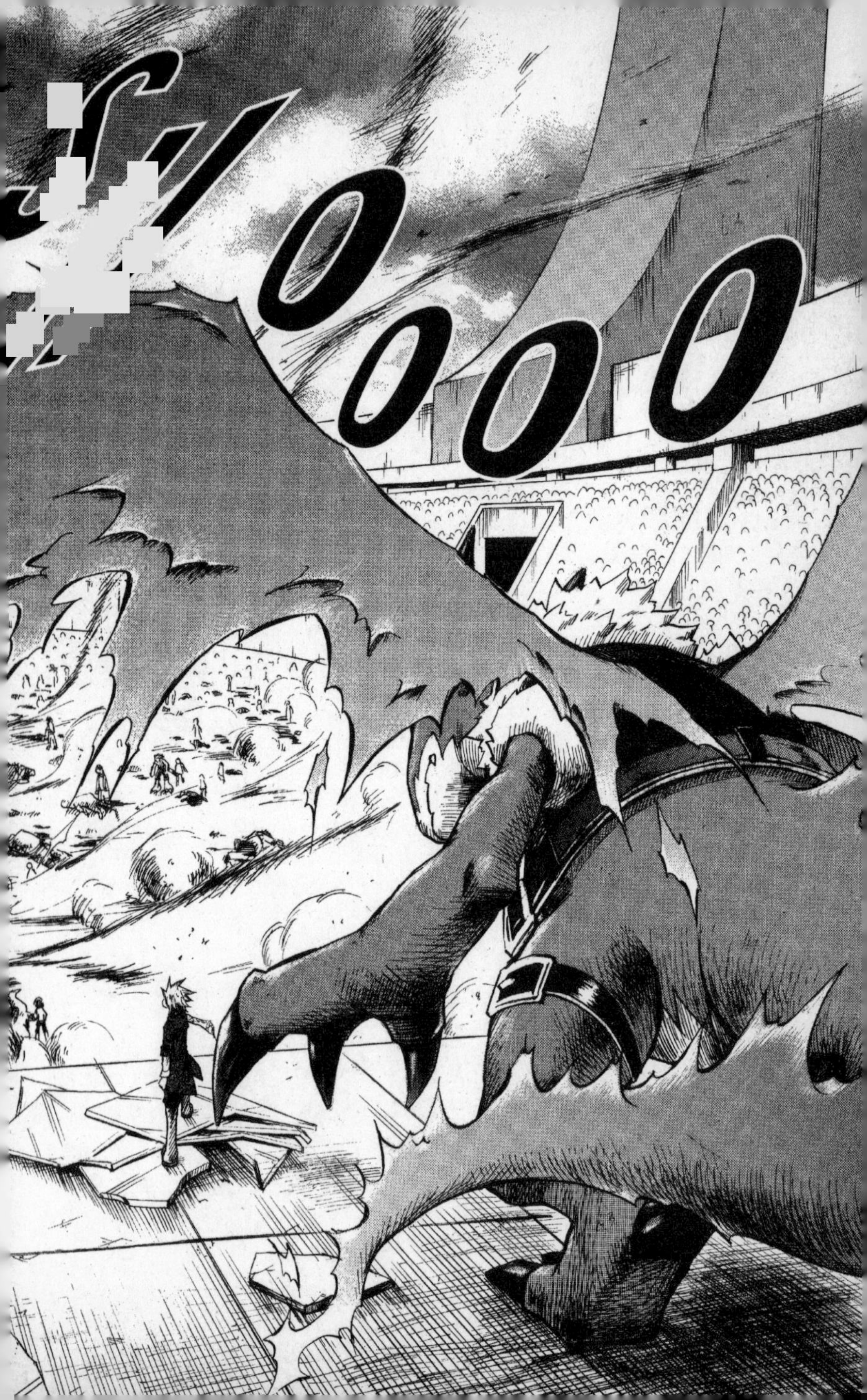
SHOOOO

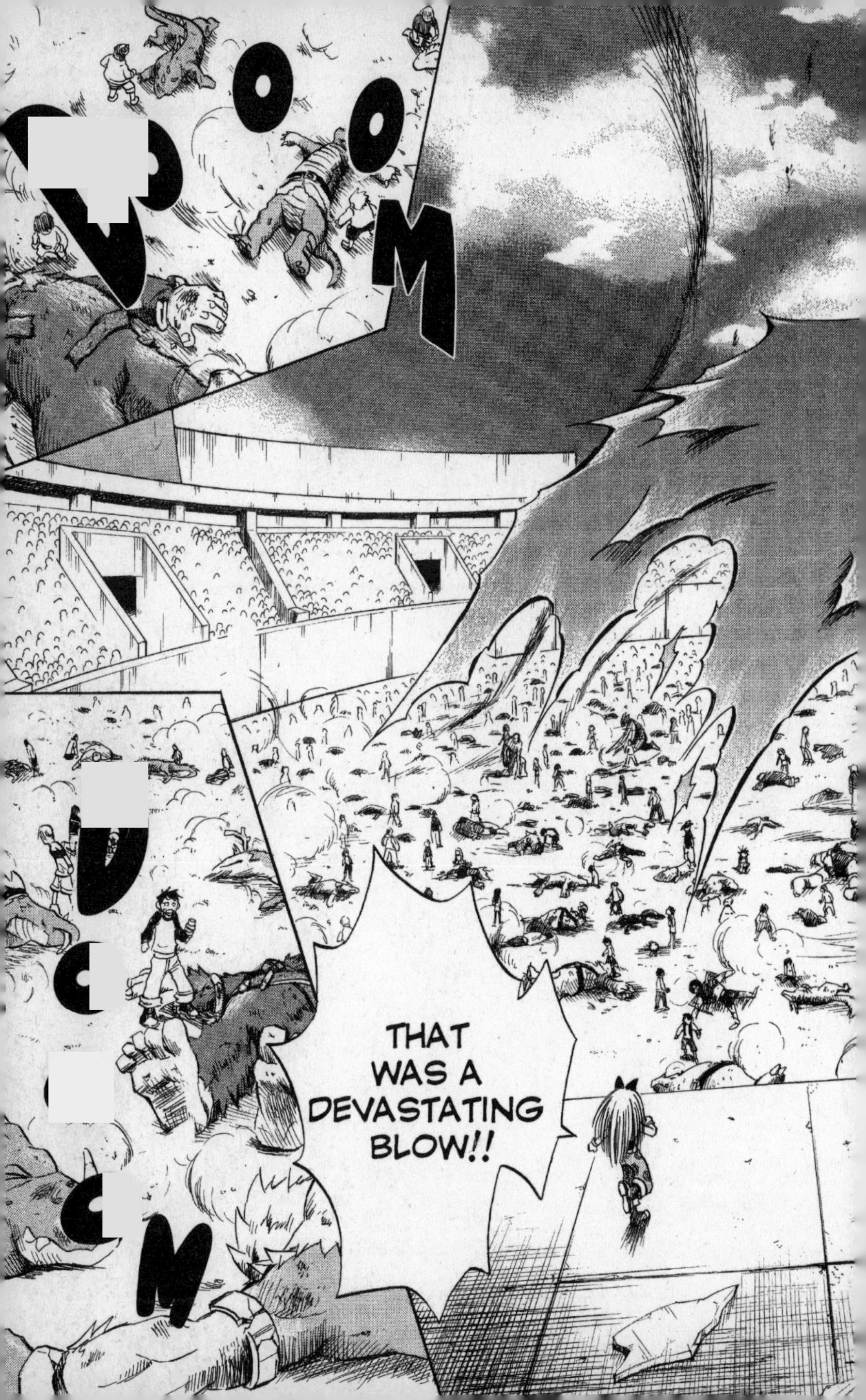
THAT WAS A DEVASTATING BLOW!!

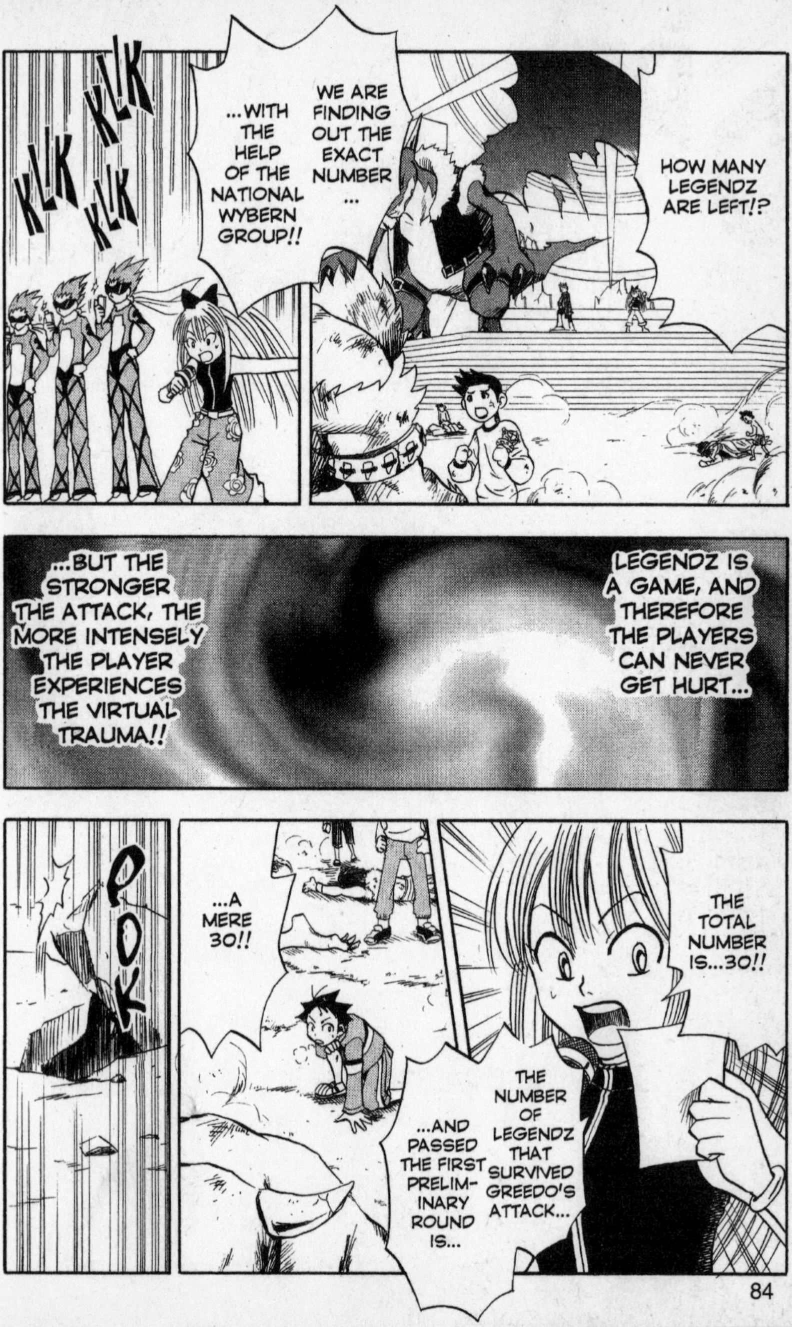
HOW MANY LEGENDZ ARE LEFT!?
WE ARE FINDING OUT THE EXACT NUMBER ...
...WITH THE HELP OF THE NATIONAL WYBERN GROUP!!
KLIK KLIK KLIK
LEGENDZ IS A GAME, AND THEREFORE THE PLAYERS CAN NEVER GET HURT...
...BUT THE STRONGER THE ATTACK, THE MORE INTENSELY THE PLAYER EXPERIENCES THE VIRTUAL TRAUMA!!
THE TOTAL NUMBER IS...30!!
THE NUMBER OF LEGENDZ THAT SURVIVED GREEDO'S ATTACK...
...AND PASSED THE FIRST PRELIMINARY ROUND IS...
...A MERE 30!!
POK

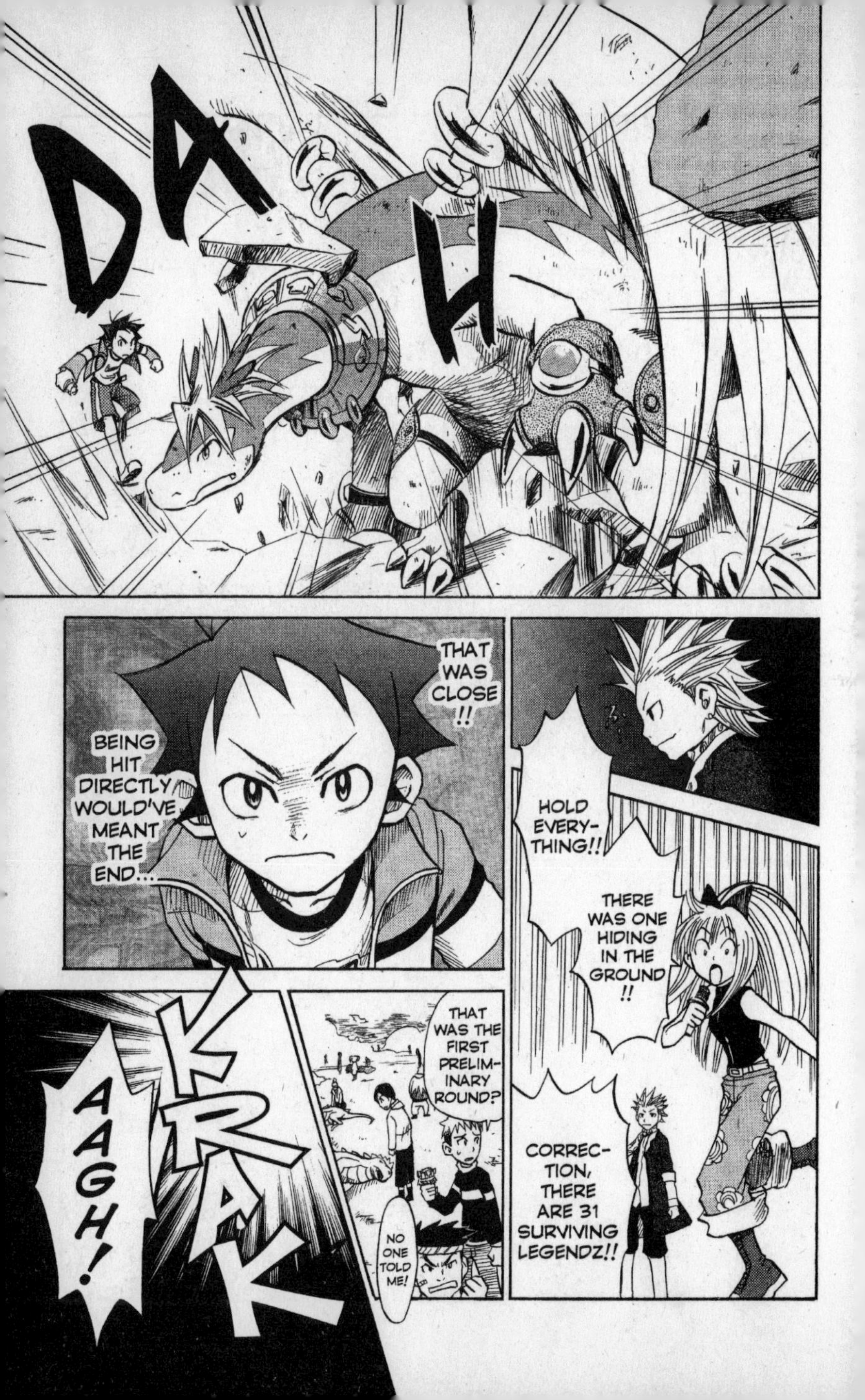
DAH
THAT WAS CLOSE!!
BEING HIT DIRECTLY WOULD'VE MEANT THE END...
HOLD EVERY-THING!!
THERE WAS ONE HIDING IN THE GROUND!!
CORRECTION, THERE ARE 31 SURVIVING LEGENDZ!!
THAT WAS THE FIRST PRELIMINARY ROUND?
NO ONE TOLD ME!
KRAK
AAGH!

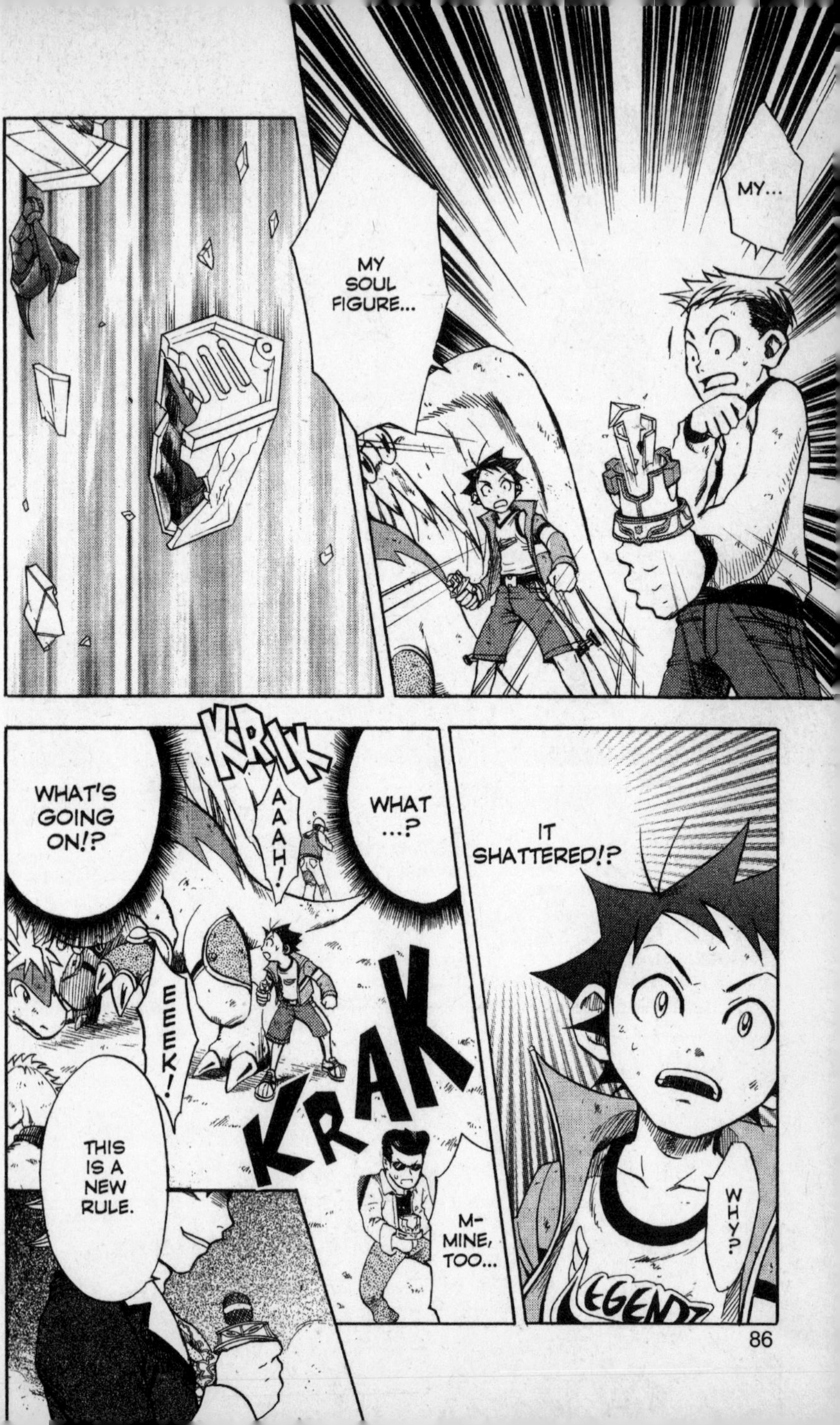
MY...
MY SOUL FIGURE...
IT SHATTERED!?
WHY?
WHAT ...?
KRIK
AAAH!
WHAT'S GOING ON!?
EEEK!
KRAK
M-MINE, TOO...
THIS IS A NEW RULE.

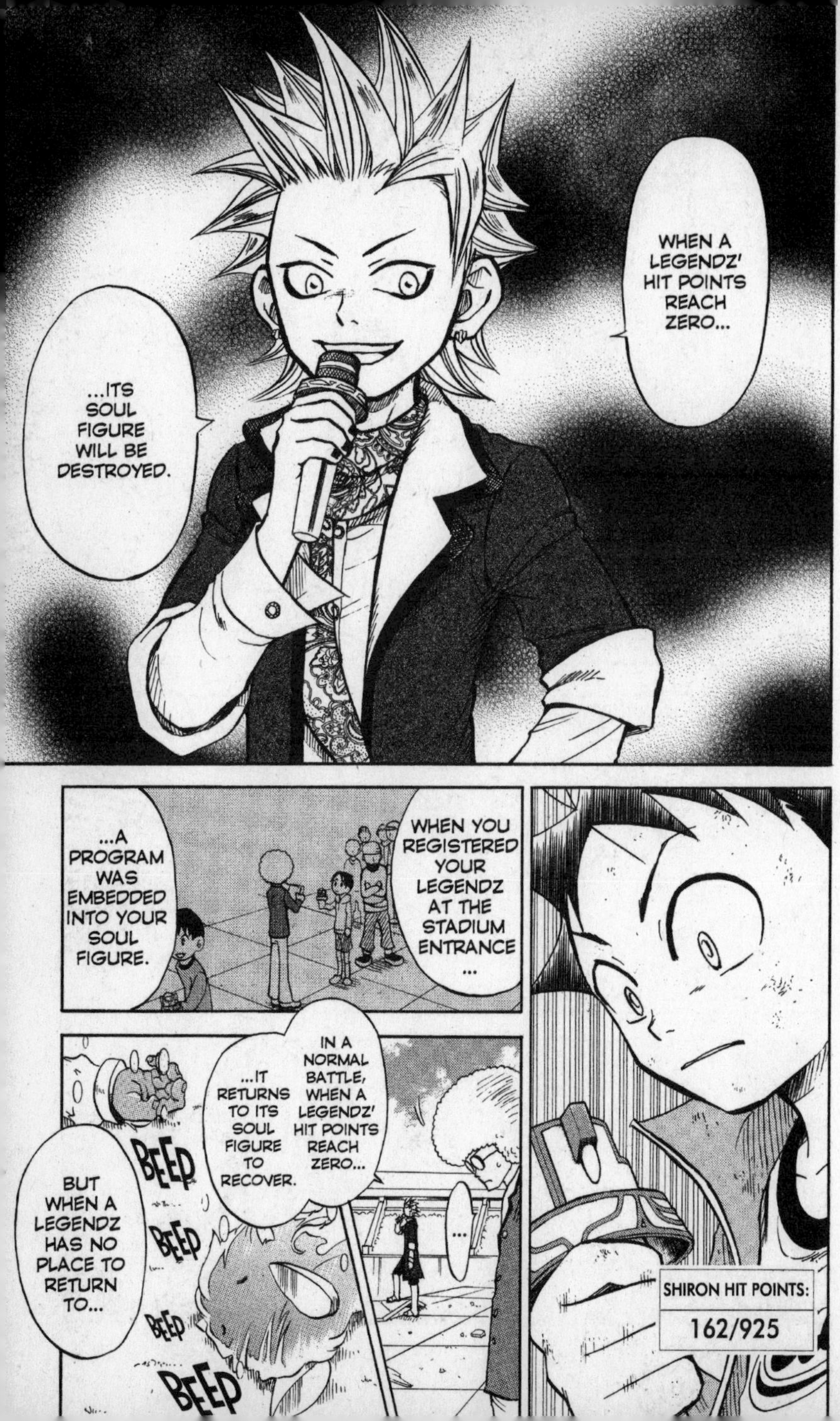
WHEN A LEGENDZ' HIT POINTS REACH ZERO...
...ITS SOUL FIGURE WILL BE DESTROYED.
SHIRON HIT POINTS:
162/925
WHEN YOU REGISTERED YOUR LEGENDZ AT THE STADIUM ENTRANCE ...
...A PROGRAM WAS EMBEDDED INTO YOUR SOUL FIGURE.
IN A NORMAL BATTLE, WHEN A LEGENDZ' HIT POINTS REACH ZERO...
...IT RETURNS TO ITS SOUL FIGURE TO RECOVER.
...
BEEP
BEEP
BEEP
BEEP
BUT WHEN A LEGENDZ HAS NO PLACE TO RETURN TO...

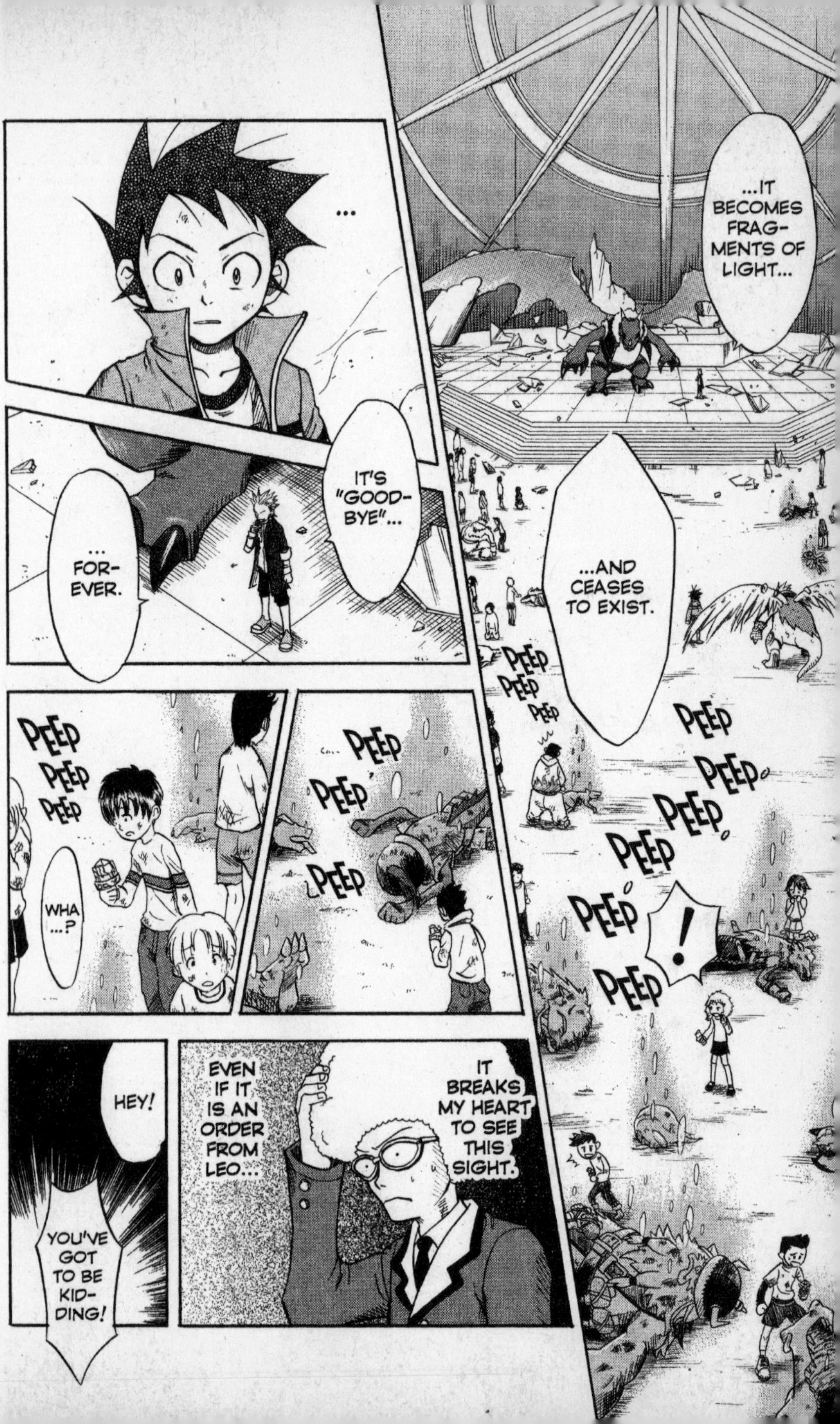
...IT BECOMES FRAG-MENTS OF LIGHT...
...AND CEASES TO EXIST.
PEEP PEEP PEEP
PEEP PEEP PEEP PEEP PEEP PEEP PEEP
!
...
IT'S "GOOD-BYE"...
... FOR-EVER.
PEEP PEEP PEEP
PEEP PEEP PEEP
WHA ...?
IT BREAKS MY HEART TO SEE THIS SIGHT.
EVEN IF IT IS AN ORDER FROM LEO...
HEY!
YOU'VE GOT TO BE KID-DING!

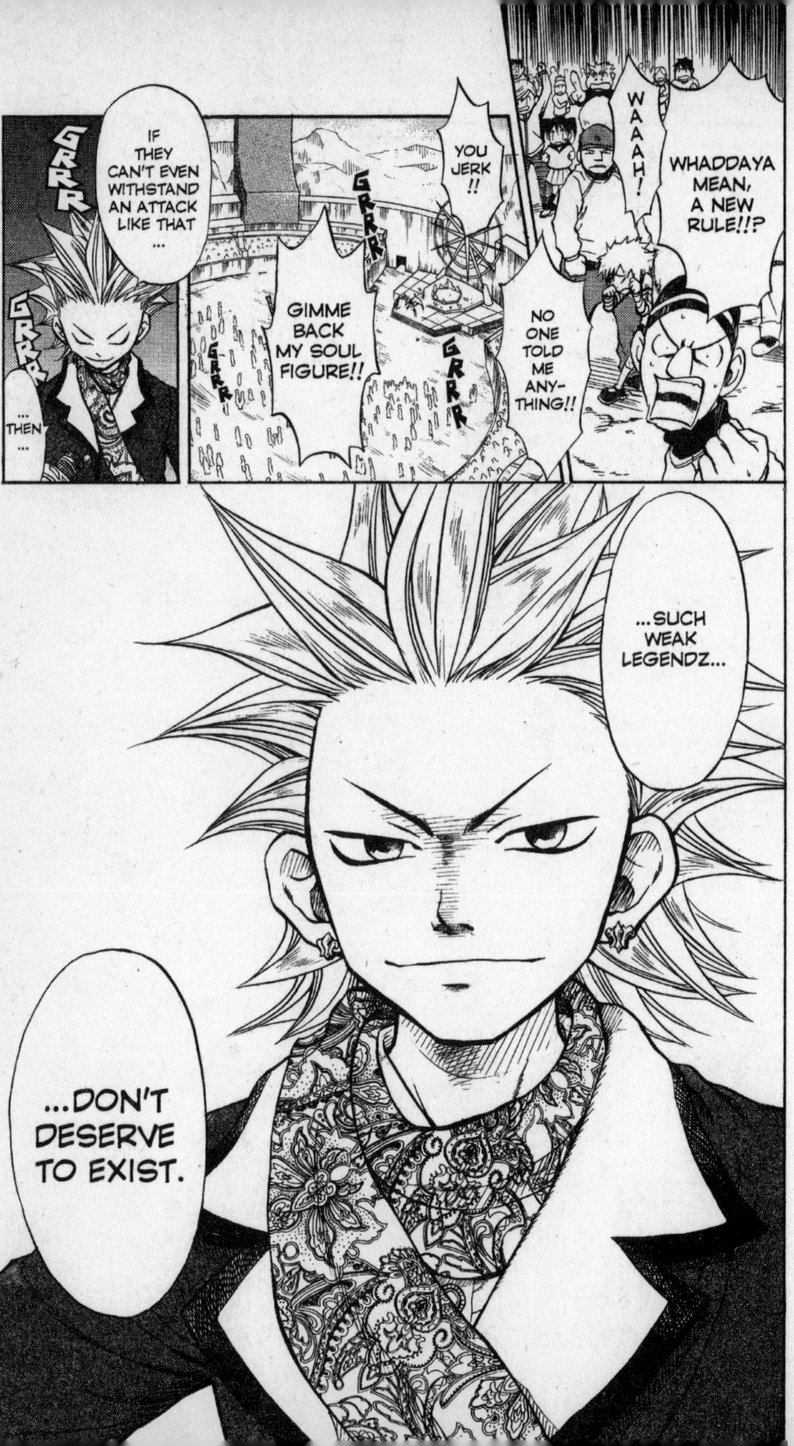
WHADDAYA MEAN, A NEW RULE!!?
WAAAH!
NO ONE TOLD ME ANYTHING!!
YOU JERK!!
GRRR
GIMME BACK MY SOUL FIGURE!!
GRRR
GRRR
IF THEY CAN'T EVEN WITHSTAND AN ATTACK LIKE THAT ...
GRRR
GRRR
... THEN ...
...SUCH WEAK LEGENDZ...
...DON'T DESERVE TO EXIST.

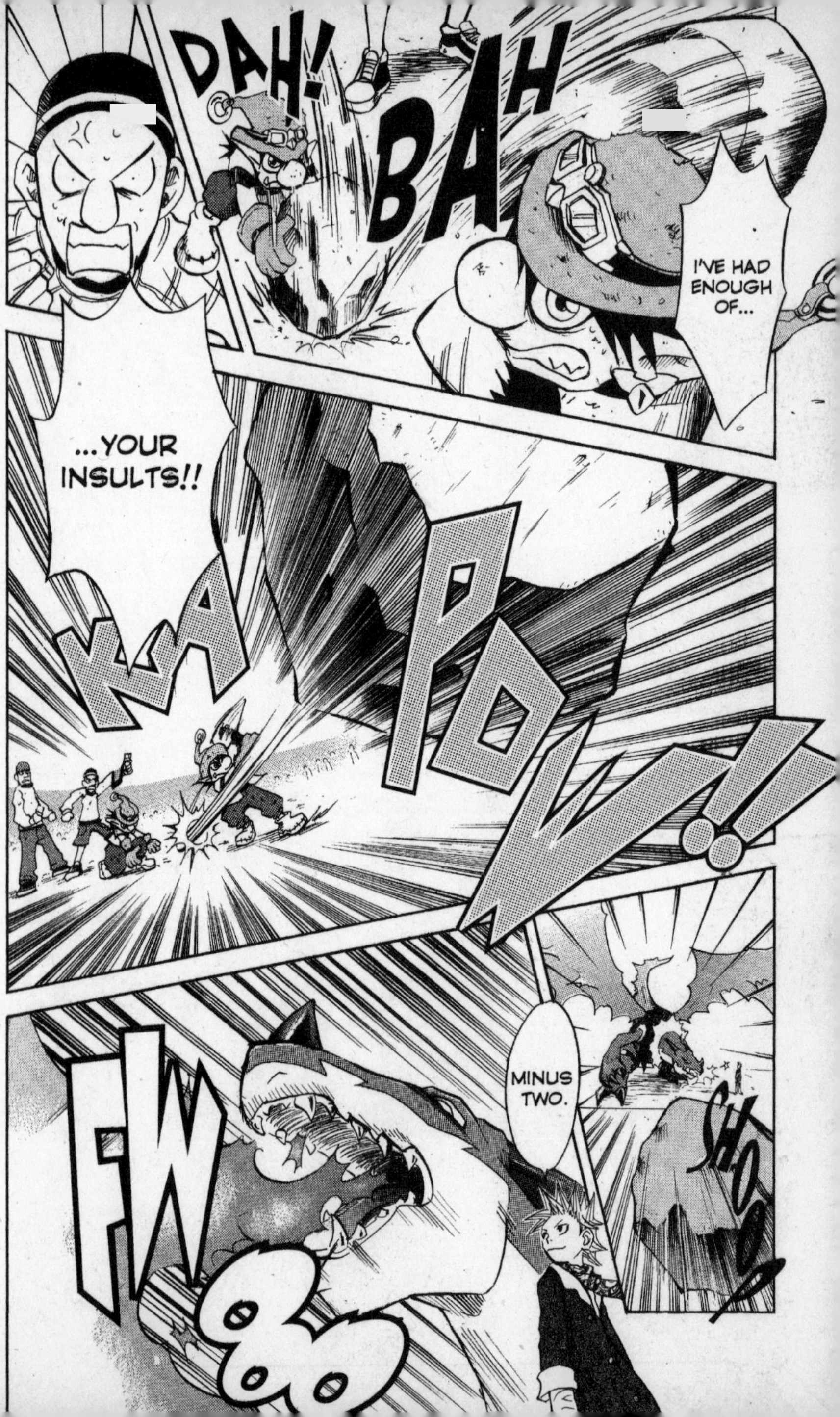

I'VE HAD ENOUGH OF...
BAH
DAH!
...YOUR INSULTS!!
KAPOW!!
SHOO
MINUS TWO.
FWOOO

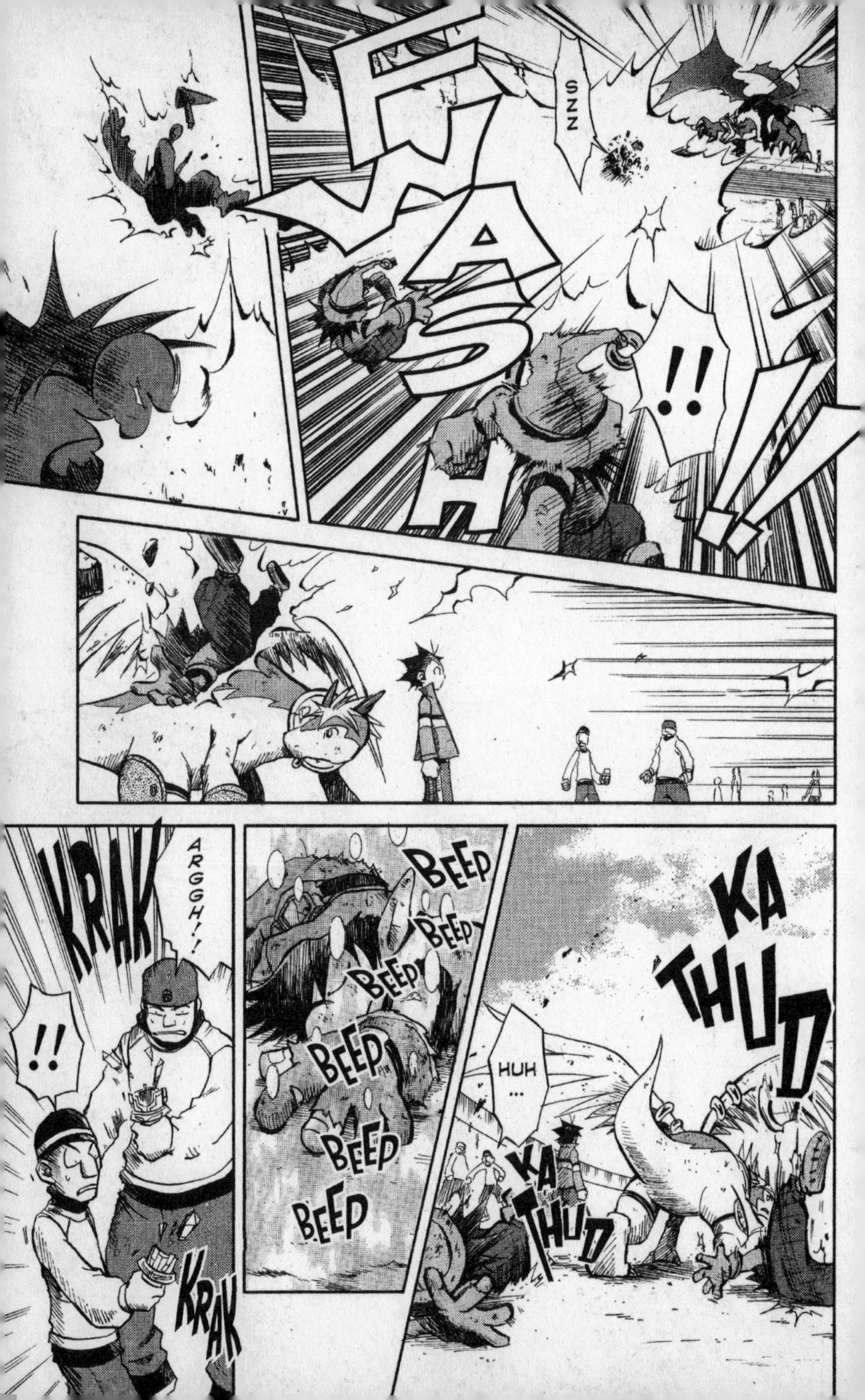
SZZ
!!
FWASH
!!
ARGGH!!
KRAK
KRAK
BEEP
BEEP
BEEP
BEEP
BEEP
BEEP
KA THUD
HUH ...
KA THUD

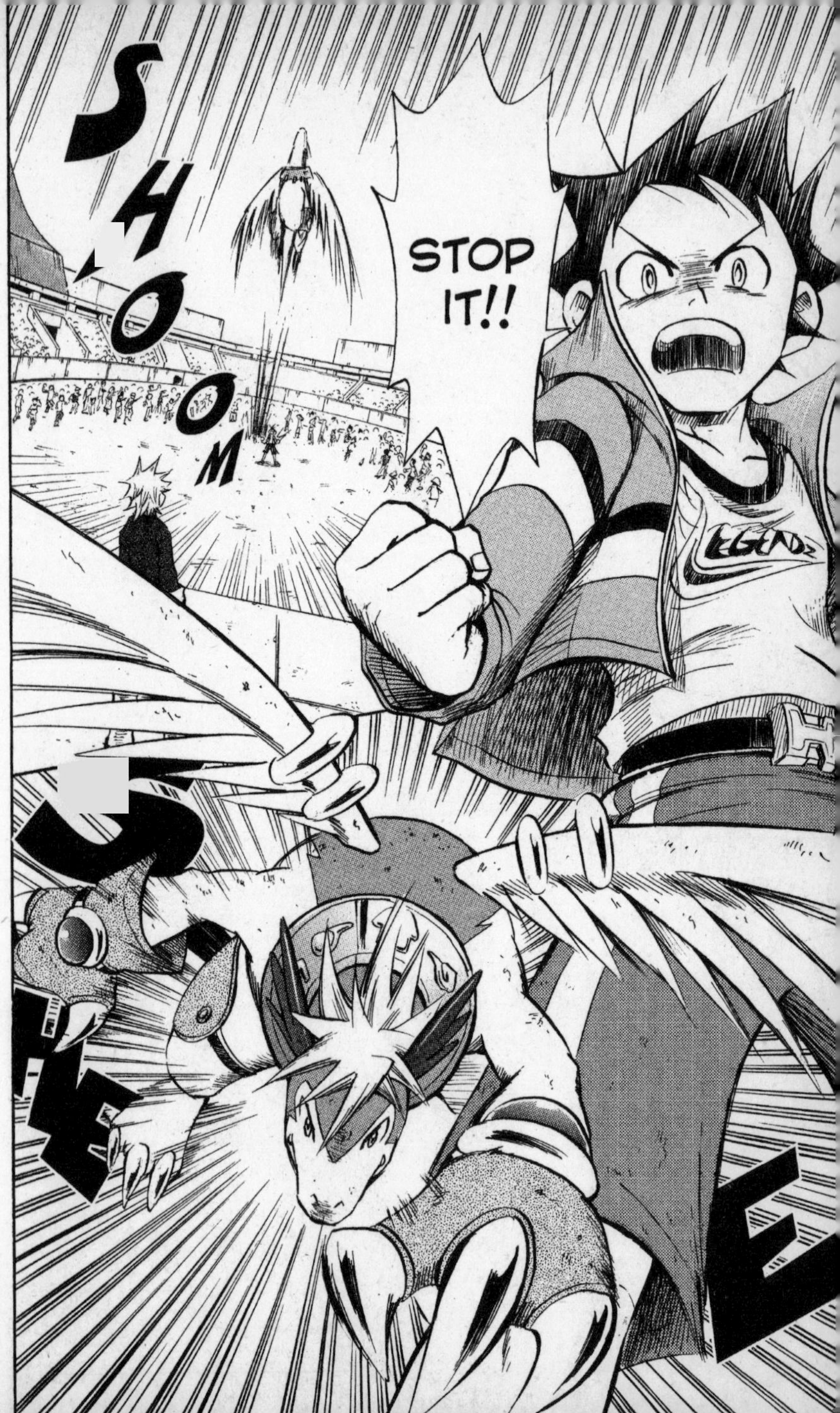
STOP IT!!
SHOOM

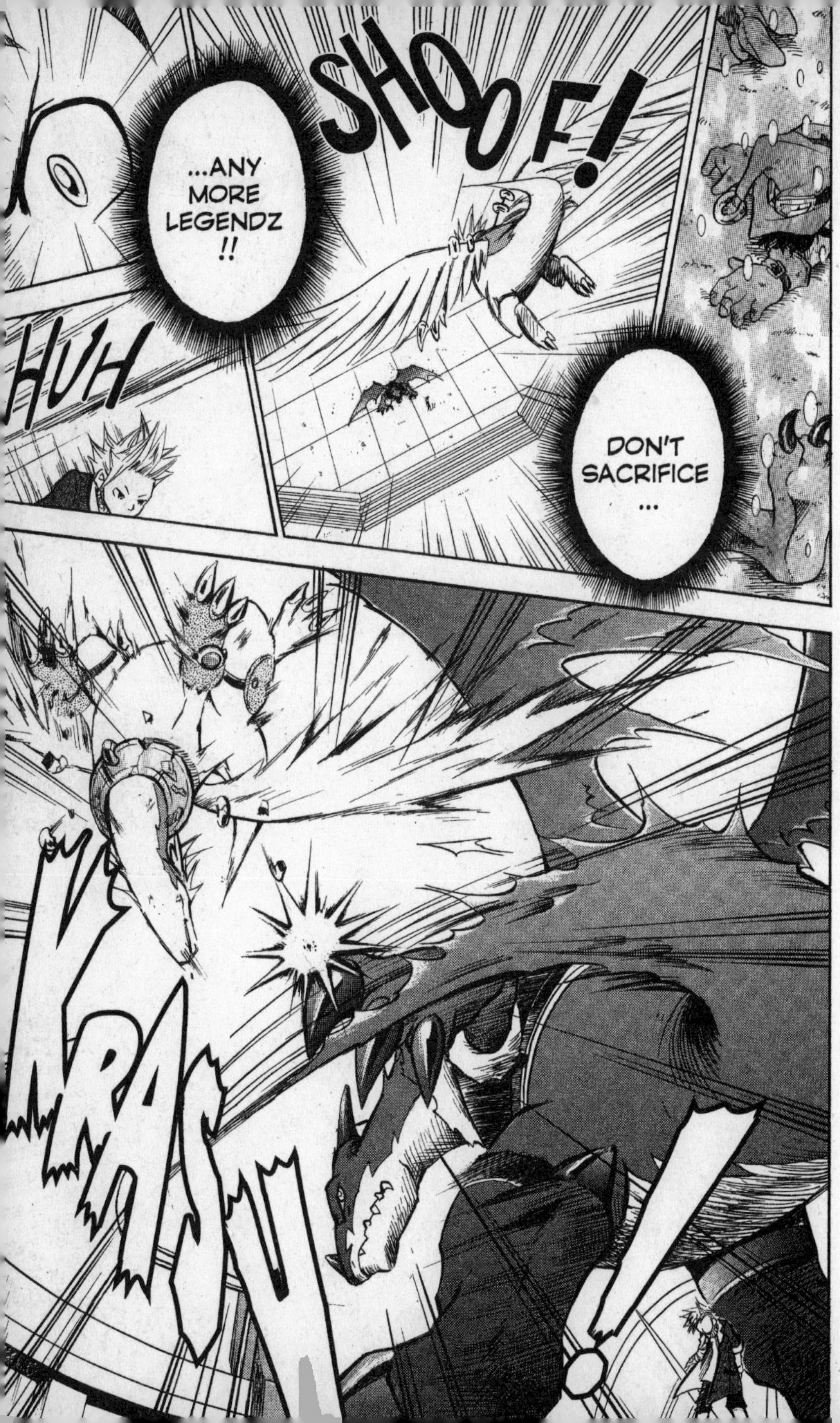
DON'T SACRIFICE ...
SHOOF!
...ANY MORE LEGENDZ !!
HUH

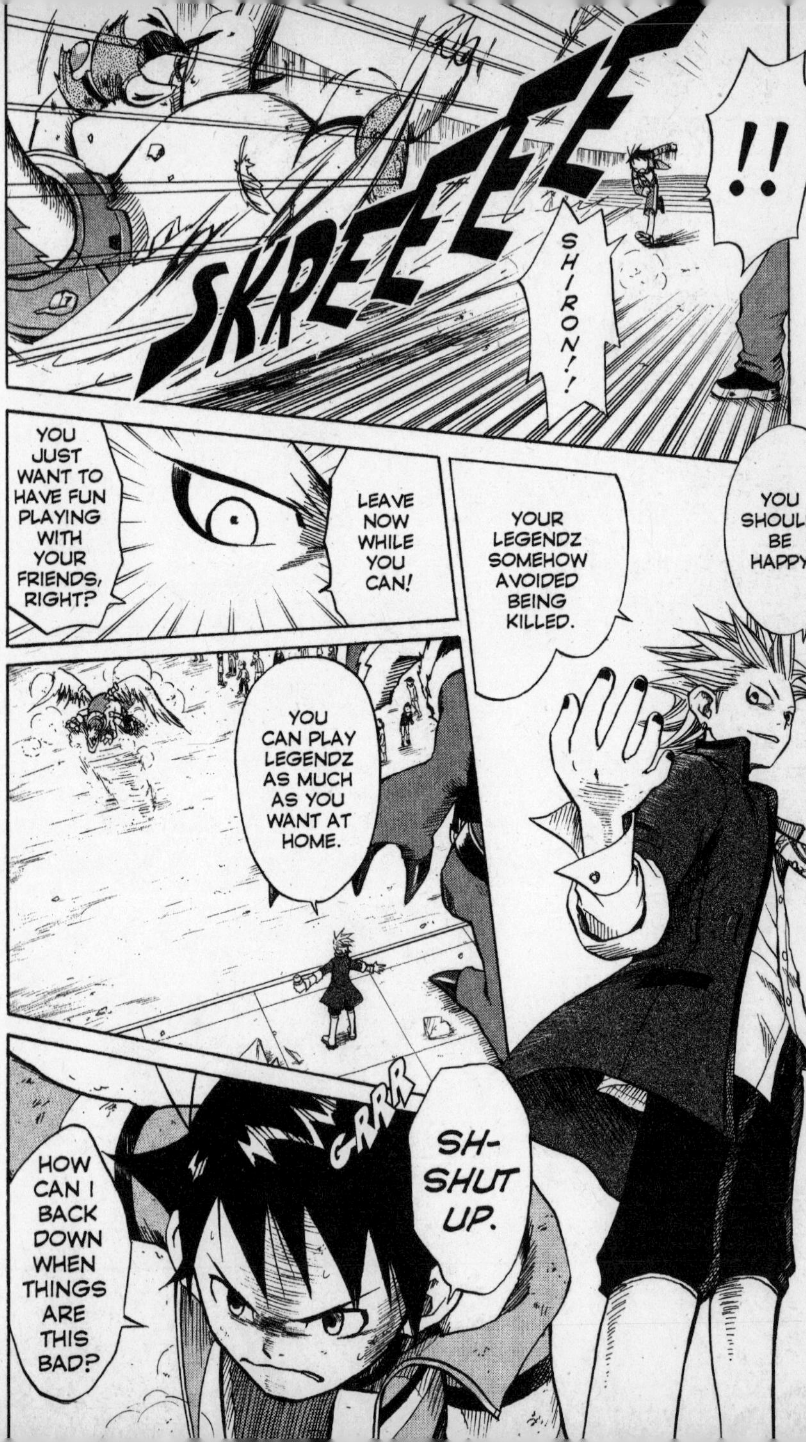
!!
SHIRON!!
SKREEEE
YOU SHOULD BE HAPPY.
YOUR LEGENDZ SOMEHOW AVOIDED BEING KILLED.
LEAVE NOW WHILE YOU CAN!
YOU JUST WANT TO HAVE FUN PLAYING WITH YOUR FRIENDS, RIGHT?
YOU CAN PLAY LEGENDZ AS MUCH AS YOU WANT AT HOME.
SH-SHUT UP.
GRRR
HOW CAN I BACK DOWN WHEN THINGS ARE THIS BAD?

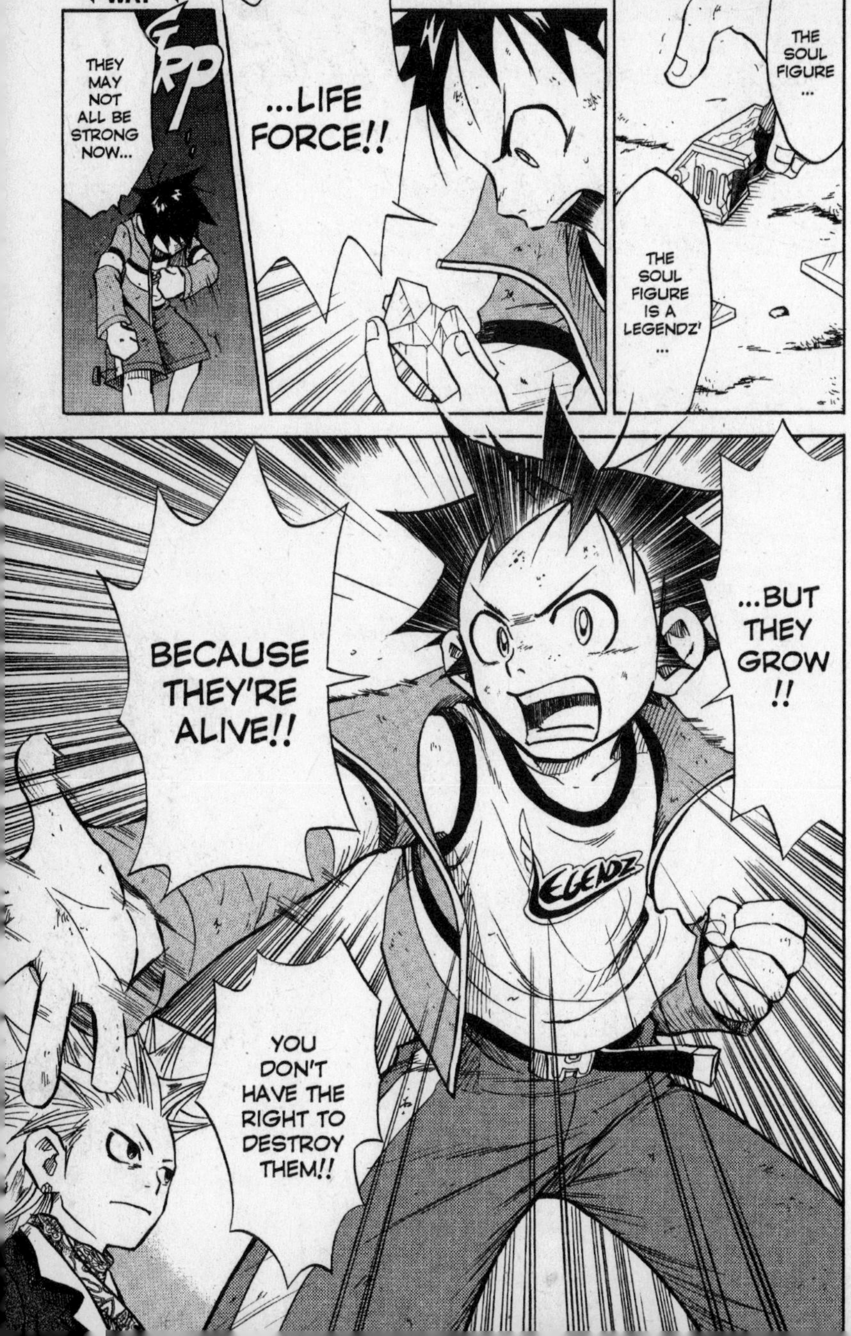
READ THIS WAY
THE SOUL FIGURE ...
THE SOUL FIGURE IS A LEGENDZ' ...
...LIFE FORCE!!
GRP
THEY MAY NOT ALL BE STRONG NOW...
...BUT THEY GROW !!
BECAUSE THEY'RE ALIVE!!
YOU DON'T HAVE THE RIGHT TO DESTROY THEM!!
LEGENDZ

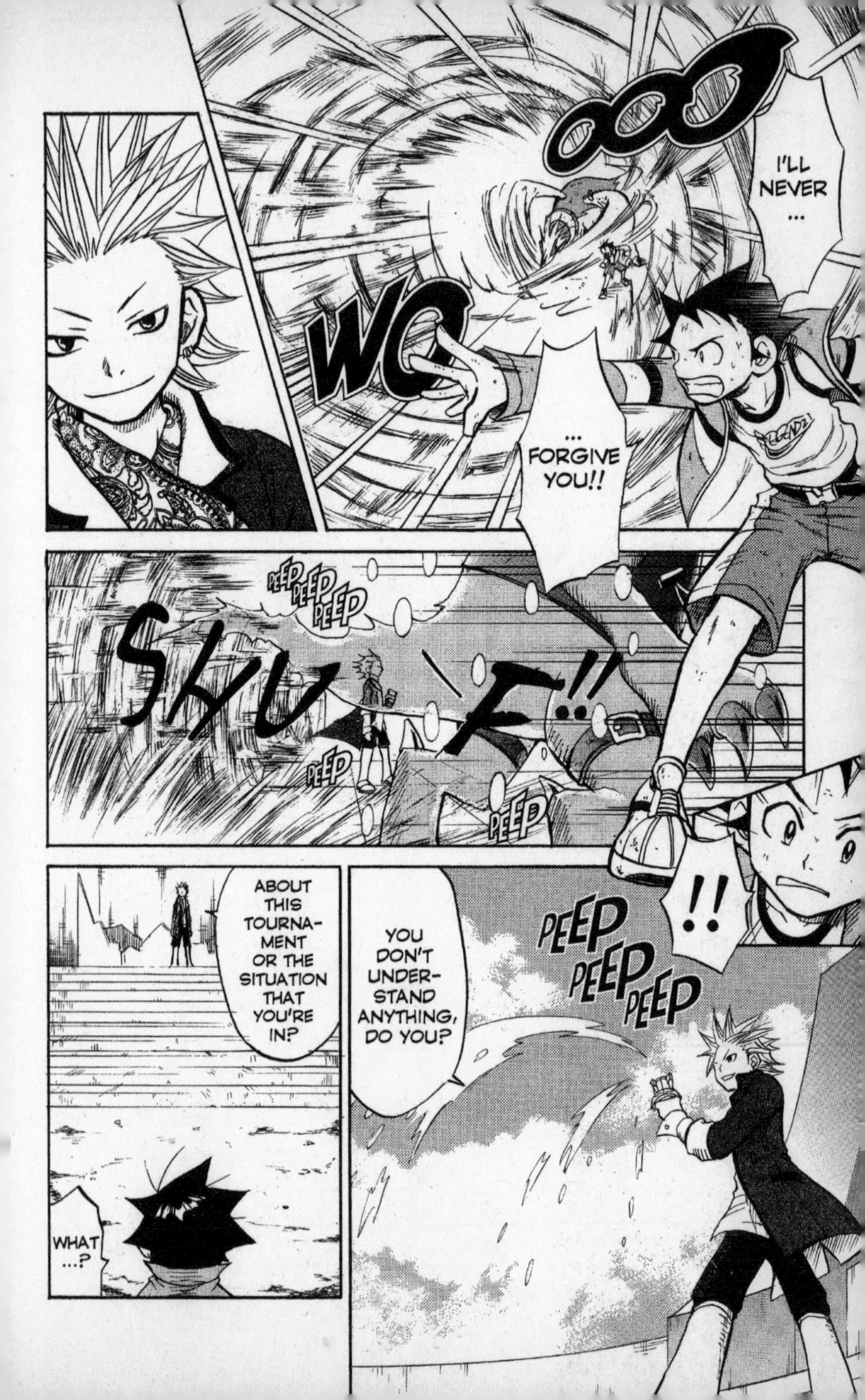
OOO
I'LL NEVER ...
WO
... FORGIVE YOU!!
!!
PEEP PEEP PEEP
SHU F!!
PEEP
PEEP
PEEP PEEP PEEP
YOU DON'T UNDERSTAND ANYTHING, DO YOU?
ABOUT THIS TOURNAMENT OR THE SITUATION THAT YOU'RE IN?
WHAT ...?

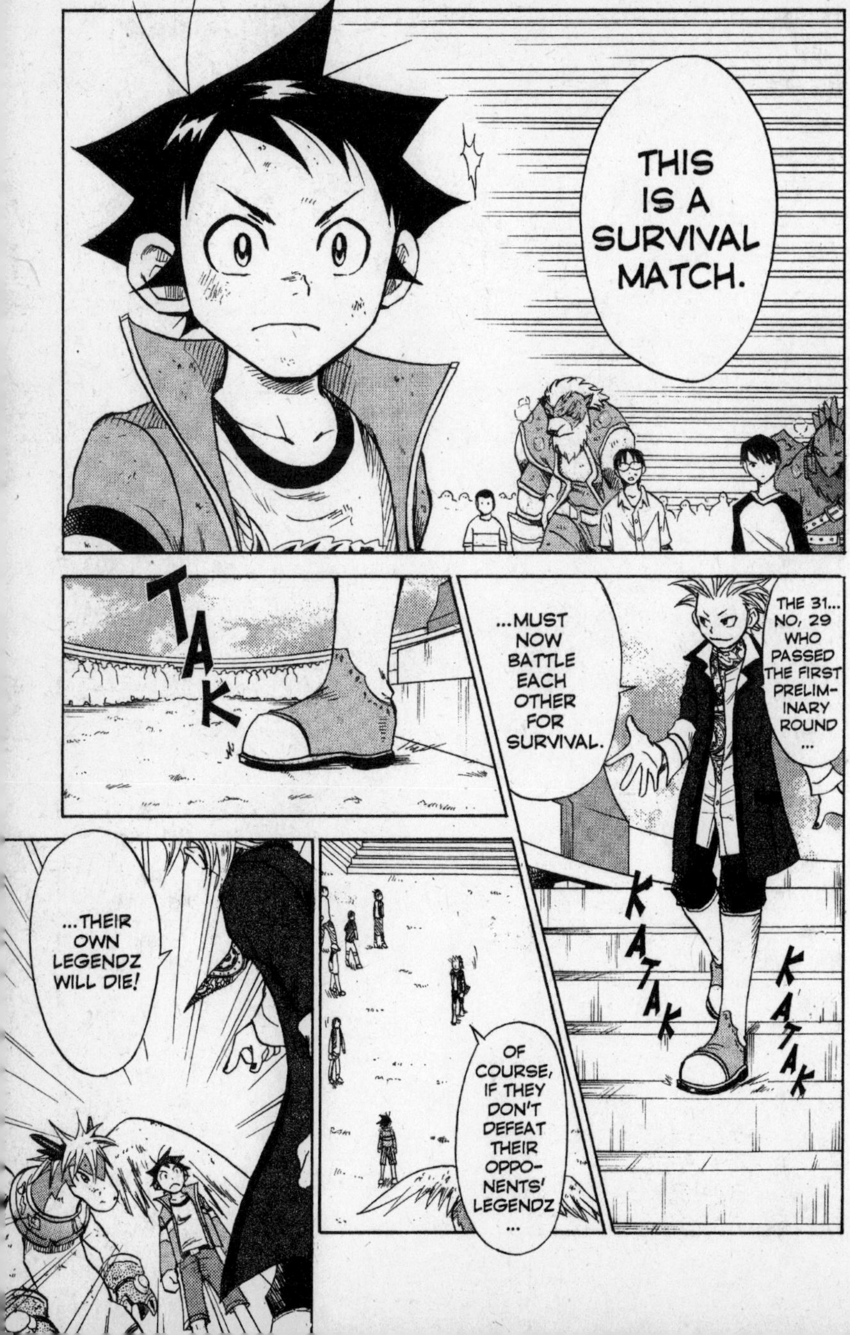
THIS IS A SURVIVAL MATCH.
THE 31... NO, 29 WHO PASSED THE FIRST PRELIM-INARY ROUND ...
...MUST NOW BATTLE EACH OTHER FOR SURVIVAL.
KATAK
KATAK
TAK
OF COURSE, IF THEY DON'T DEFEAT THEIR OPPO-NENTS' LEGENDZ ...
...THEIR OWN LEGENDZ WILL DIE!

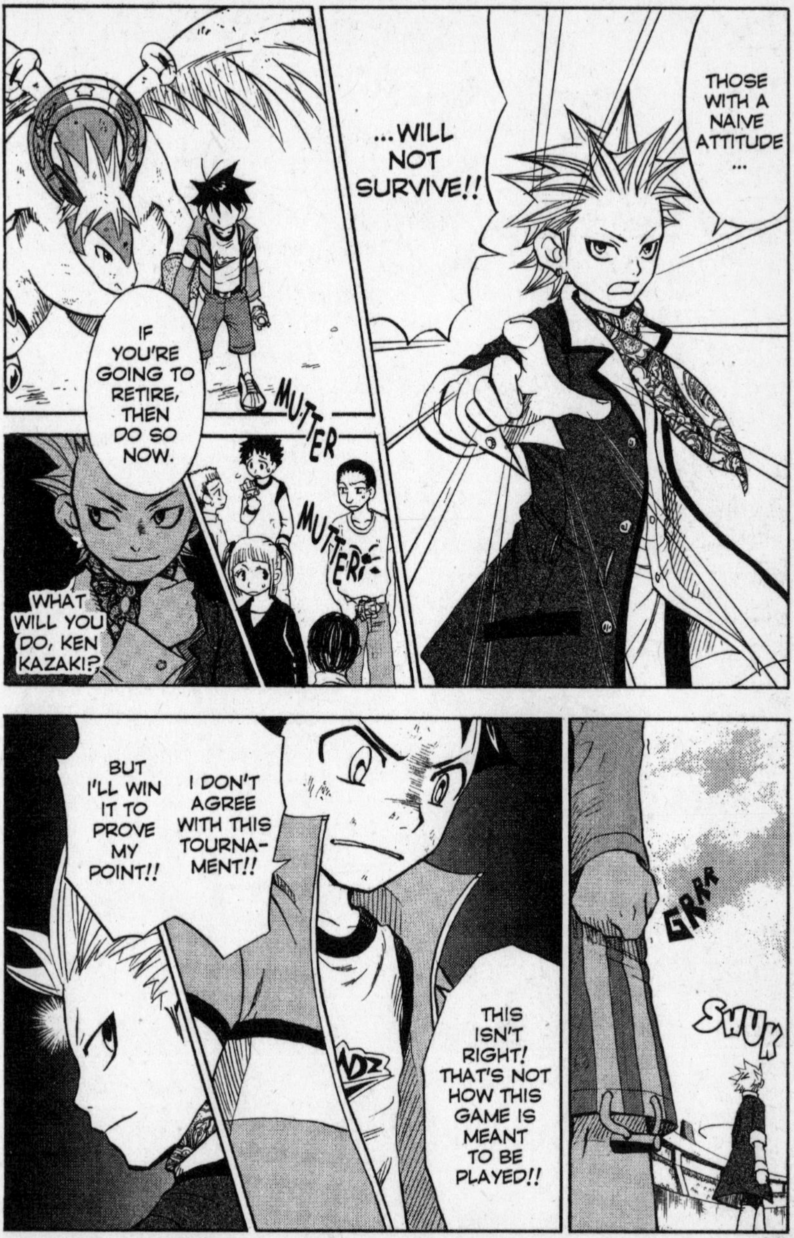
THOSE WITH A NAIVE ATTITUDE ...
...WILL NOT SURVIVE!!
IF YOU'RE GOING TO RETIRE, THEN DO SO NOW.
MUTTER
MUTTER
WHAT WILL YOU DO, KEN KAZAKI!?
GRRR
SHUK
I DON'T AGREE WITH THIS TOURNAMENT!!
BUT I'LL WIN IT TO PROVE MY POINT!!
THIS ISN'T RIGHT! THAT'S NOT HOW THIS GAME IS MEANT TO BE PLAYED!!

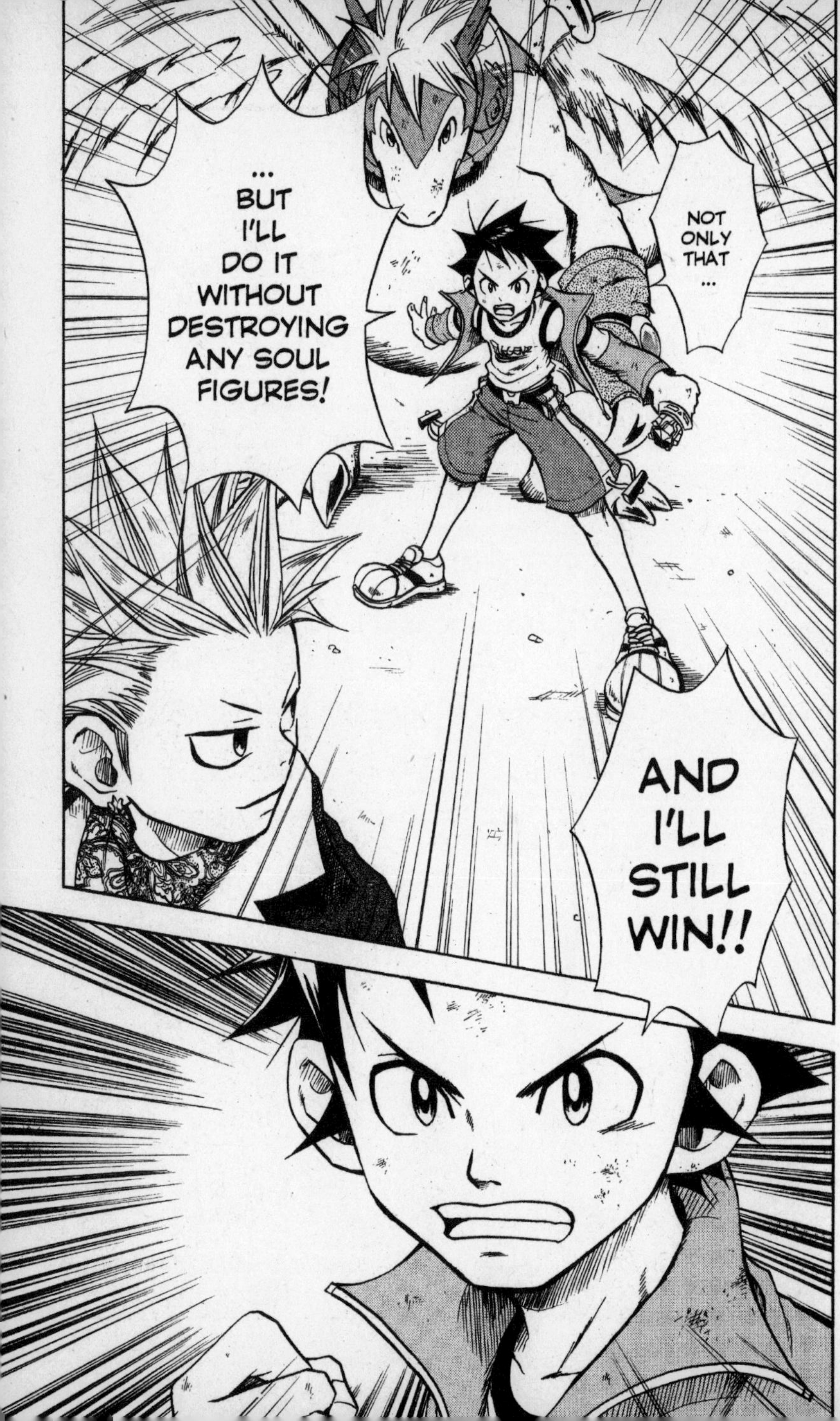
NOT ONLY THAT ...
... BUT I'LL DO IT WITHOUT DESTROYING ANY SOUL FIGURES!
AND I'LL STILL WIN!!

LEO

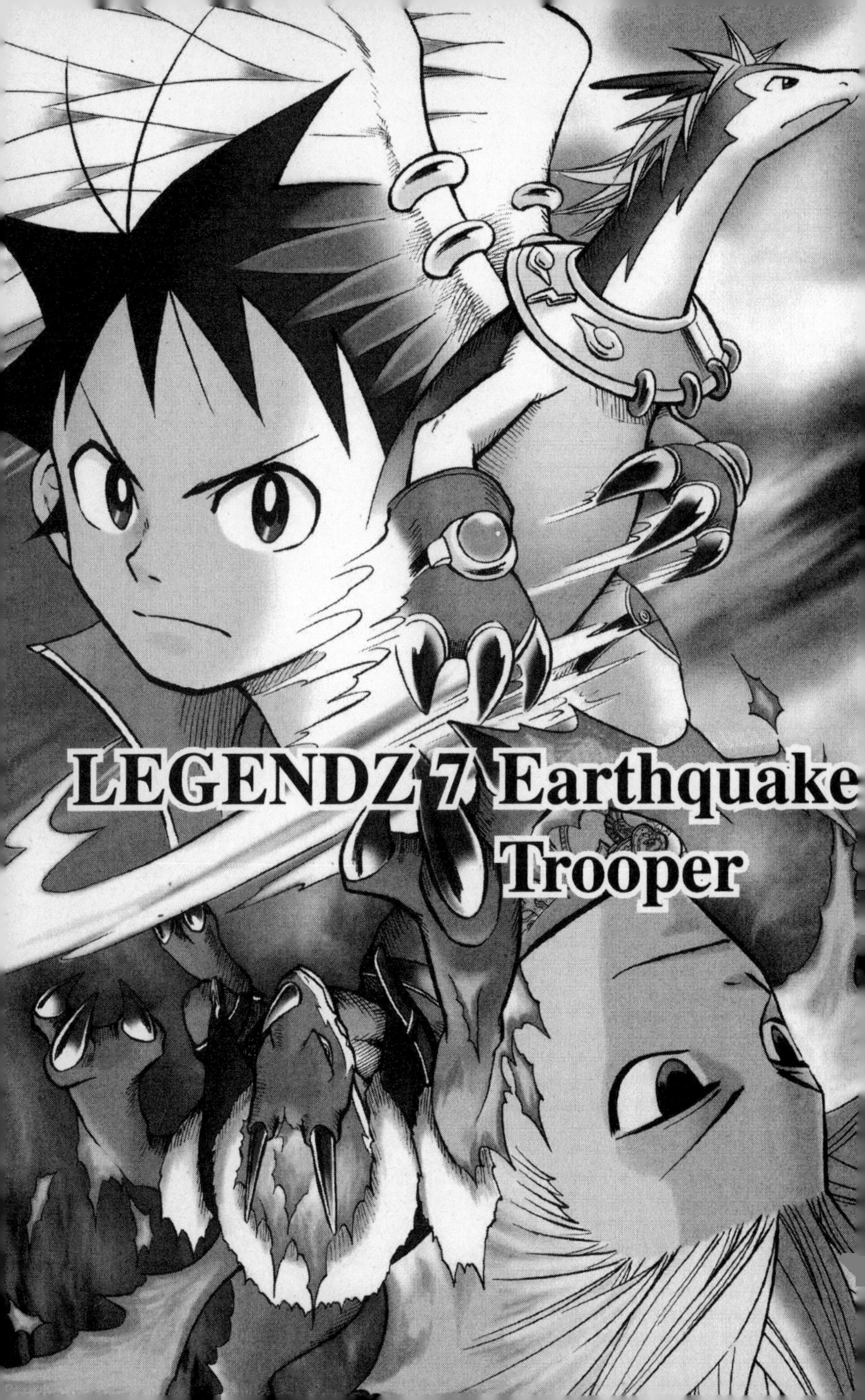
LEGENDZ 7 Earthquake Trooper

LEGENDZ™

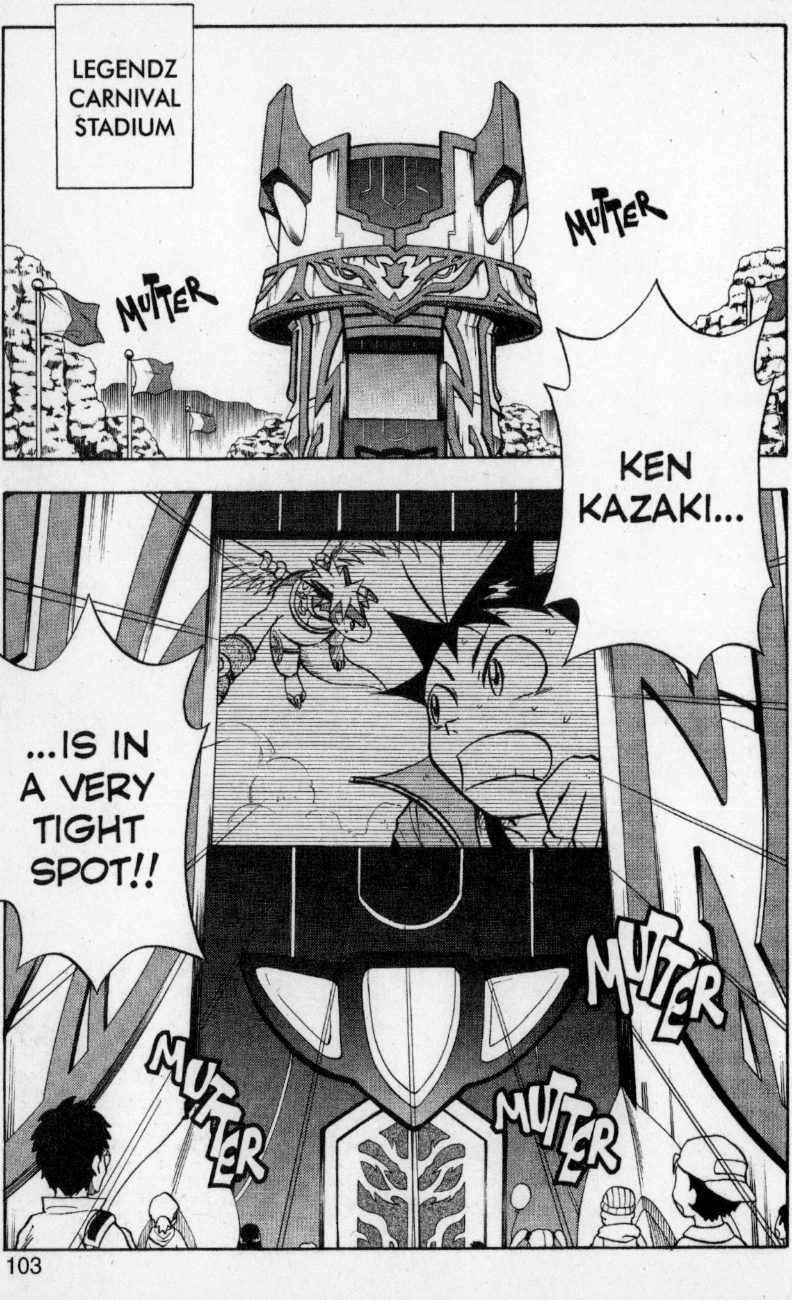
LEGENDZ CARNIVAL STADIUM
MUTTER
MUTTER
KEN KAZAKI...
...IS IN A VERY TIGHT SPOT!!
MUTTER
MUTTER
MUTTER

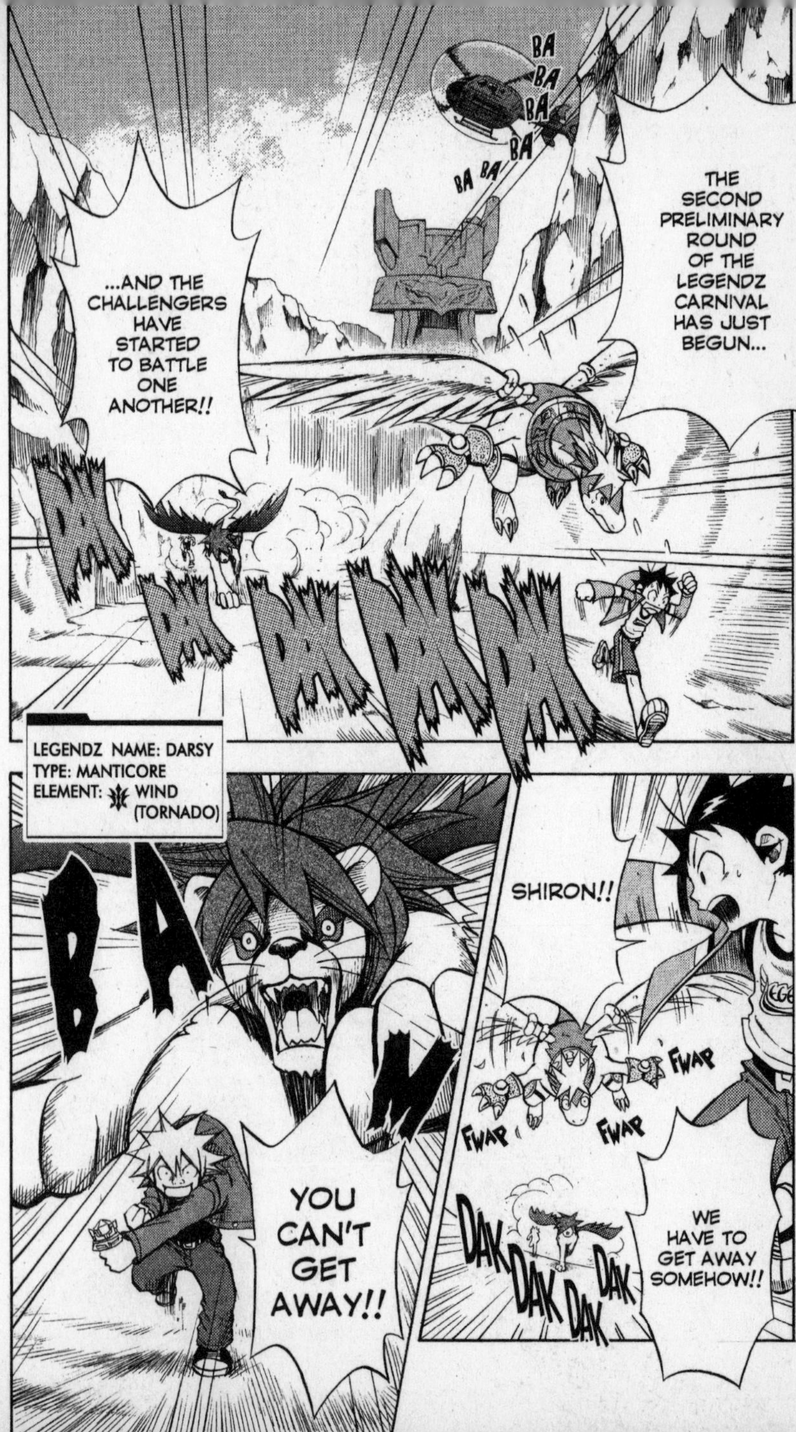
BA BA BA BA BA BA BA
THE SECOND PRELIMINARY ROUND OF THE LEGENDZ CARNIVAL HAS JUST BEGUN...
...AND THE CHALLENGERS HAVE STARTED TO BATTLE ONE ANOTHER!!
DAK DAK DAK DAK DAK
SHIRON!!
FWAP FWAP FWAP
WE HAVE TO GET AWAY SOMEHOW!!
DAK DAK DAK DAK
LEGENDZ NAME: DARSY
TYPE: MANTICORE
ELEMENT: WIND (TORNADO)
BAM
YOU CAN'T GET AWAY!!

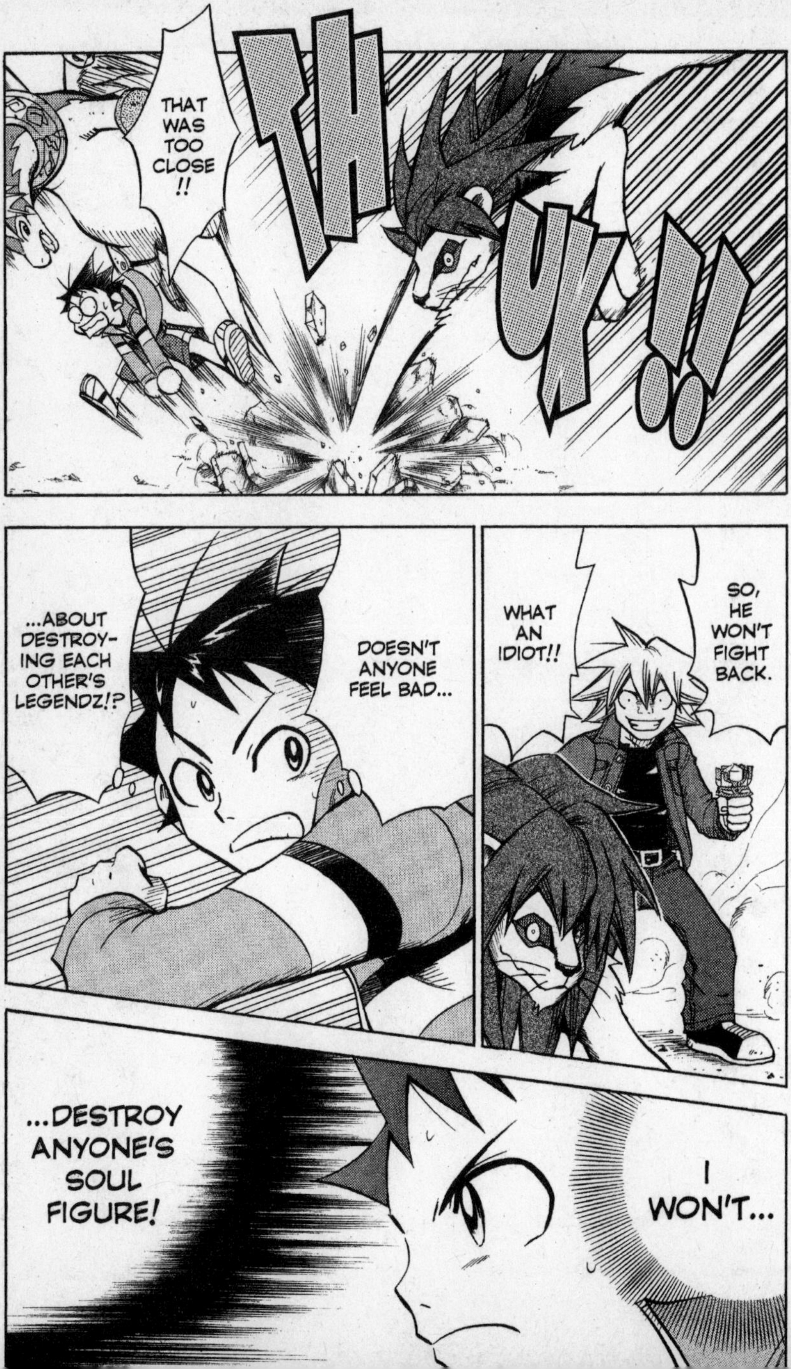
THUK!!
THAT WAS TOO CLOSE!!
SO, HE WON'T FIGHT BACK.
WHAT AN IDIOT!!
DOESN'T ANYONE FEEL BAD...
...ABOUT DESTROYING EACH OTHER'S LEGENDZ!?
I WON'T...
...DESTROY ANYONE'S SOUL FIGURE!

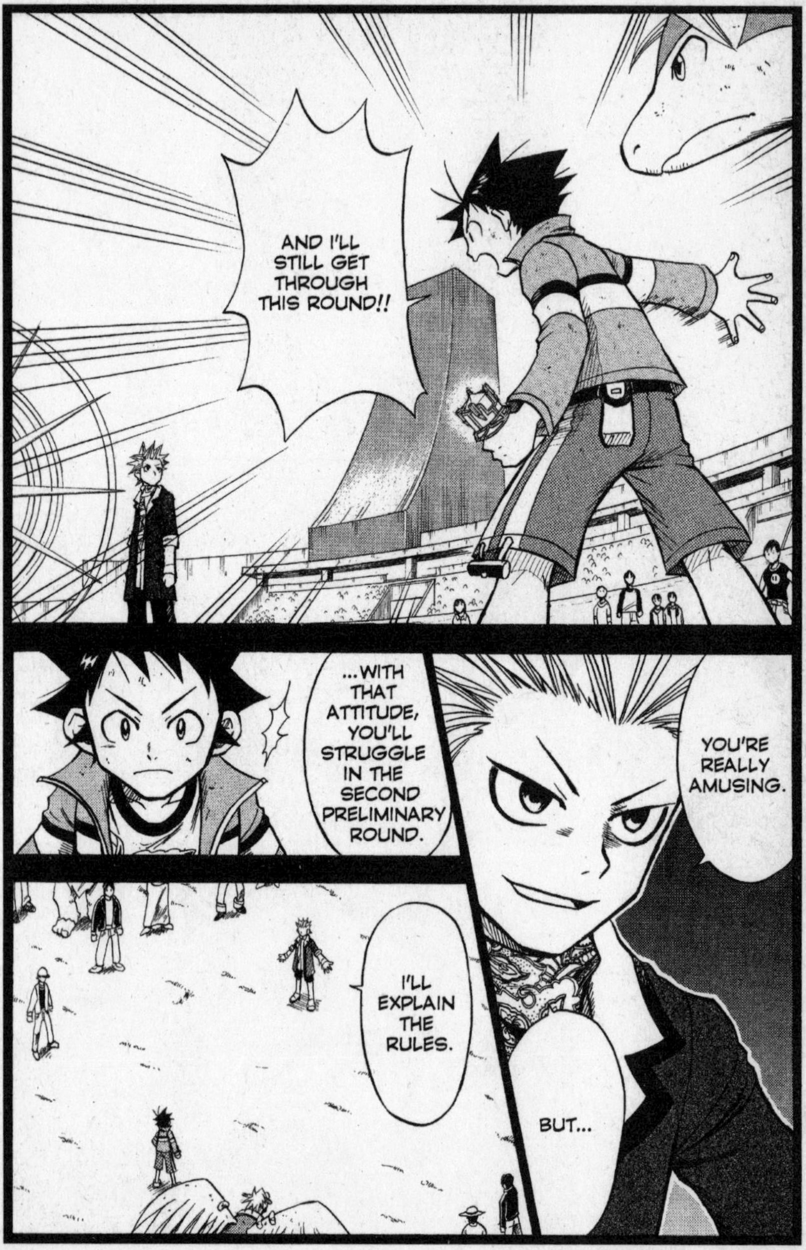
AND I'LL STILL GET THROUGH THIS ROUND!!
YOU'RE REALLY AMUSING.
BUT...
...WITH THAT ATTITUDE, YOU'LL STRUGGLE IN THE SECOND PRELIMINARY ROUND.
I'LL EXPLAIN THE RULES.

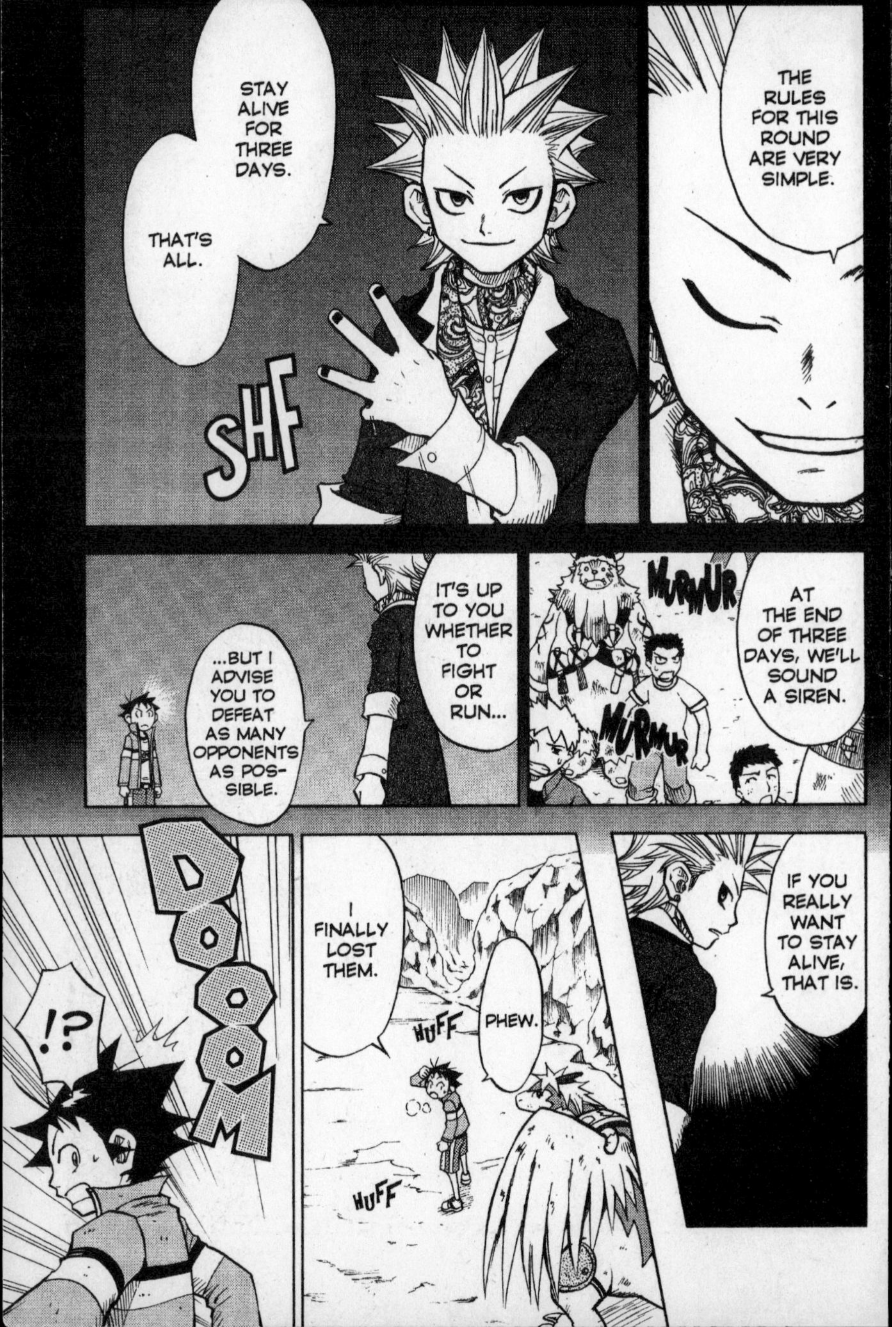
THE RULES FOR THIS ROUND ARE VERY SIMPLE.
STAY ALIVE FOR THREE DAYS.
THAT'S ALL.
SHF
AT THE END OF THREE DAYS, WE'LL SOUND A SIREN.
MURMUR
MURMUR
IT'S UP TO YOU WHETHER TO FIGHT OR RUN...
...BUT I ADVISE YOU TO DEFEAT AS MANY OPPONENTS AS POS-SIBLE.
IF YOU REALLY WANT TO STAY ALIVE, THAT IS.
I FINALLY LOST THEM.
PHEW.
HUFF
HUFF
DOOOOM
!?

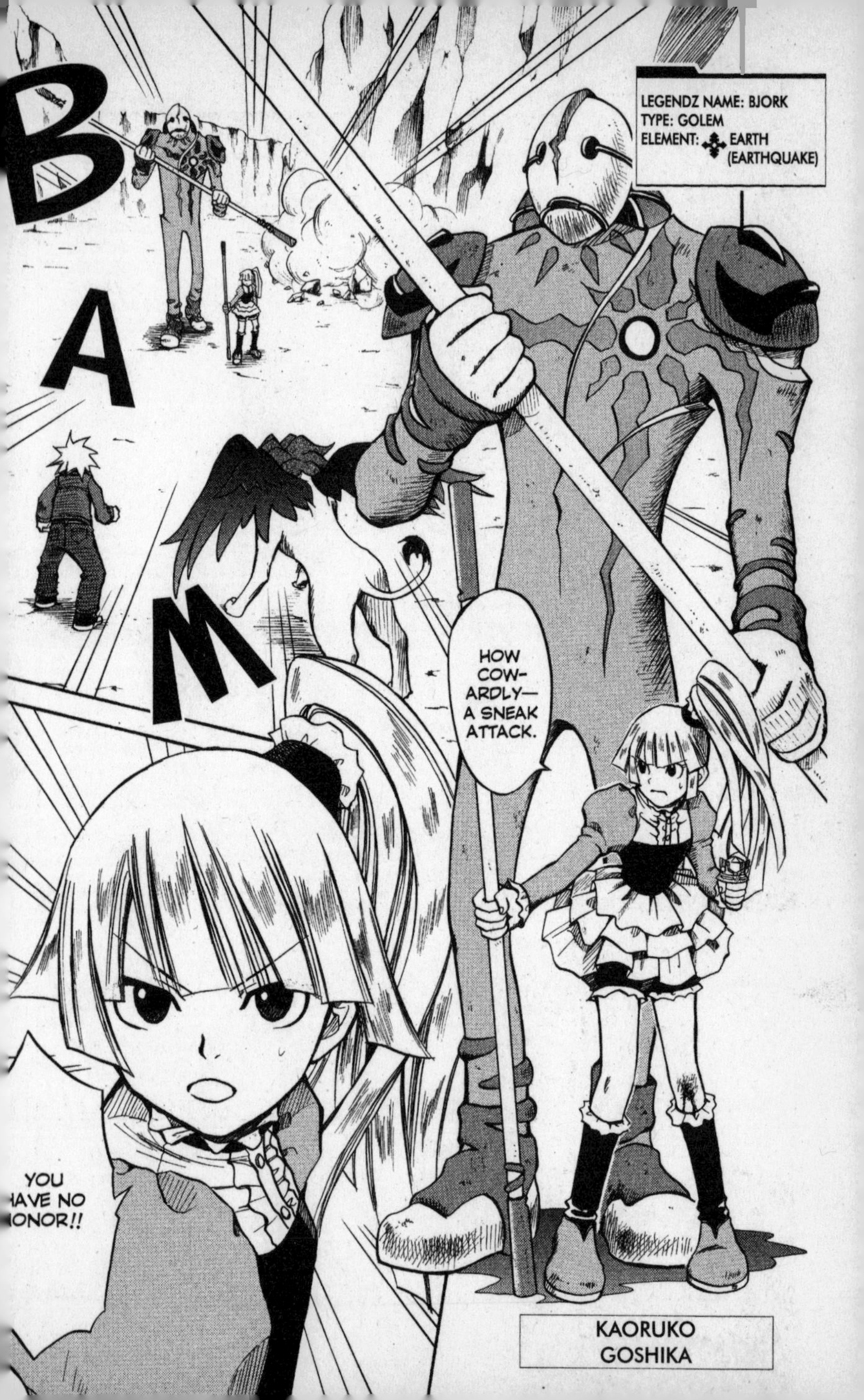
LEGENDZ NAME: BJORK
TYPE: GOLEM
ELEMENT: EARTH (EARTHQUAKE)
BAM
HOW COWARDLY— A SNEAK ATTACK.
KAORUKO GOSHIKA
YOU HAVE NO HONOR!!

READ THIS WAY

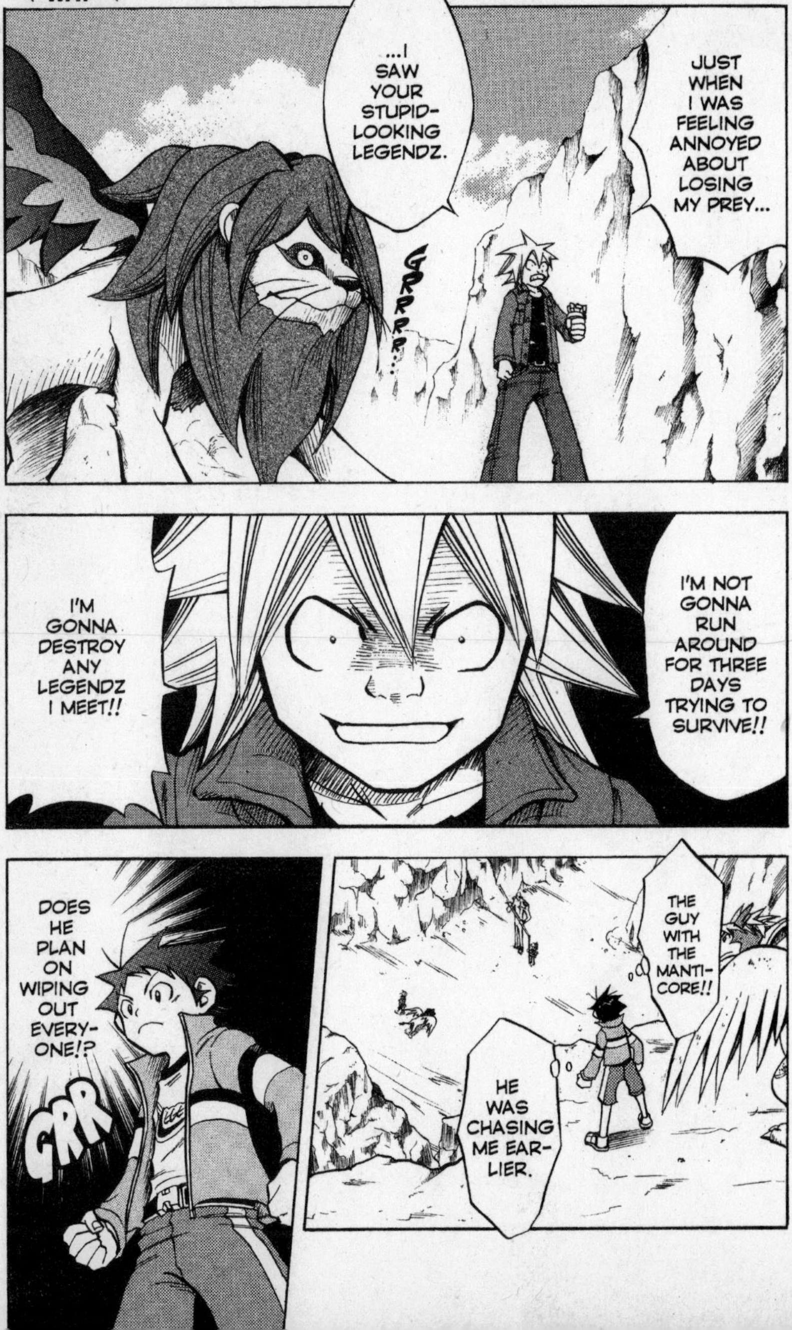
JUST WHEN I WAS FEELING ANNOYED ABOUT LOSING MY PREY...
...I SAW YOUR STUPID-LOOKING LEGENDZ.
GRRRR...
I'M NOT GONNA RUN AROUND FOR THREE DAYS TRYING TO SURVIVE!!
I'M GONNA DESTROY ANY LEGENDZ I MEET!!
THE GUY WITH THE MANTICORE!!
HE WAS CHASING ME EARLIER.
DOES HE PLAN ON WIPING OUT EVERYONE!?
GRR

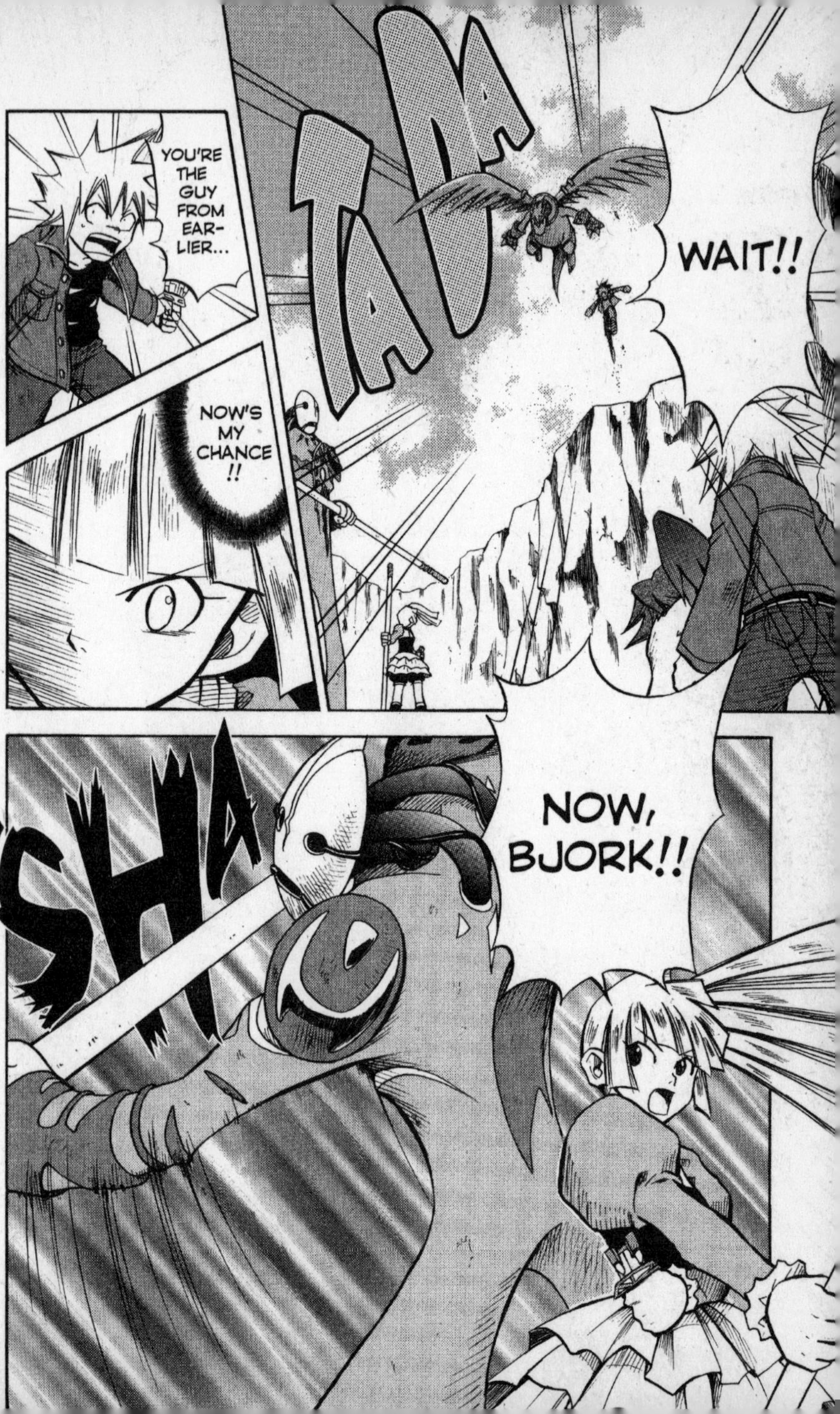
WAIT!!
TA DA
YOU'RE THE GUY FROM EARLIER...
NOW'S MY CHANCE!!
NOW, BJORK!!
SHA

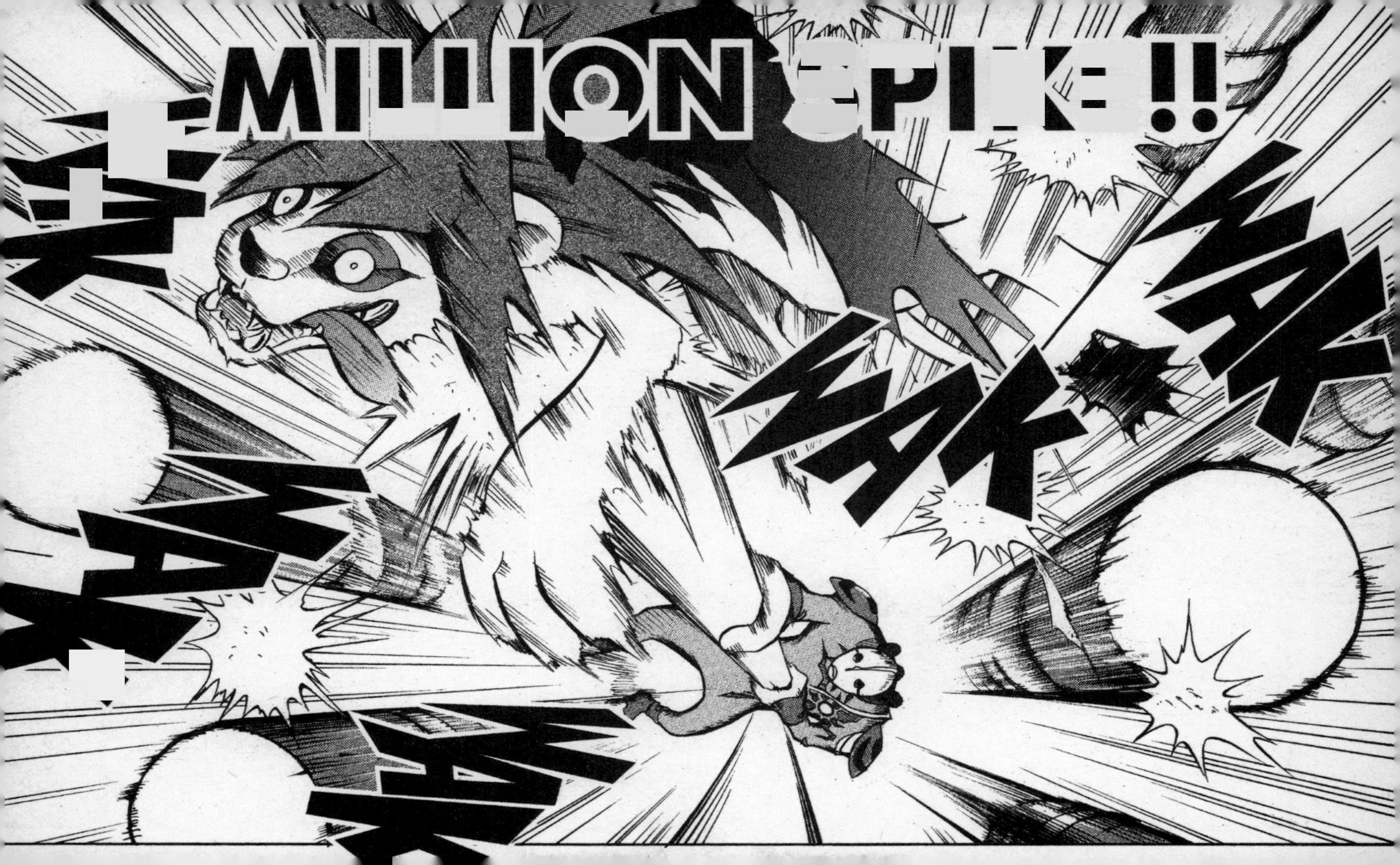
MILLION SPIKE!!
WAK
WAK
WAK
WAK
WAK

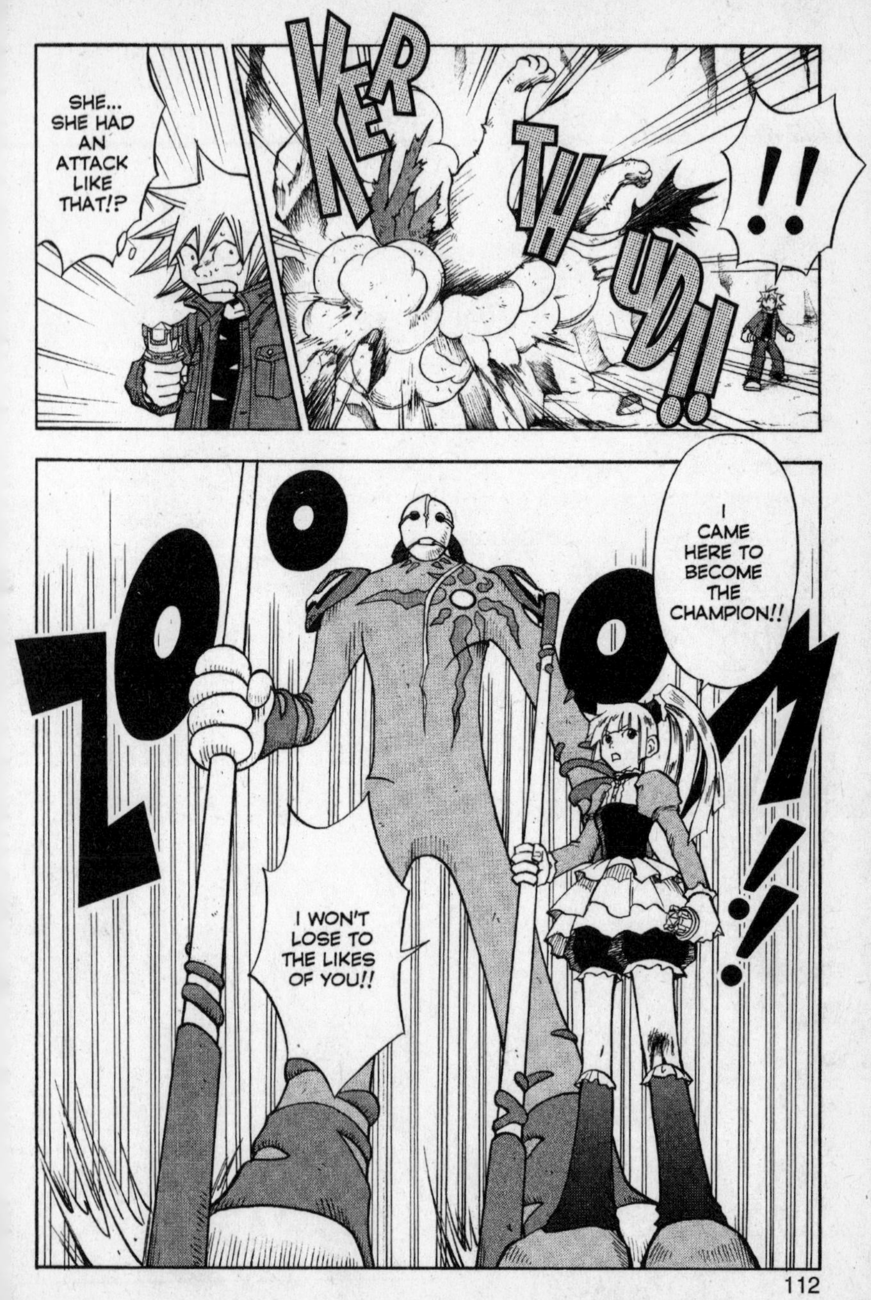
!!
KER THUD!!
SHE... SHE HAD AN ATTACK LIKE THAT!?
I CAME HERE TO BECOME THE CHAMPION!!
ZOOOOM!!
I WON'T LOSE TO THE LIKES OF YOU!!

READ THIS WAY

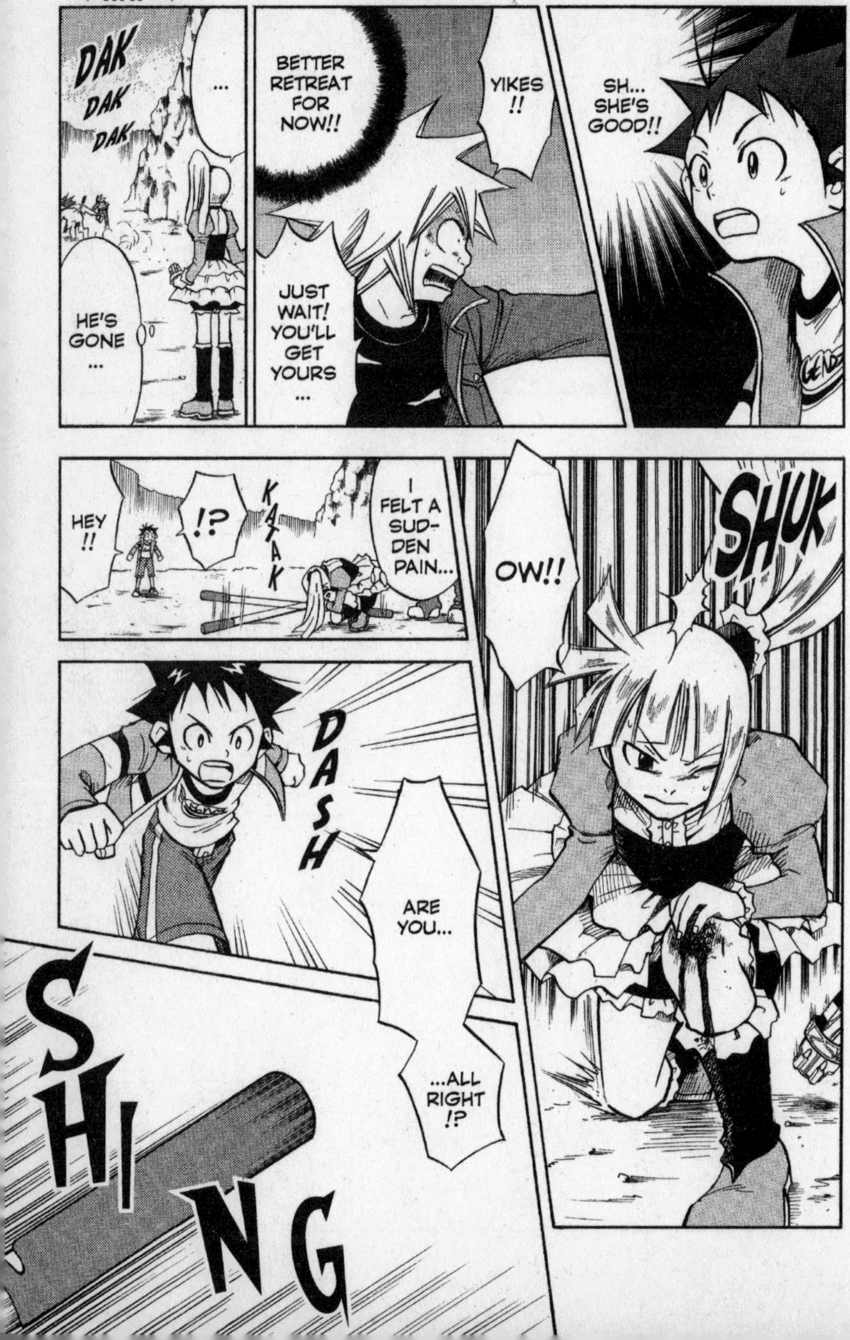
SH... SHE'S GOOD!!
YIKES !!
BETTER RETREAT FOR NOW!!
JUST WAIT! YOU'LL GET YOURS ...
...
DAK DAK DAK
HE'S GONE ...
SHUK
OW!!
I FELT A SUD-DEN PAIN...
KATAK
!?
HEY !!
DASH
ARE YOU...
...ALL RIGHT !?
SHING

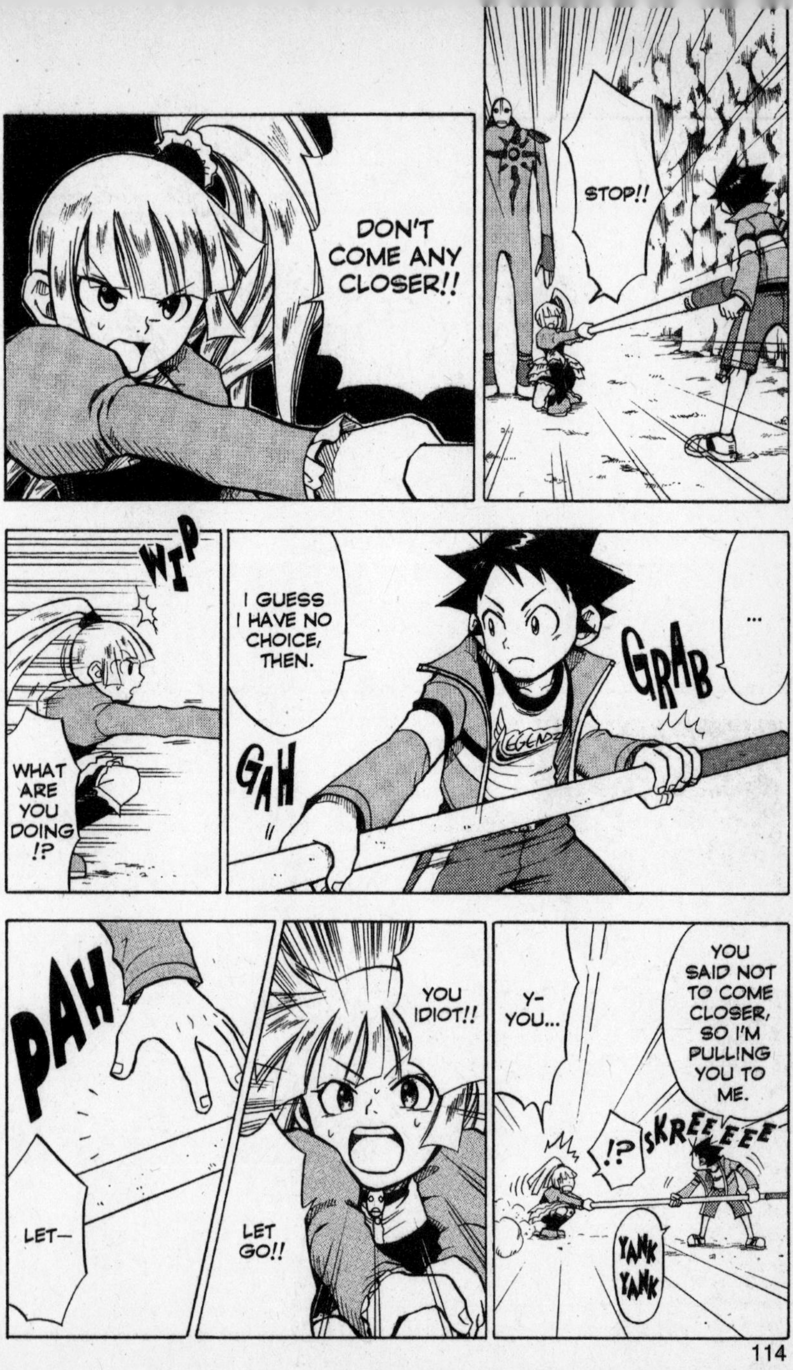
STOP!!
DON'T COME ANY CLOSER!!
...
GRAB
I GUESS I HAVE NO CHOICE, THEN.
GAH
WIP
WHAT ARE YOU DOING!?
YOU SAID NOT TO COME CLOSER, SO I'M PULLING YOU TO ME.
Y- YOU...
!?
SKREEEEEE
YANK YANK
YOU IDIOT!!
LET GO!!
PAH
LET—

READ THIS WAY

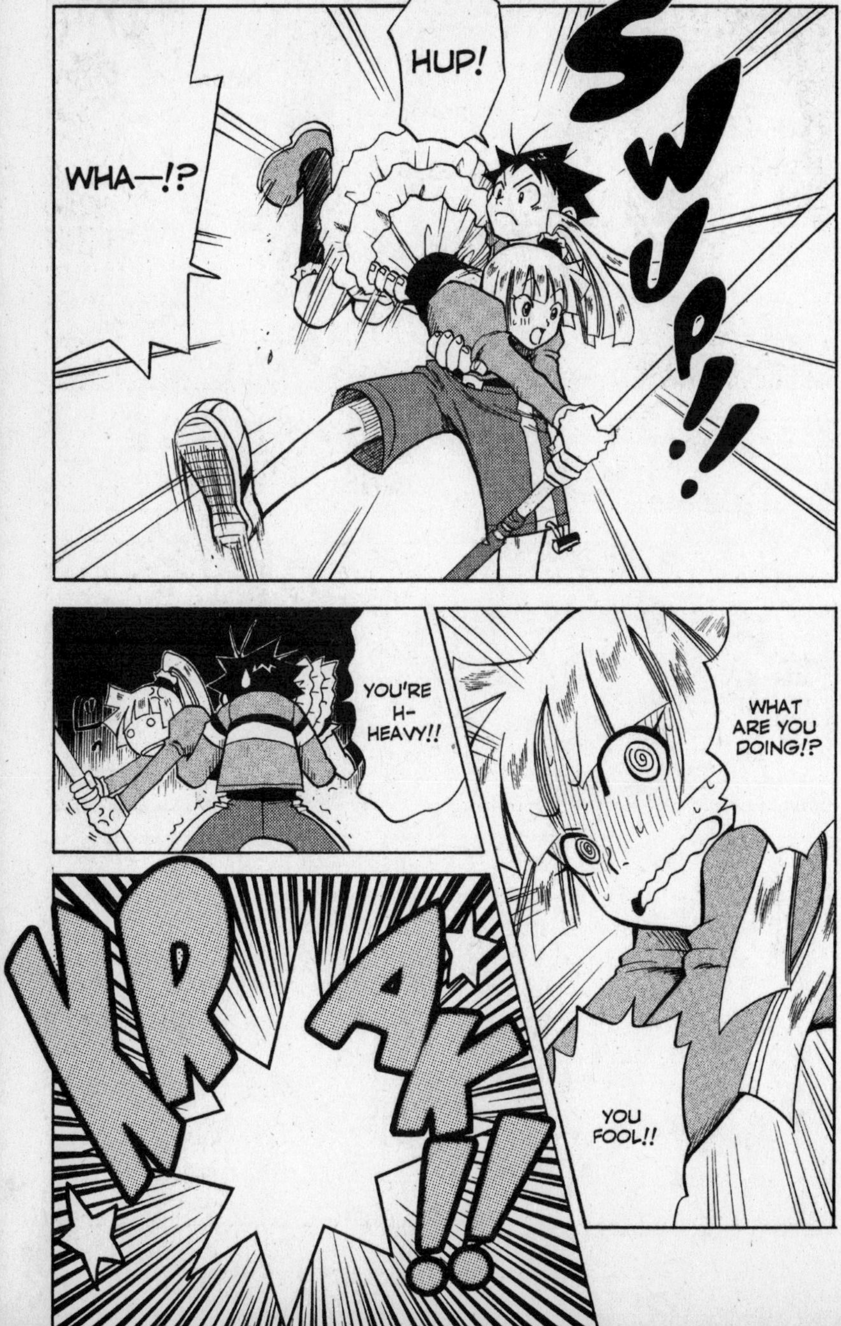

SWUP!!
HUP!
WHA—!?
WHAT ARE YOU DOING!?
YOU FOOL!!
YOU'RE H-HEAVY!!
KRAK!!

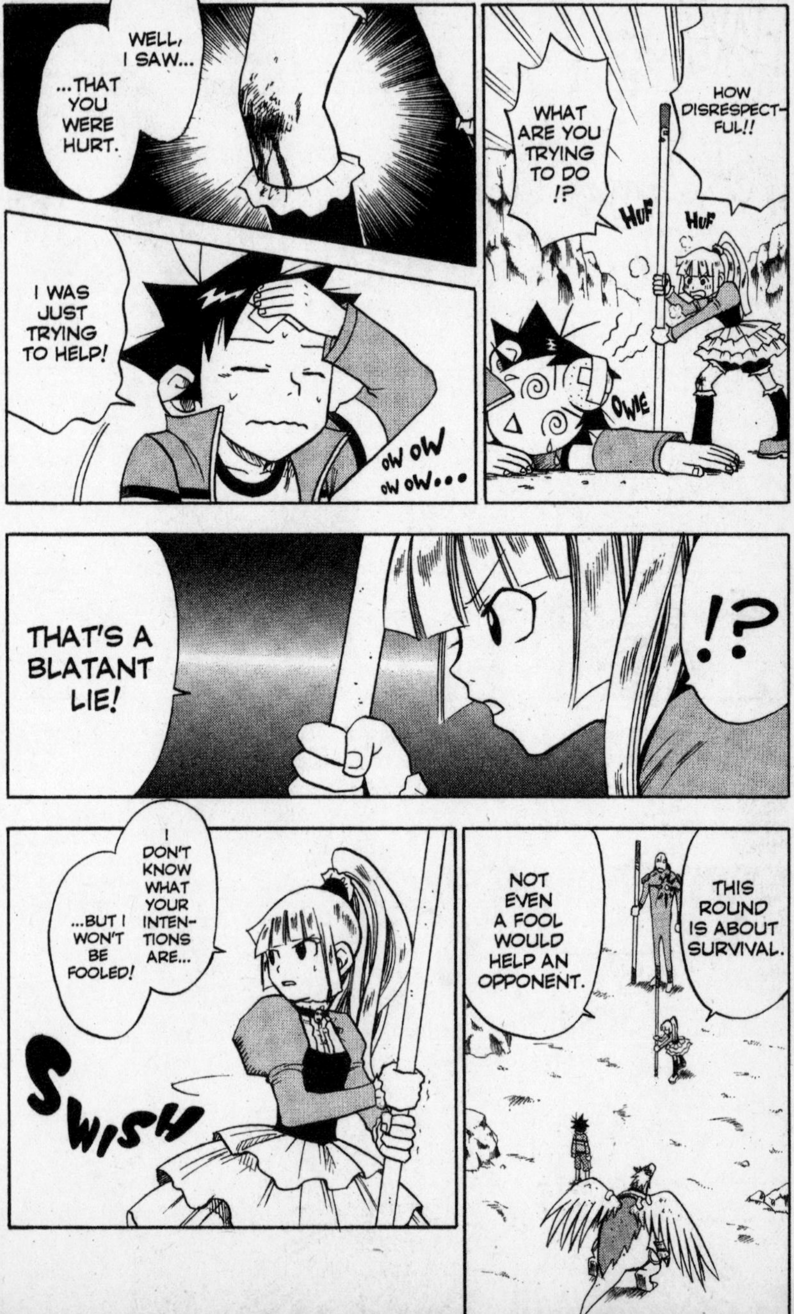
HOW DISRESPECTFUL!!
WHAT ARE YOU TRYING TO DO !?
HUF
HUF
OWIE
WELL, I SAW...
...THAT YOU WERE HURT.
I WAS JUST TRYING TO HELP!
OW OW OW OW...
!?
THAT'S A BLATANT LIE!
THIS ROUND IS ABOUT SURVIVAL.
NOT EVEN A FOOL WOULD HELP AN OPPONENT.
I DON'T KNOW WHAT YOUR INTENTIONS ARE...
...BUT I WON'T BE FOOLED!
SWISH

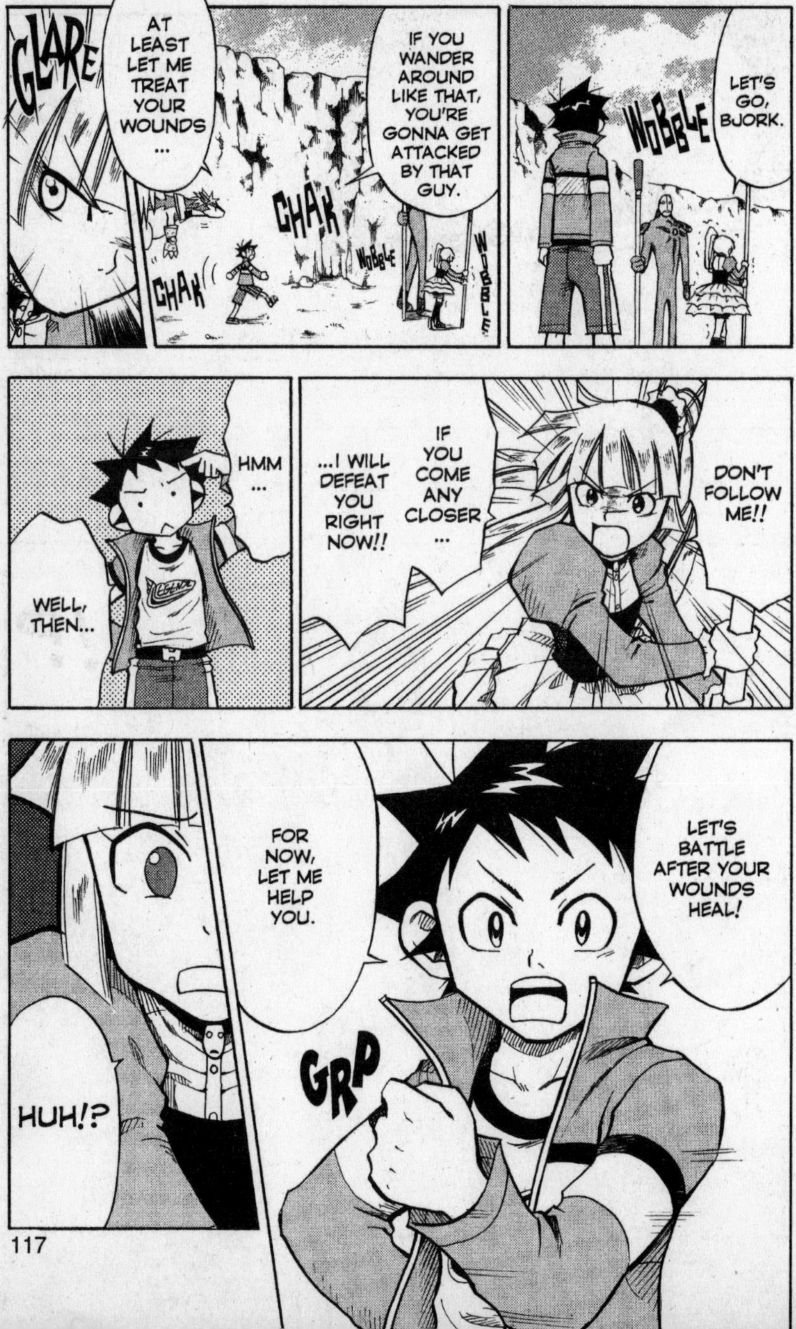
LET'S GO, BJORK.
WOBBLE
IF YOU WANDER AROUND LIKE THAT, YOU'RE GONNA GET ATTACKED BY THAT GUY.
WOBBLE
WOBBLE
CHAK
CHAK
AT LEAST LET ME TREAT YOUR WOUNDS ...
GLARE
DON'T FOLLOW ME!!
IF YOU COME ANY CLOSER ...
...I WILL DEFEAT YOU RIGHT NOW!!
HMM ...
WELL, THEN...
LET'S BATTLE AFTER YOUR WOUNDS HEAL!
FOR NOW, LET ME HELP YOU.
GRP
HUH!?

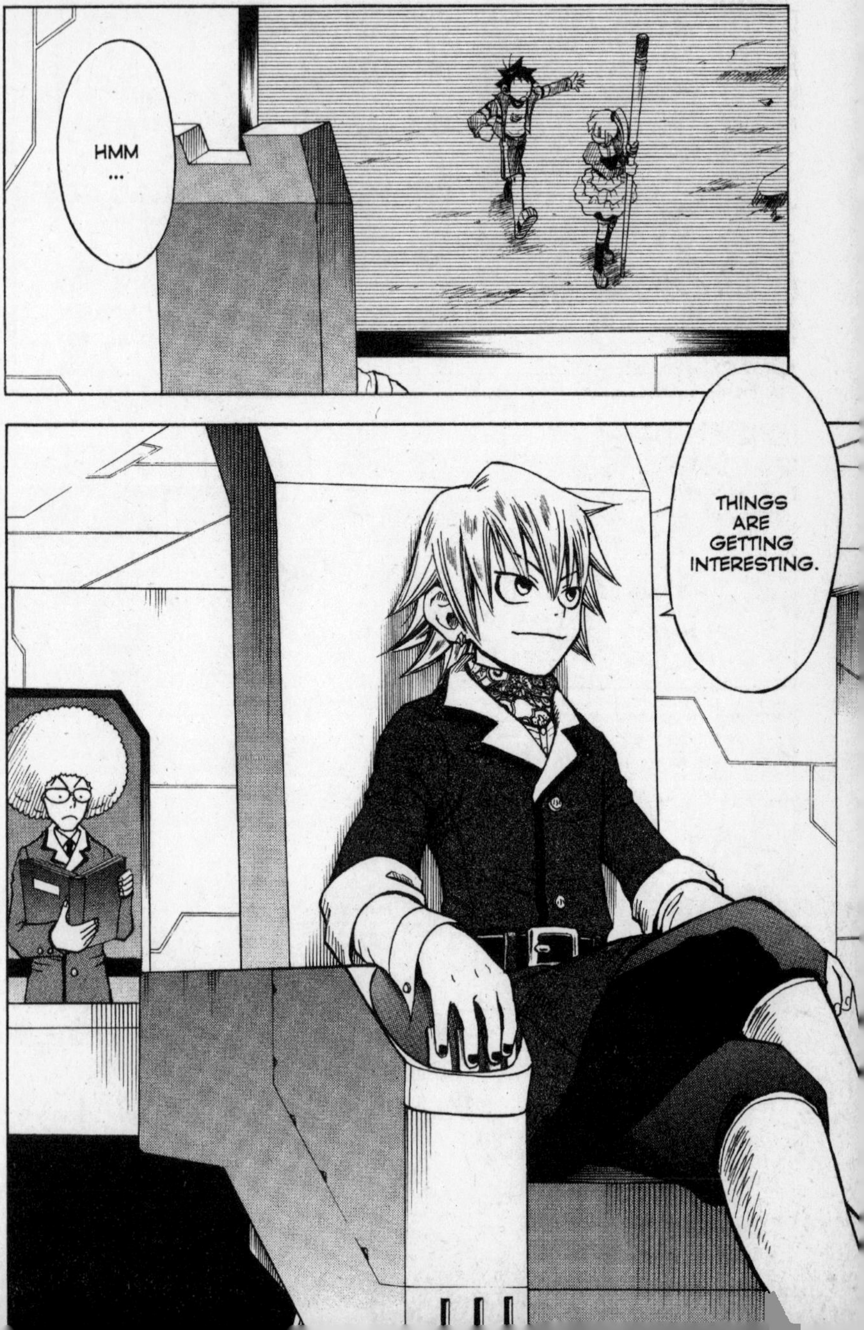
HMM ...
THINGS ARE GETTING INTERESTING.

READ THIS WAY

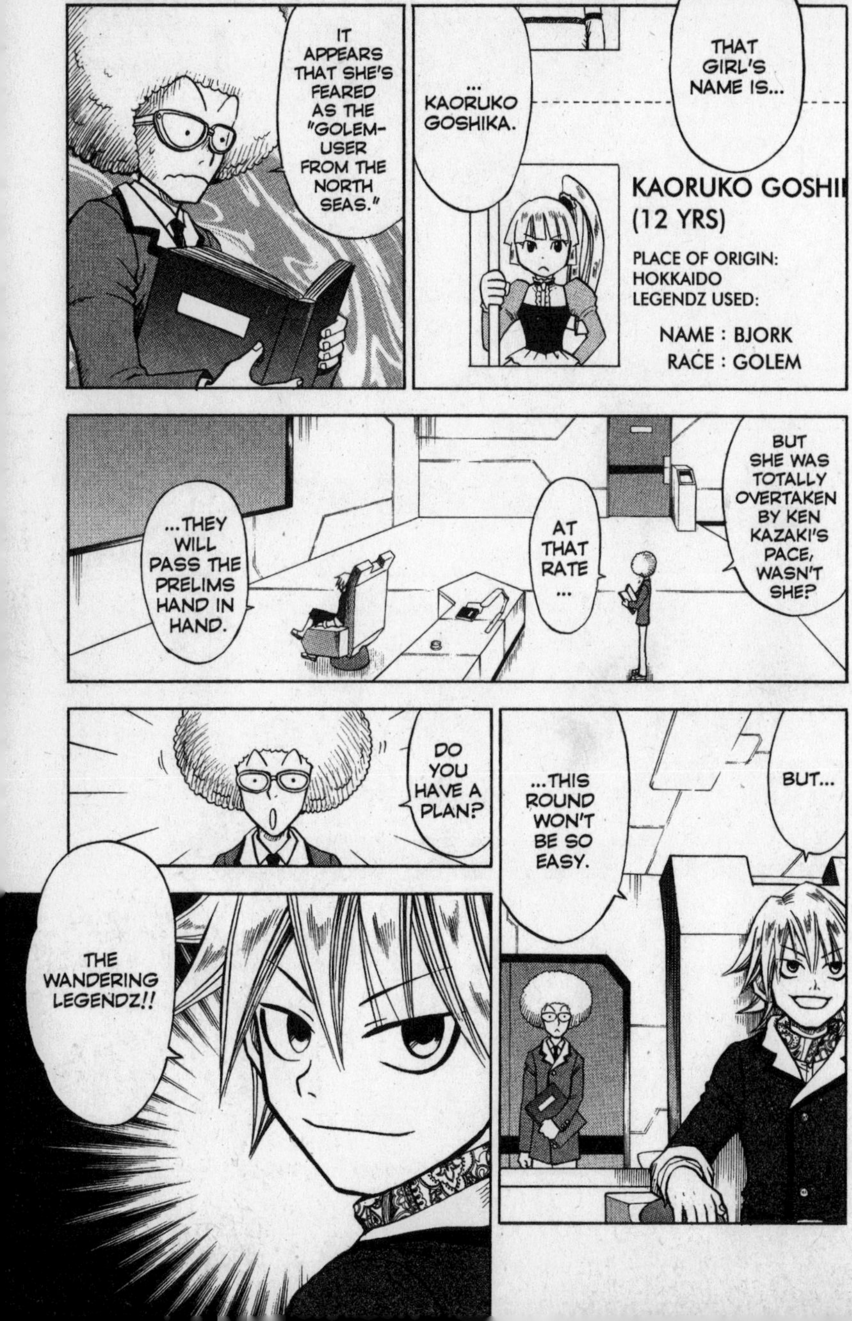
THAT GIRL'S NAME IS...
...KAORUKO GOSHIKA.
KAORUKO GOSHII
(12 YRS)
PLACE OF ORIGIN: HOKKAIDO
LEGENDZ USED:
NAME : BJORK
RACE : GOLEM
IT APPEARS THAT SHE'S FEARED AS THE "GOLEM-USER FROM THE NORTH SEAS."
BUT SHE WAS TOTALLY OVERTAKEN BY KEN KAZAKI'S PACE, WASN'T SHE?
AT THAT RATE...
...THEY WILL PASS THE PRELIMS HAND IN HAND.
BUT...
...THIS ROUND WON'T BE SO EASY.
DO YOU HAVE A PLAN?
THE WANDERING LEGENDZ!!

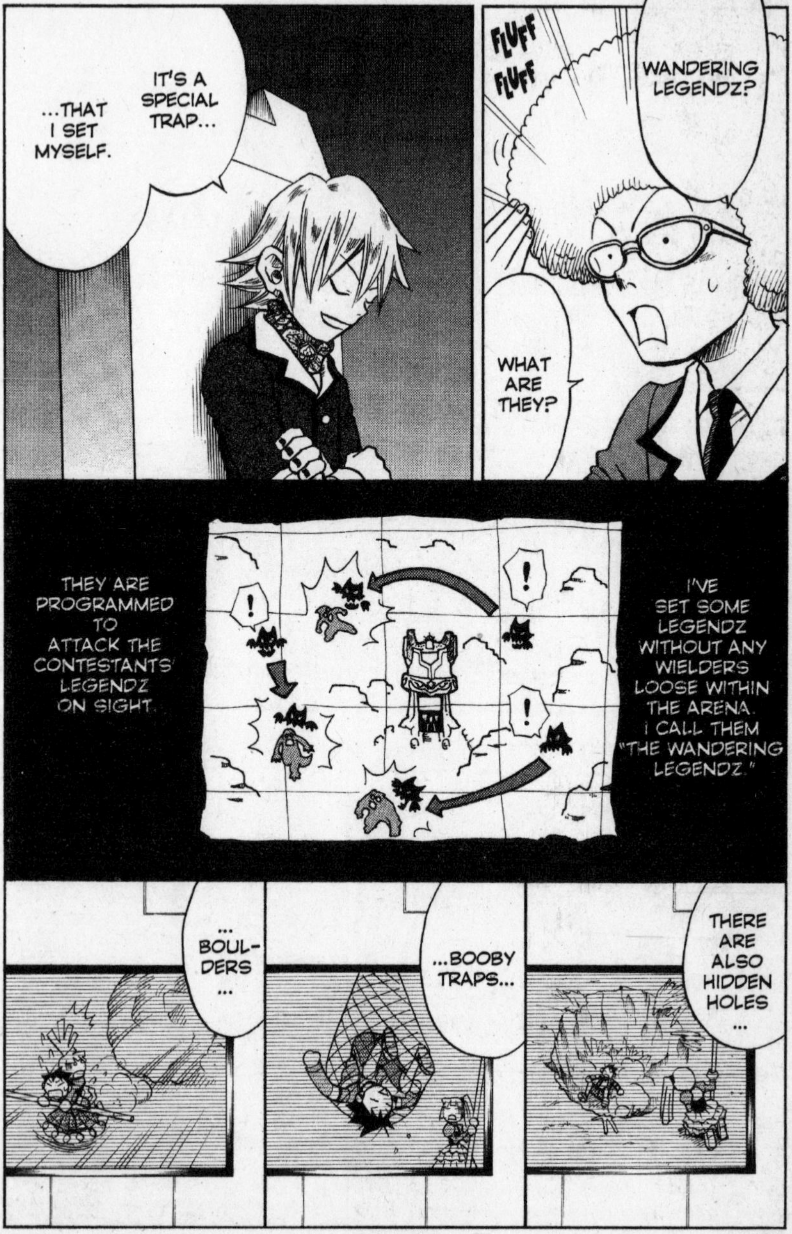
FLUFF
FLUFF
WANDERING LEGENDZ?
WHAT ARE THEY?
IT'S A SPECIAL TRAP...
...THAT I SET MYSELF.
I'VE SET SOME LEGENDZ WITHOUT ANY WIELDERS LOOSE WITHIN THE ARENA. I CALL THEM "THE WANDERING LEGENDZ."
THEY ARE PROGRAMMED TO ATTACK THE CONTESTANTS' LEGENDZ ON SIGHT.
THERE ARE ALSO HIDDEN HOLES ...
...BOOBY TRAPS...
... BOUL-DERS ...

READ THIS WAY

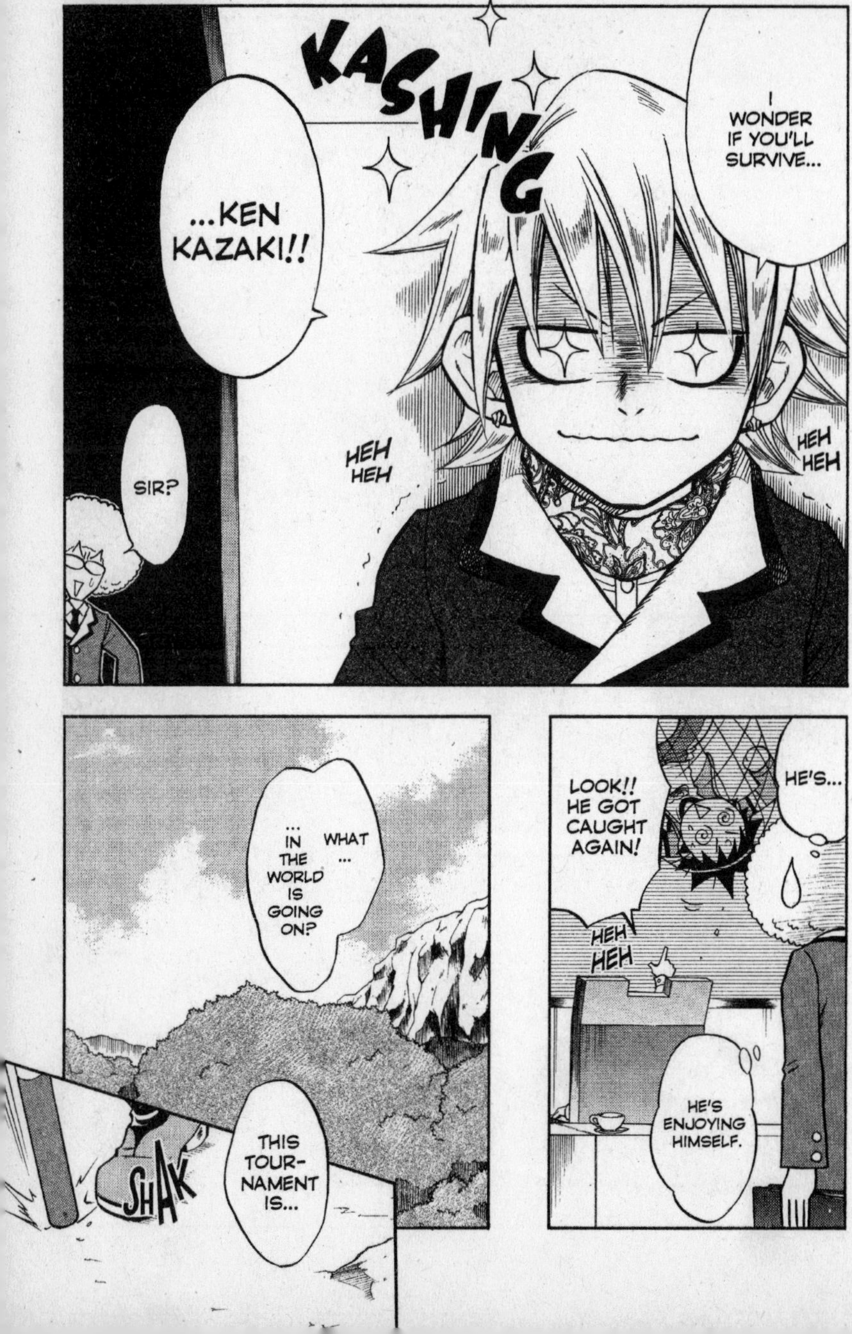
I WONDER IF YOU'LL SURVIVE...
KASHING
...KEN KAZAKI!!
HEH HEH
HEH HEH
SIR?
HE'S...
LOOK!! HE GOT CAUGHT AGAIN!
HEH HEH
HE'S ENJOYING HIMSELF.
WHAT ... IN THE WORLD IS GOING ON?
THIS TOURNAMENT IS...
SHAK

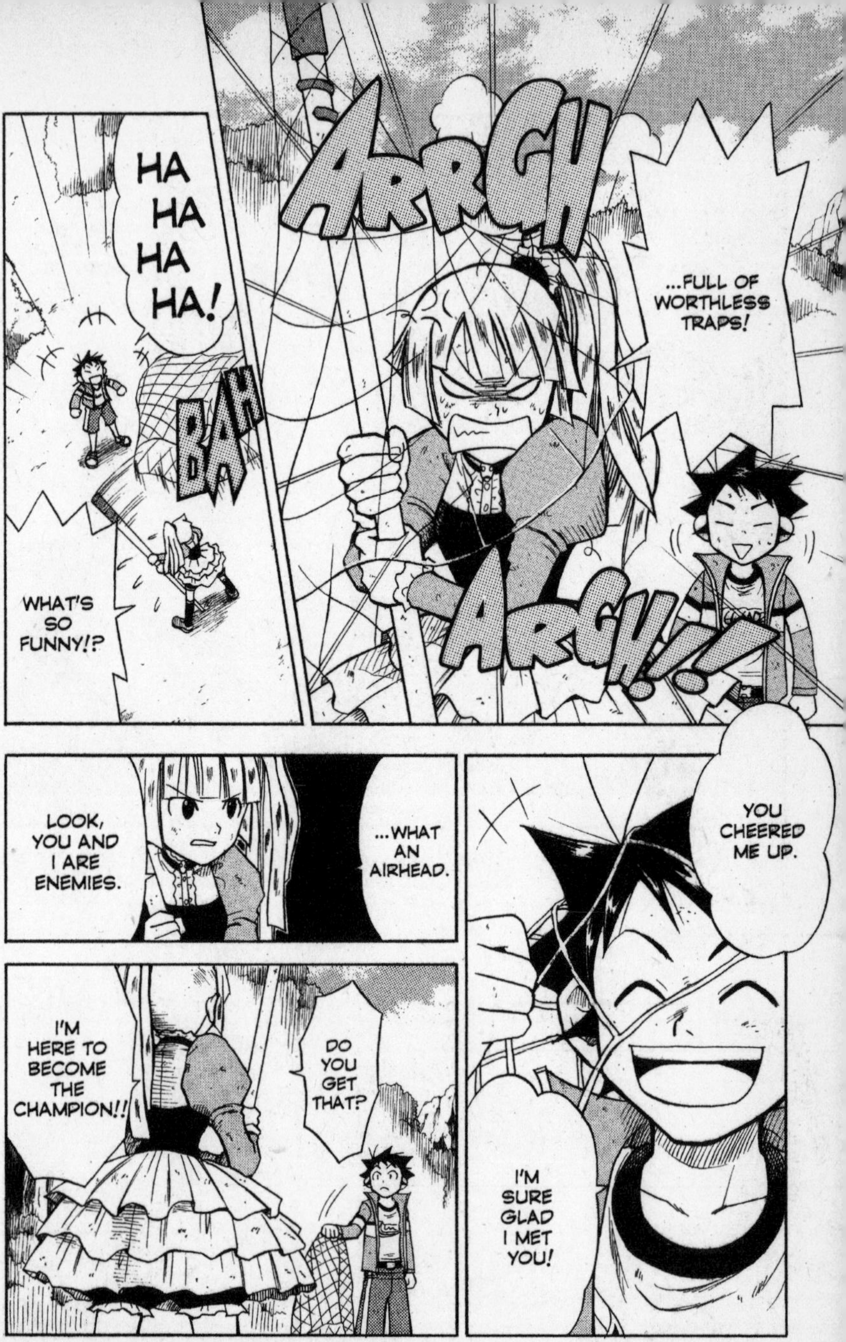
ARRGH
...FULL OF WORTHLESS TRAPS!
ARGH!!!
HA HA HA HA!
BAH
WHAT'S SO FUNNY!?
YOU CHEERED ME UP.
I'M SURE GLAD I MET YOU!
...WHAT AN AIRHEAD.
LOOK, YOU AND I ARE ENEMIES.
DO YOU GET THAT?
I'M HERE TO BECOME THE CHAMPION!!

READ THIS WAY

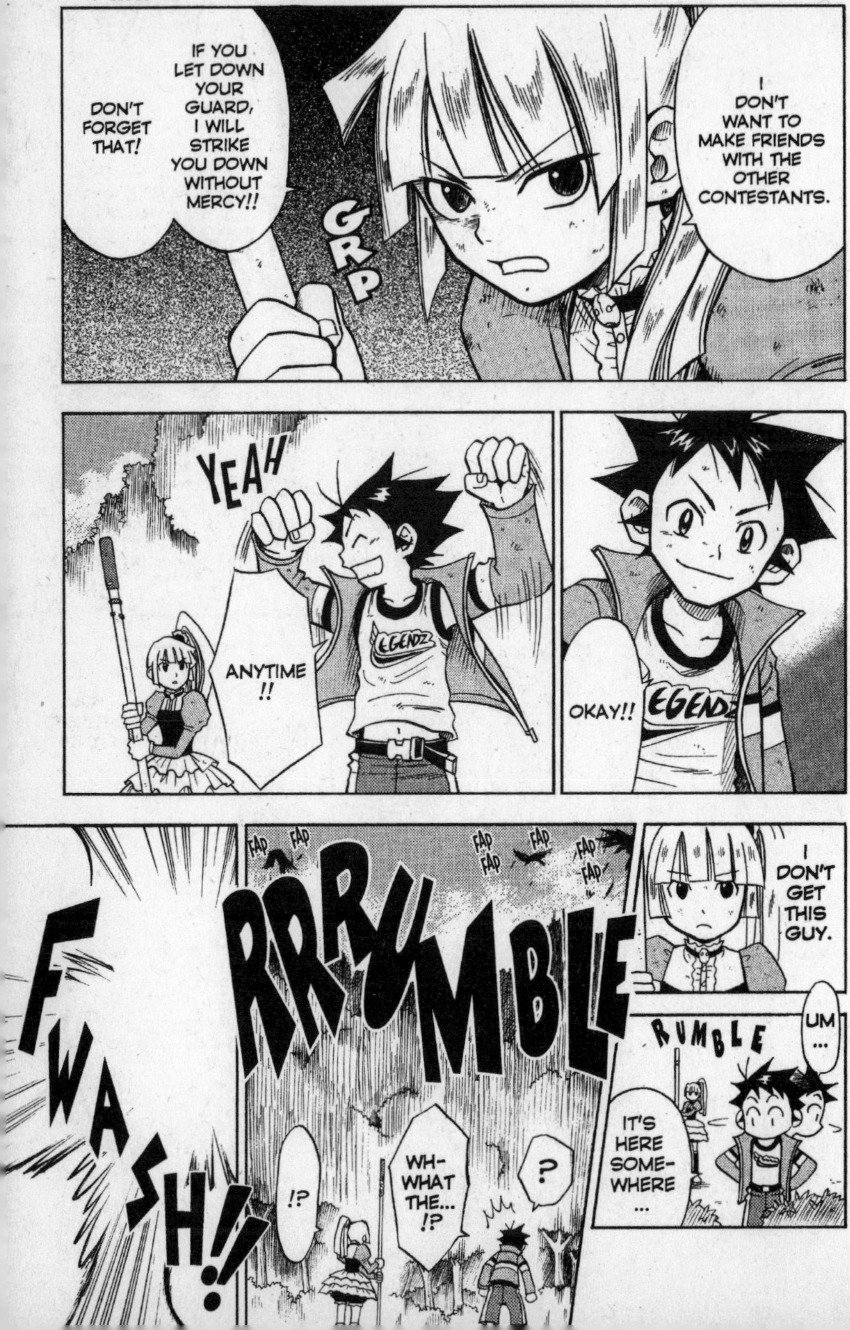
I DON'T WANT TO MAKE FRIENDS WITH THE OTHER CONTESTANTS.
GRP
IF YOU LET DOWN YOUR GUARD, I WILL STRIKE YOU DOWN WITHOUT MERCY!!
DON'T FORGET THAT!
OKAY!!
YEAH
ANYTIME !!
I DON'T GET THIS GUY.
UM ...
RUMBLE
IT'S HERE SOME- WHERE ...
FAP FAP FAP FAP FAP FAP FAP FAP
RRRUMBLE
?
WH- WHAT THE... !?
!?
FWASH!!

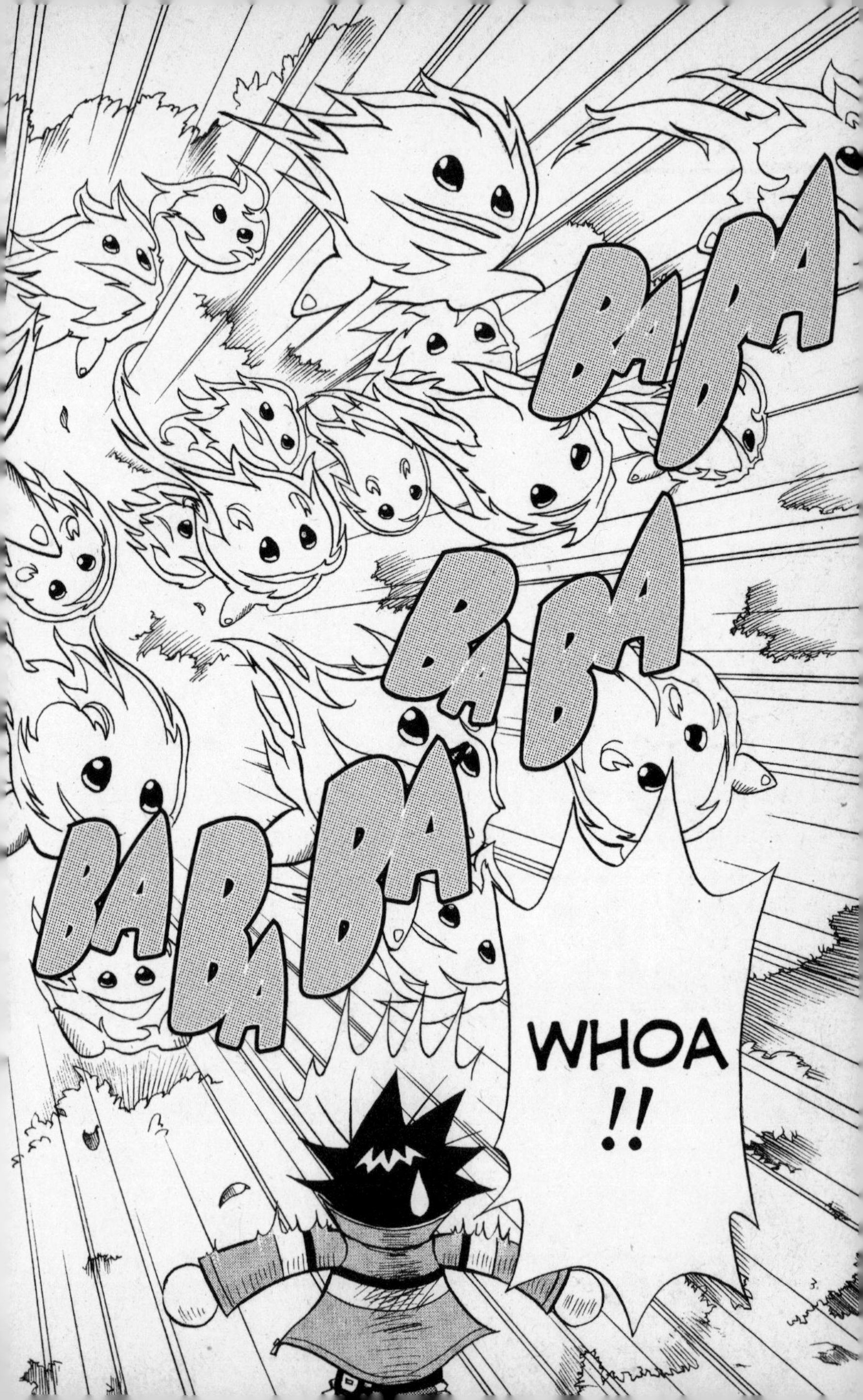
WHOA !!

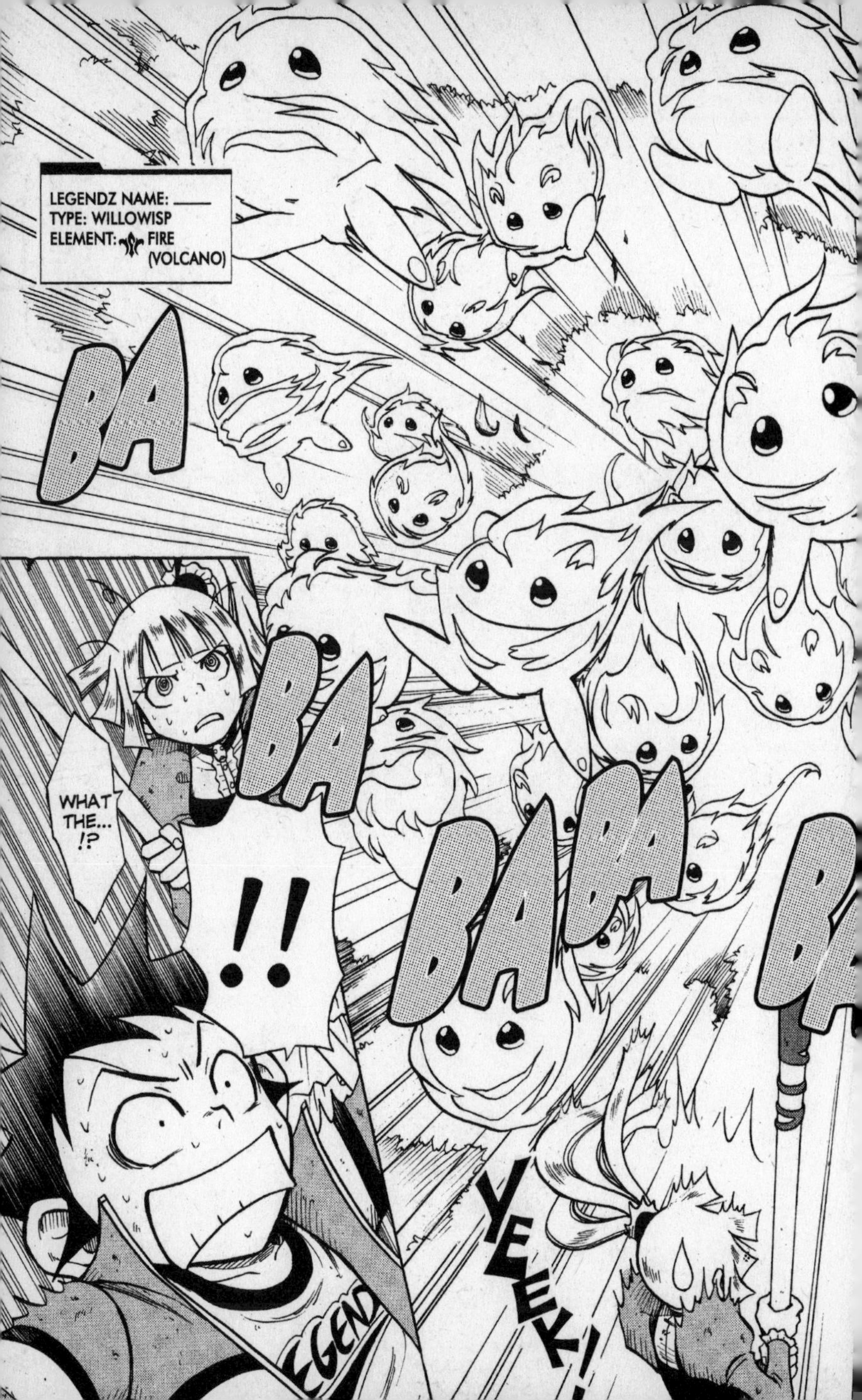
LEGENDZ NAME: ____
TYPE: WILLOWISP
ELEMENT: FIRE (VOLCANO)
BA
BA BA
BA BA
BA
YEEEK!
WHAT THE... !?
!!

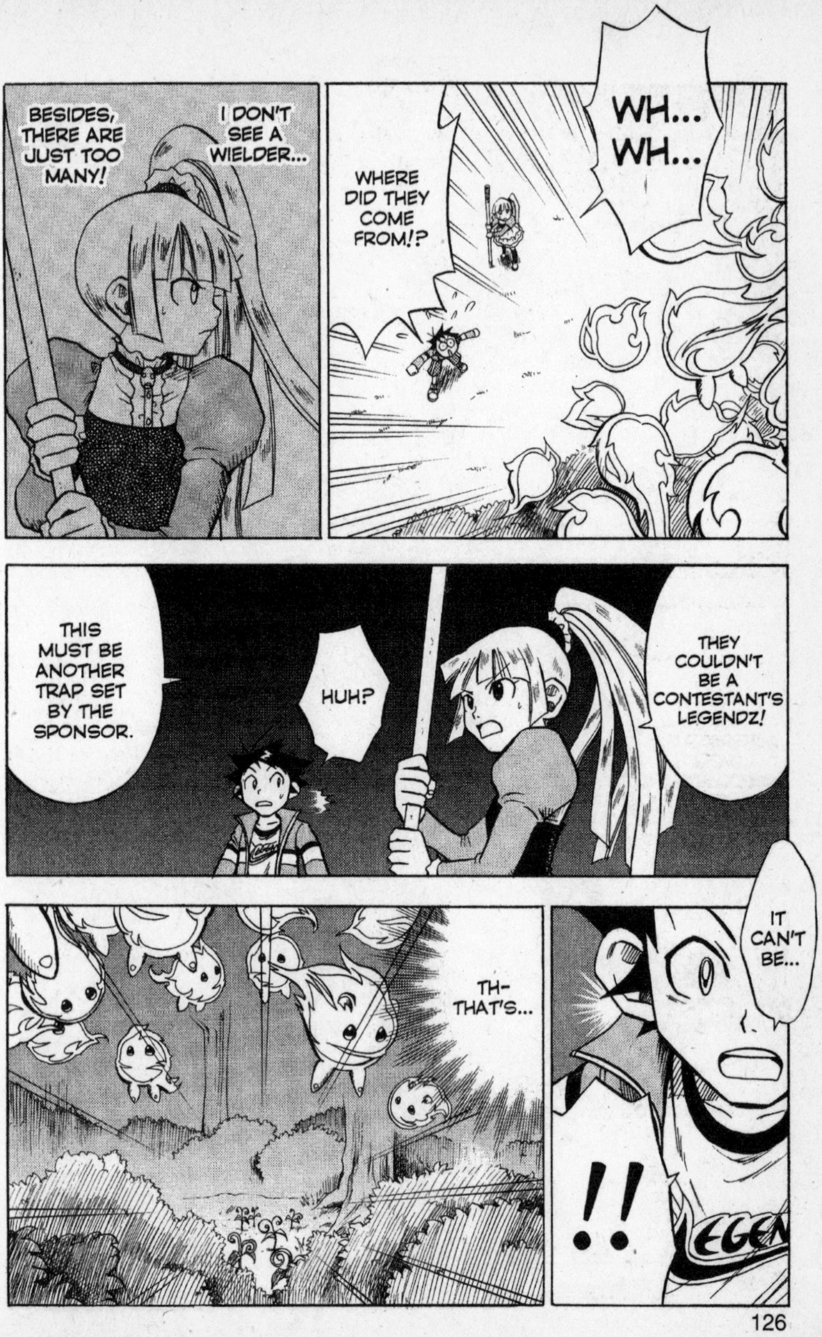
WH... WH...
WHERE DID THEY COME FROM!?
I DON'T SEE A WIELDER...
BESIDES, THERE ARE JUST TOO MANY!
THEY COULDN'T BE A CONTESTANT'S LEGENDZ!
HUH?
THIS MUST BE ANOTHER TRAP SET BY THE SPONSOR.
IT CAN'T BE...
!!
TH- THAT'S...

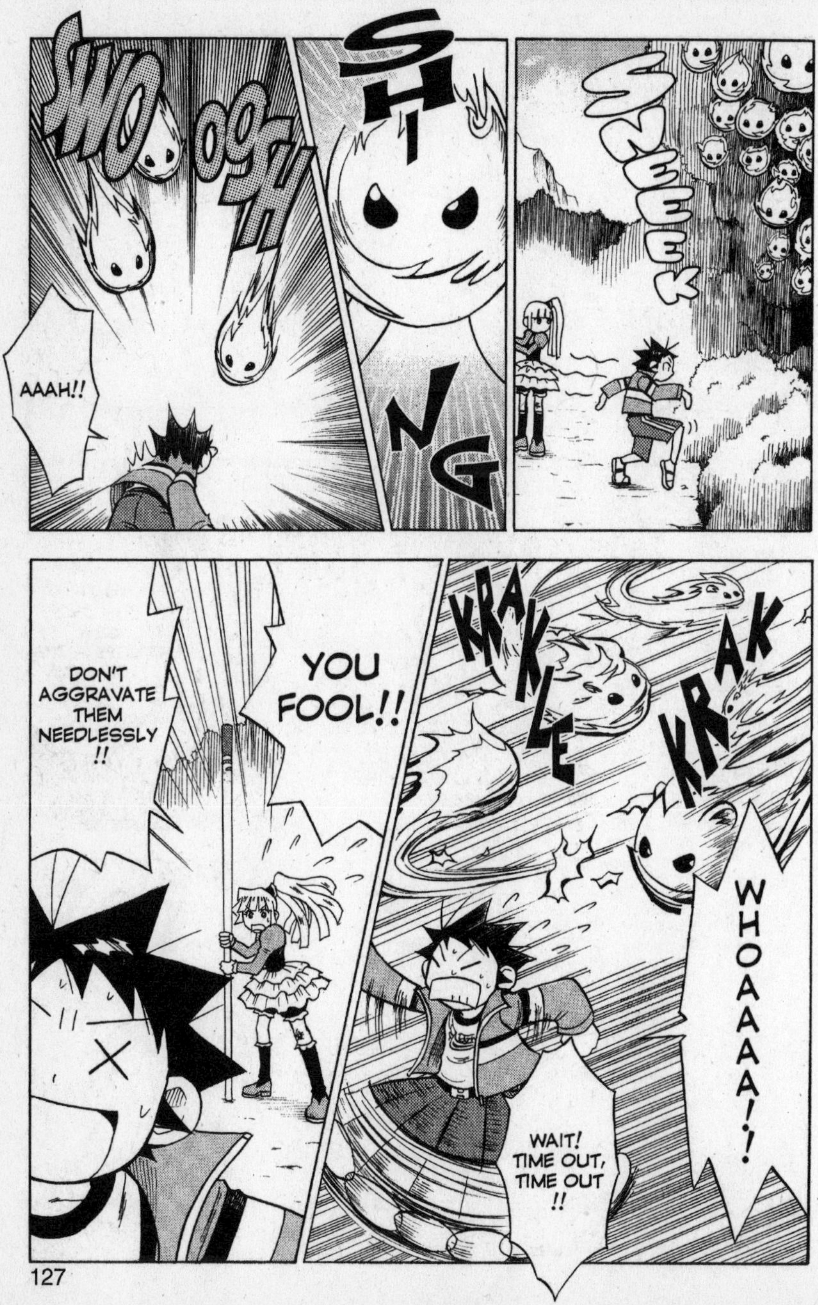
SNEEK
SHING
SWOOOSH
AAAH!!
KRAK
KRAKLE
WHOAAAA!!
WAIT! TIME OUT, TIME OUT!!
YOU FOOL!!
DON'T AGGRAVATE THEM NEEDLESSLY!!

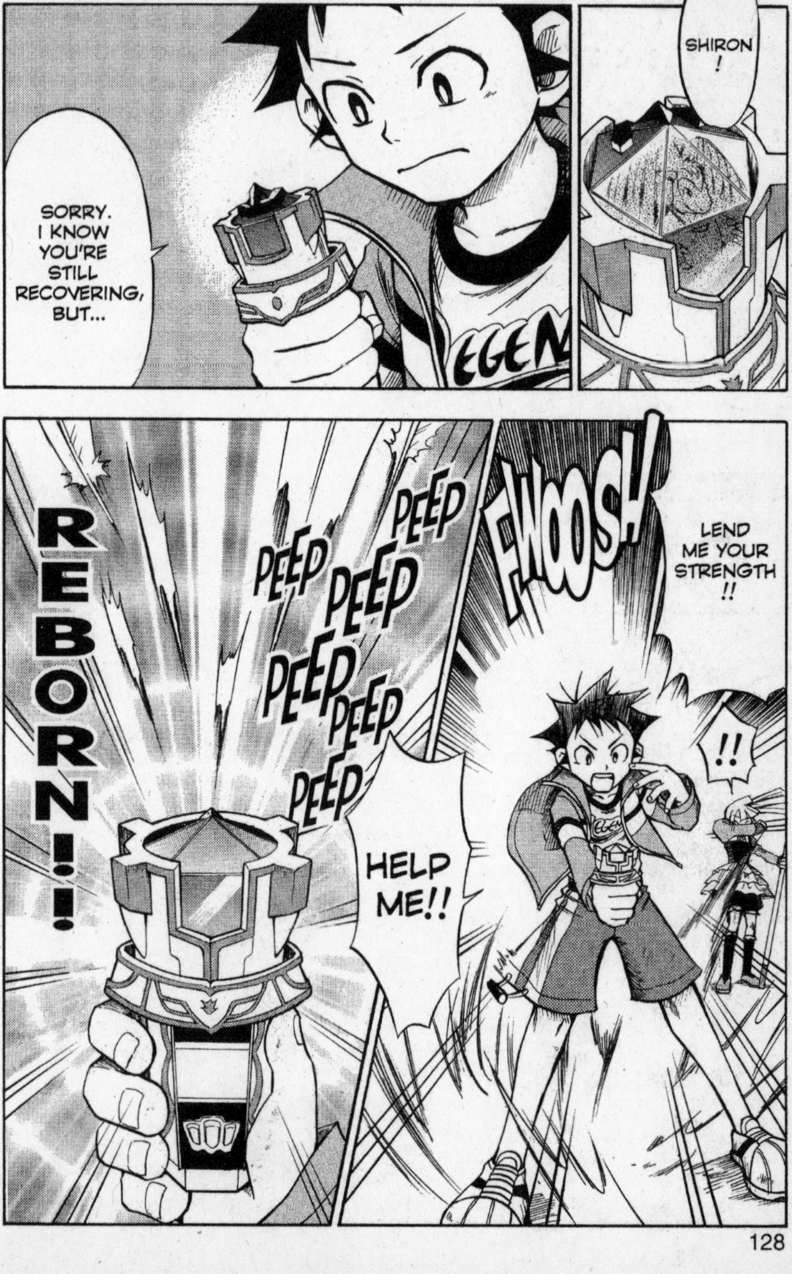
SHIRON!
SORRY. I KNOW YOU'RE STILL RECOVERING, BUT...
LEND ME YOUR STRENGTH!!
FWOOSH!
!!
HELP ME!!
PEEP PEEP PEEP PEEP PEEP PEEP
REBORN!!!

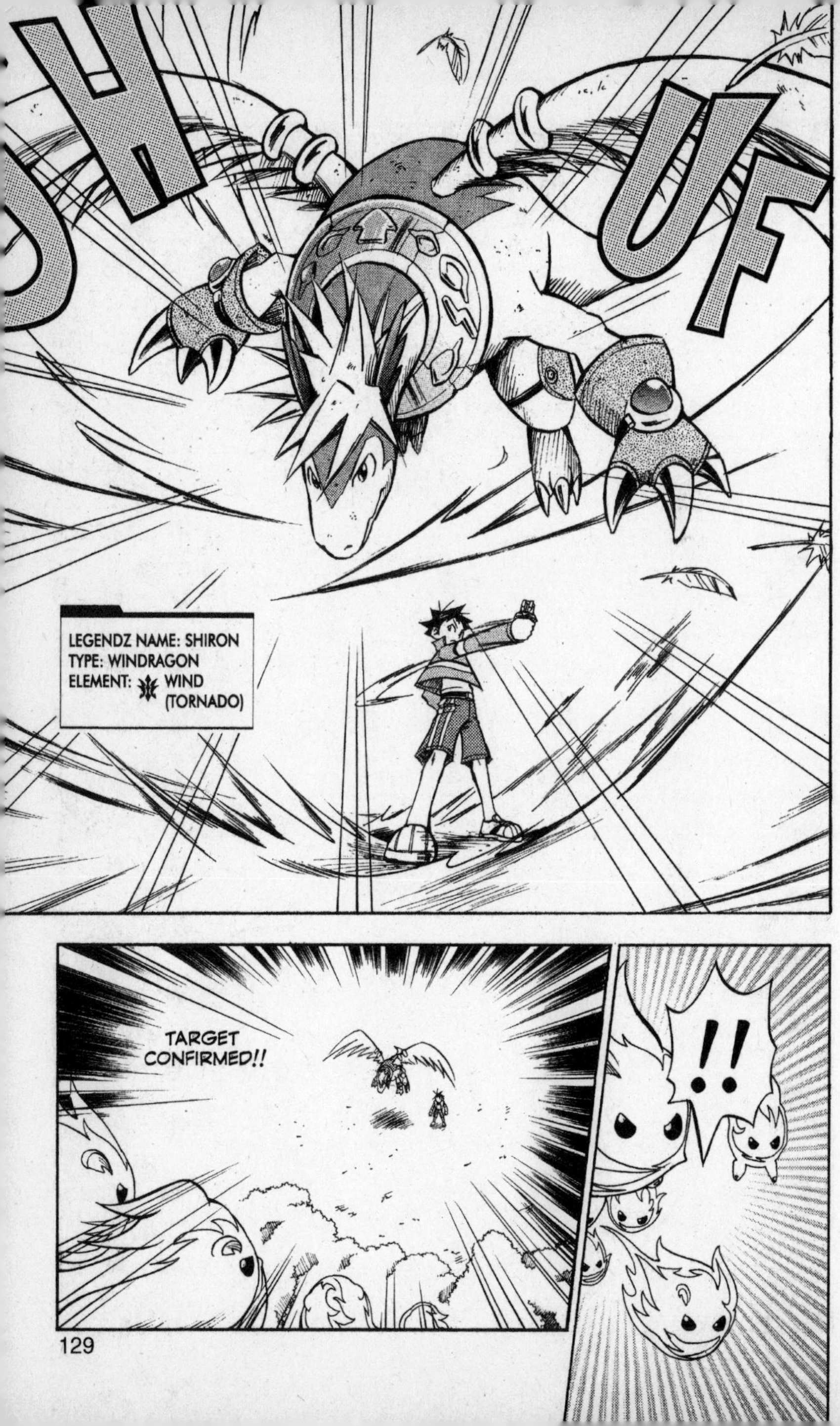
SHUF
LEGENDZ NAME: SHIRON
TYPE: WINDRAGON
ELEMENT: WIND (TORNADO)
!!
TARGET CONFIRMED!!

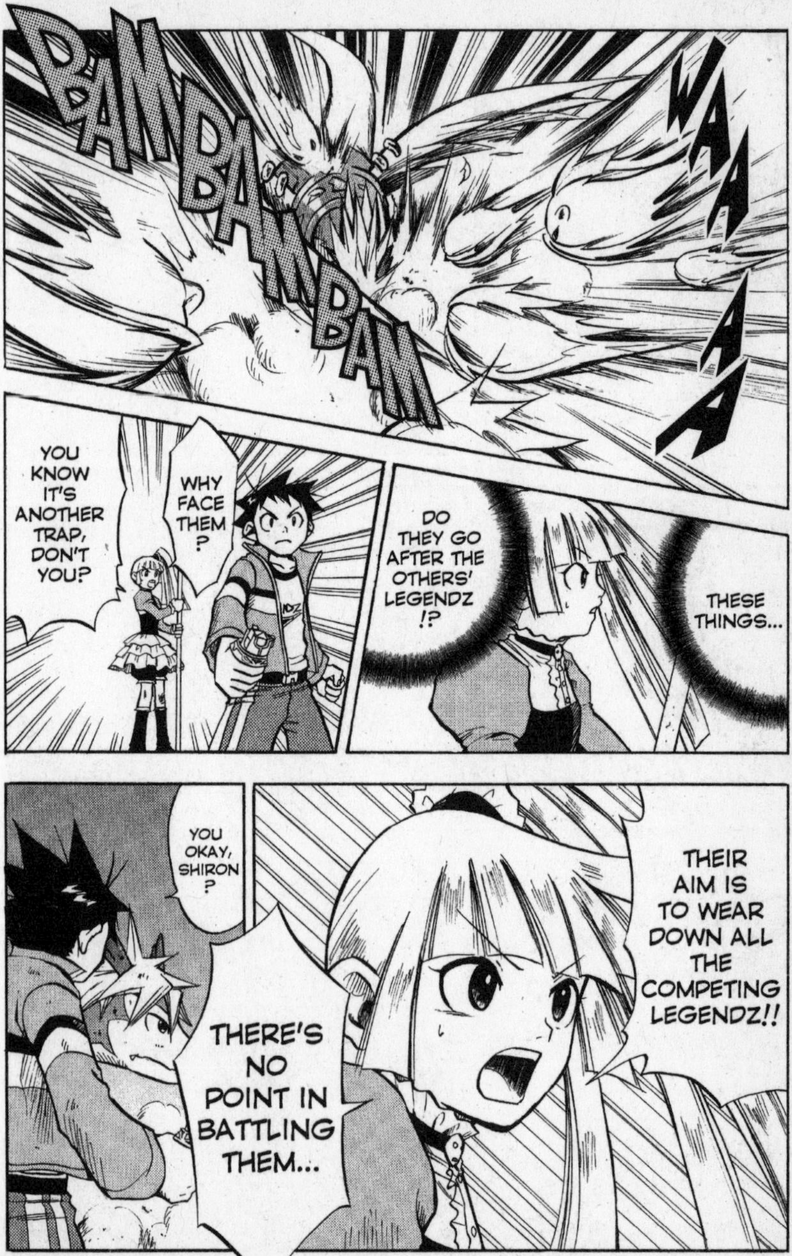
WAAAAA
BAMBAMBAMBAM
THESE THINGS...
DO THEY GO AFTER THE OTHERS' LEGENDZ!?
WHY FACE THEM?
YOU KNOW IT'S ANOTHER TRAP, DON'T YOU?
THEIR AIM IS TO WEAR DOWN ALL THE COMPETING LEGENDZ!!
THERE'S NO POINT IN BATTLING THEM...
YOU OKAY, SHIRON?

READ THIS WAY

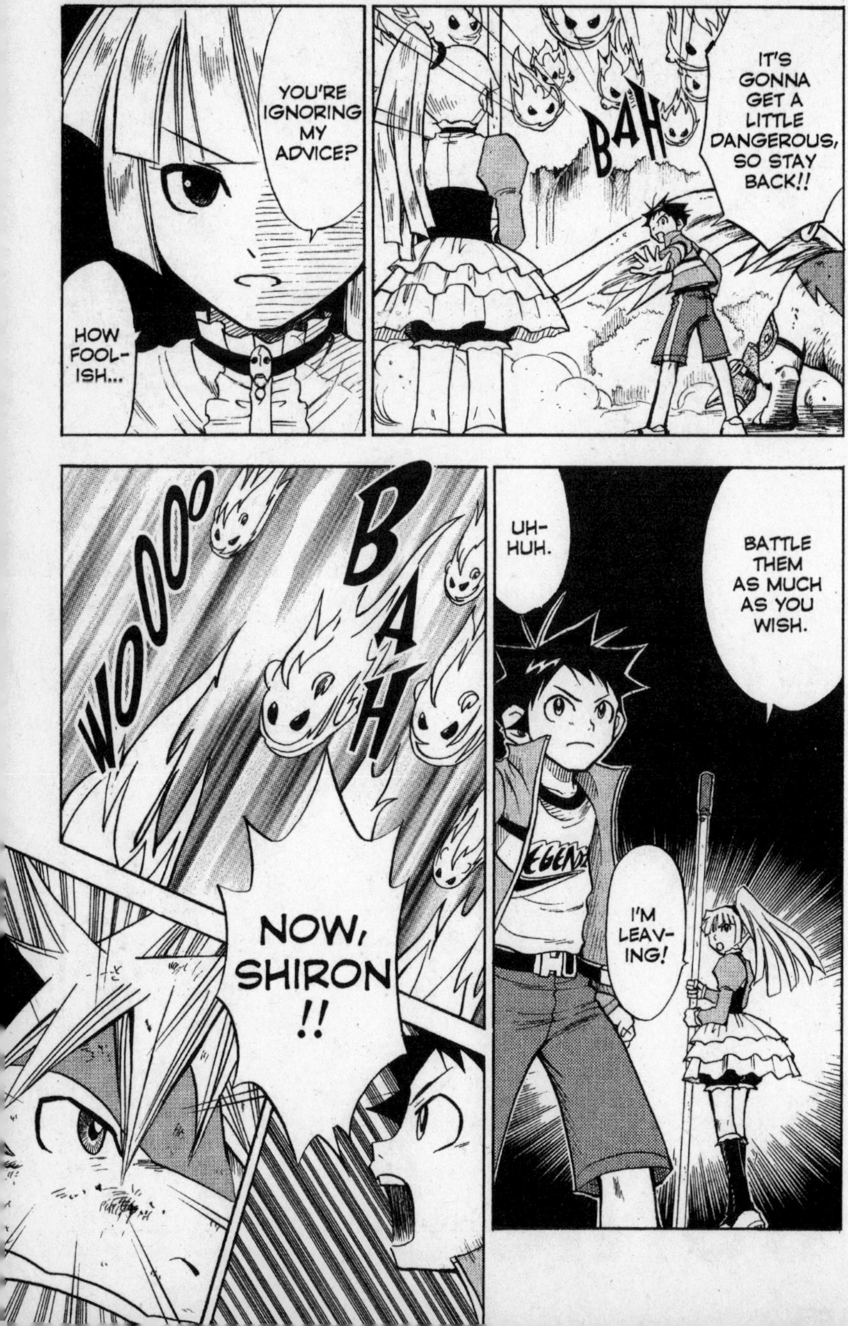
IT'S GONNA GET A LITTLE DANGEROUS, SO STAY BACK!!
BAH
YOU'RE IGNORING MY ADVICE?
HOW FOOL-ISH...
BATTLE THEM AS MUCH AS YOU WISH.
UH-HUH.
I'M LEAV-ING!
WOOOO
BAH
NOW, SHIRON!!

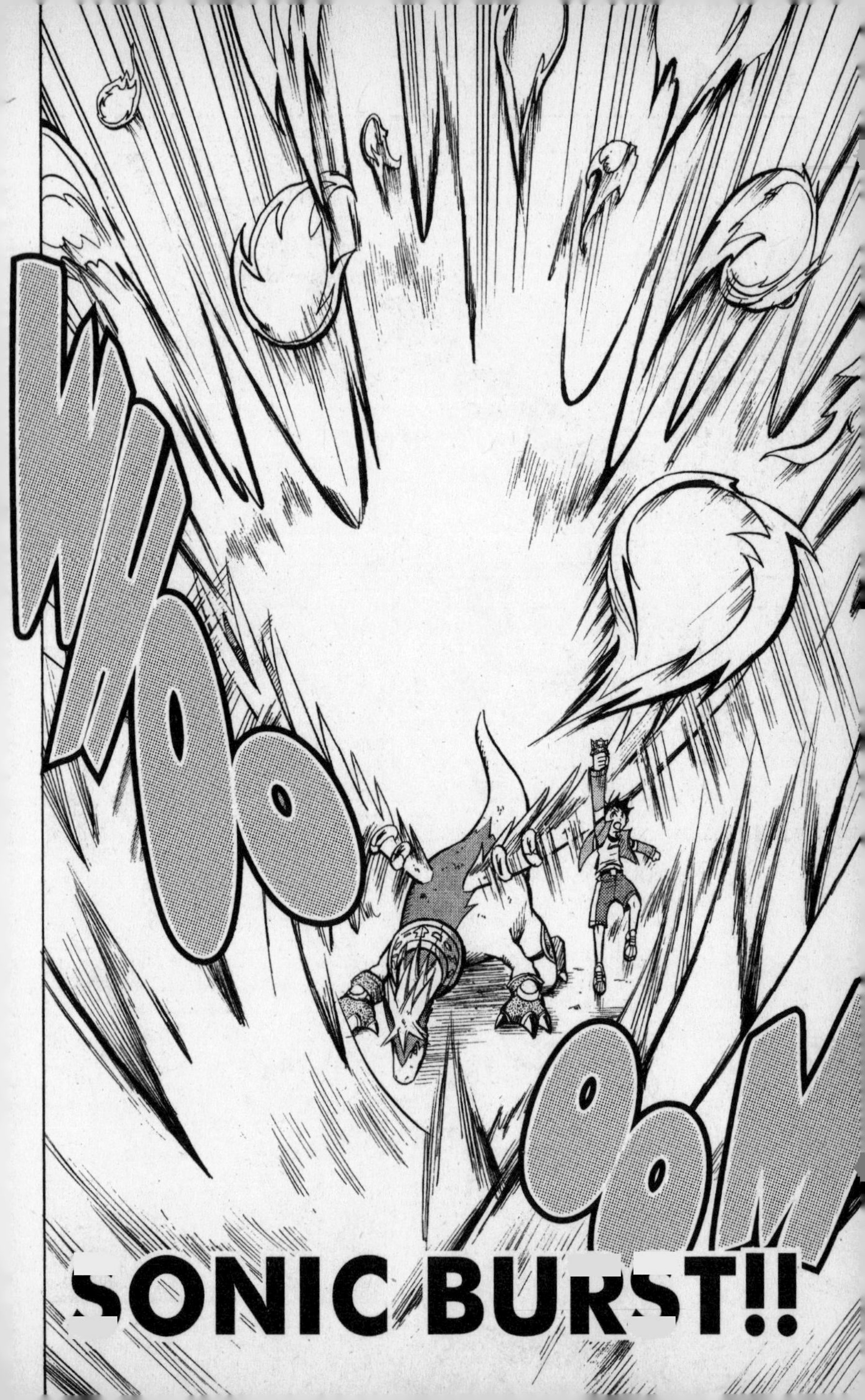
WHOOOOOOM
SONIC BURST!!

READ THIS WAY

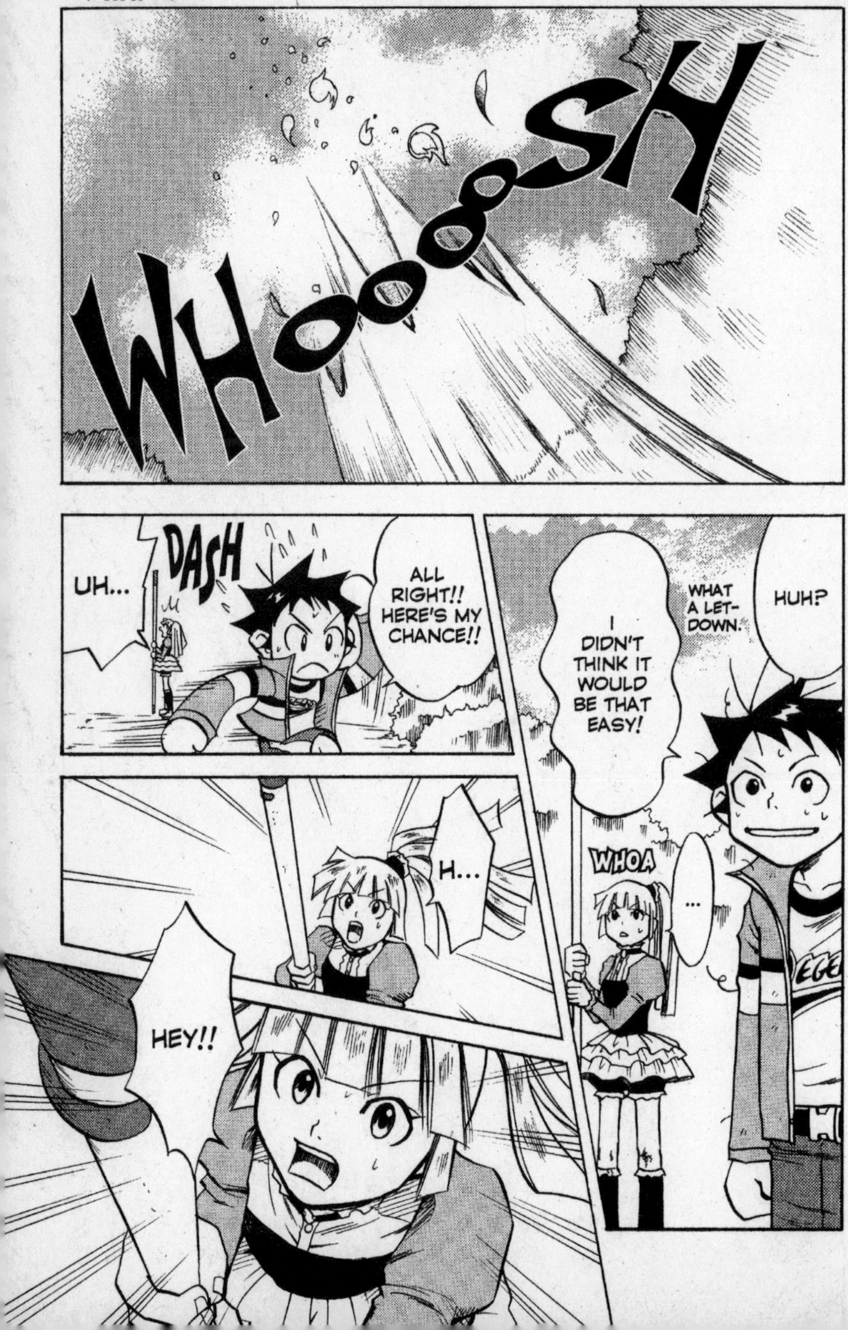
WHOOOO-SH
HUH?
WHAT A LET-DOWN.
I DIDN'T THINK IT WOULD BE THAT EASY!
...
WHOA
ALL RIGHT!! HERE'S MY CHANCE!!
DASH
UH...
H...
HEY!!

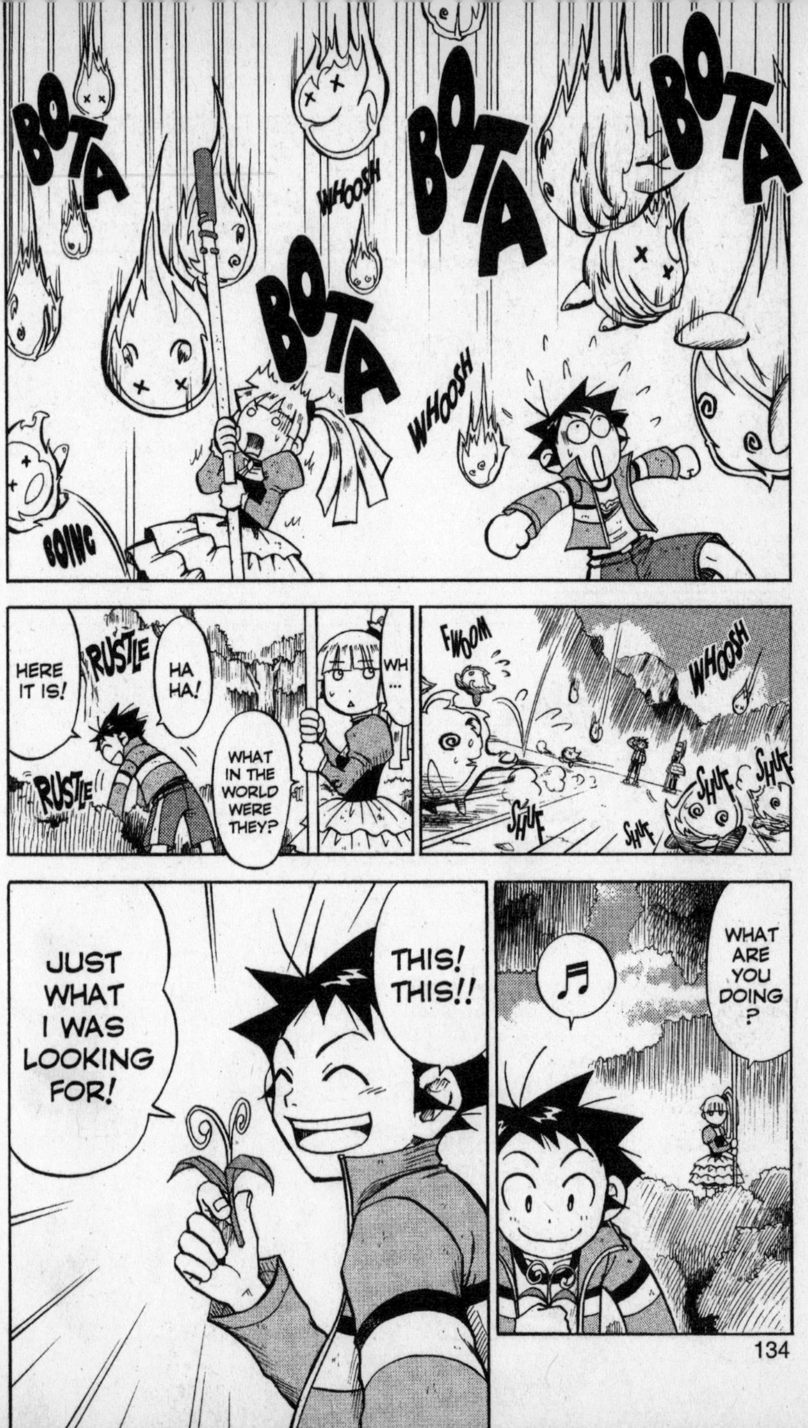
BOTA
BOTA
BOTA
WHOOSH
BOTA
WHOOSH
BOING
FWOOM
WHOOSH
SHUF
SHUF
SHUF
SHUF
WH ...
WHAT IN THE WORLD WERE THEY?
HA HA!
RUSTLE
HERE IT IS!
RUSTLE
WHAT ARE YOU DOING?
♪
THIS! THIS!!
JUST WHAT I WAS LOOKING FOR!

READ THIS WAY

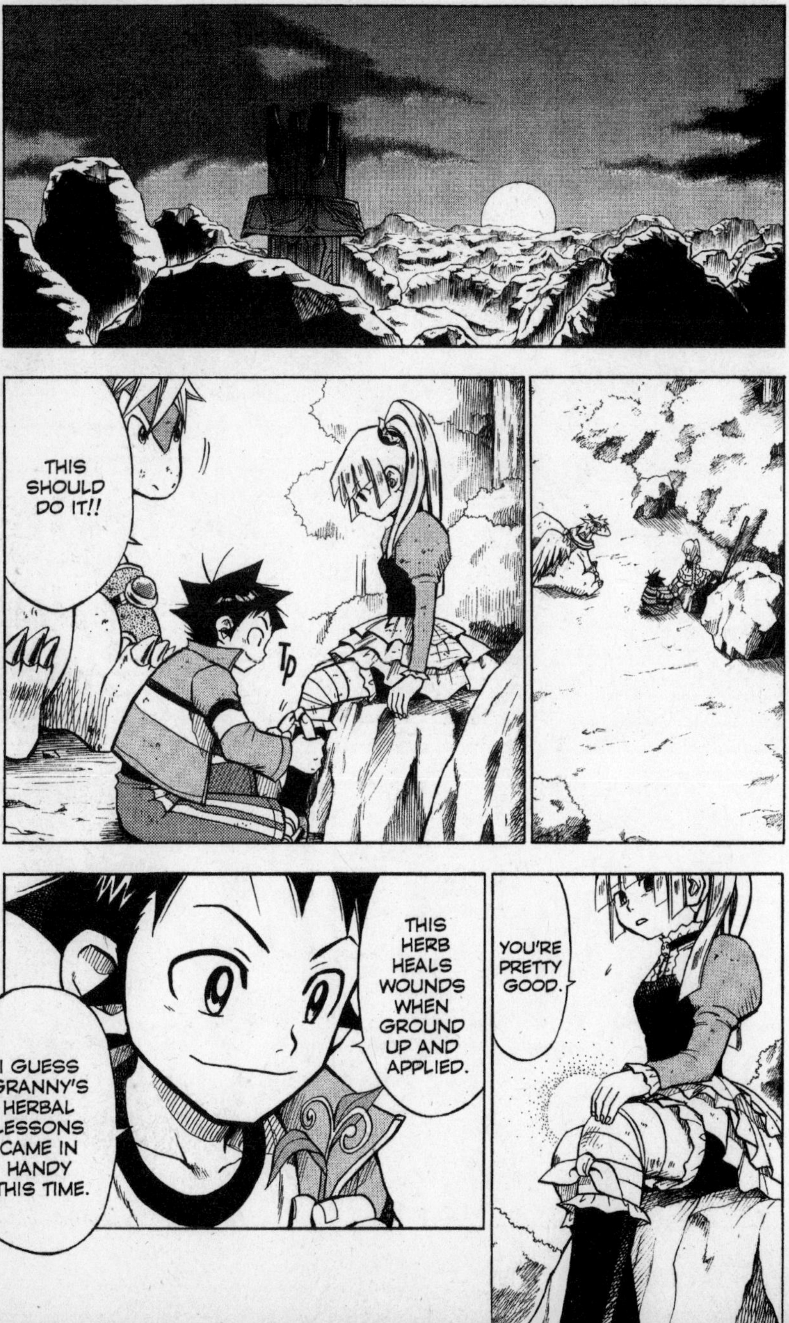
THIS SHOULD DO IT!!
TP
YOU'RE PRETTY GOOD.
THIS HERB HEALS WOUNDS WHEN GROUND UP AND APPLIED.
I GUESS GRANNY'S HERBAL LESSONS CAME IN HANDY THIS TIME.

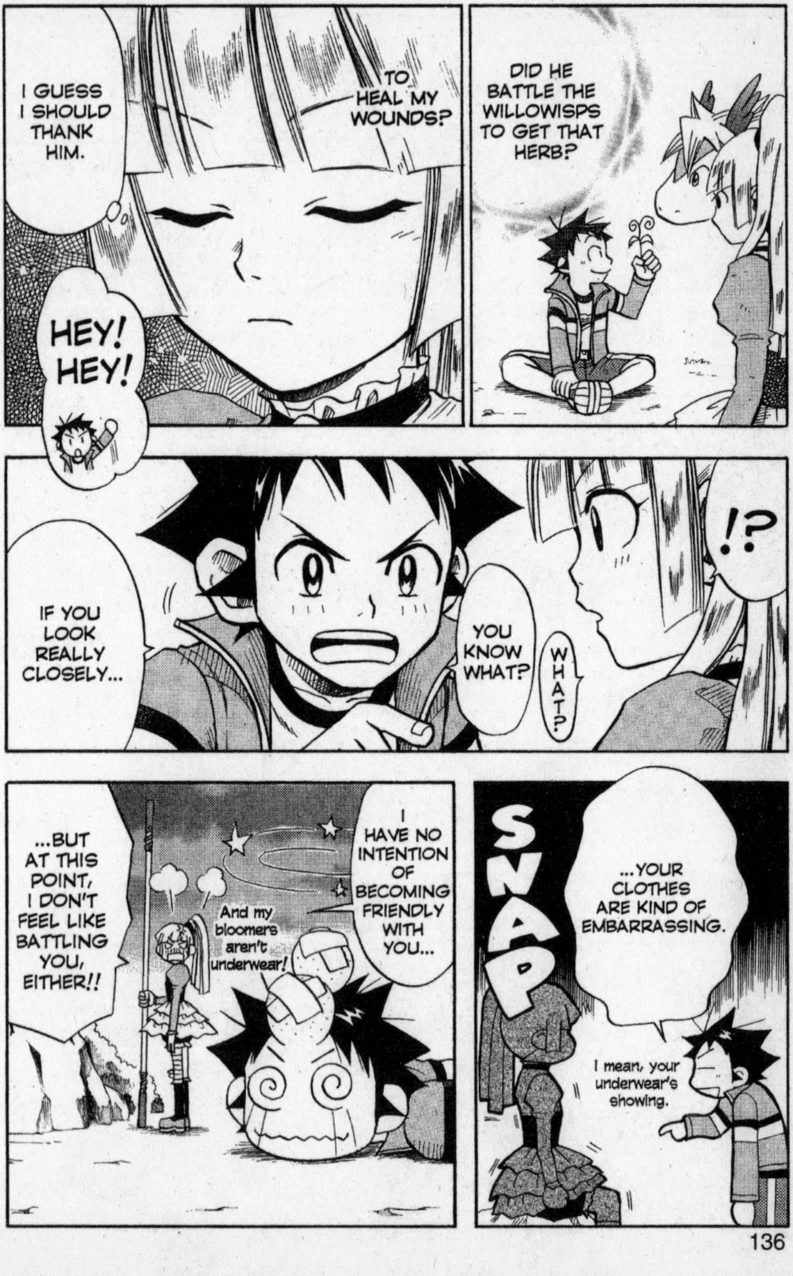
DID HE BATTLE THE WILLOWISPS TO GET THAT HERB?
TO HEAL MY WOUNDS?
I GUESS I SHOULD THANK HIM.
HEY! HEY!
!?
WHAT?
YOU KNOW WHAT?
IF YOU LOOK REALLY CLOSELY...
SNAP
...YOUR CLOTHES ARE KIND OF EMBARRASSING.
I mean, your underwear's showing.
I HAVE NO INTENTION OF BECOMING FRIENDLY WITH YOU...
And my bloomers aren't underwear!
...BUT AT THIS POINT, I DON'T FEEL LIKE BATTLING YOU, EITHER!!

READ THIS WAY

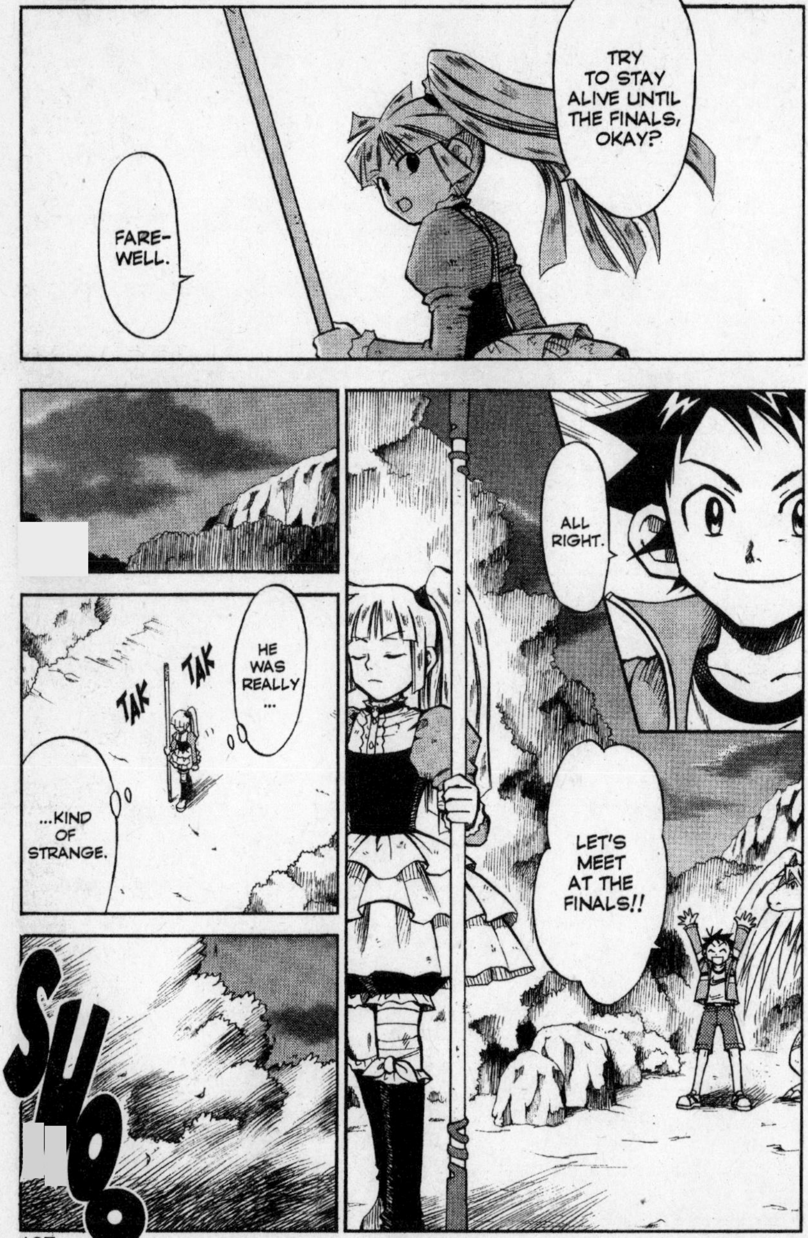
TRY TO STAY ALIVE UNTIL THE FINALS, OKAY?
FARE-WELL.
ALL RIGHT.
LET'S MEET AT THE FINALS!!
HE WAS REALLY ...
TAK
TAK
...KIND OF STRANGE.
SHOO

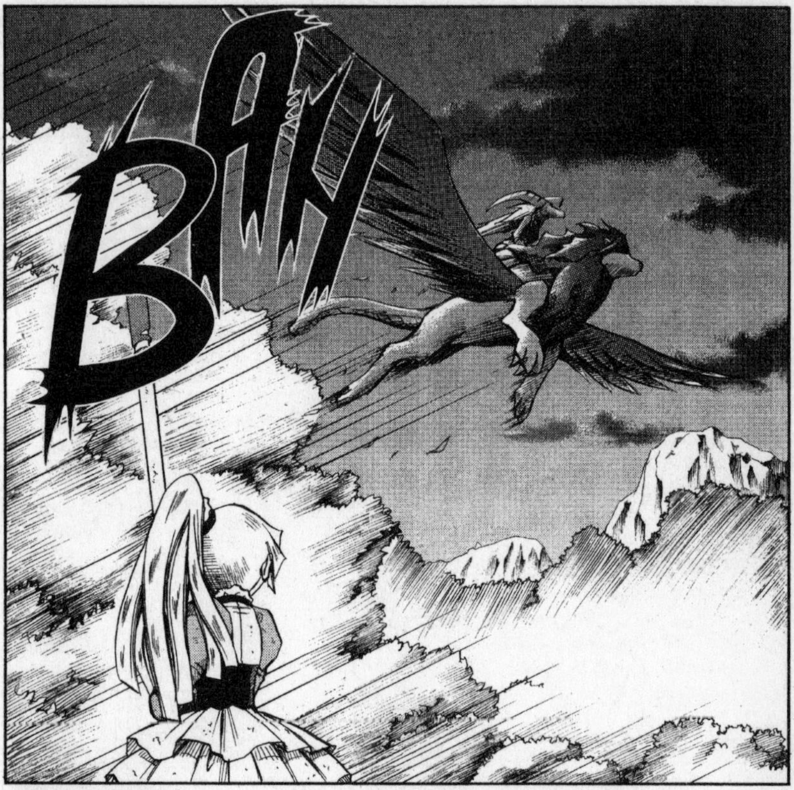
BAM
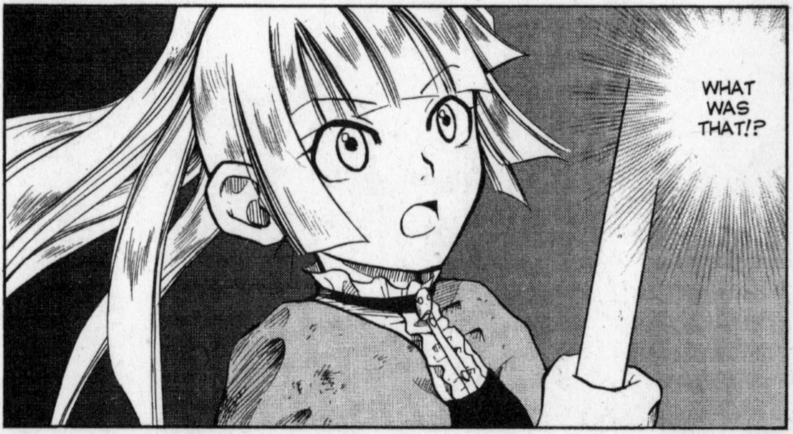
WHAT WAS THAT!?

READ THIS WAY

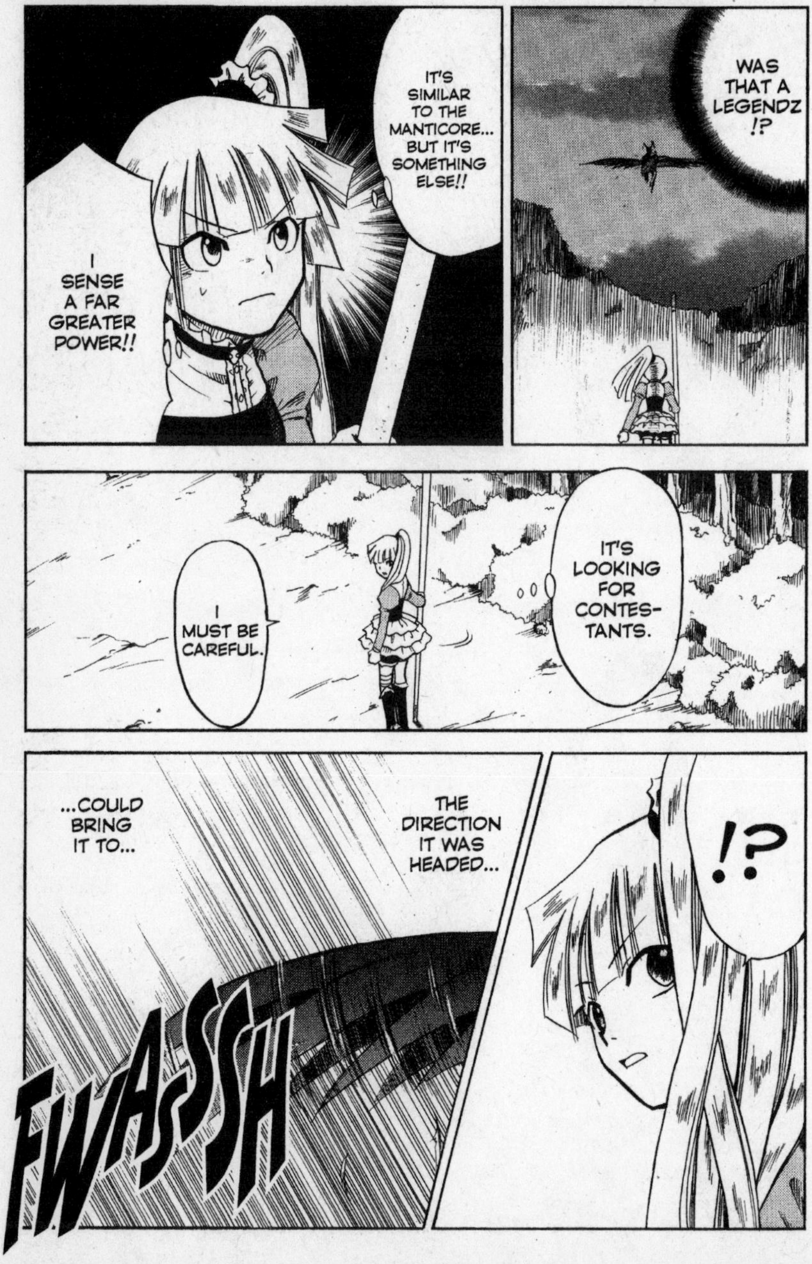
WAS THAT A LEGENDZ !?
IT'S SIMILAR TO THE MANTICORE... BUT IT'S SOMETHING ELSE!!
I SENSE A FAR GREATER POWER!!
IT'S LOOKING FOR CONTES-TANTS.
I MUST BE CAREFUL.
!?
THE DIRECTION IT WAS HEADED...
...COULD BRING IT TO...
FWASSH

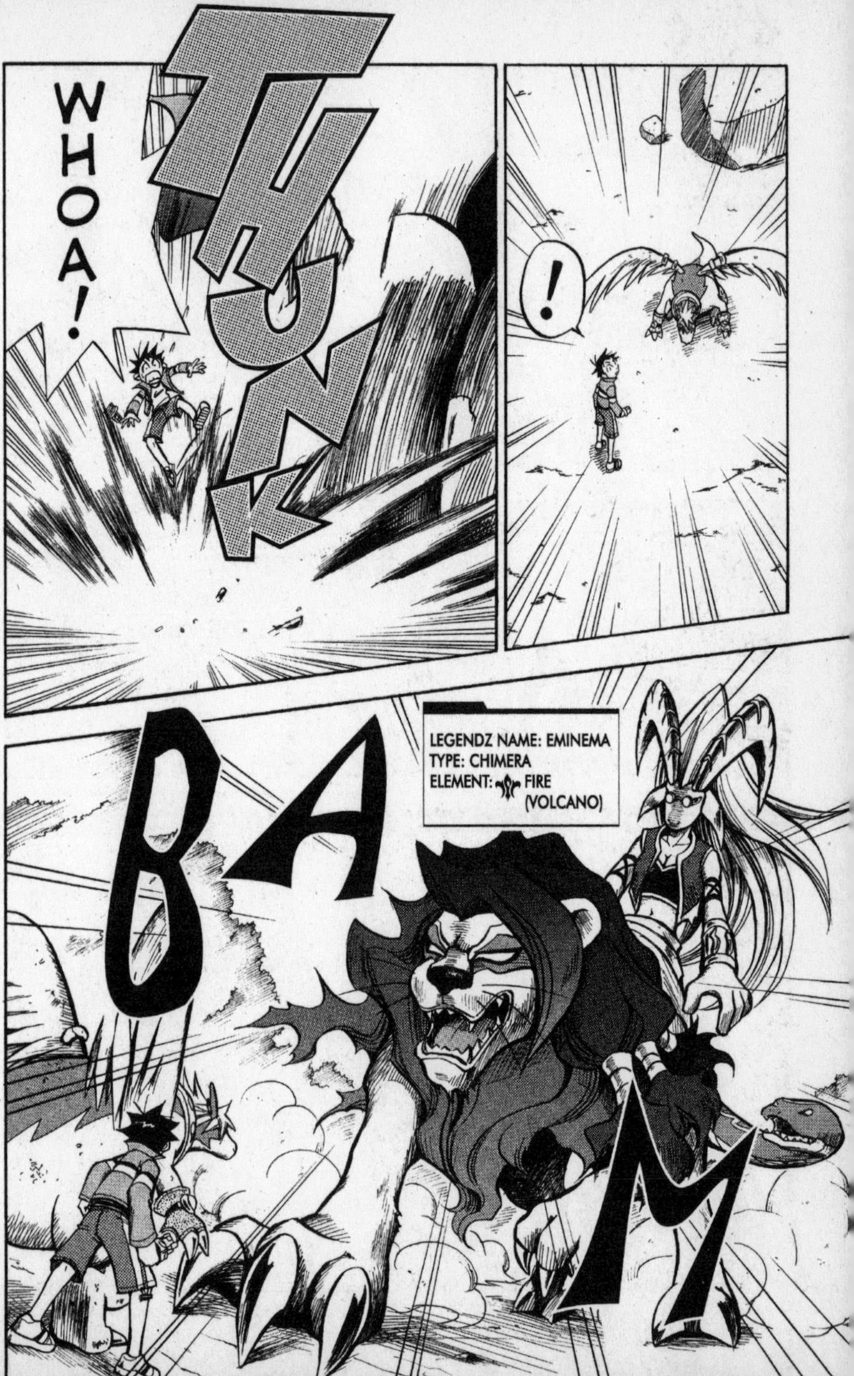
!
WHOA!
THUNK
LEGENDZ NAME: EMINEMA
TYPE: CHIMERA
ELEMENT: FIRE (VOLCANO)
BAM

READ THIS WAY

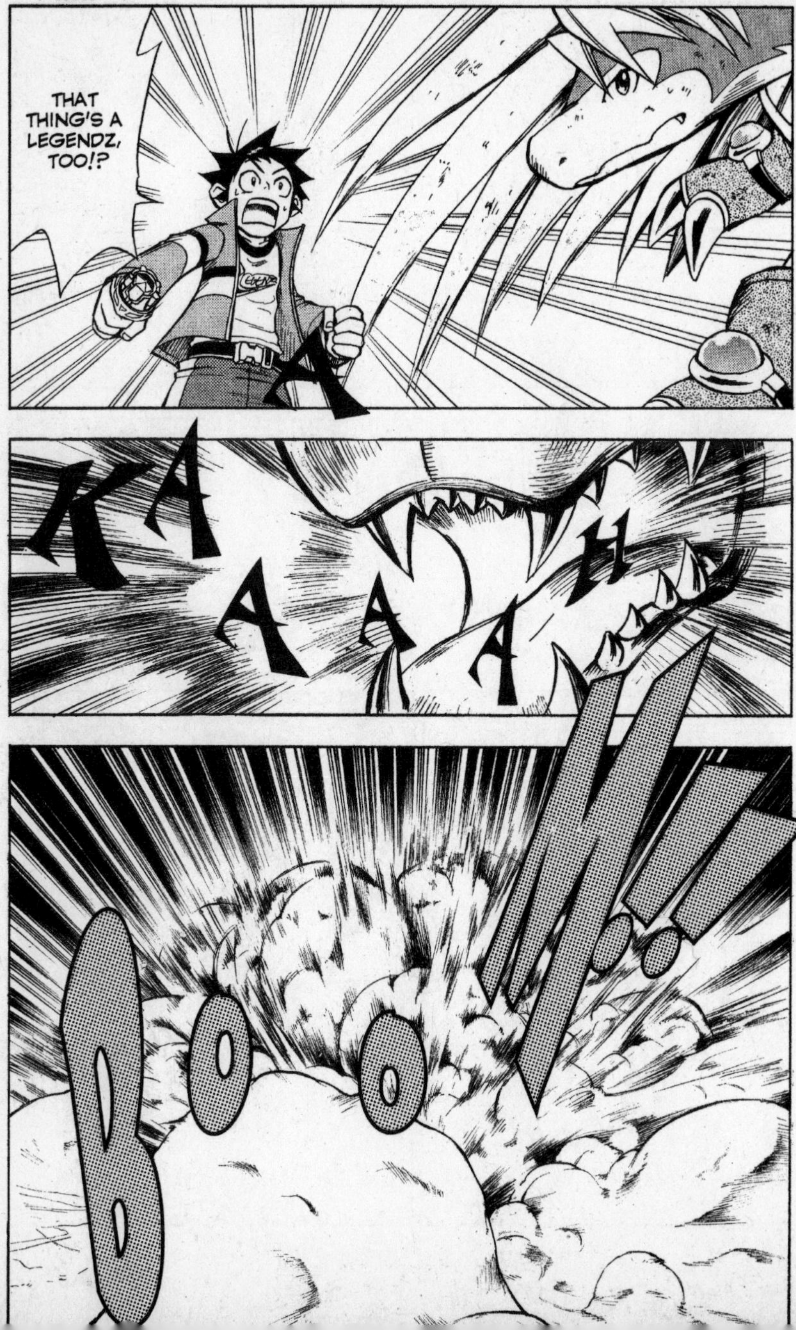
THAT THING'S A LEGENDZ, TOO!?
A
KAAAAH
BOOM!!

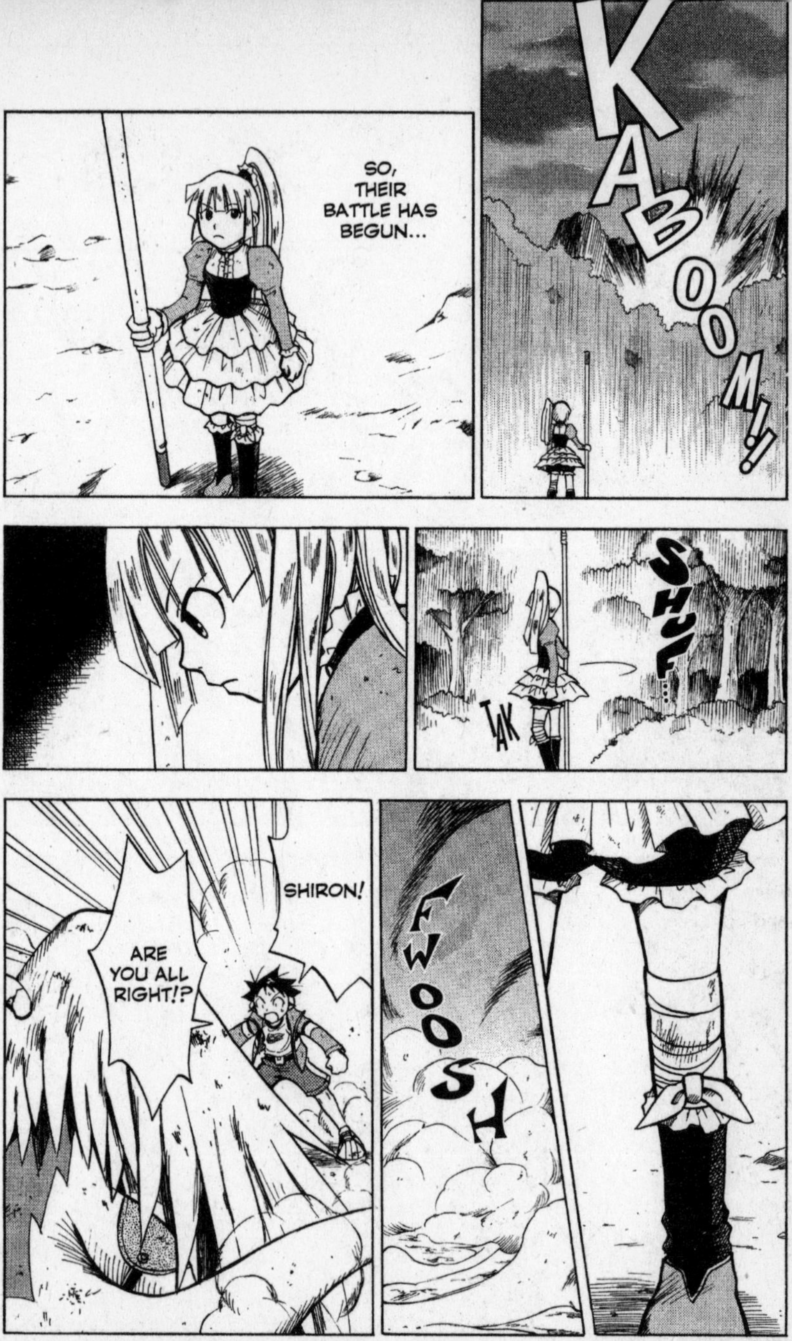
KABOOM!!
SO, THEIR BATTLE HAS BEGUN...
SHUF...
TAK
FWOOSH
SHIRON!
ARE YOU ALL RIGHT!?

READ THIS WAY

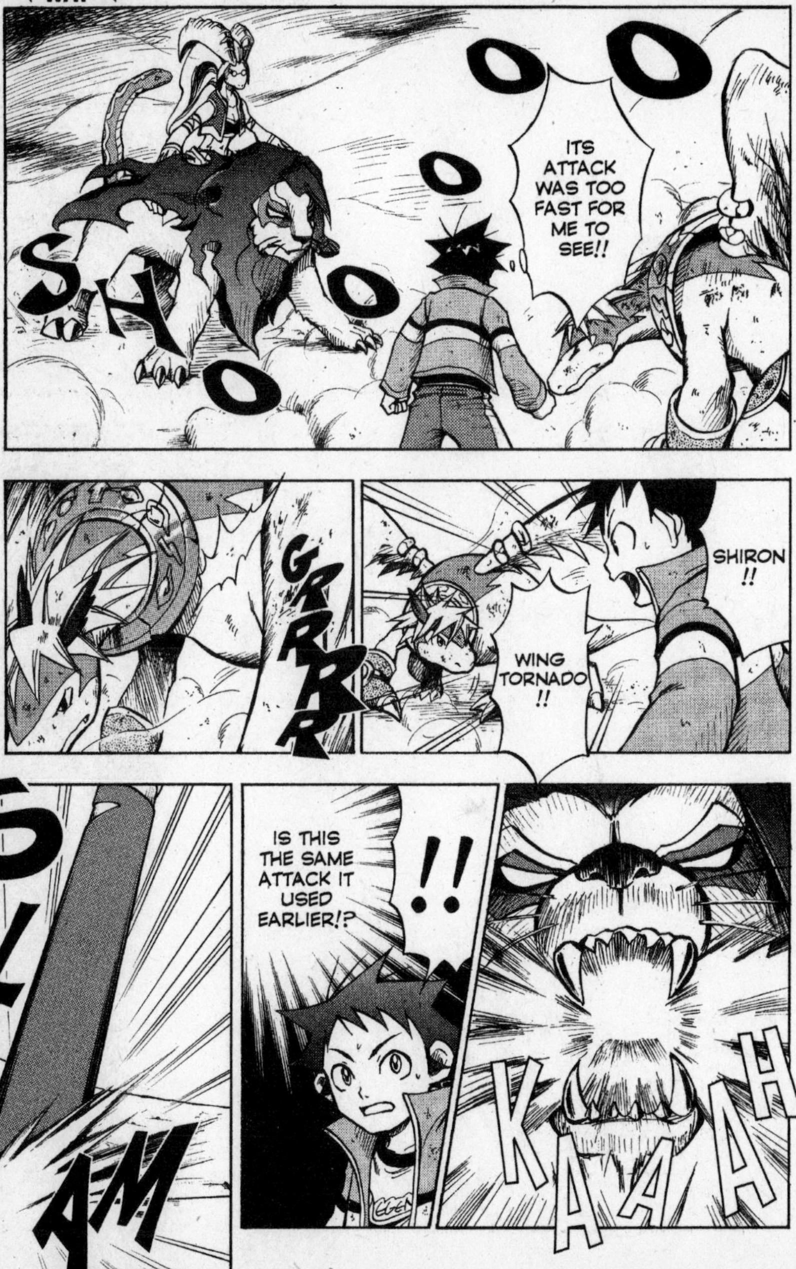
ITS ATTACK WAS TOO FAST FOR ME TO SEE!!
SHOOOOOOO
SHIRON!!
WING TORNADO!!
GRRRR
KAAAAH
!!
IS THIS THE SAME ATTACK IT USED EARLIER!?
SLAM

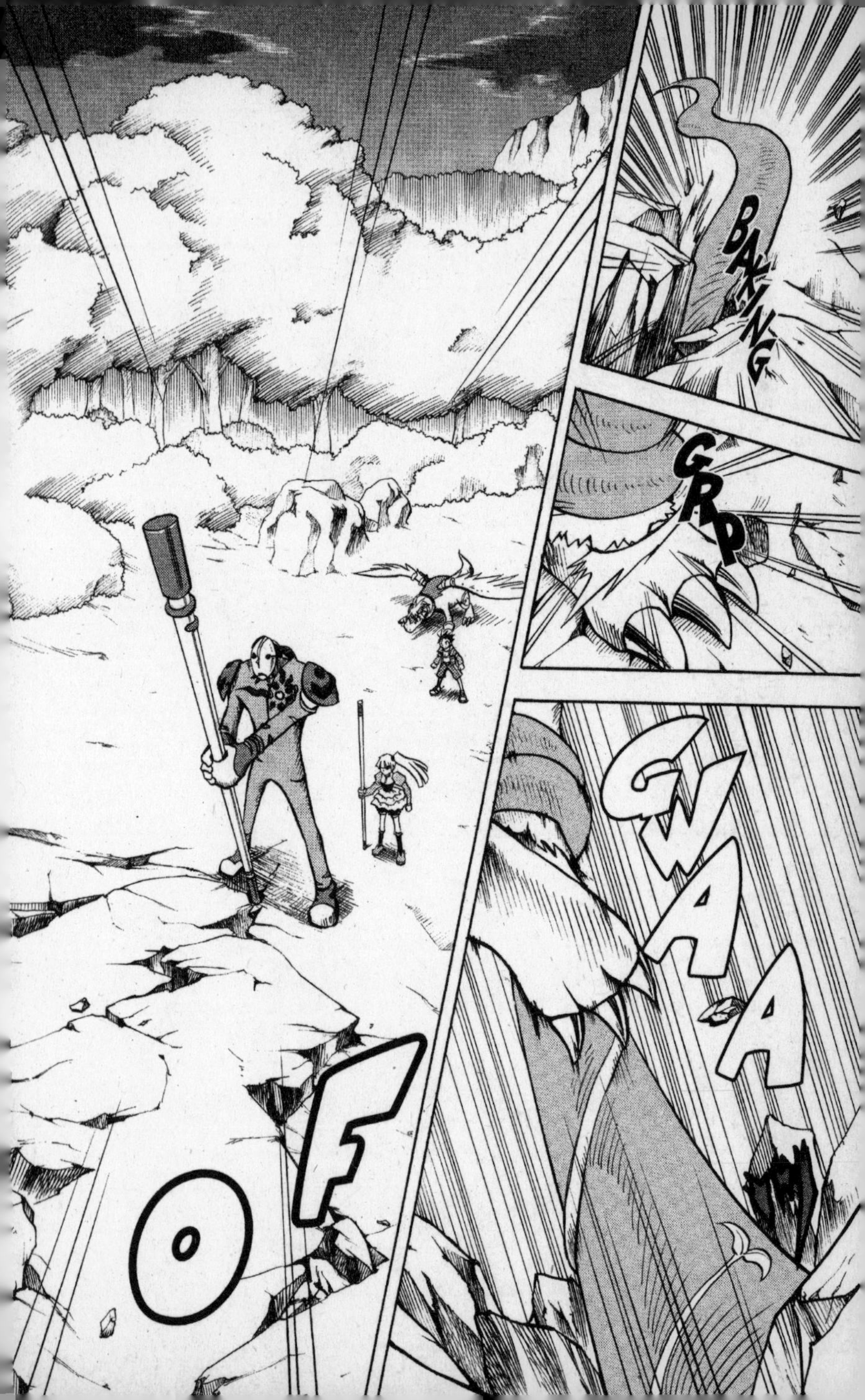
BAKING
GRP
GWAA
OF

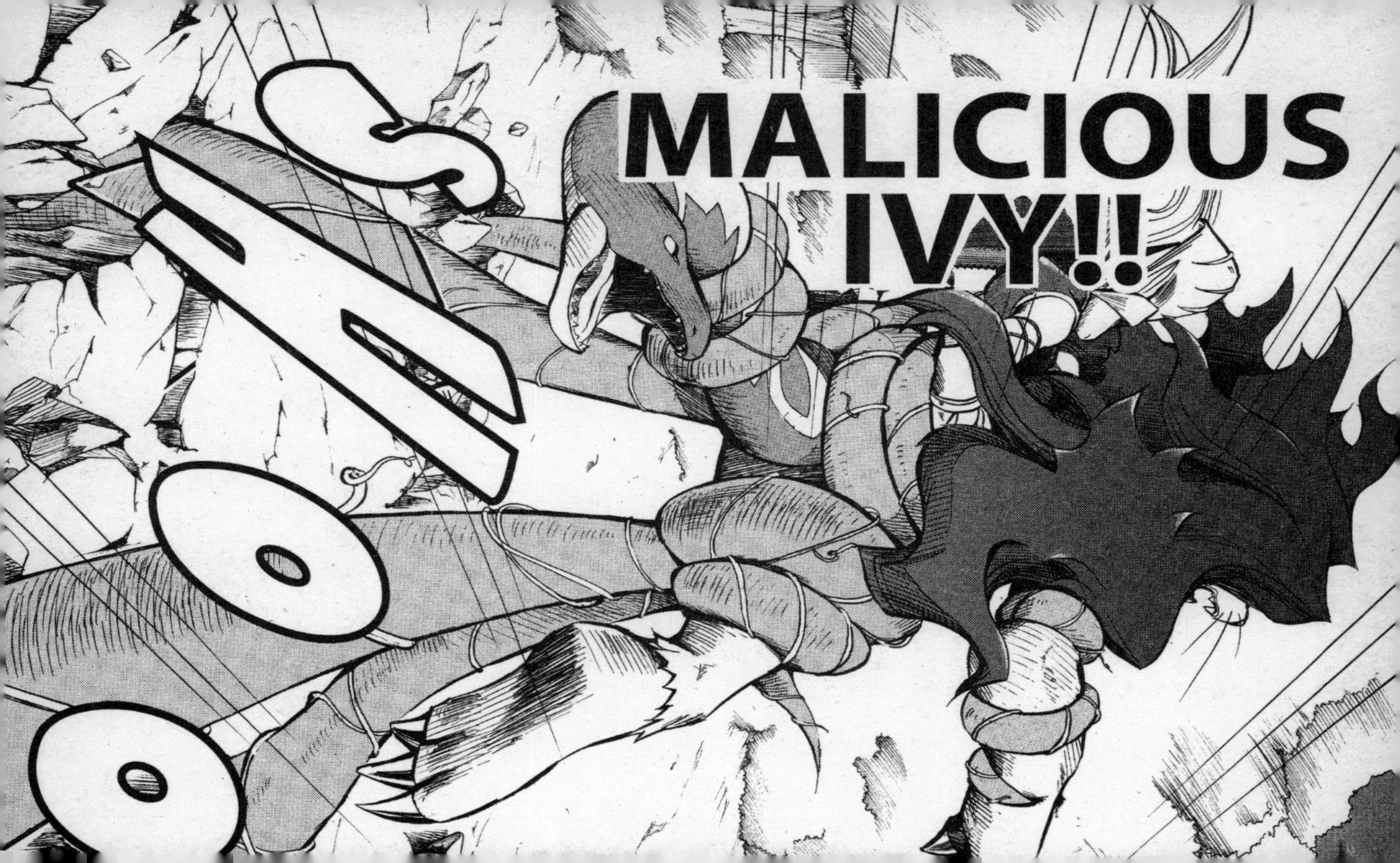
MALICIOUS IVY!!
SHOO

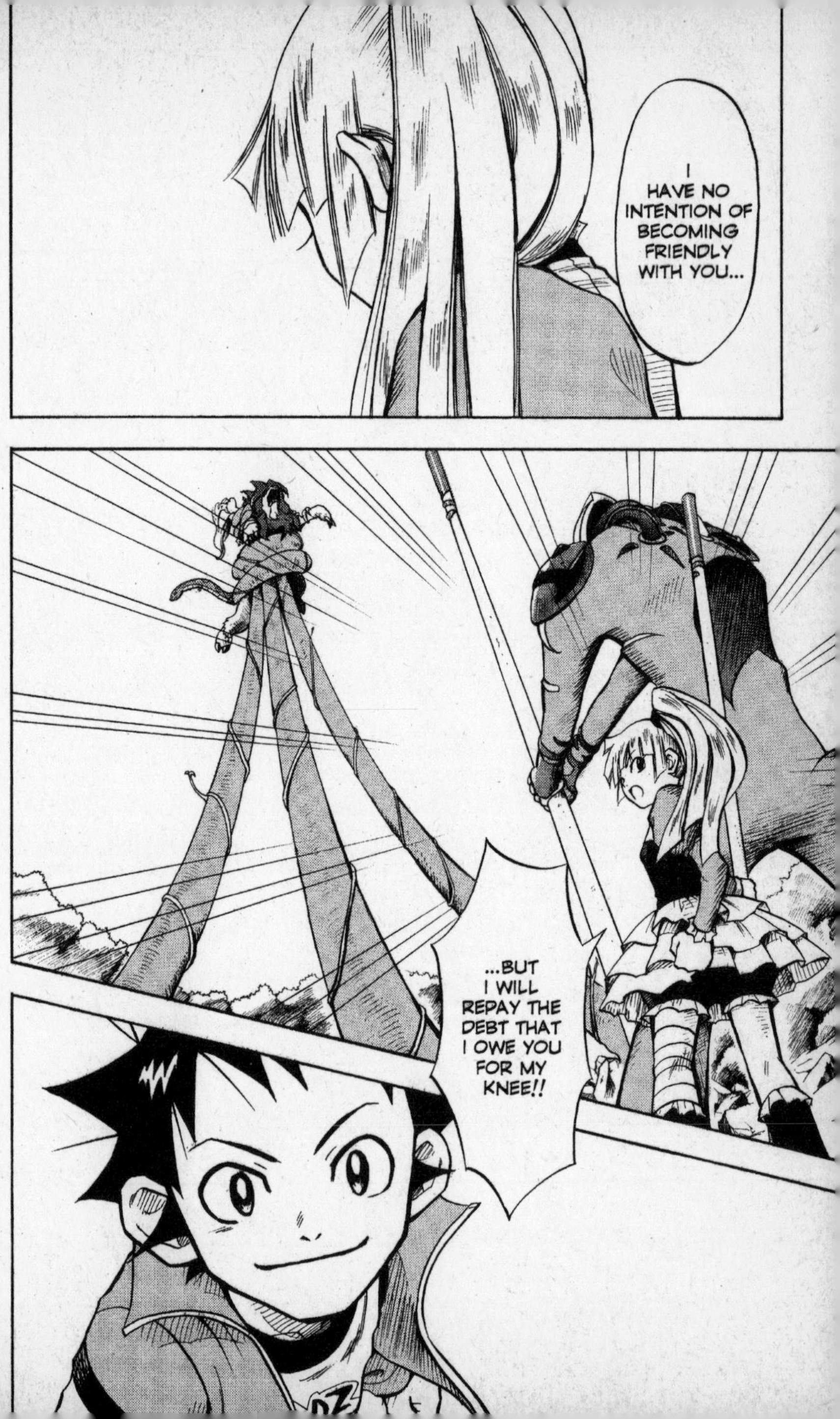
I HAVE NO INTENTION OF BECOMING FRIENDLY WITH YOU...
...BUT I WILL REPAY THE DEBT THAT I OWE YOU FOR MY KNEE!!

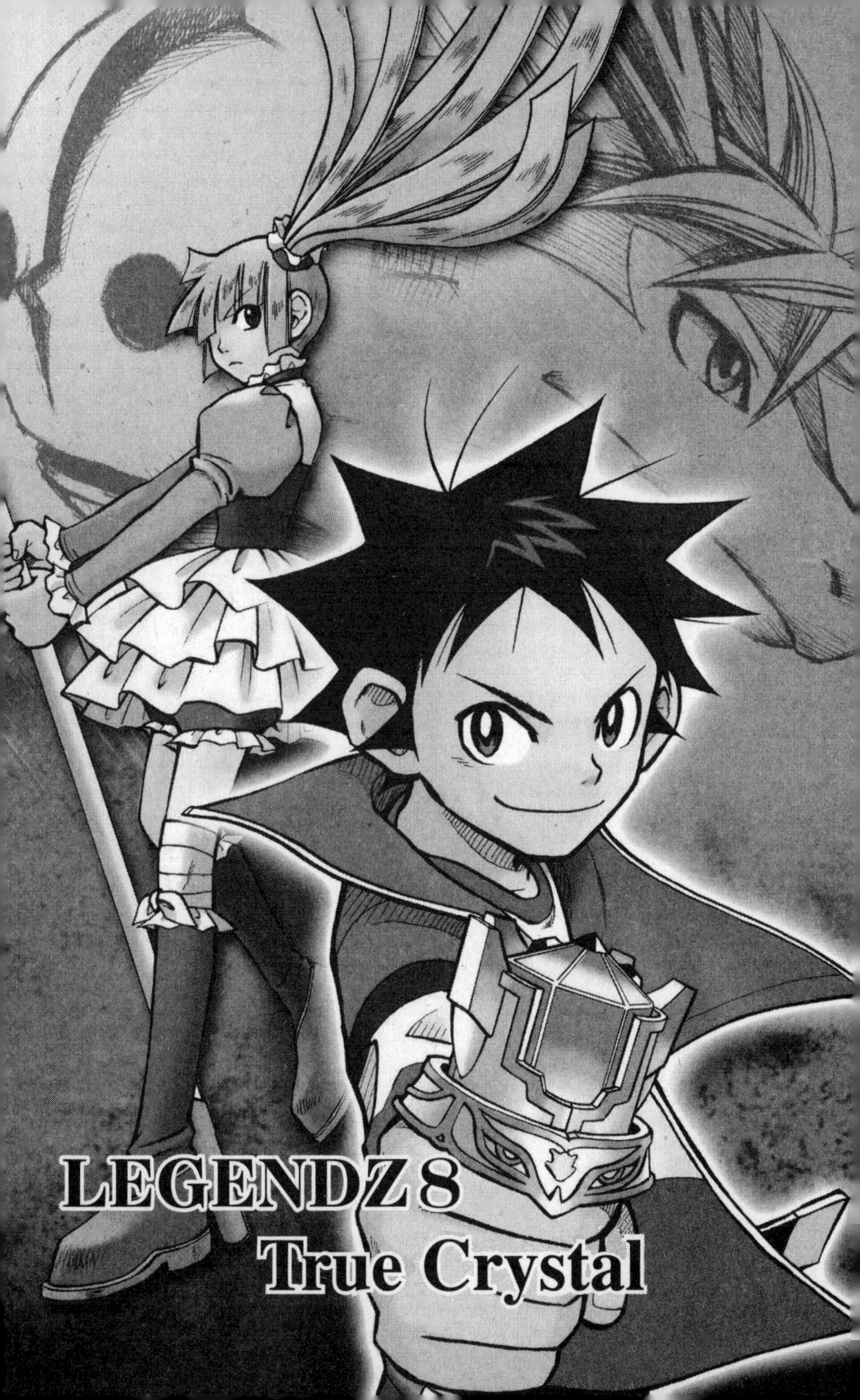
LEGENDZ 8
True Crystal

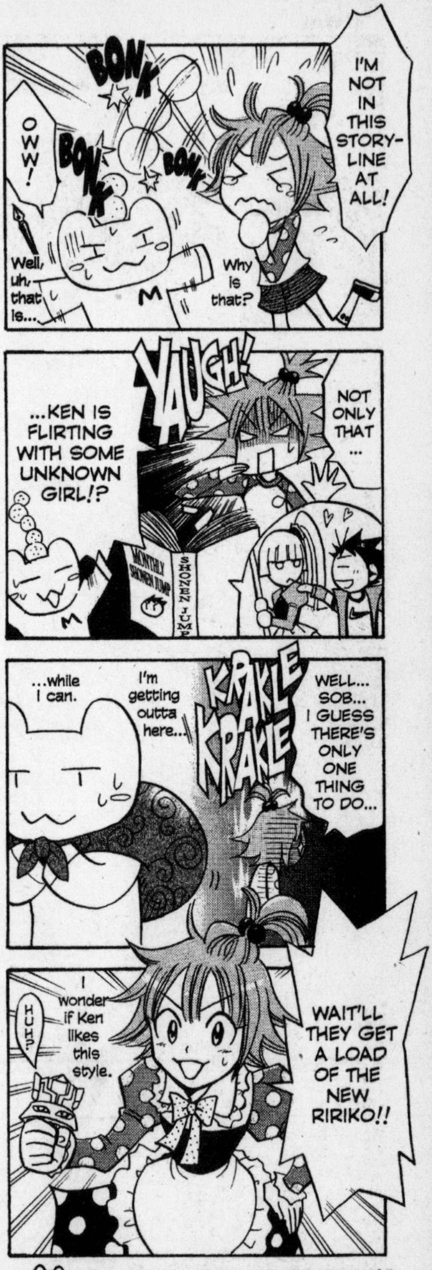
I'M NOT IN THIS STORY-LINE AT ALL!
BONK
BONK
BONK
OWW!
Why is that?
Well, uh, that is...
YAUGH!
NOT ONLY THAT ...
...KEN IS FLIRTING WITH SOME UNKNOWN GIRL!?
MONTHLY SHONEN JUMP
SHONEN JUMP
WELL... SOB... I GUESS THERE'S ONLY ONE THING TO DO...
KRAKLE KRAKLE
I'm getting outta here...
...while I can.
WAIT'LL THEY GET A LOAD OF THE NEW RIRIKO!!
I wonder if Ken likes this style.
HUH?

WILL RIRIKO GET HER REVENGE!?

READ THIS WAY

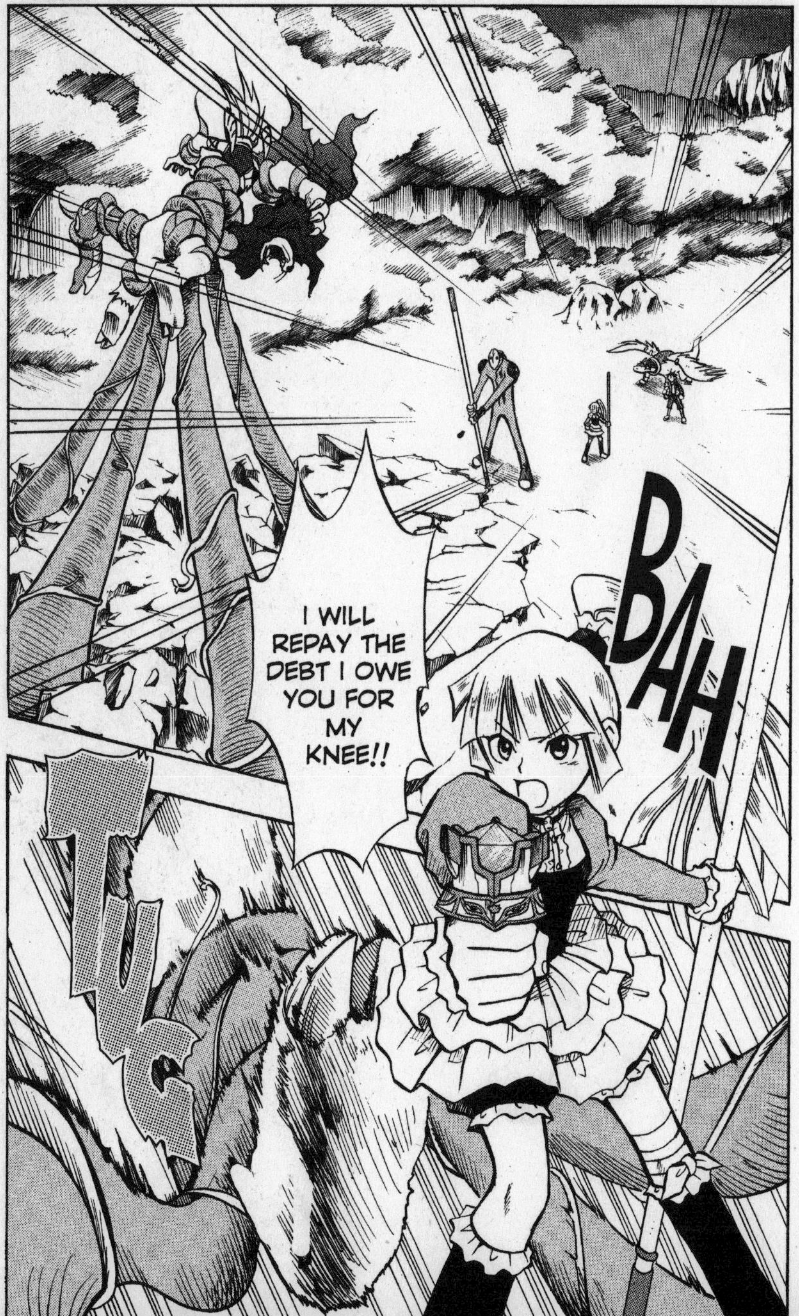
BAH
I WILL REPAY THE DEBT I OWE YOU FOR MY KNEE!!
TUG

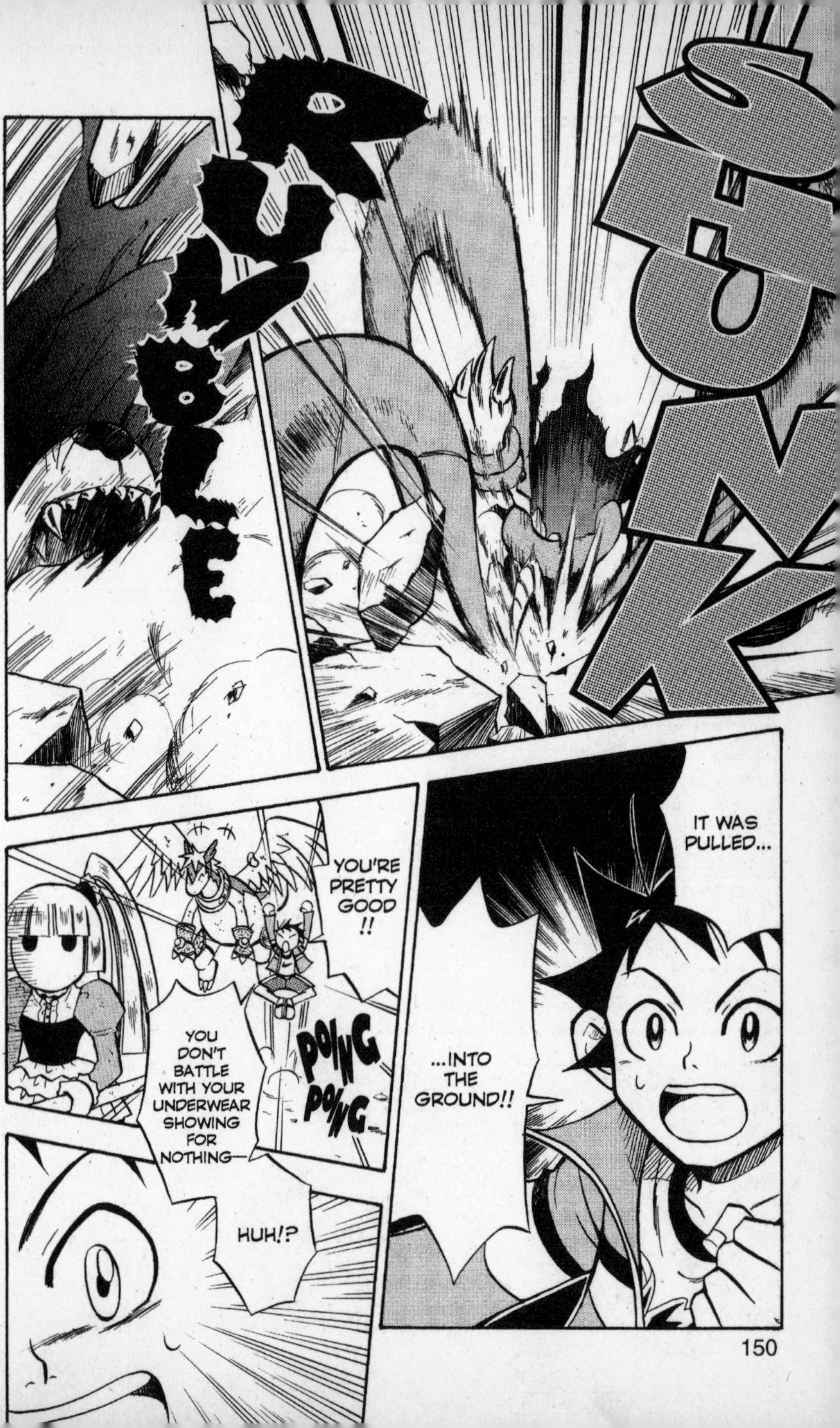
SHUNK
IT WAS PULLED...
...INTO THE GROUND!!
YOU'RE PRETTY GOOD!!
POING POING
YOU DON'T BATTLE WITH YOUR UNDERWEAR SHOWING FOR NOTHING—
HUH!?

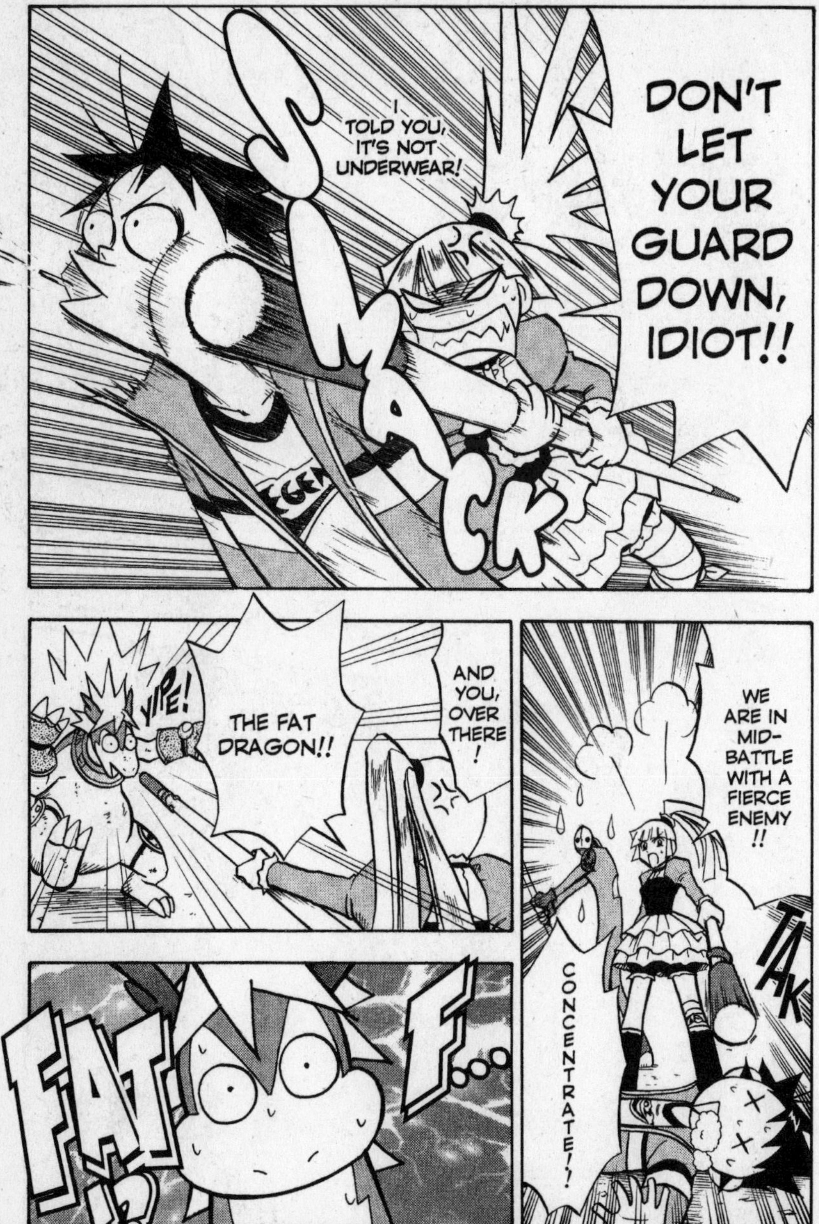
DON'T LET YOUR GUARD DOWN, IDIOT!!
I TOLD YOU, IT'S NOT UNDERWEAR!
SMACK
WE ARE IN MID-BATTLE WITH A FIERCE ENEMY!!
TAK
CONCENTRATE!!
AND YOU, OVER THERE!
THE FAT DRAGON!!
YIPE!
F...
FAT!?

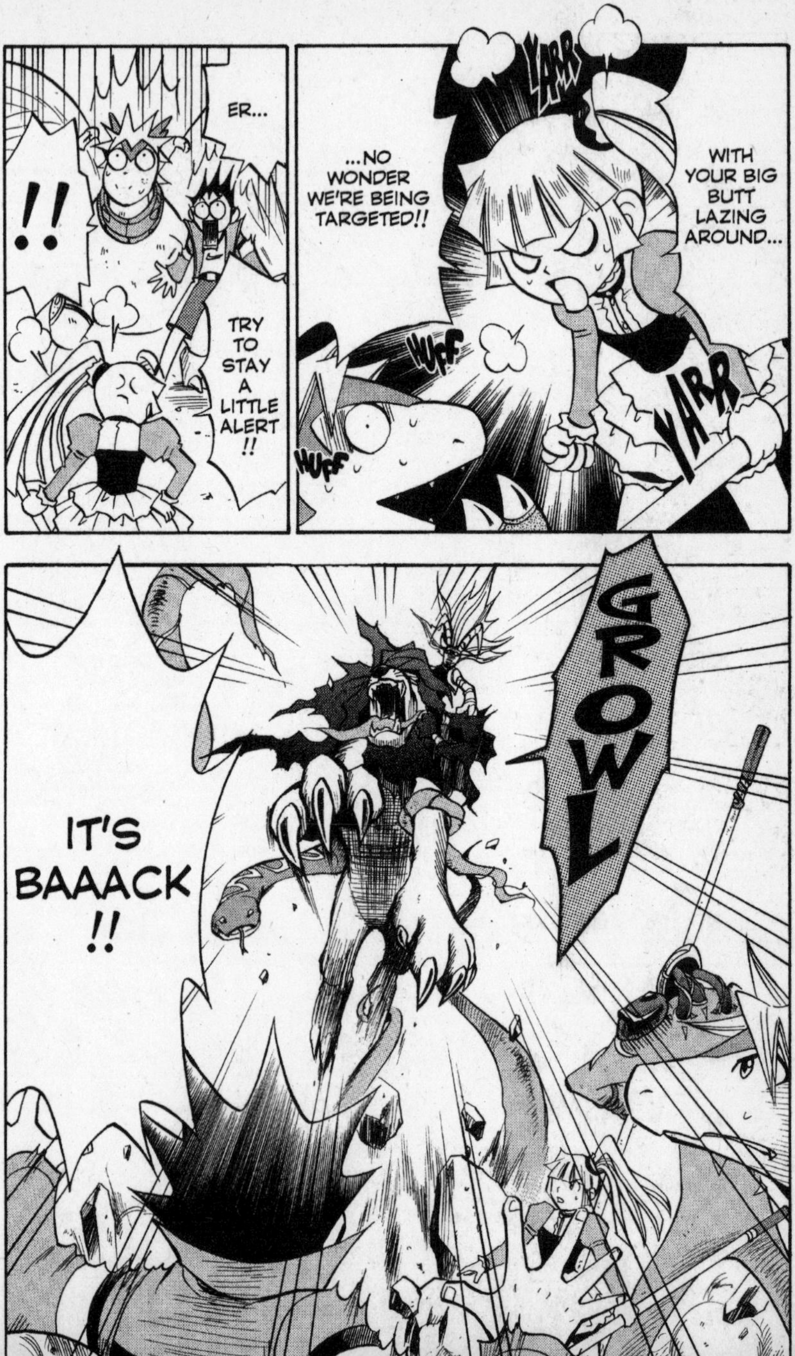
YARR
WITH YOUR BIG BUTT LAZING AROUND...
...NO WONDER WE'RE BEING TARGETED!!
YARR
HUFF
HUFF
ER...
!!
TRY TO STAY A LITTLE ALERT!!
GROWL
IT'S BAAACK!!

READ THIS WAY

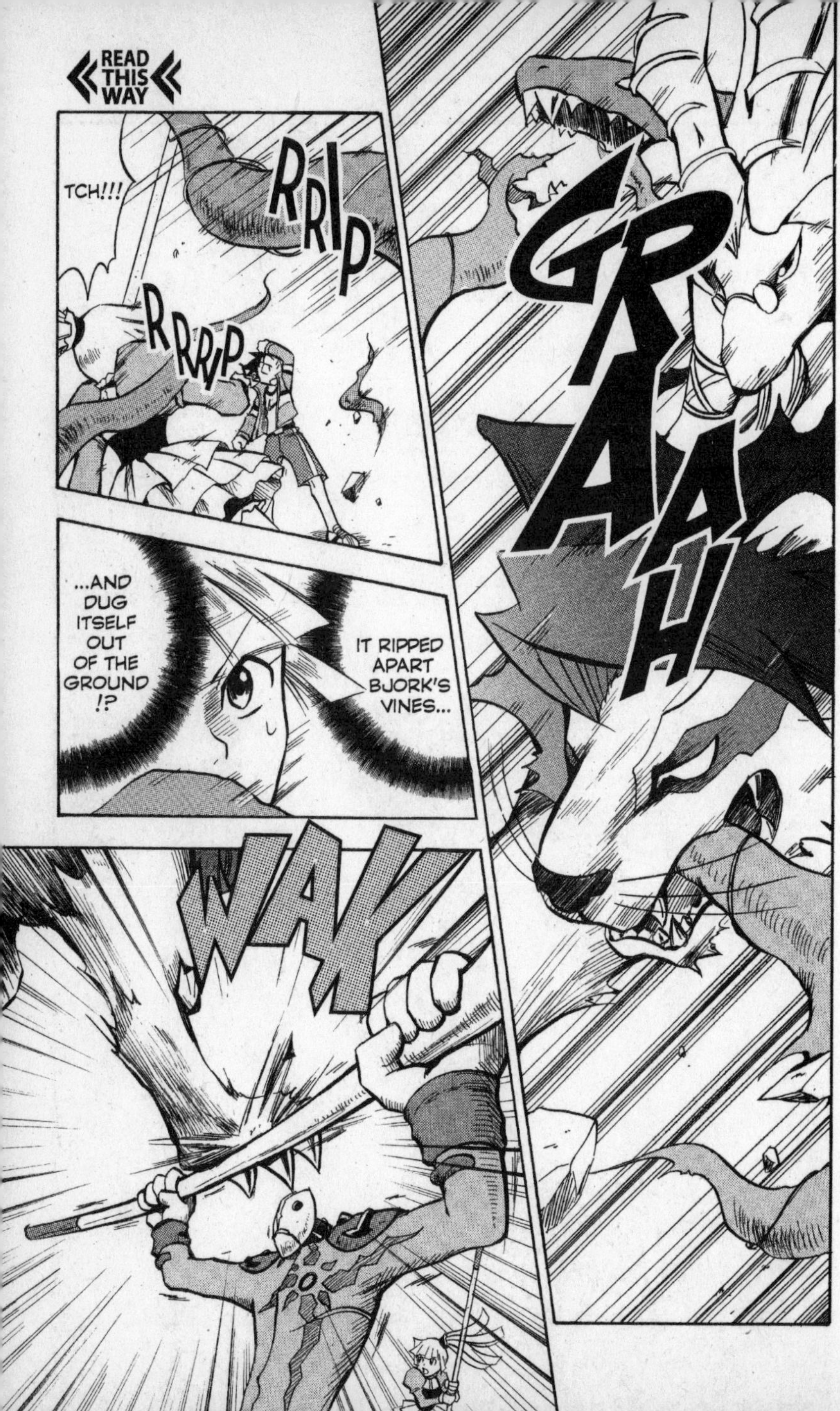
GRAAAH
RRIP
TCH!!!
RRRIP
IT RIPPED APART BJORK'S VINES...
...AND DUG ITSELF OUT OF THE GROUND!?
WAK

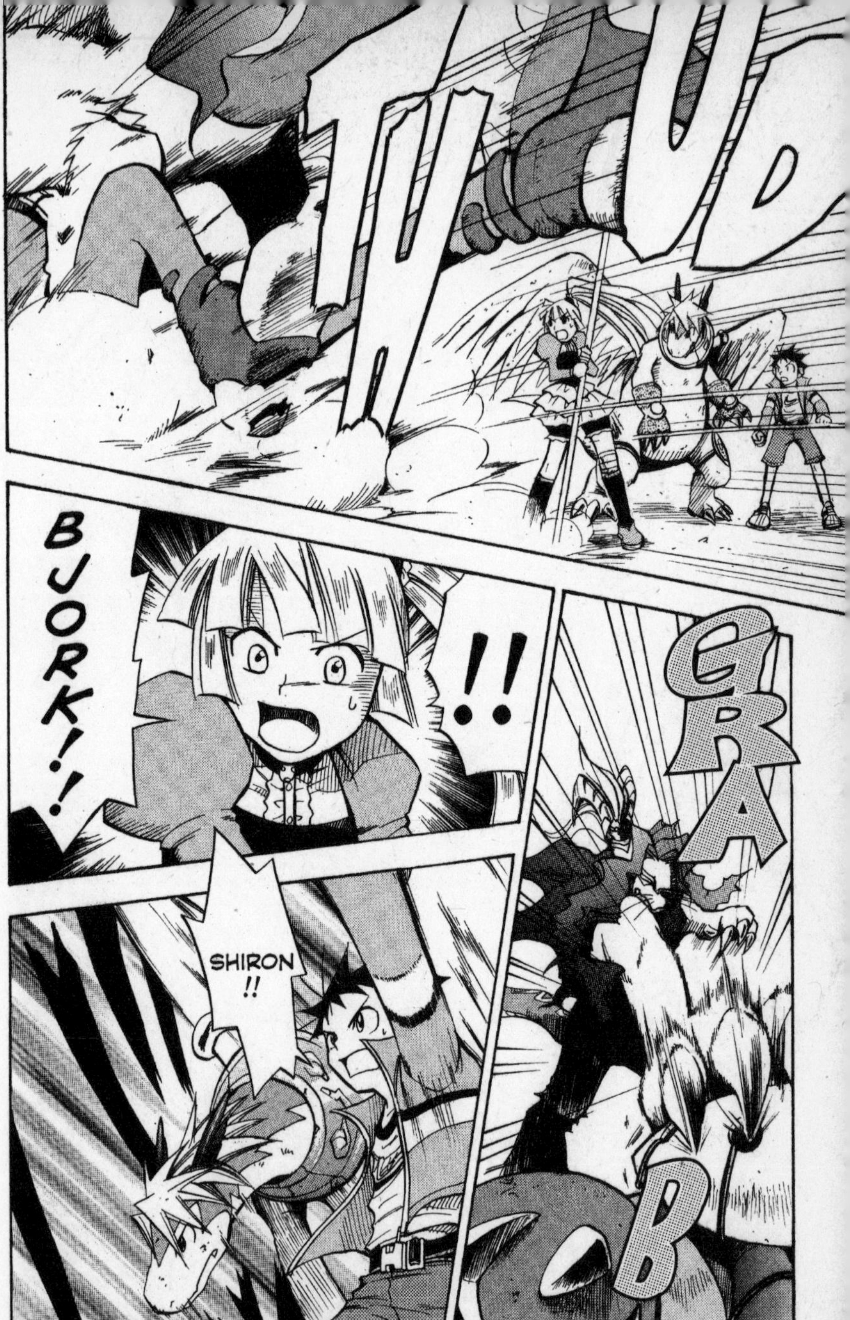
THUD
GRAB
!!
BJORK!!!
SHIRON !!

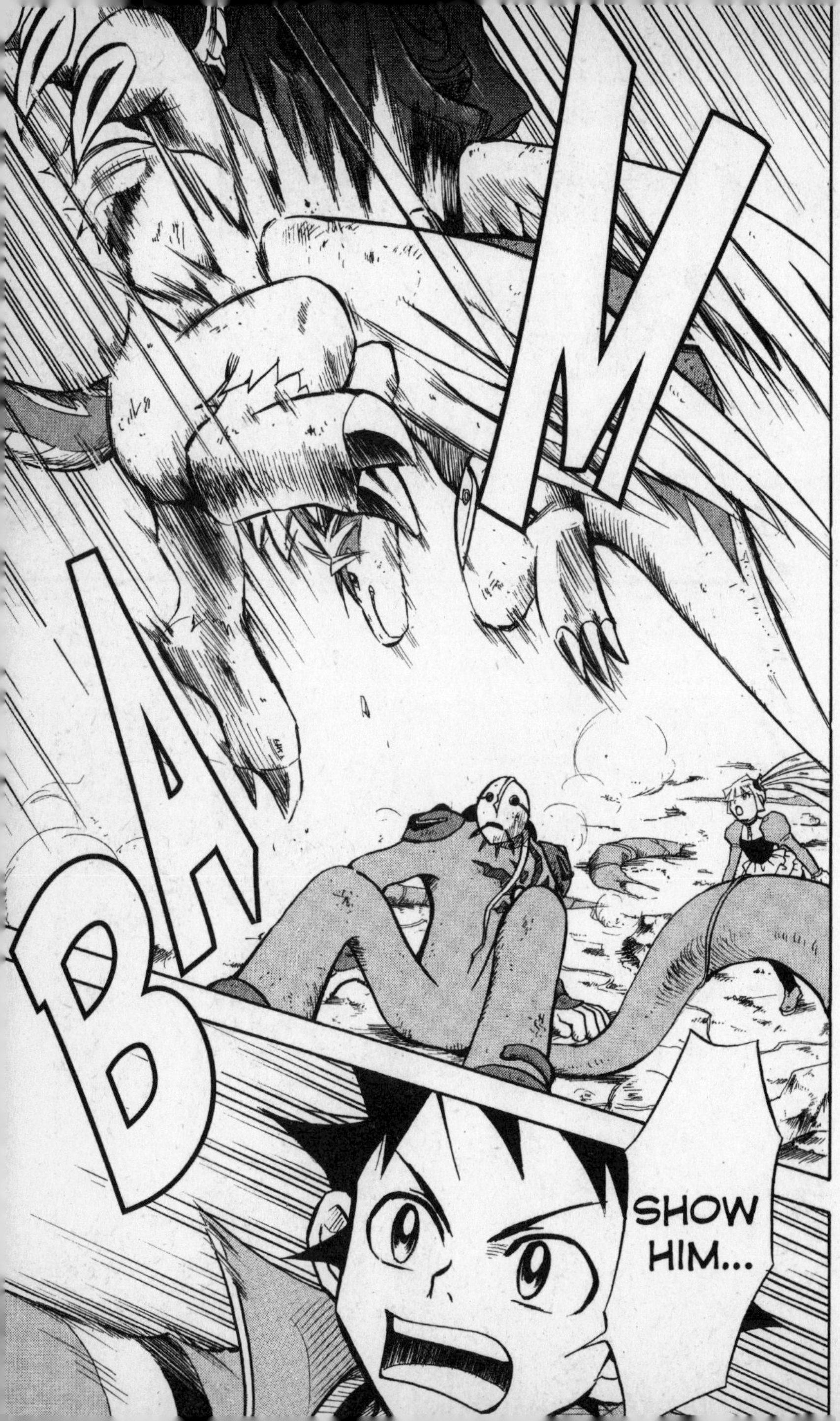
BAM
SHOW HIM...

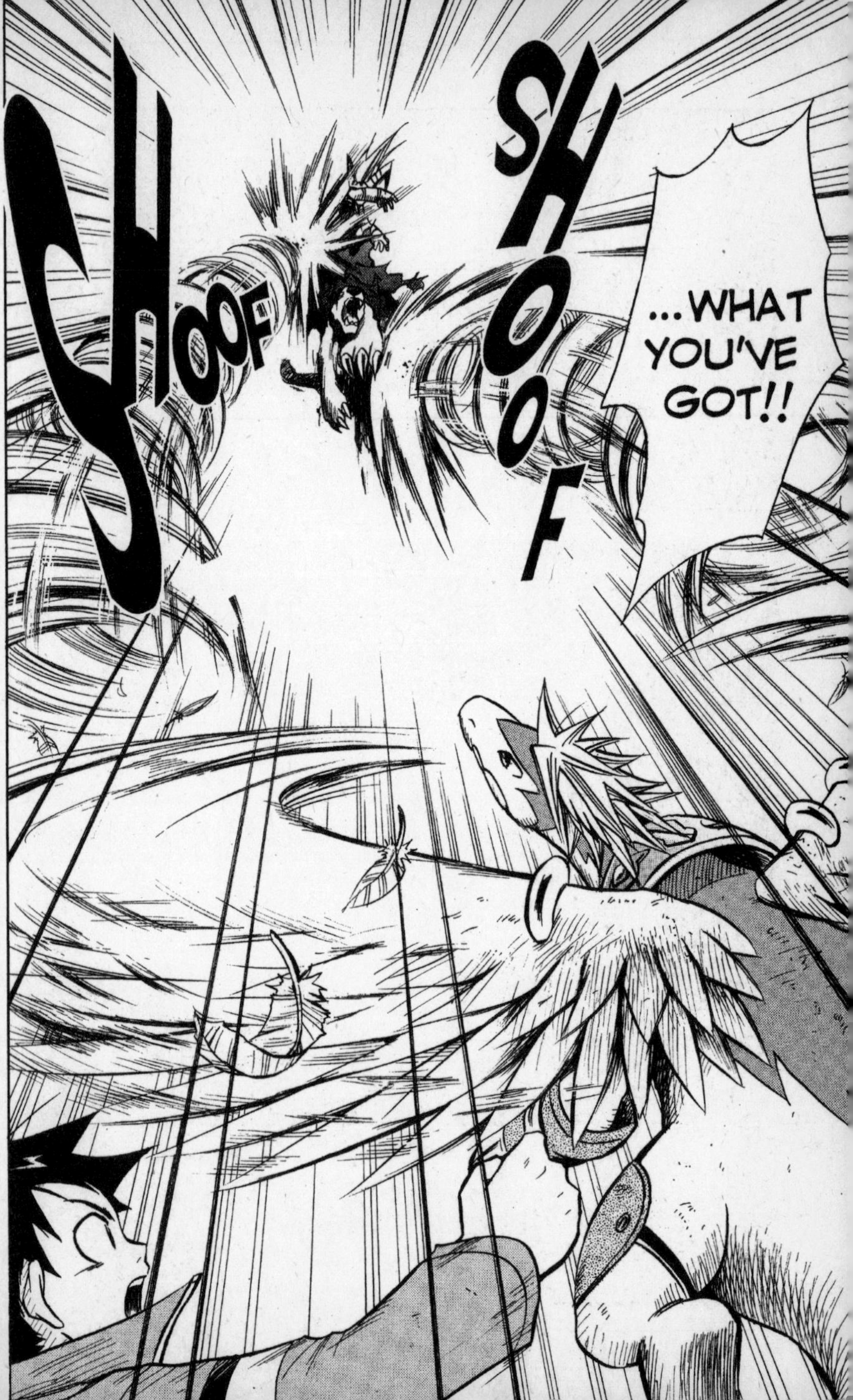
...WHAT YOU'VE GOT!!
SHOOOF
SHOOF

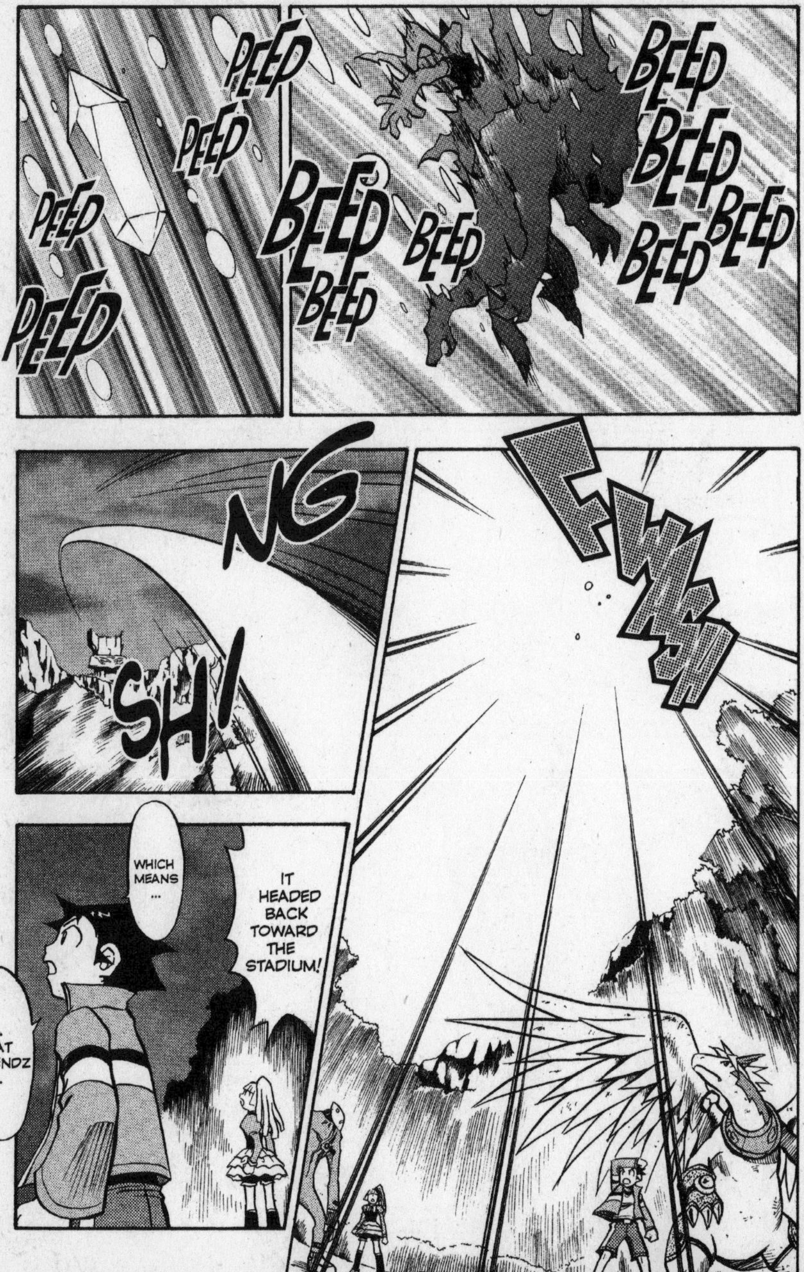
BEEP
BEEP
BEEP
BEEP
BEEP
BEEP
BEEP
PEEP
PEEP
PEEP
PEEP
FWASH
NG
SH!
IT HEADED BACK TOWARD THE STADIUM!
WHICH MEANS ...
... THAT LEGENDZ ...

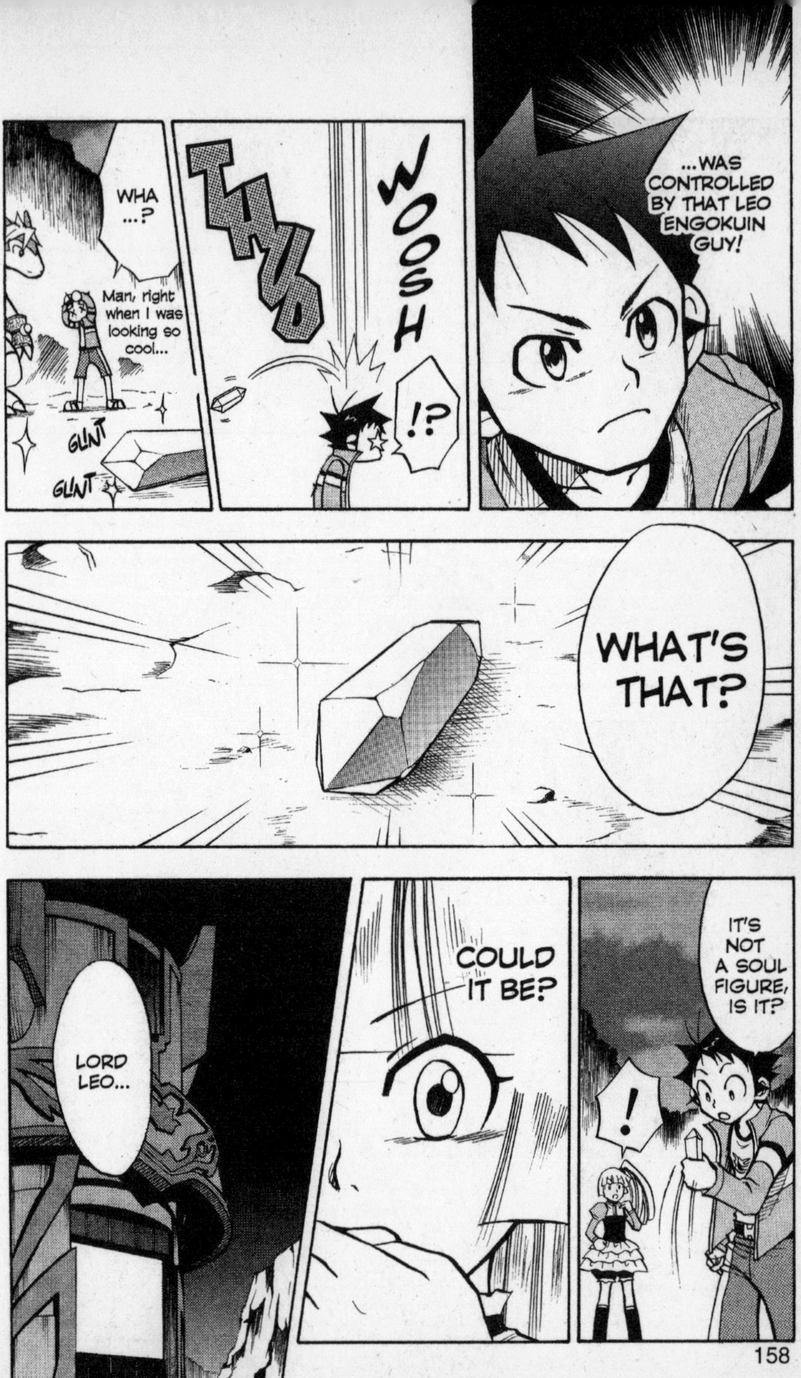

...WAS CONTROLLED BY THAT LEO ENGOKUIN GUY!
WOOSH
THUD
!?
WHA ...?
Man, right when I was looking so cool...
GLINT
GLINT
WHAT'S THAT?
IT'S NOT A SOUL FIGURE, IS IT?
!
COULD IT BE?
LORD LEO...

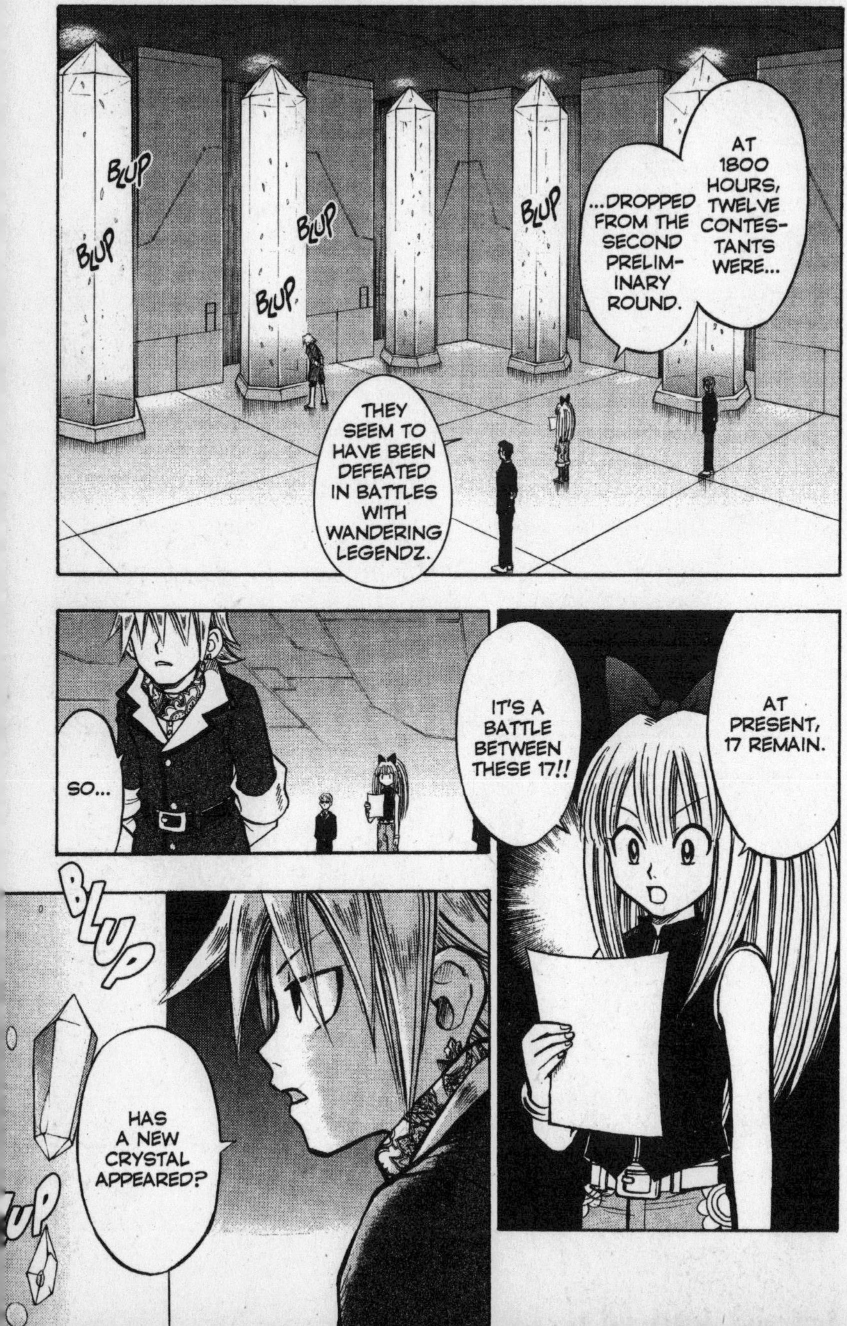
AT 1800 HOURS, TWELVE CONTES- TANTS WERE...
...DROPPED FROM THE SECOND PRELIM- INARY ROUND.
BLUP
BLUP
BLUP
BLUP
BLUP
THEY SEEM TO HAVE BEEN DEFEATED IN BATTLES WITH WANDERING LEGENDZ.
AT PRESENT, 17 REMAIN.
IT'S A BATTLE BETWEEN THESE 17!!
SO...
BLUP
HAS A NEW CRYSTAL APPEARED?

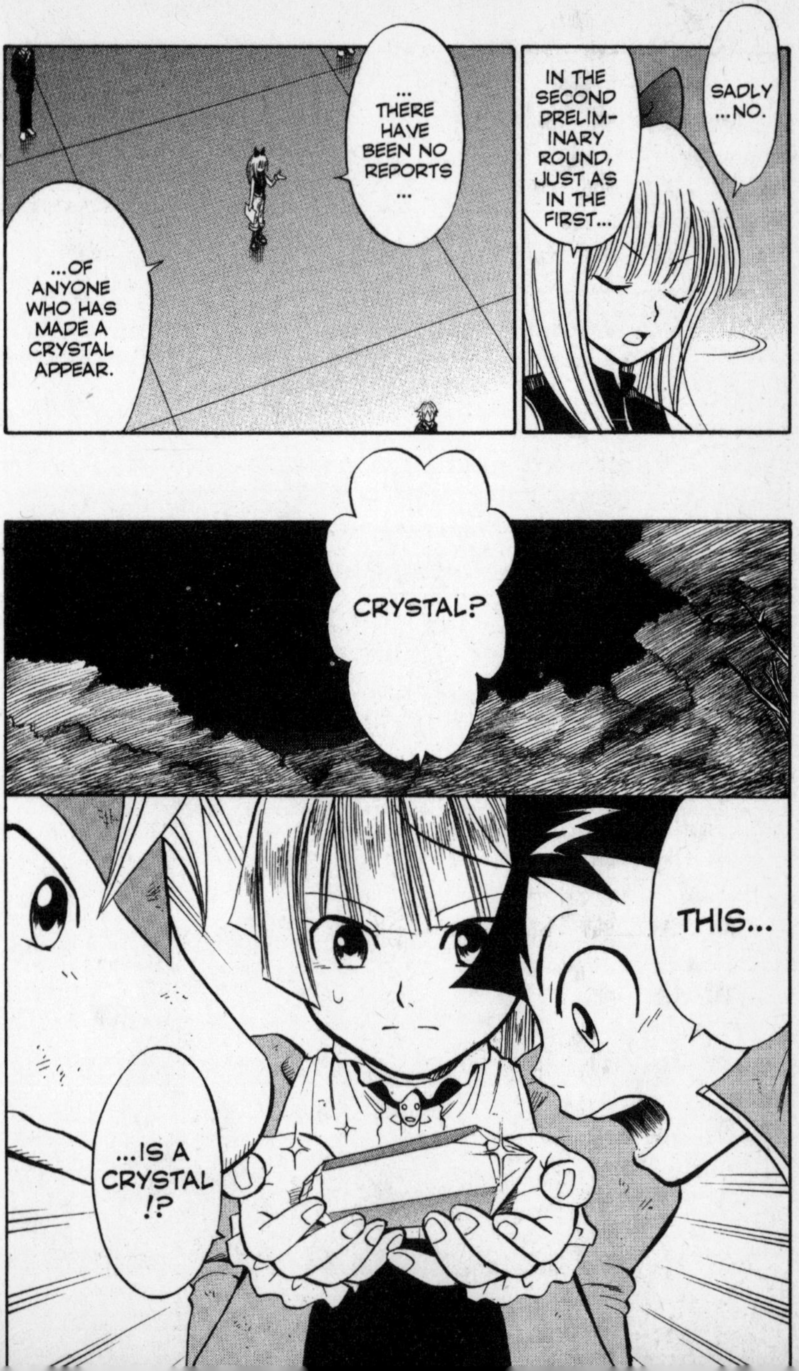
SADLY ...NO.
IN THE SECOND PRELIMINARY ROUND, JUST AS IN THE FIRST...
... THERE HAVE BEEN NO REPORTS ...
...OF ANYONE WHO HAS MADE A CRYSTAL APPEAR.
CRYSTAL?
THIS...
...IS A CRYSTAL !?

READ THIS WAY

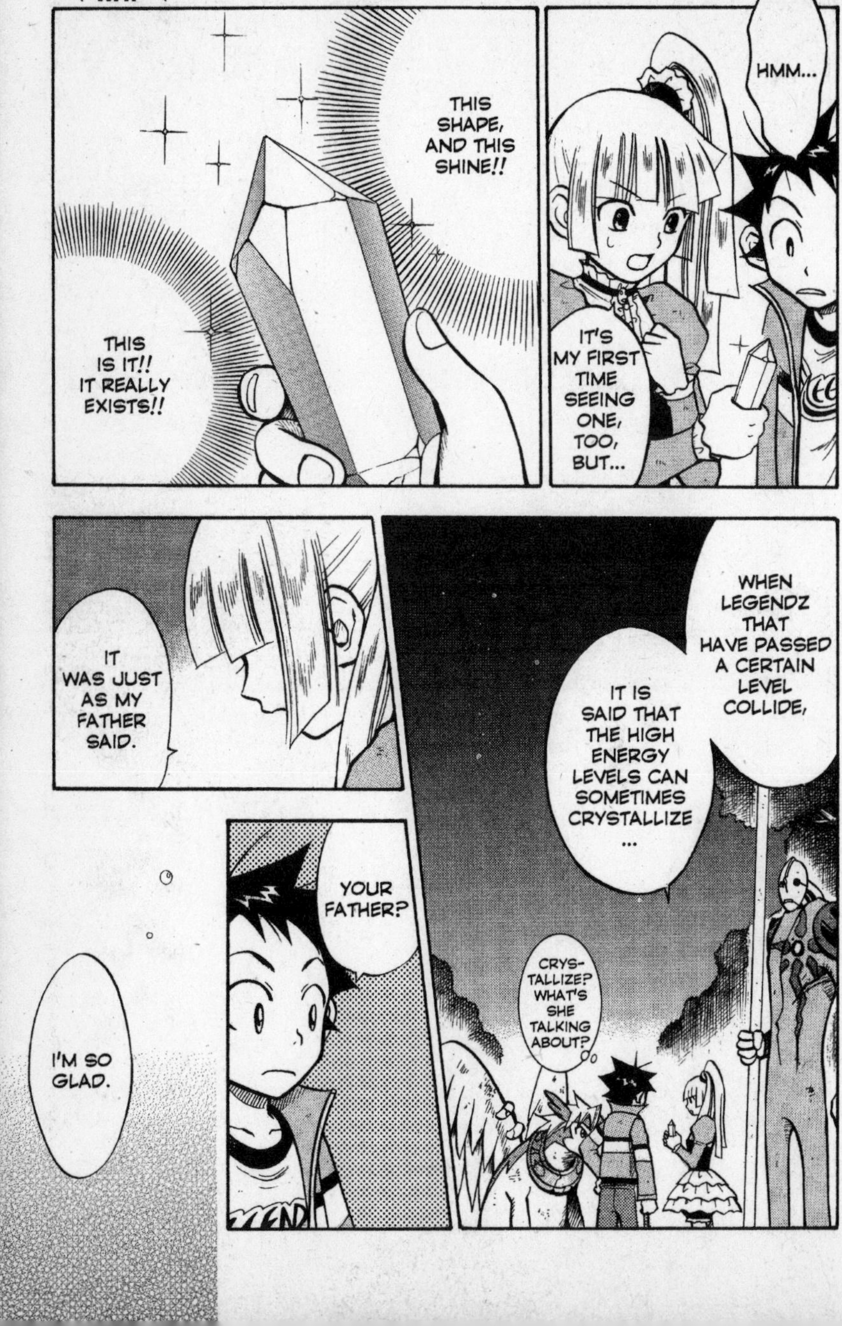

HMM...
IT'S MY FIRST TIME SEEING ONE, TOO, BUT...
THIS SHAPE, AND THIS SHINE!!
THIS IS IT!! IT REALLY EXISTS!!
WHEN LEGENDZ THAT HAVE PASSED A CERTAIN LEVEL COLLIDE,
IT IS SAID THAT THE HIGH ENERGY LEVELS CAN SOMETIMES CRYSTALLIZE ...
CRYS-TALLIZE? WHAT'S SHE TALKING ABOUT?
IT WAS JUST AS MY FATHER SAID.
YOUR FATHER?
I'M SO GLAD.

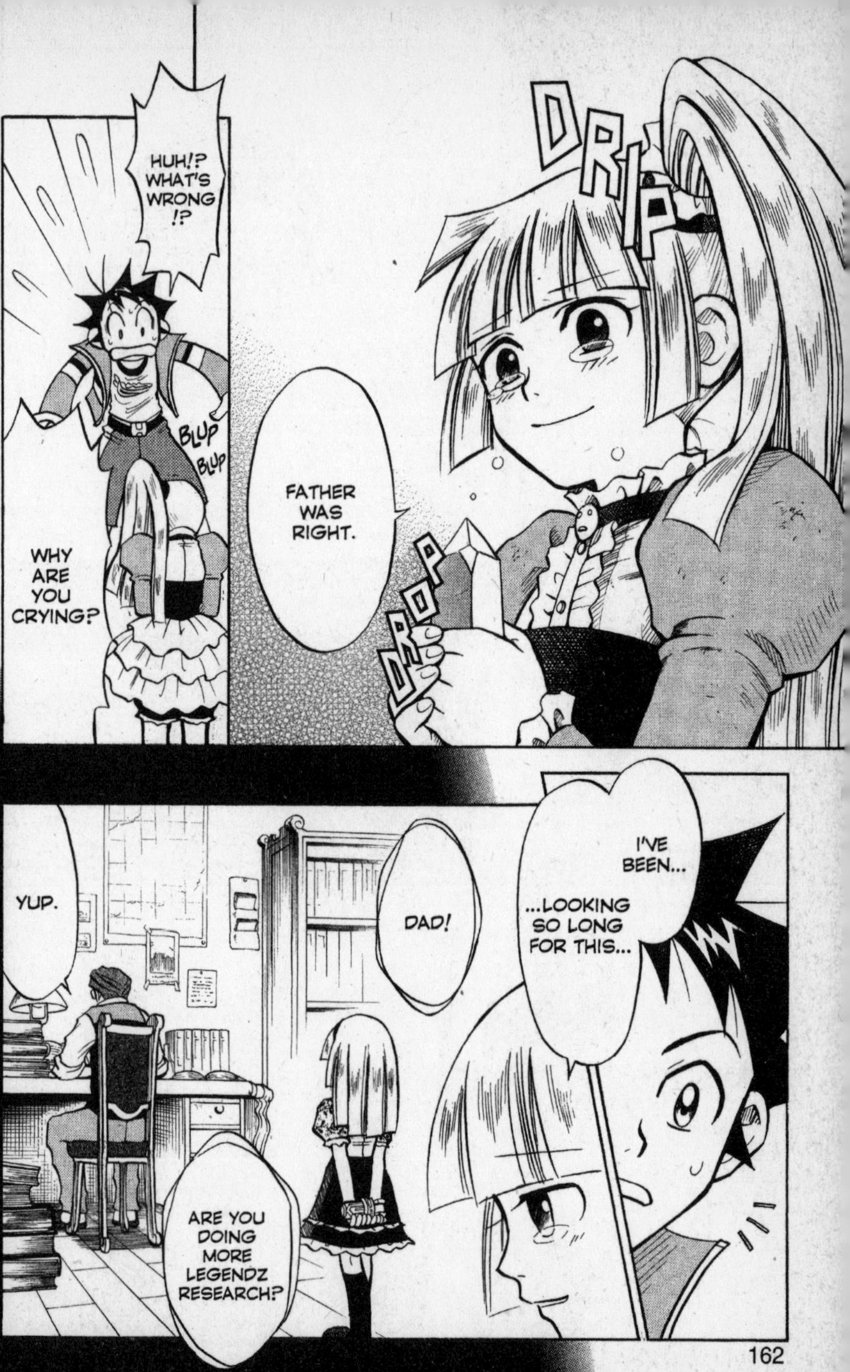
DRIP
FATHER WAS RIGHT.
DROP
HUH!? WHAT'S WRONG !?
BLUP
BLUP
WHY ARE YOU CRYING?
I'VE BEEN...
...LOOKING SO LONG FOR THIS...
DAD!
ARE YOU DOING MORE LEGENDZ RESEARCH?
YUP.

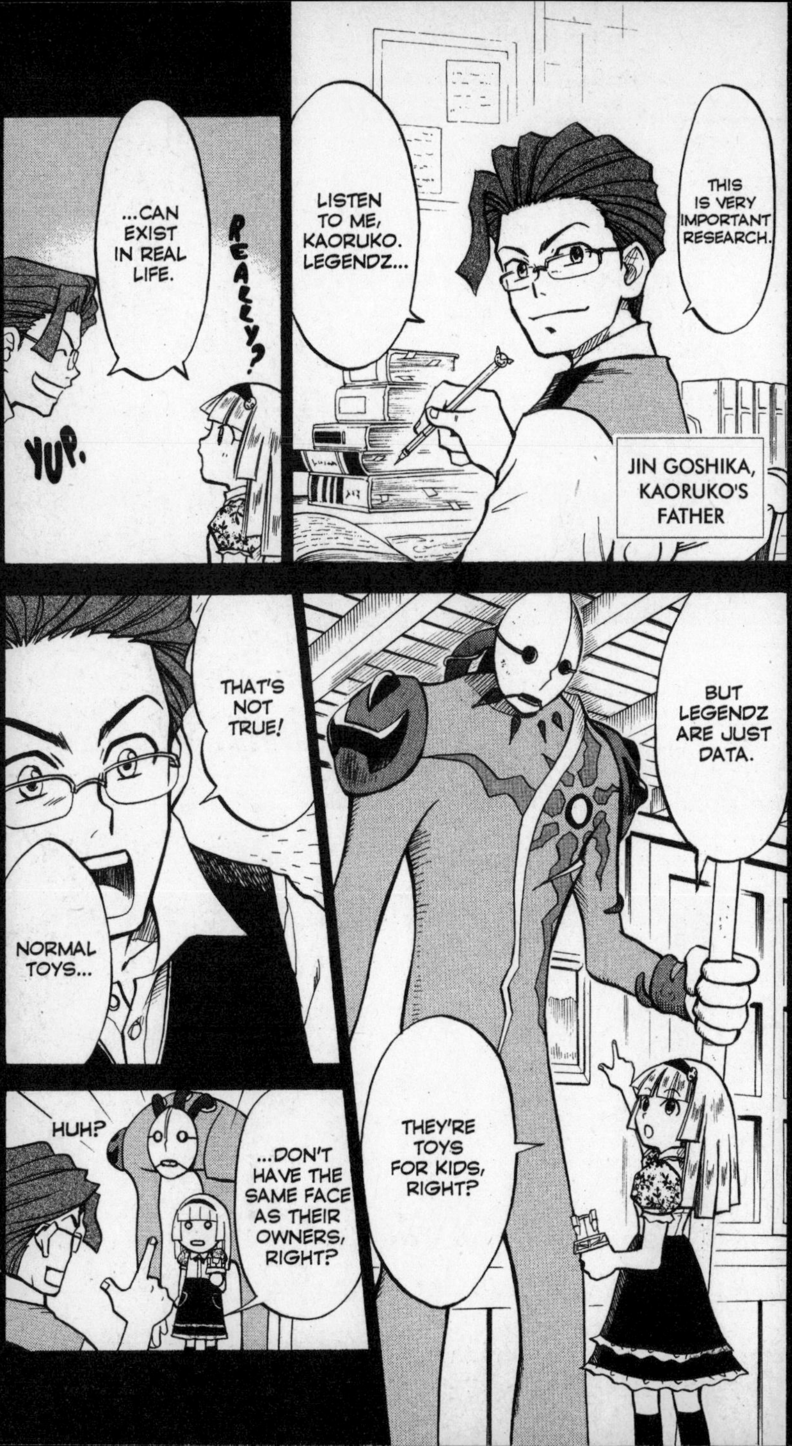
THIS IS VERY IMPORTANT RESEARCH.
JIN GOSHIKA, KAORUKO'S FATHER
LISTEN TO ME, KAORUKO. LEGENDZ...
...CAN EXIST IN REAL LIFE.
REALLY?
YUP.
BUT LEGENDZ ARE JUST DATA.
THEY'RE TOYS FOR KIDS, RIGHT?
THAT'S NOT TRUE!
NORMAL TOYS...
...DON'T HAVE THE SAME FACE AS THEIR OWNERS, RIGHT?
HUH?

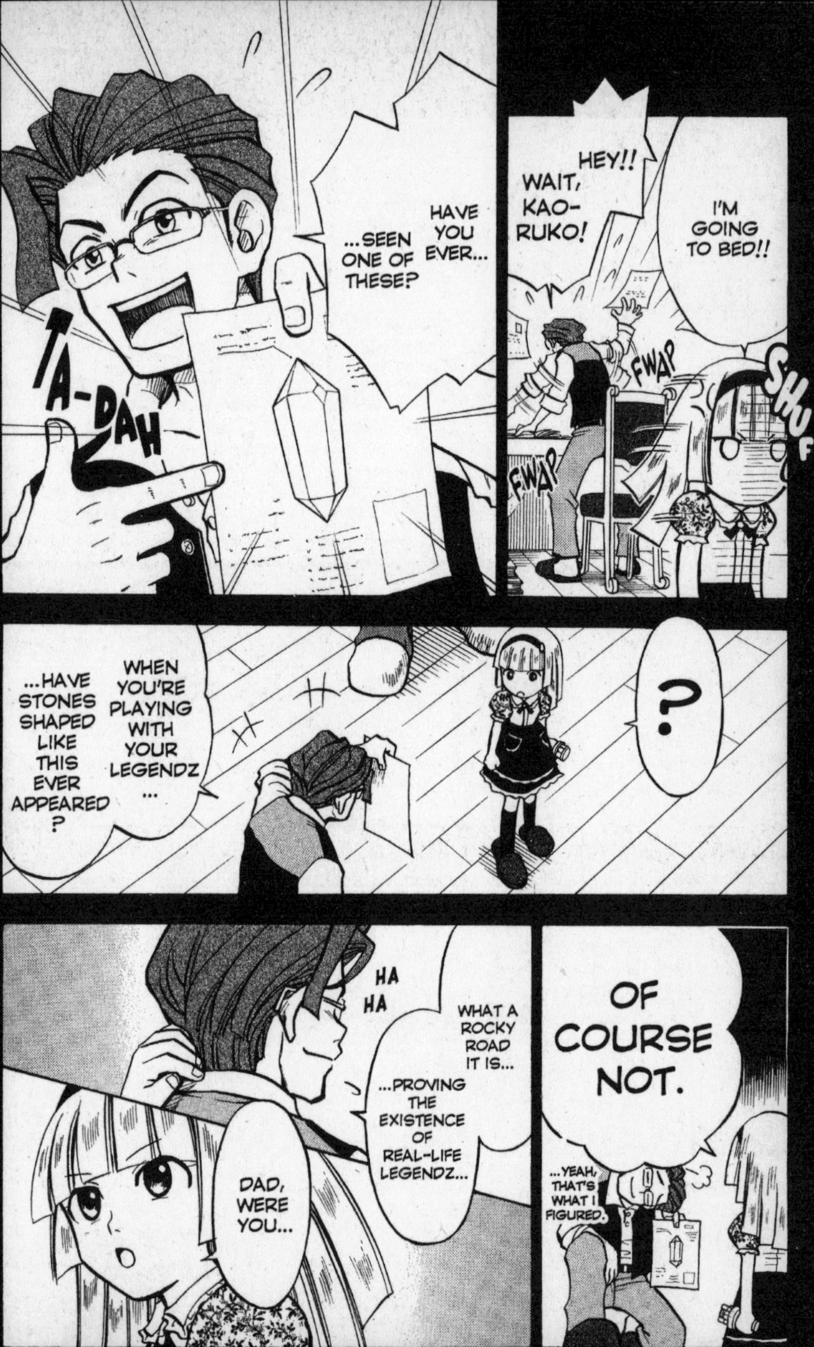
I'M GOING TO BED!!
HEY!! WAIT, KAO-RUKO!
FWAP
SHUF
FWAP
HAVE YOU EVER... ...SEEN ONE OF THESE?
TA-DAH
?
WHEN YOU'RE PLAYING WITH YOUR LEGENDZ... ...HAVE STONES SHAPED LIKE THIS EVER APPEARED?
OF COURSE NOT.
...YEAH, THAT'S WHAT I FIGURED.
HA HA
WHAT A ROCKY ROAD IT IS... ...PROVING THE EXISTENCE OF REAL-LIFE LEGENDZ...
DAD, WERE YOU...

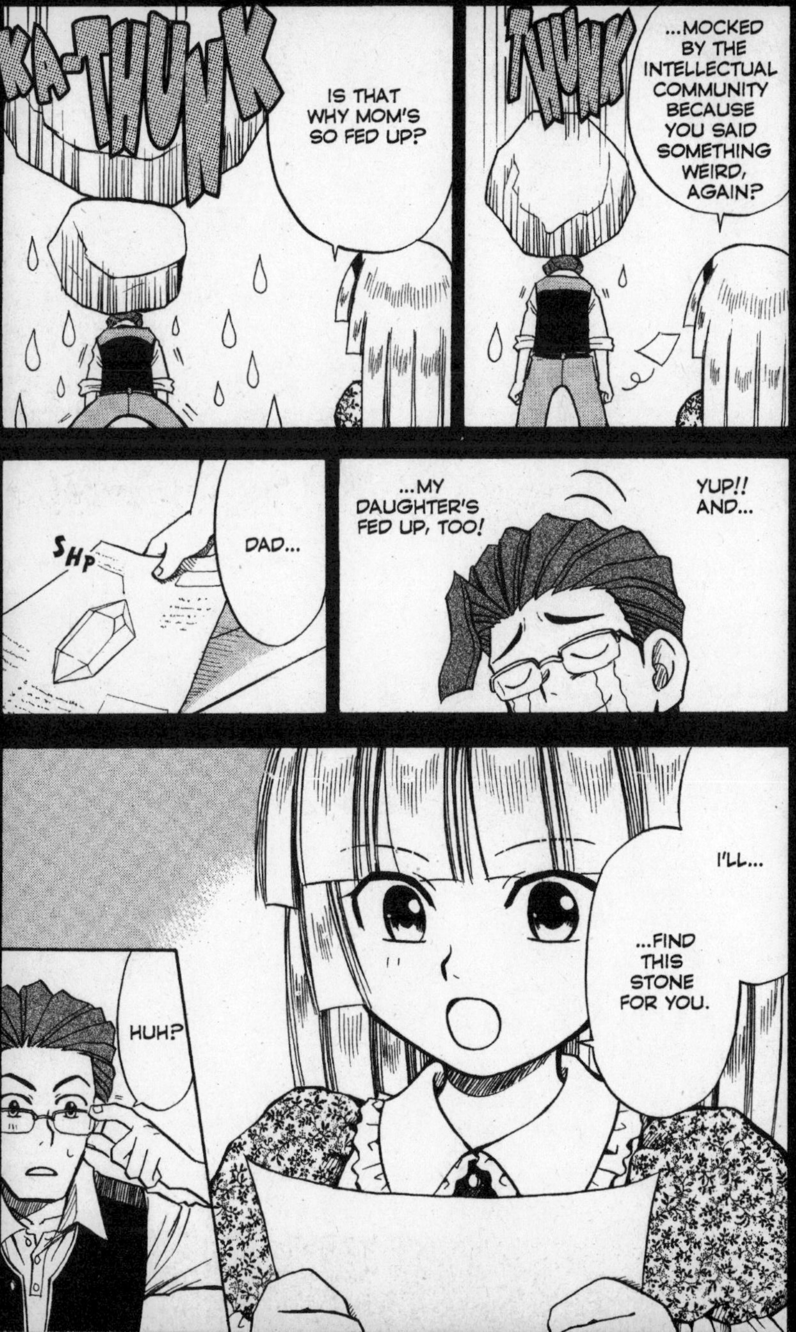
THUNK
...MOCKED BY THE INTELLECTUAL COMMUNITY BECAUSE YOU SAID SOMETHING WEIRD, AGAIN?
KA-THUNK
IS THAT WHY MOM'S SO FED UP?
YUP!! AND...
...MY DAUGHTER'S FED UP, TOO!
DAD...
SHP
I'LL...
...FIND THIS STONE FOR YOU.
HUH?

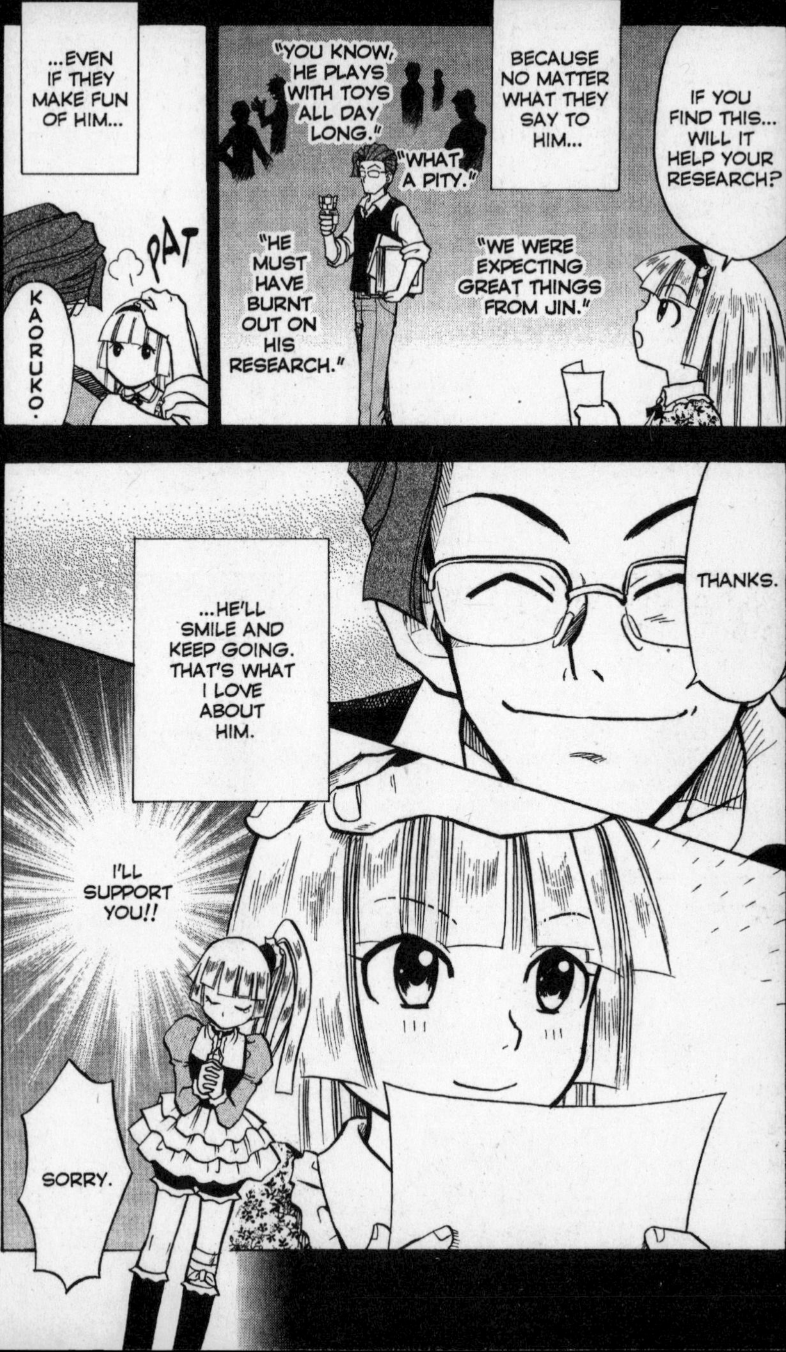
IF YOU FIND THIS... WILL IT HELP YOUR RESEARCH?
BECAUSE NO MATTER WHAT THEY SAY TO HIM...
"YOU KNOW, HE PLAYS WITH TOYS ALL DAY LONG."
"WHAT A PITY."
"WE WERE EXPECTING GREAT THINGS FROM JIN."
"HE MUST HAVE BURNT OUT ON HIS RESEARCH."
...EVEN IF THEY MAKE FUN OF HIM...
PAT
KAORUKO.
THANKS.
...HE'LL SMILE AND KEEP GOING. THAT'S WHAT I LOVE ABOUT HIM.
I'LL SUPPORT YOU!!
SORRY.

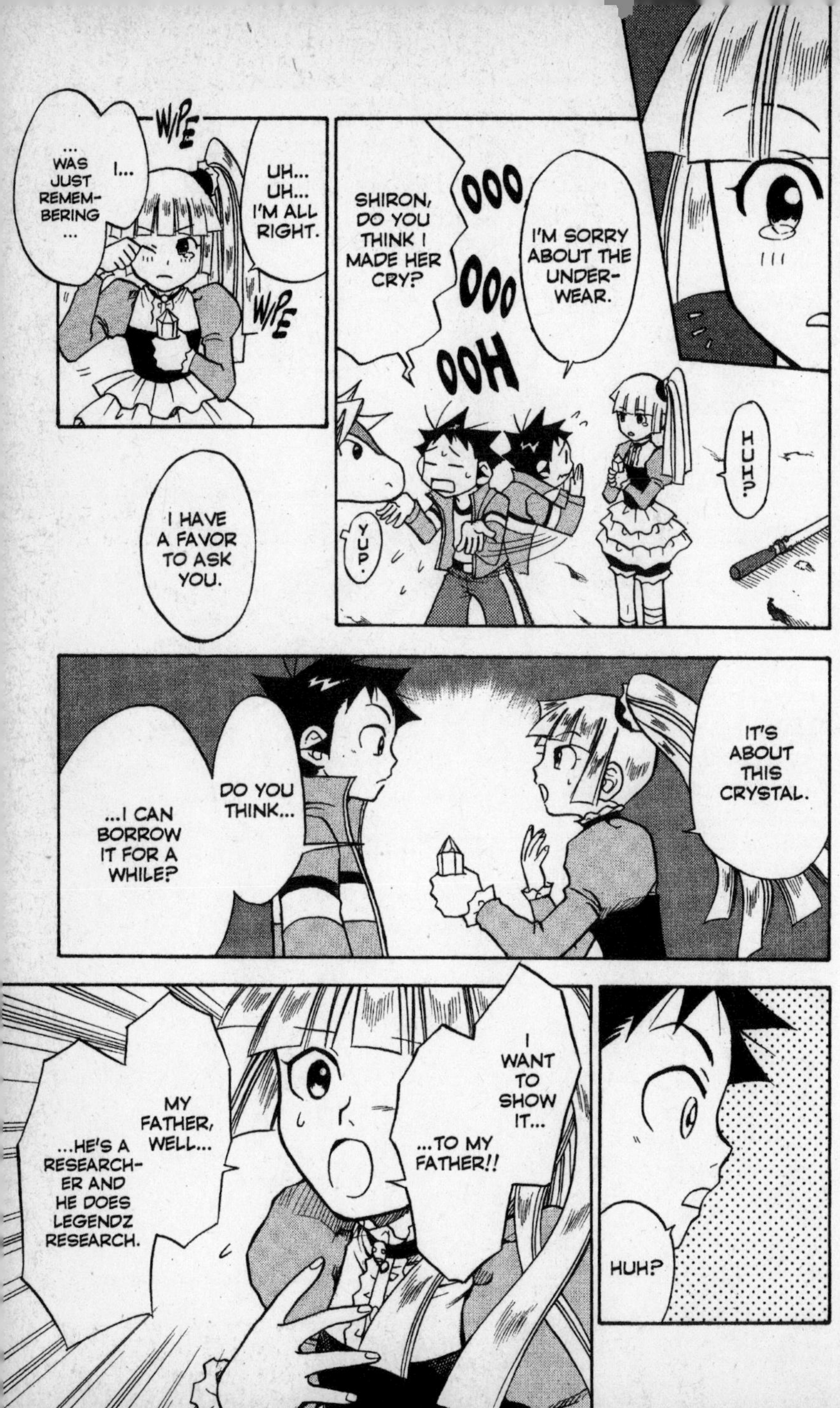
I'M SORRY ABOUT THE UNDERWEAR.
OOOOOOOOH
SHIRON, DO YOU THINK I MADE HER CRY?
HUH?
YUP.
UH... UH... I'M ALL RIGHT.
WIPE
I...
...WAS JUST REMEMBERING...
WIPE
I HAVE A FAVOR TO ASK YOU.
IT'S ABOUT THIS CRYSTAL.
DO YOU THINK...
...I CAN BORROW IT FOR A WHILE?
HUH?
I WANT TO SHOW IT...
...TO MY FATHER!!
MY FATHER, WELL...
...HE'S A RESEARCHER AND HE DOES LEGENDZ RESEARCH.

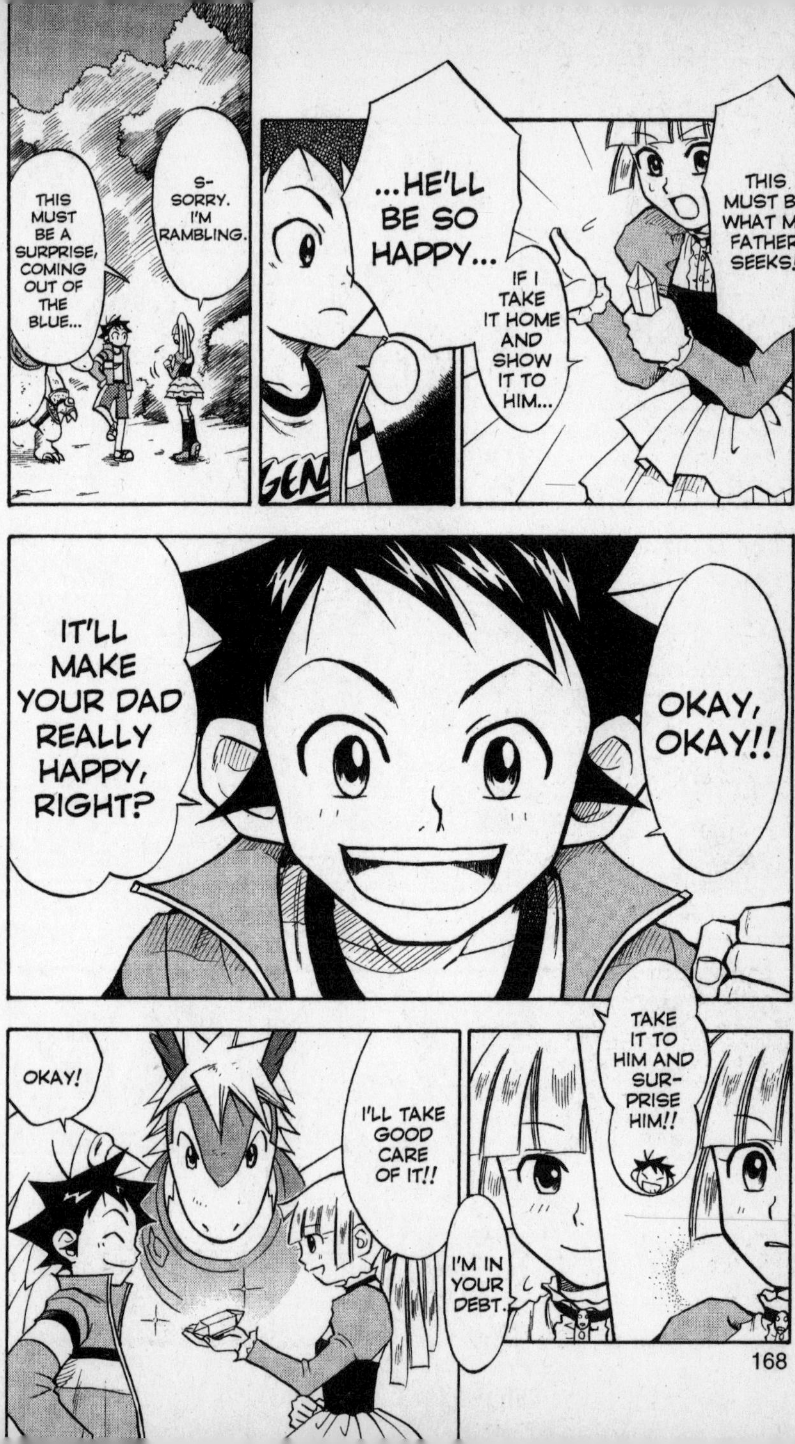
THIS MUST BE WHAT MY FATHER SEEKS!!
IF I TAKE IT HOME AND SHOW IT TO HIM...
...HE'LL BE SO HAPPY...
S-SORRY. I'M RAMBLING.
THIS MUST BE A SURPRISE, COMING OUT OF THE BLUE...
OKAY, OKAY!!
IT'LL MAKE YOUR DAD REALLY HAPPY, RIGHT?
TAKE IT TO HIM AND SUR-PRISE HIM!!
I'M IN YOUR DEBT.
I'LL TAKE GOOD CARE OF IT!!
OKAY!

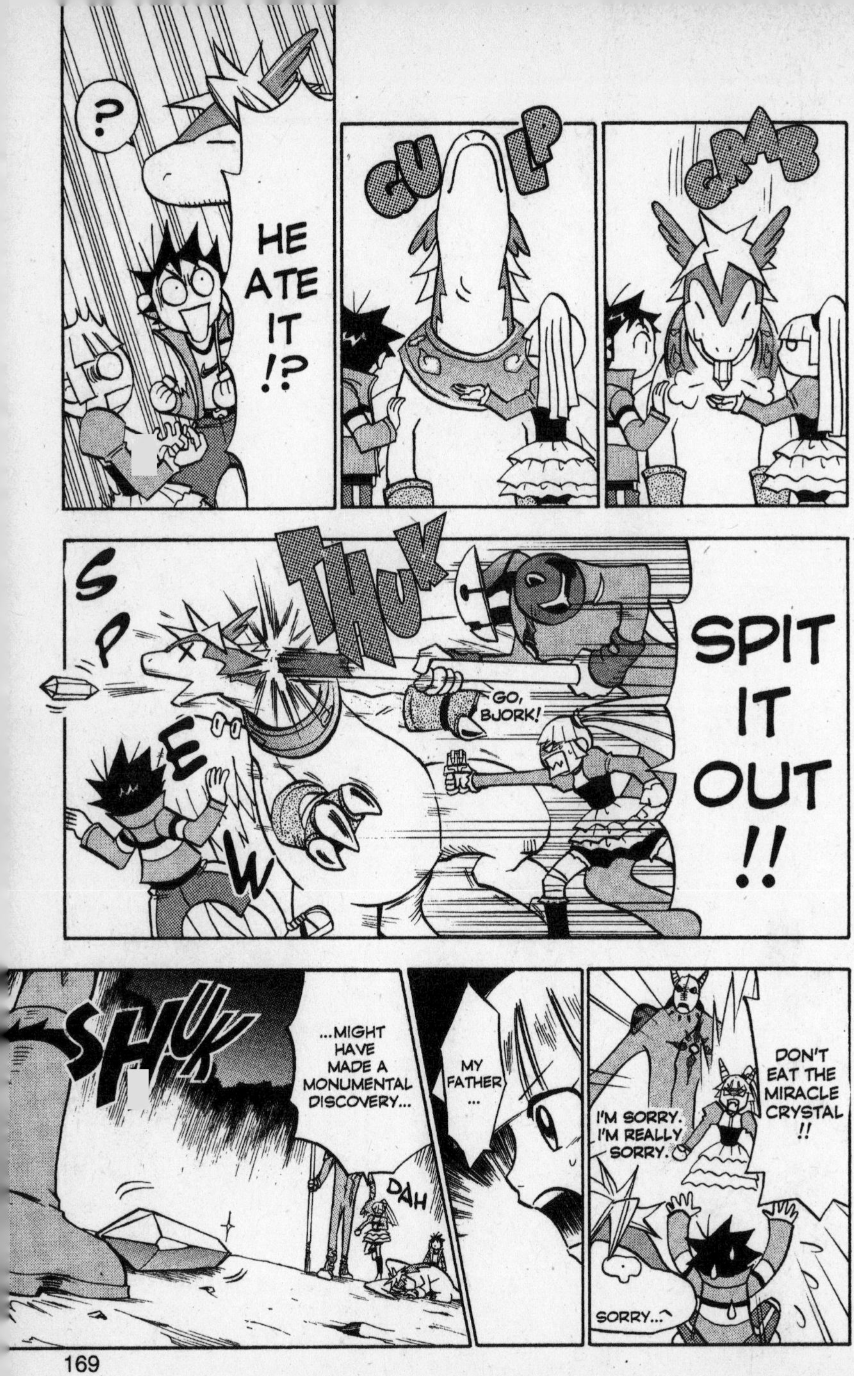
GRAB
GULP
?
HE ATE IT!?
SPIT IT OUT!!
THUK
GO, BJORK!
SPEW
DON'T EAT THE MIRACLE CRYSTAL!!
I'M SORRY. I'M REALLY SORRY.
SORRY...
MY FATHER...
...MIGHT HAVE MADE A MONUMENTAL DISCOVERY...
DAH
SHUK

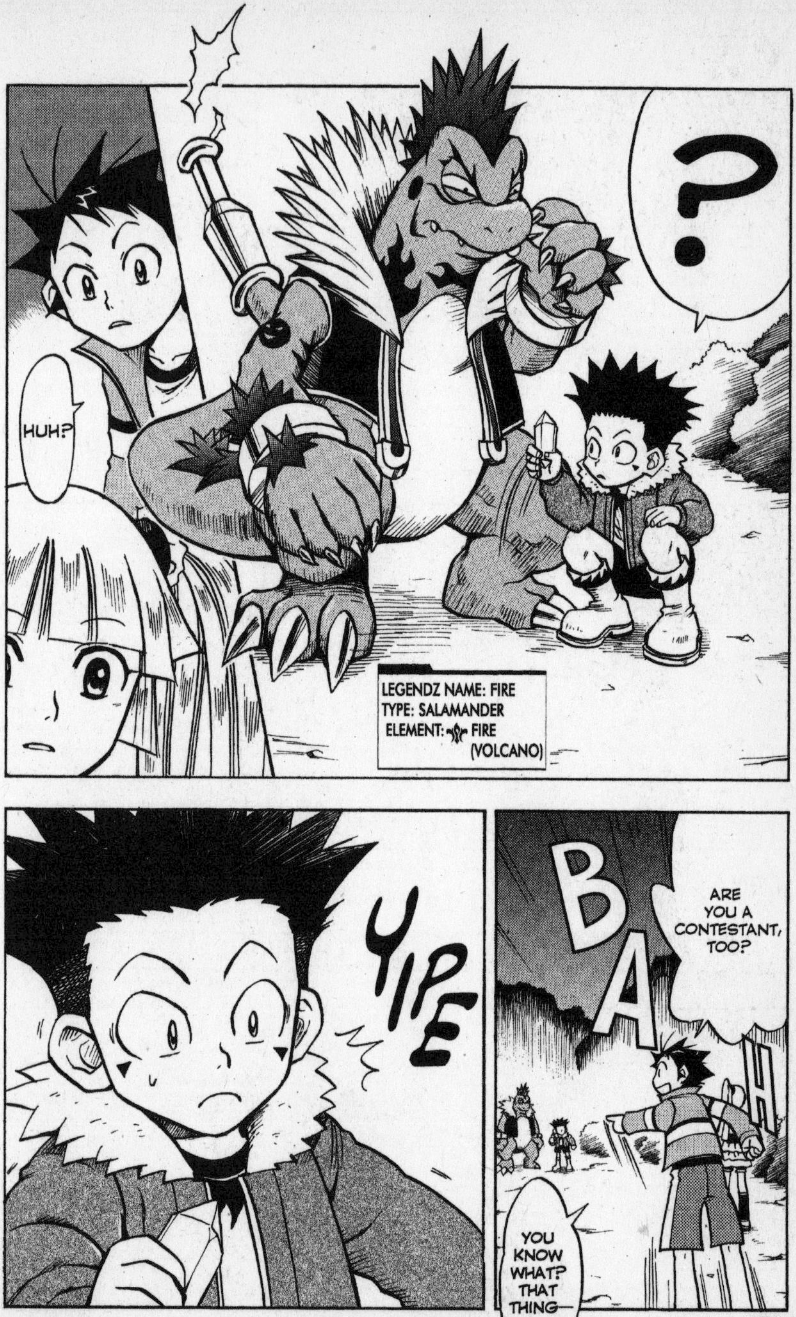
?
HUH?
LEGENDZ NAME: FIRE
TYPE: SALAMANDER
ELEMENT: FIRE (VOLCANO)
BAAH
ARE YOU A CONTESTANT, TOO?
YOU KNOW WHAT? THAT THING—
YIPE

READ THIS WAY

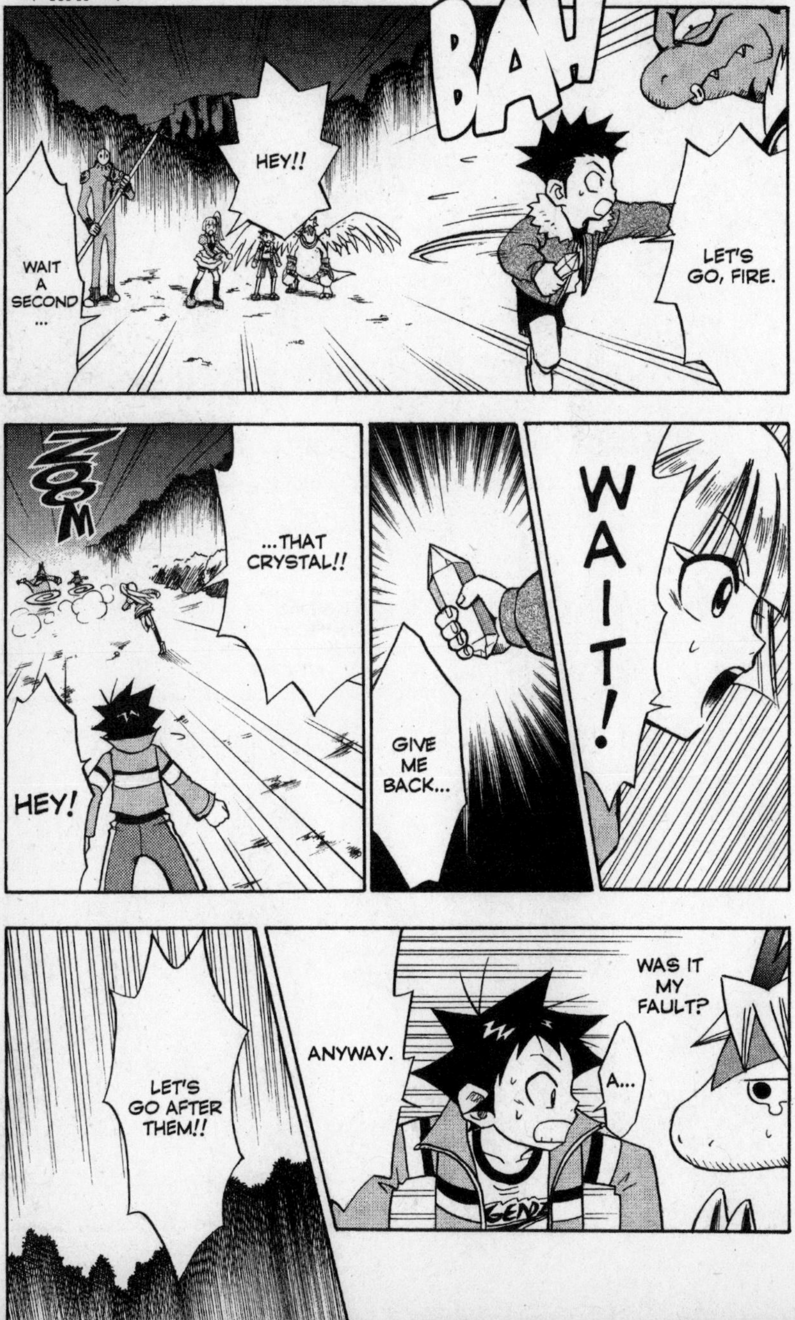

LET'S GO, FIRE.
BAH
HEY!!
WAIT A SECOND...
WAIT!
GIVE ME BACK...
...THAT CRYSTAL!!
ZOOM
HEY!
WAS IT MY FAULT?
A...
ANYWAY.
LET'S GO AFTER THEM!!

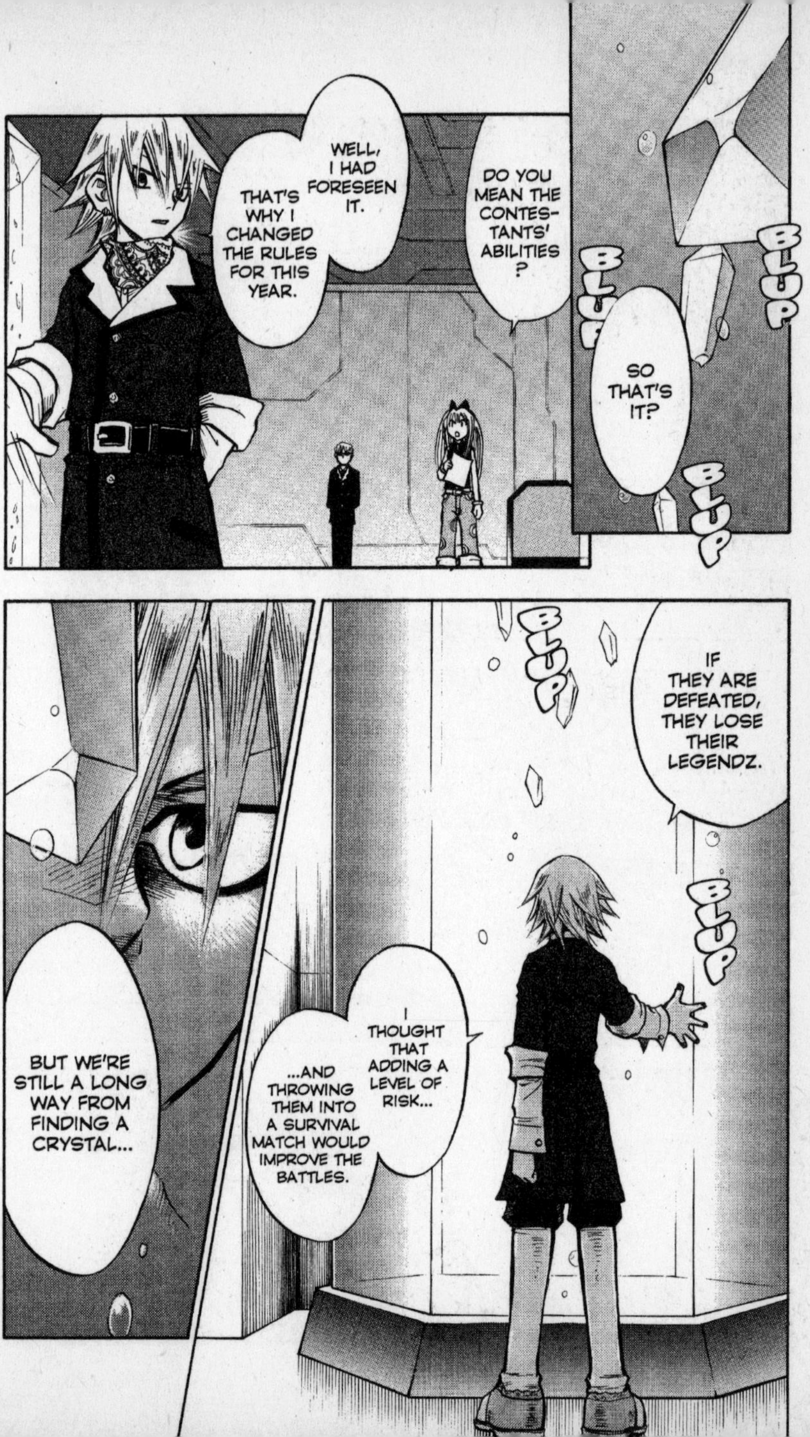
BLUP
BLUP
SO THAT'S IT?
BLUP
DO YOU MEAN THE CONTESTANTS' ABILITIES?
WELL, I HAD FORESEEN IT.
THAT'S WHY I CHANGED THE RULES FOR THIS YEAR.
BLUP
IF THEY ARE DEFEATED, THEY LOSE THEIR LEGENDZ.
BLUP
I THOUGHT THAT ADDING A LEVEL OF RISK...
...AND THROWING THEM INTO A SURVIVAL MATCH WOULD IMPROVE THE BATTLES.
BUT WE'RE STILL A LONG WAY FROM FINDING A CRYSTAL...

READ THIS WAY

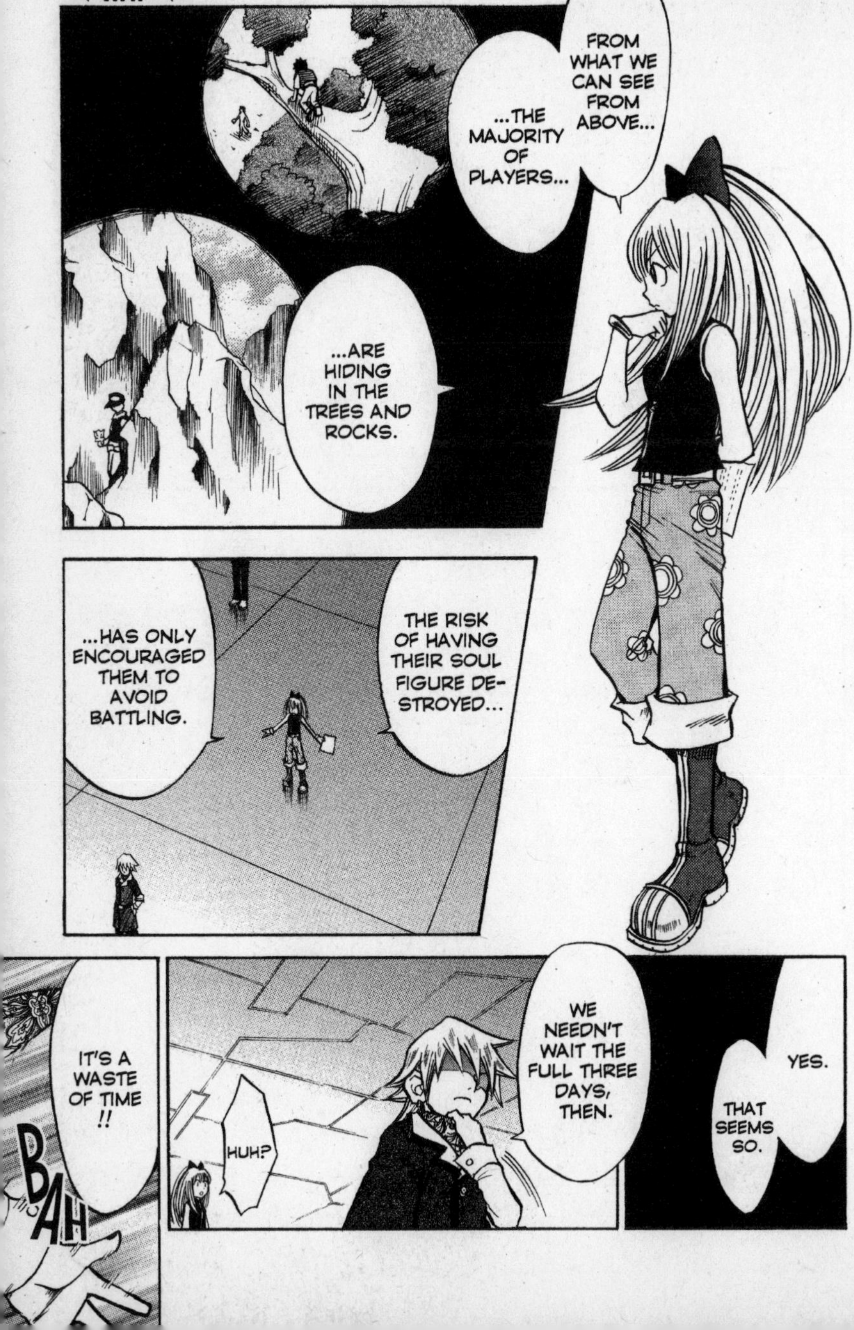

FROM WHAT WE CAN SEE FROM ABOVE...
...THE MAJORITY OF PLAYERS...
...ARE HIDING IN THE TREES AND ROCKS.
THE RISK OF HAVING THEIR SOUL FIGURE DE-STROYED...
...HAS ONLY ENCOURAGED THEM TO AVOID BATTLING.
YES.
THAT SEEMS SO.
WE NEEDN'T WAIT THE FULL THREE DAYS, THEN.
HUH?
IT'S A WASTE OF TIME !!
BAH

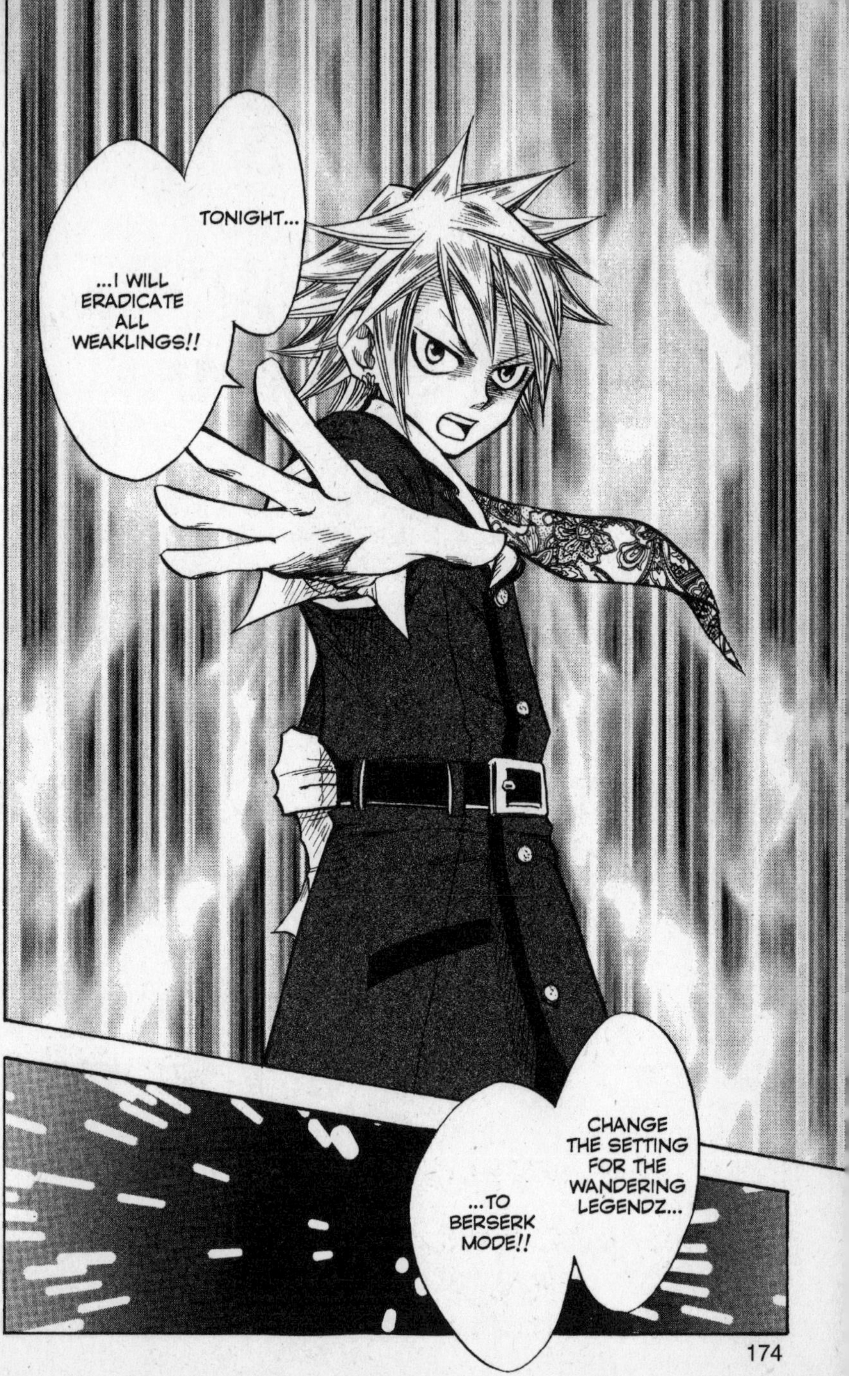
TONIGHT...
...I WILL ERADICATE ALL WEAKLINGS!!
CHANGE THE SETTING FOR THE WANDERING LEGENDZ...
...TO BERSERK MODE!!

READ THIS WAY

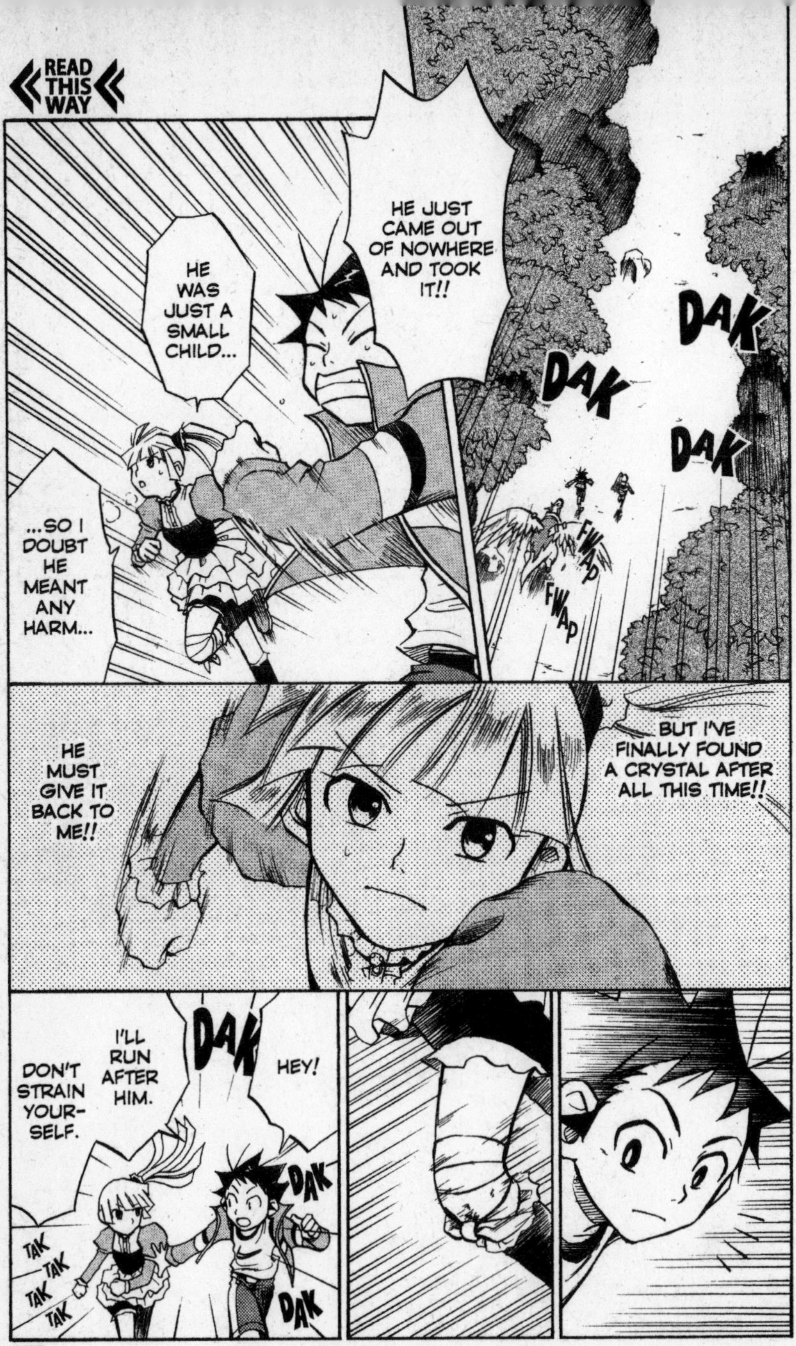
HE JUST CAME OUT OF NOWHERE AND TOOK IT!!
HE WAS JUST A SMALL CHILD...
...SO I DOUBT HE MEANT ANY HARM...
DAK
DAK
DAK
FWAP
FWAP
BUT I'VE FINALLY FOUND A CRYSTAL AFTER ALL THIS TIME!!
HE MUST GIVE IT BACK TO ME!!
HEY!
DAK
I'LL RUN AFTER HIM.
DON'T STRAIN YOUR-SELF.
DAK
DAK
TAK
TAK
TAK
TAK

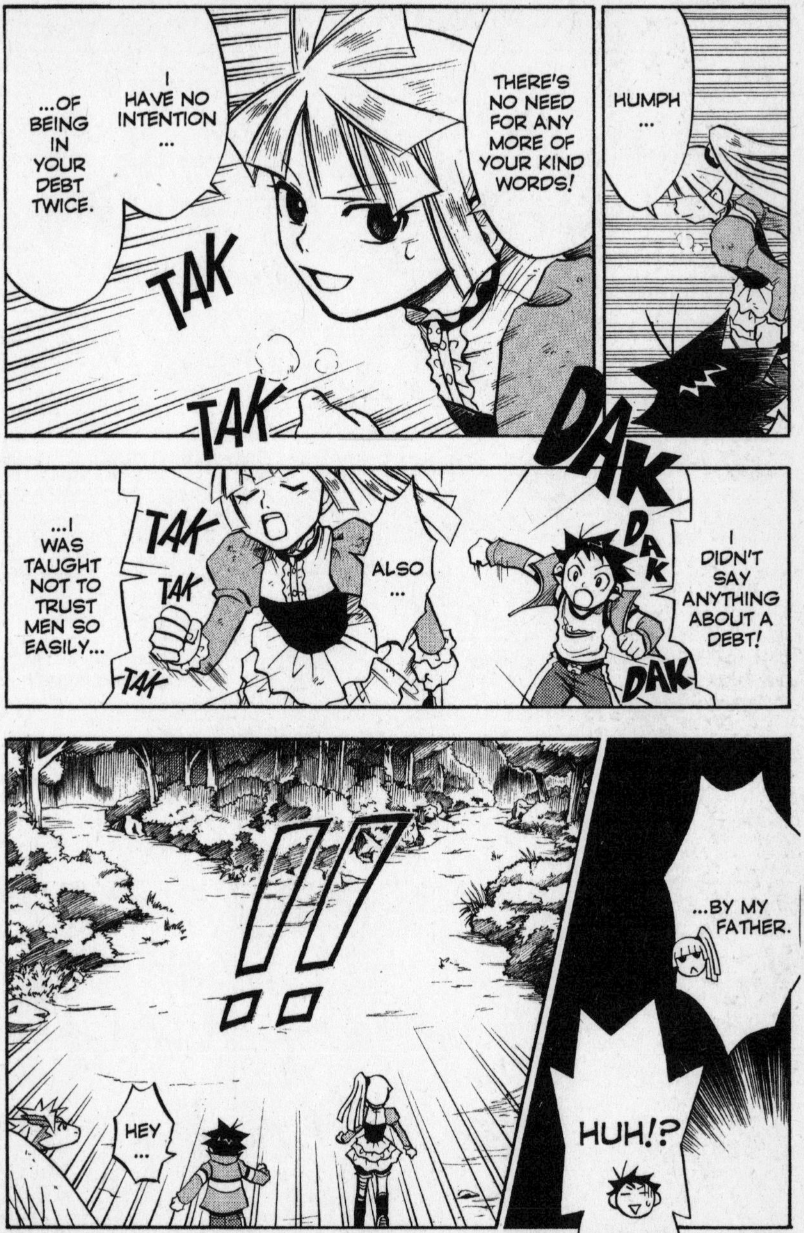
HUMPH ...
THERE'S NO NEED FOR ANY MORE OF YOUR KIND WORDS!
I HAVE NO INTENTION ...
...OF BEING IN YOUR DEBT TWICE.
TAK
TAK
DAK
DAK
I DIDN'T SAY ANYTHING ABOUT A DEBT!
DAK
ALSO ...
...I WAS TAUGHT NOT TO TRUST MEN SO EASILY...
TAK
TAK
TAK
...BY MY FATHER.
HUH!?
!!
HEY ...

READ THIS WAY

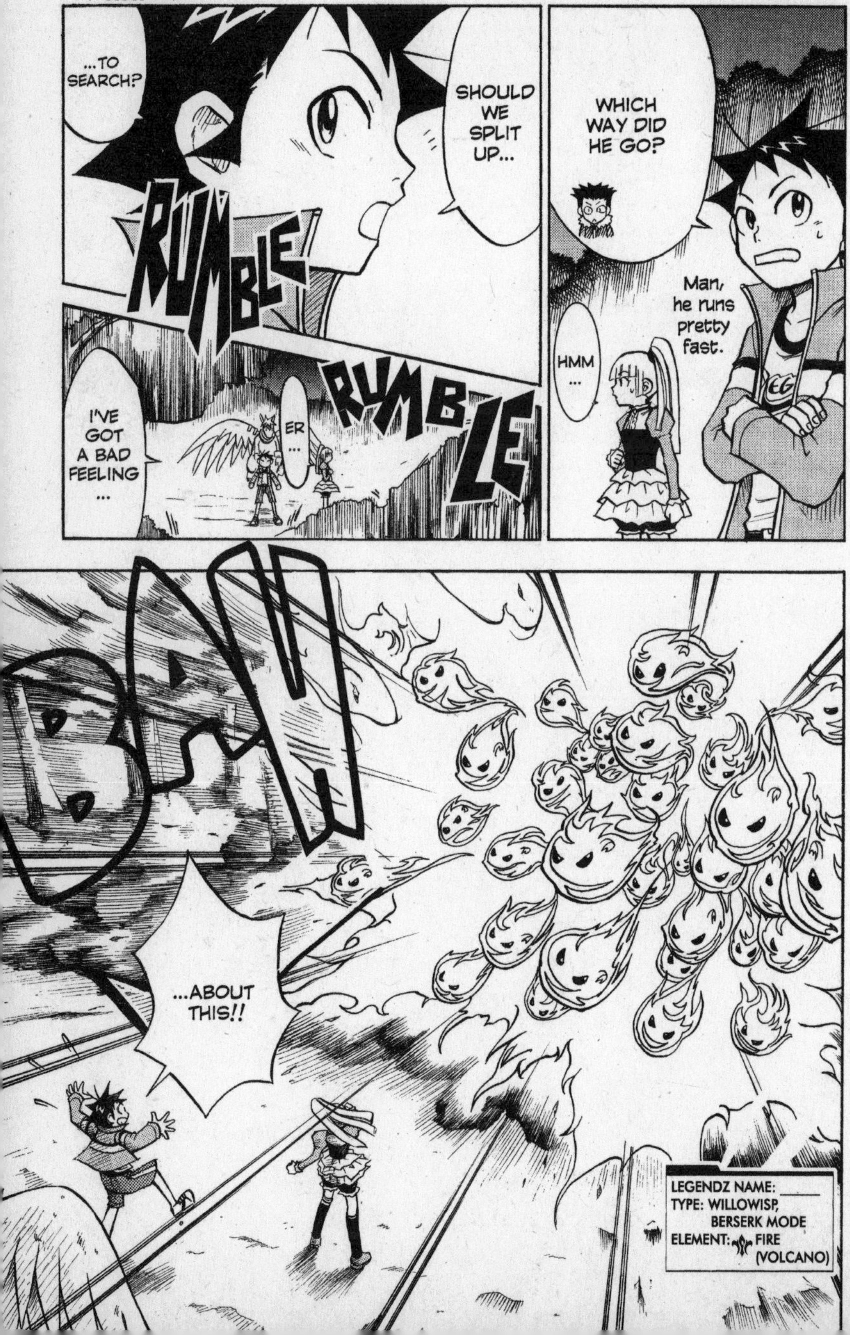
WHICH WAY DID HE GO?
Man, he runs pretty fast.
HMM ...
SHOULD WE SPLIT UP...
...TO SEARCH?
RUMBLE
RUMBLE
ER ...
I'VE GOT A BAD FEELING ...
...ABOUT THIS!!
LEGENDZ NAME: _____
TYPE: WILLOWISP, BERSERK MODE
ELEMENT: FIRE (VOLCANO)

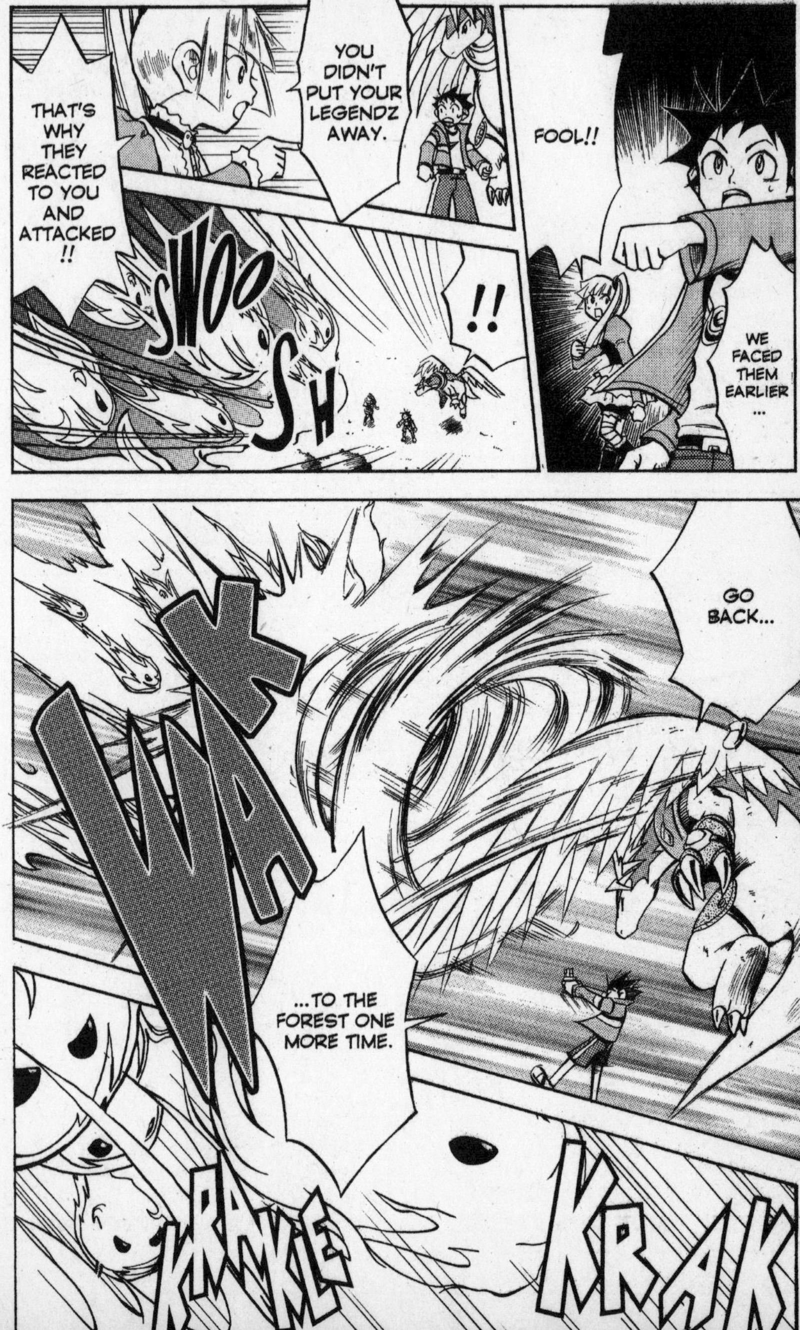
FOOL!!
WE FACED THEM EARLIER ...
YOU DIDN'T PUT YOUR LEGENDZ AWAY.
THAT'S WHY THEY REACTED TO YOU AND ATTACKED !!
!!
SWOOSH
GO BACK...
WHAK
...TO THE FOREST ONE MORE TIME.
KRAK
KRAKLE

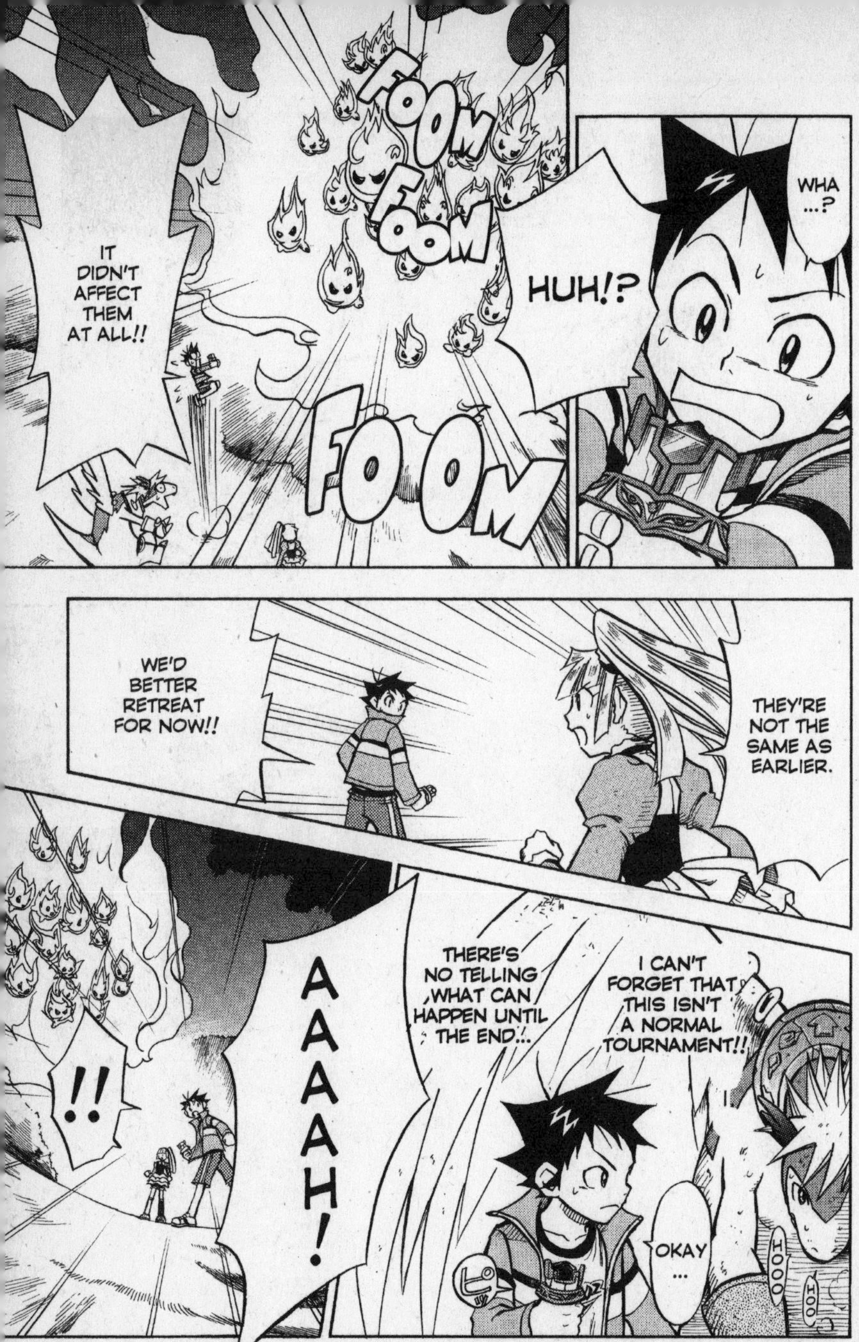
WHA ...?
HUH!?
FOOM FOOM
FOOM
IT DIDN'T AFFECT THEM AT ALL!!
THEY'RE NOT THE SAME AS EARLIER.
WE'D BETTER RETREAT FOR NOW!!
I CAN'T FORGET THAT THIS ISN'T A NORMAL TOURNAMENT!!
THERE'S NO TELLING WHAT CAN HAPPEN UNTIL THE END...
OKAY ...
HOOO
HOO
AAAAH!
!!

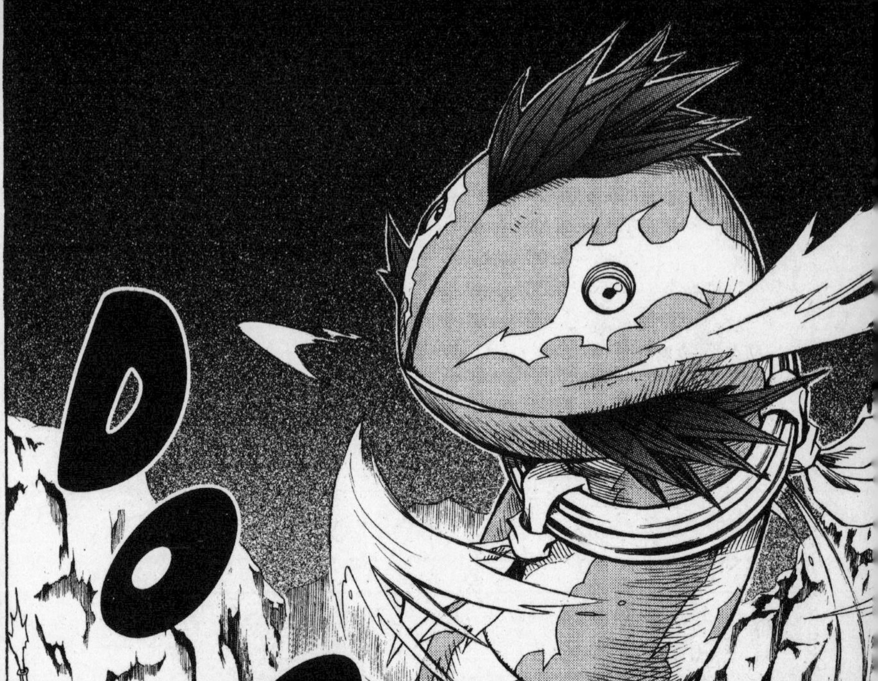
DOOOOOM
LEGENDZ NAME: KUPA
TYPE: STORM WORM,
BERSERK MODE
ELEMENT: WATER
(STORM)

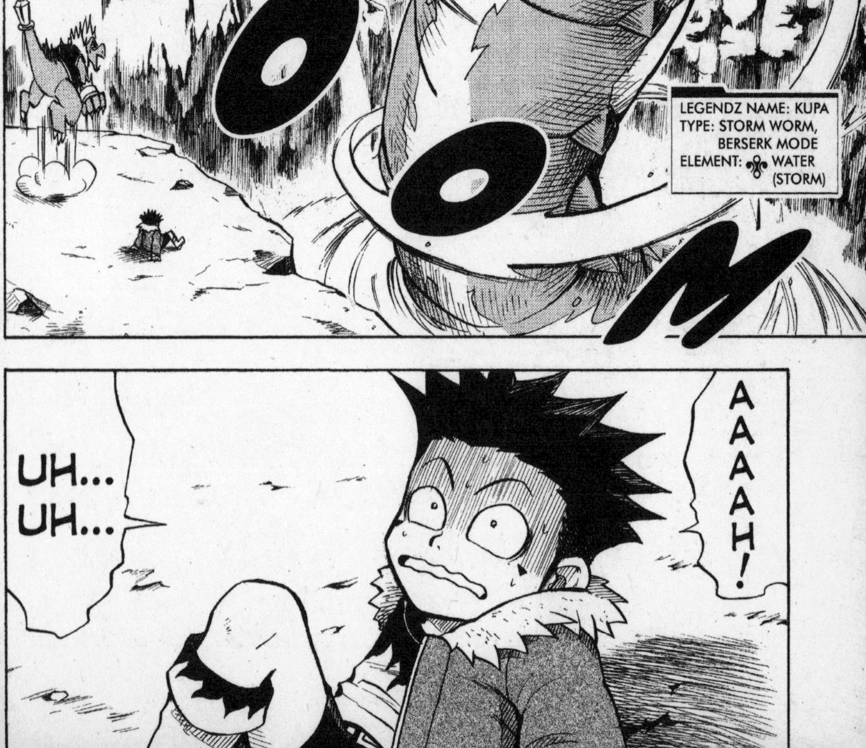
AAAAH!
UH...
UH...

READ THIS WAY

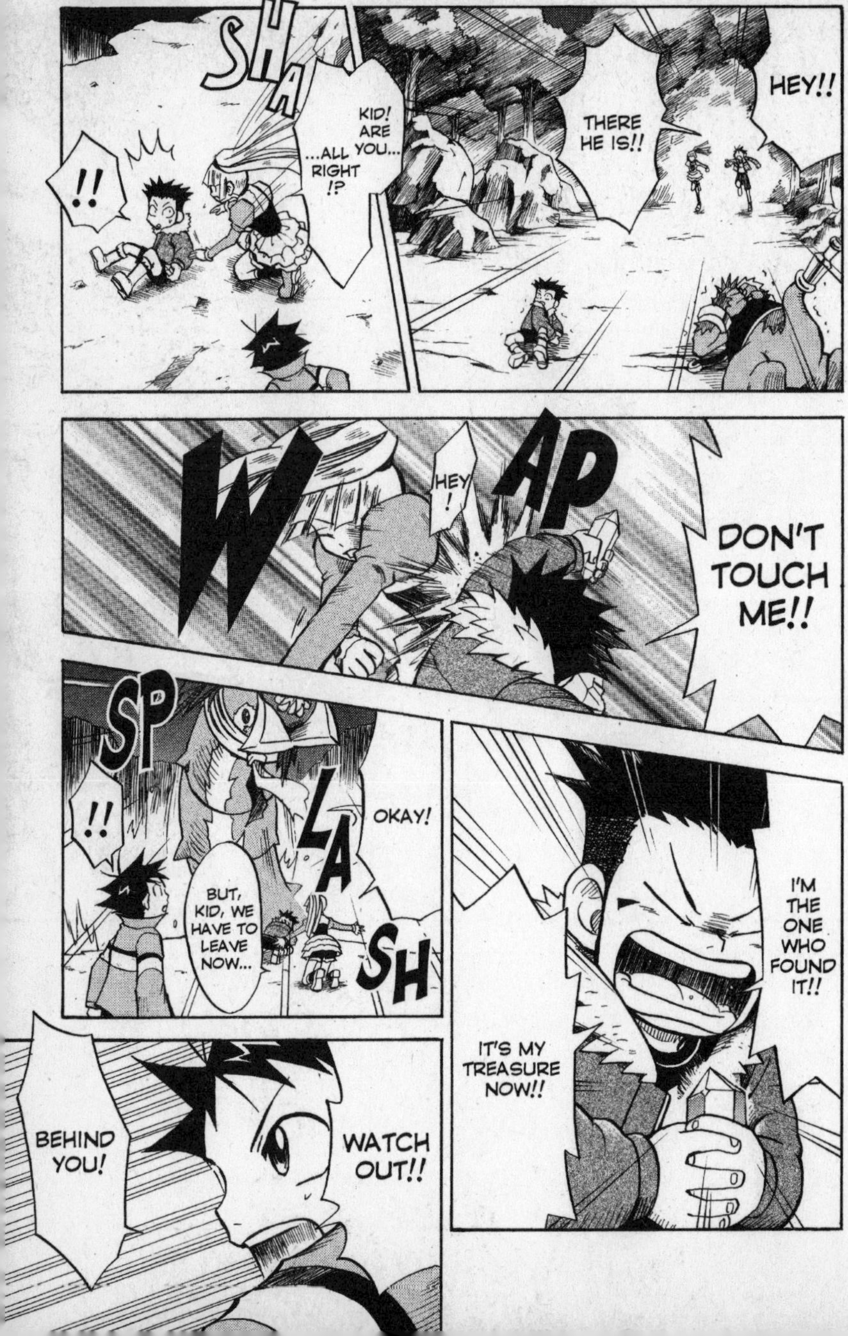
HEY!!
THERE HE IS!!
SHA
KID! ARE YOU... ...ALL RIGHT!?
!!
WAP
DON'T TOUCH ME!!
HEY!
I'M THE ONE WHO FOUND IT!!
IT'S MY TREASURE NOW!!
SPLASH
OKAY!
BUT, KID, WE HAVE TO LEAVE NOW...
!!
WATCH OUT!!
BEHIND YOU!

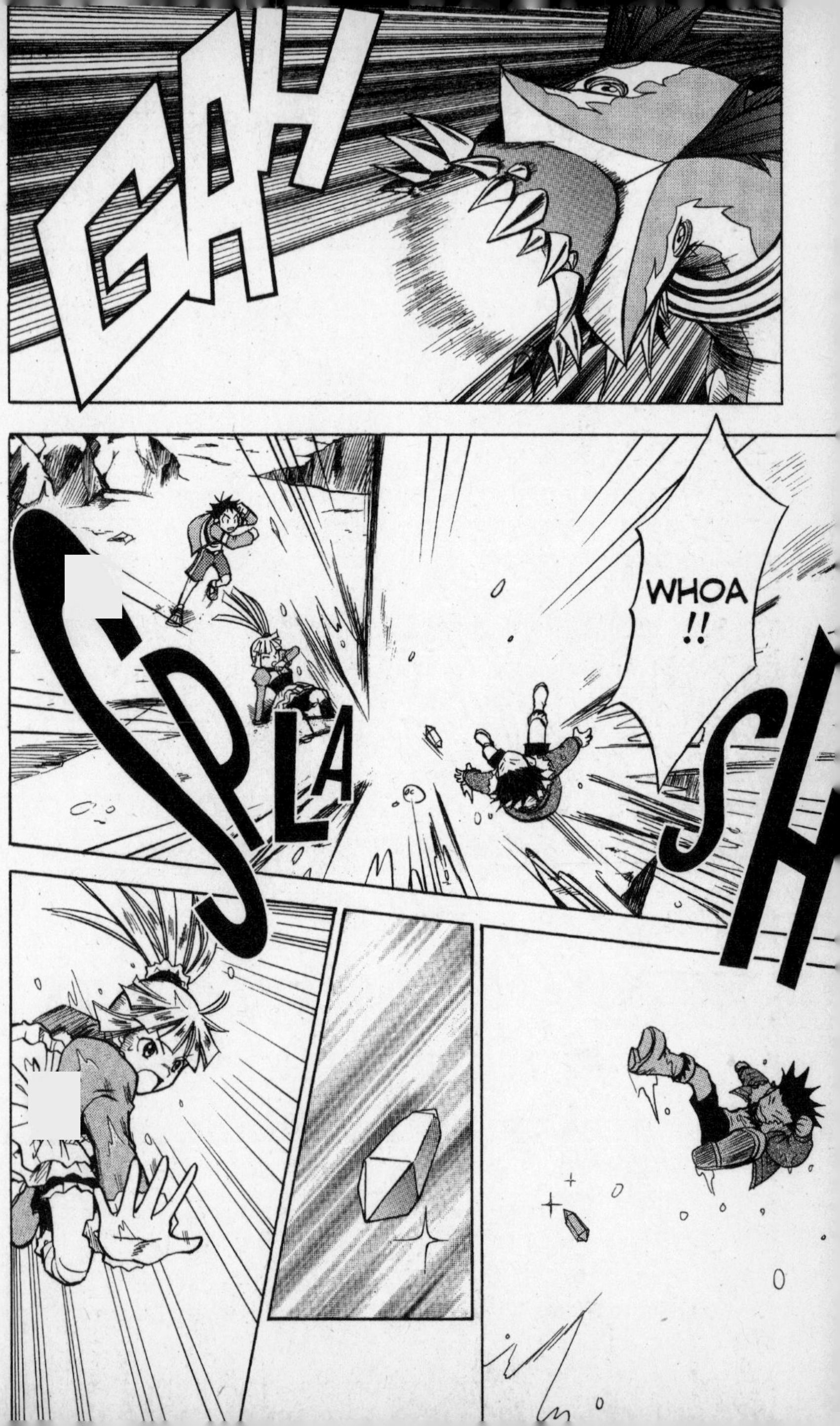
GAH
WHOA !!
SPLASH

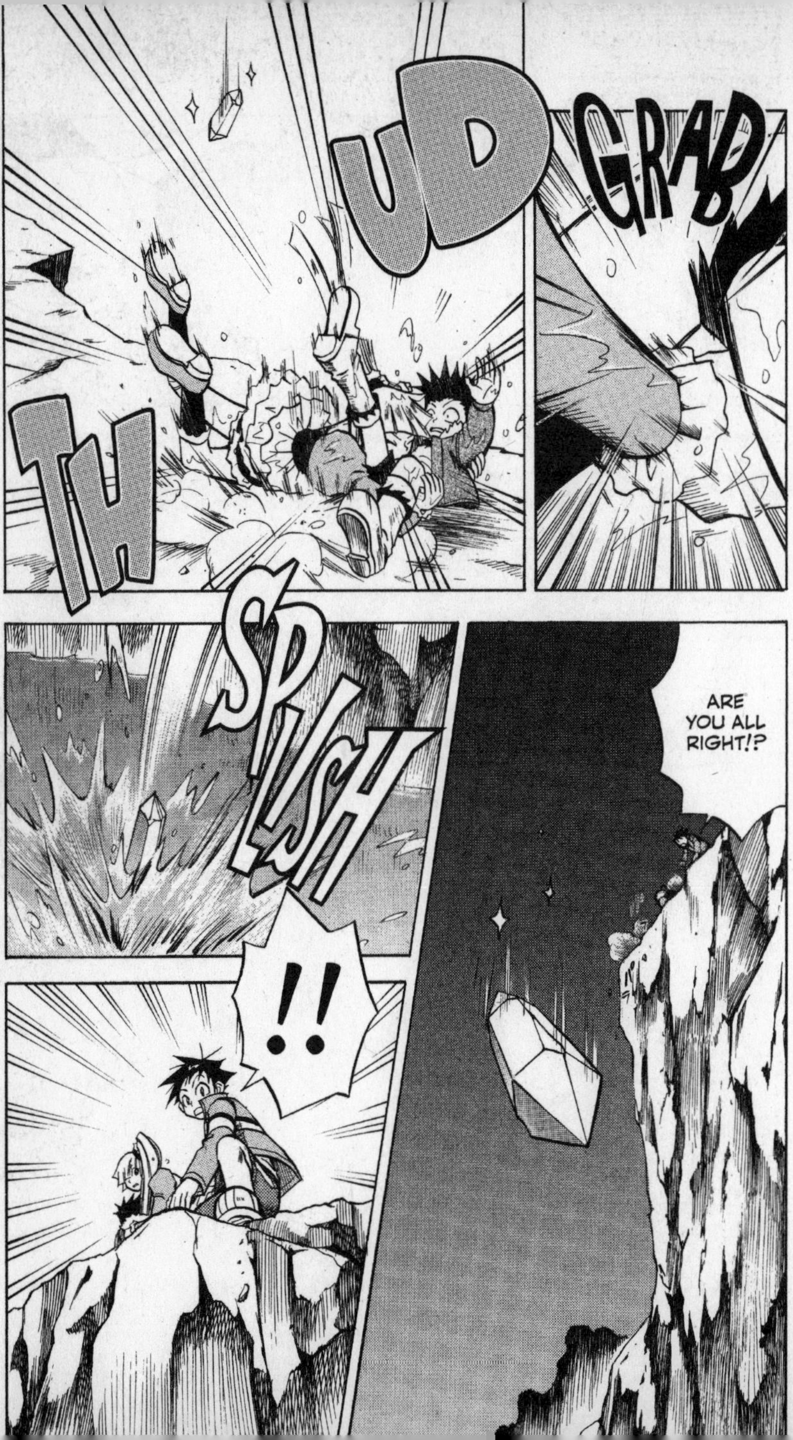
GRAB
THUD
ARE YOU ALL RIGHT!?
SPLISH
!!

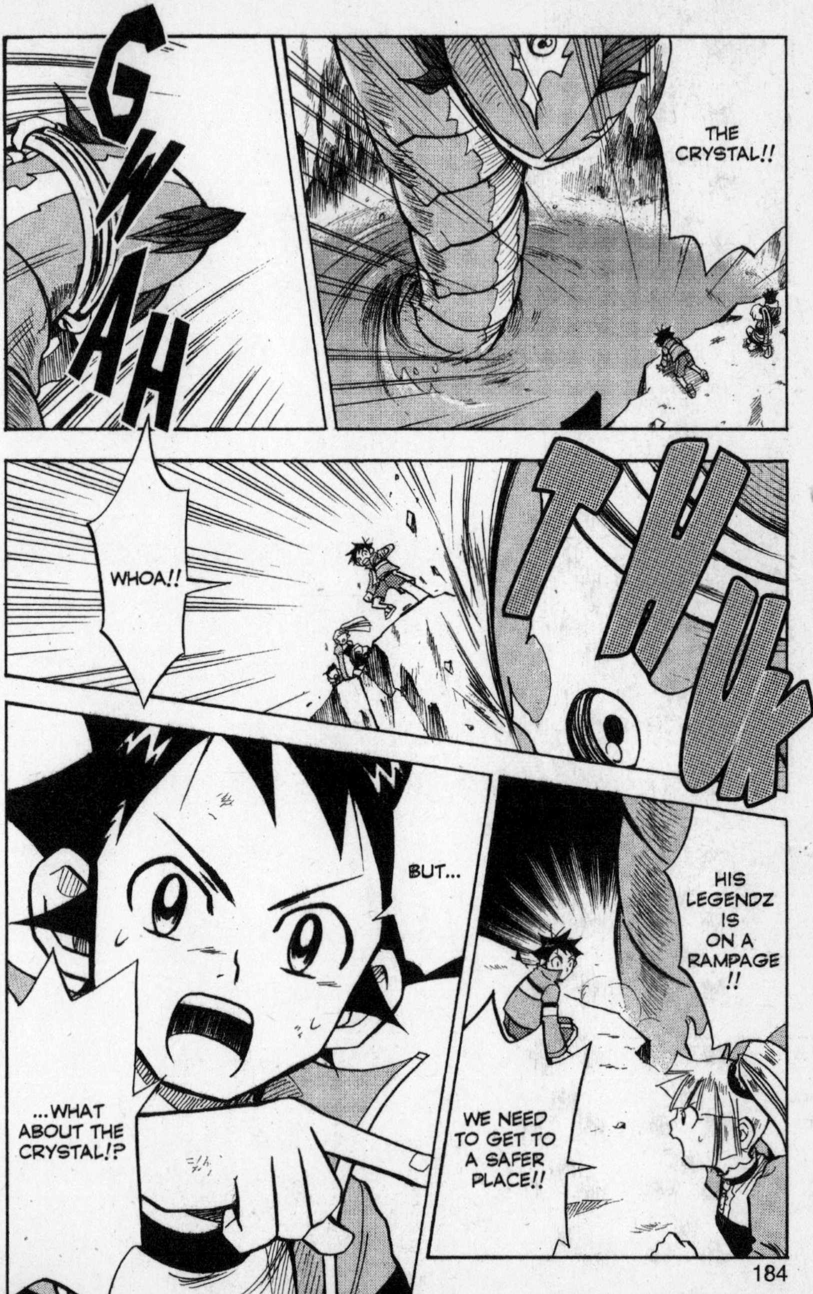
THE CRYSTAL!!
GWAH
THUNK
WHOA!!
HIS LEGENDZ IS ON A RAMPAGE!!
WE NEED TO GET TO A SAFER PLACE!!
BUT...
...WHAT ABOUT THE CRYSTAL!?

READ THIS WAY

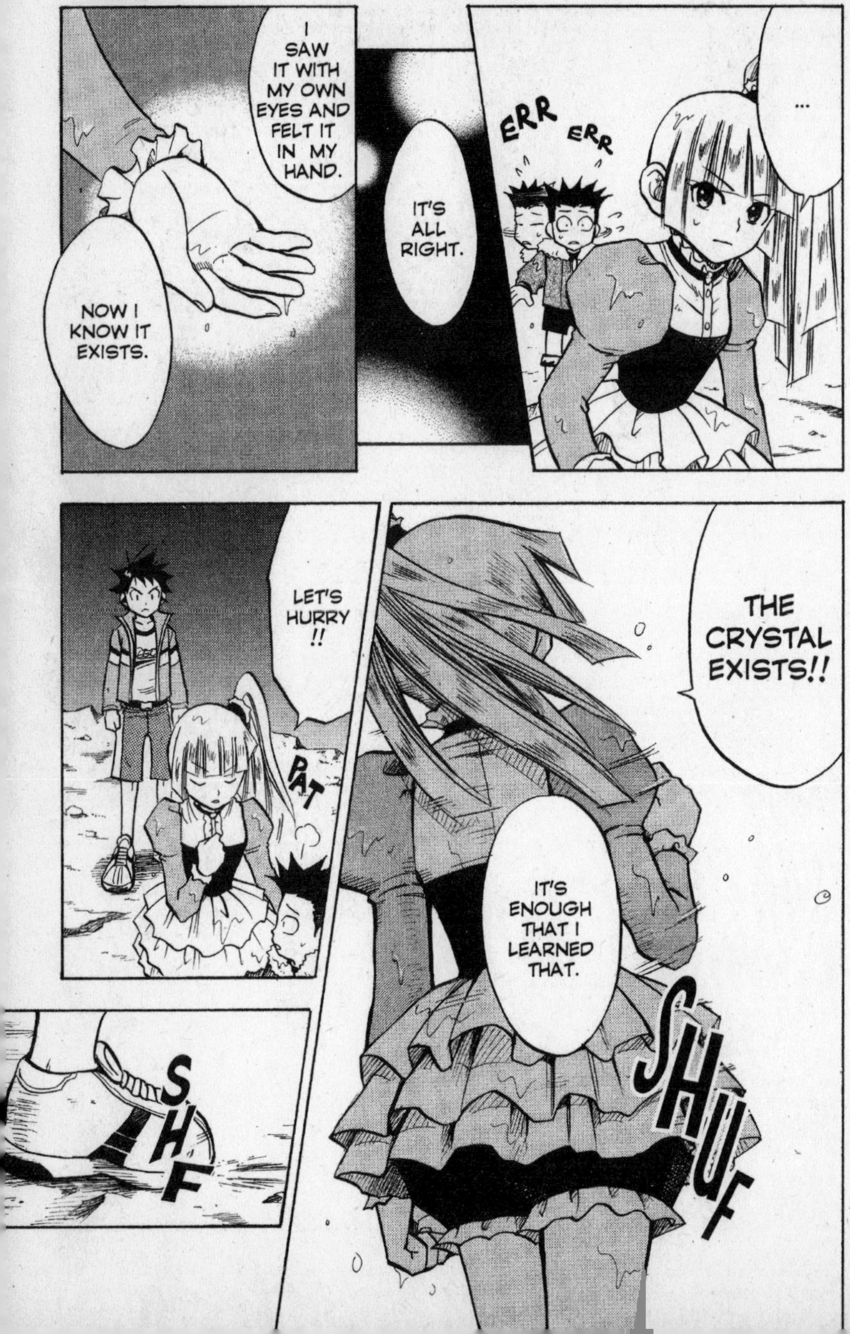
...
ERR ERR
IT'S ALL RIGHT.
I SAW IT WITH MY OWN EYES AND FELT IT IN MY HAND.
NOW I KNOW IT EXISTS.
THE CRYSTAL EXISTS!!
IT'S ENOUGH THAT I LEARNED THAT.
SHUF
LET'S HURRY!!
PAT
SHF

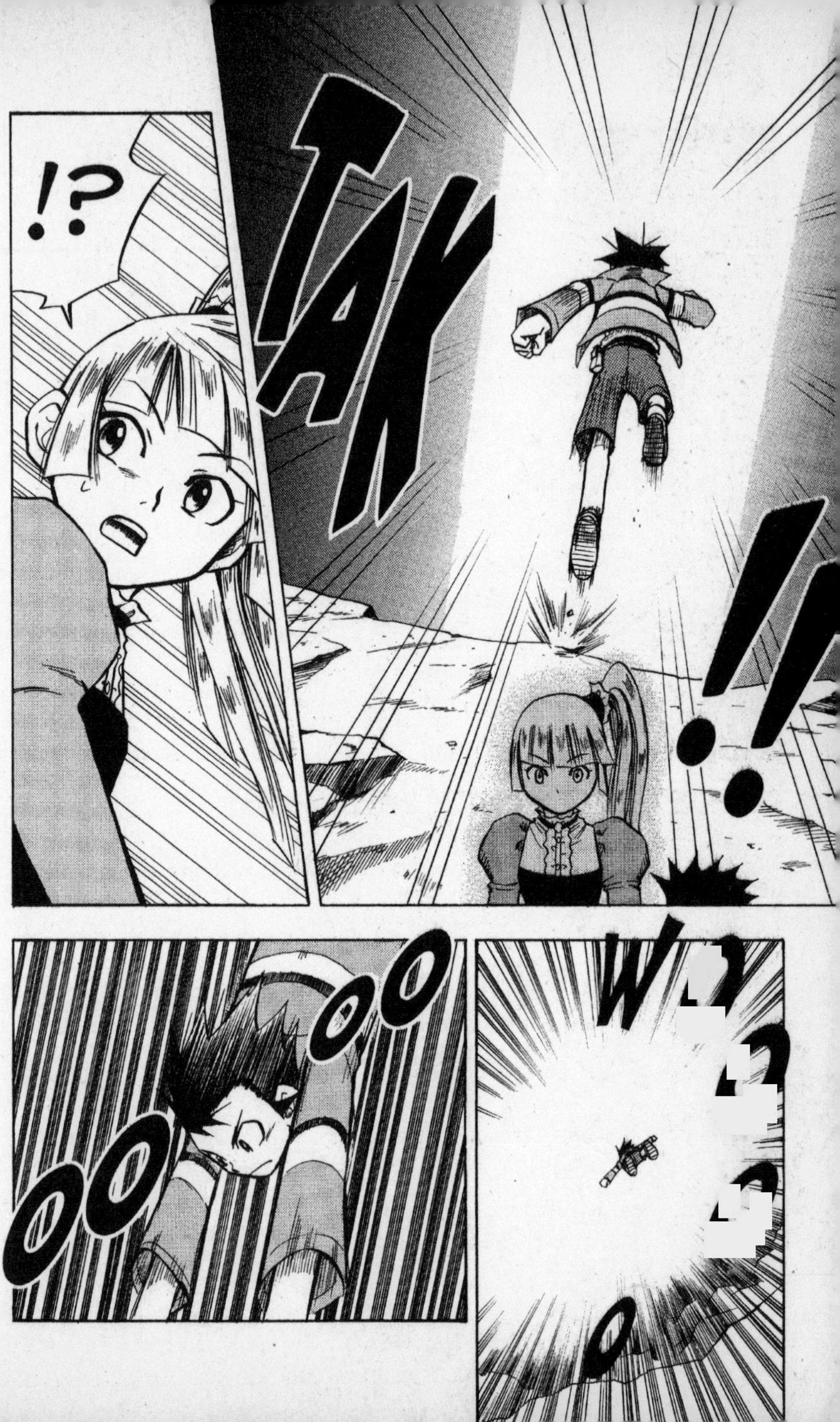
TAK
!!
!?
OOOO

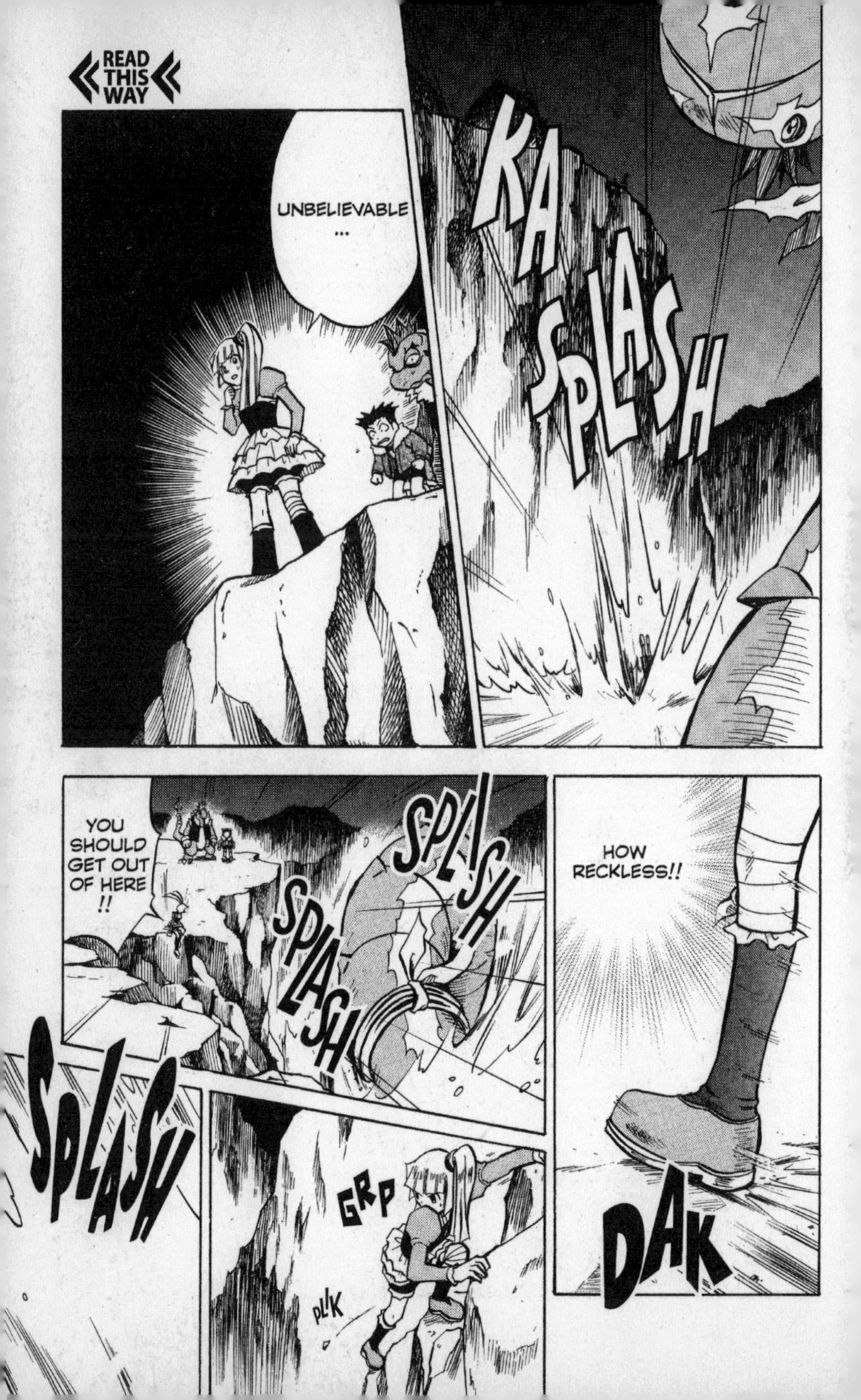
READ THIS WAY
KA SPLASH
UNBELIEVABLE ...
HOW RECKLESS!!
DAK
SPLASH
SPLASH
YOU SHOULD GET OUT OF HERE !!
SPLASH
GRP
PLIK

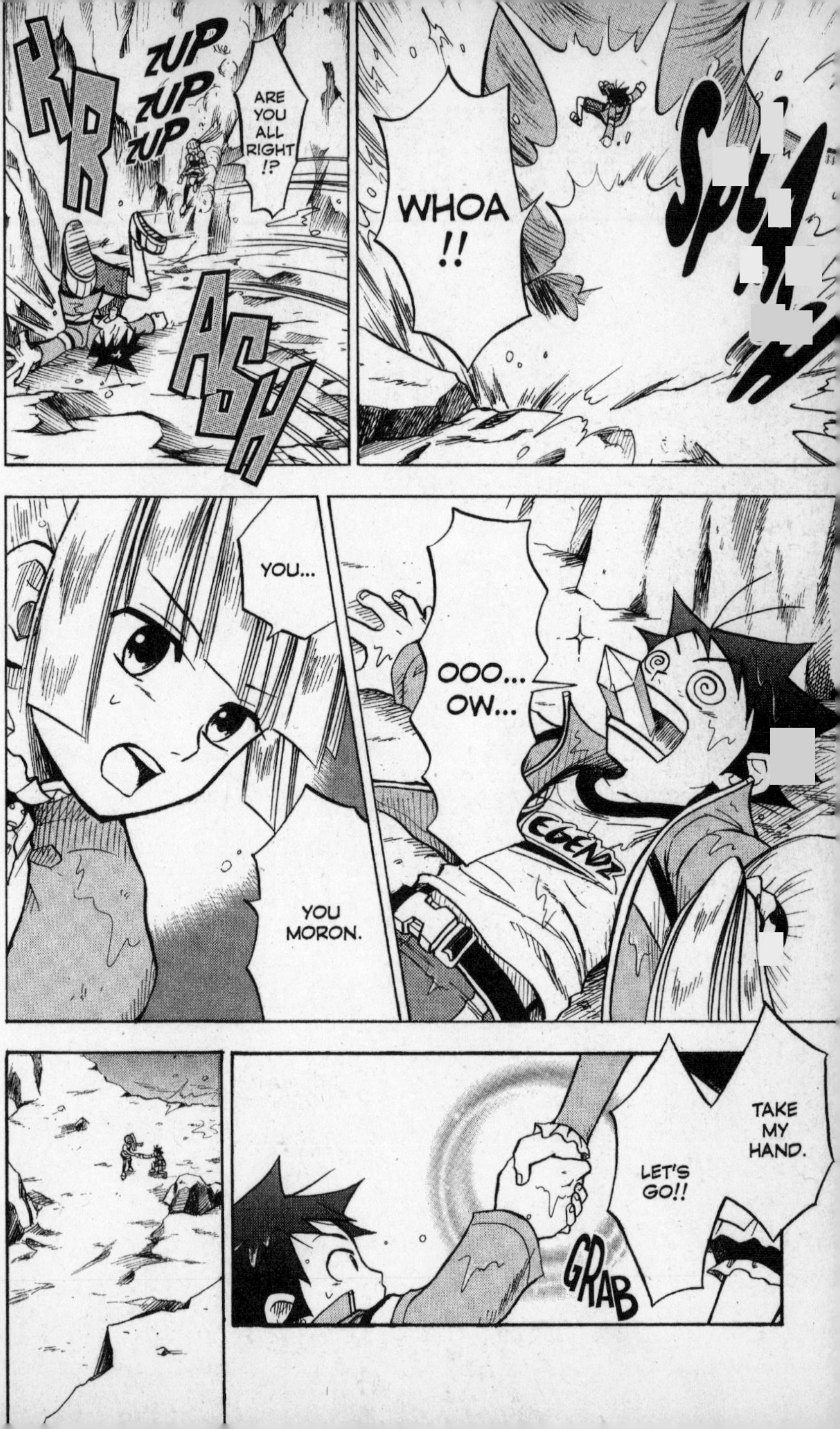
WHOA !!
ARE YOU ALL RIGHT !?
ZUP ZUP ZUP
KR ASH
OOO... OW...
YOU...
YOU MORON.
TAKE MY HAND.
LET'S GO!!
GRAB

READ THIS WAY

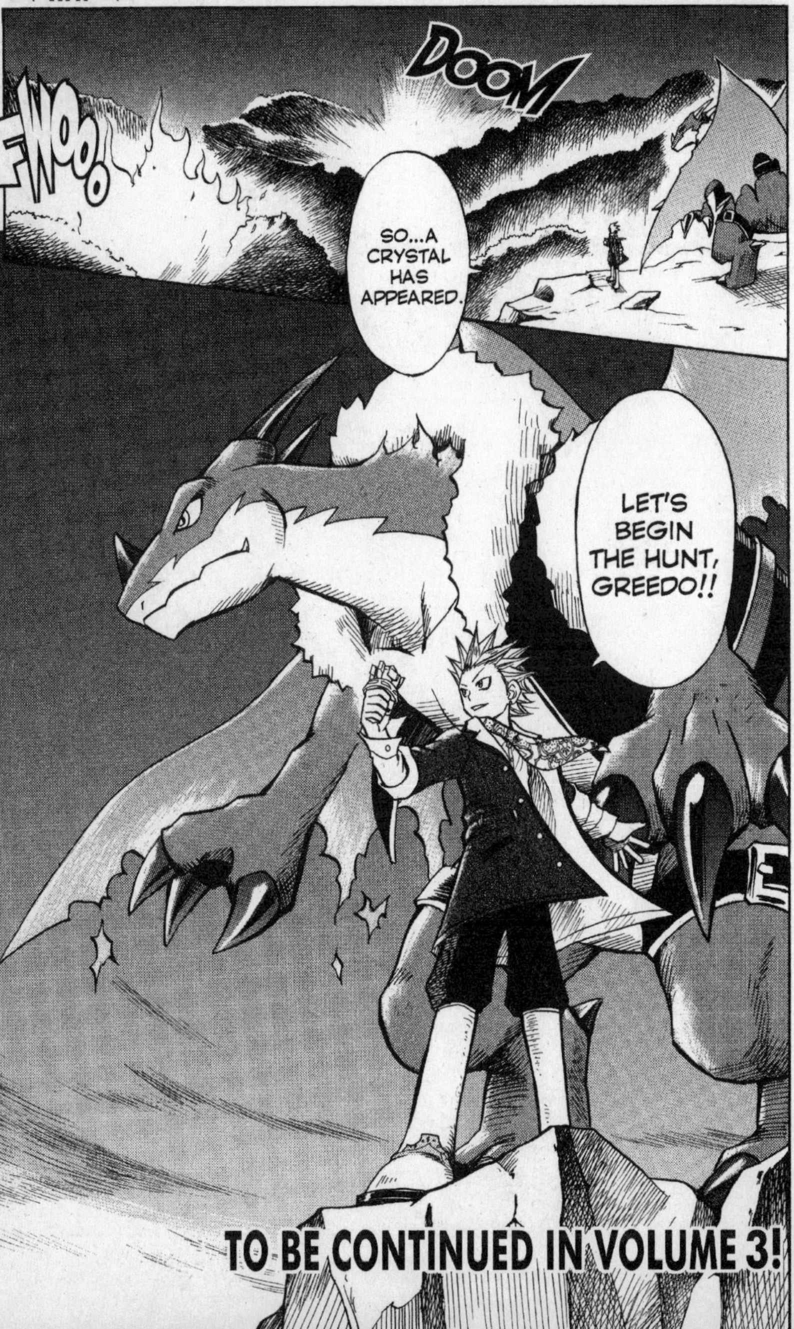
DOOM
SO...A CRYSTAL HAS APPEARED.
FWOOO
LET'S BEGIN THE HUNT, GREEDO!!
TO BE CONTINUED IN VOLUME 3!

LEGENDZ COLLECTION

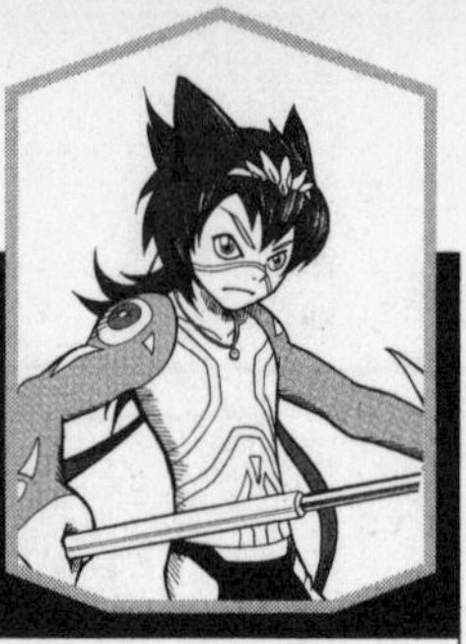

ELEMENT: WATER (STORM)
TYPE: TRITON
HIT POINTS: 600
FAVORITE ATTACK: MAELSTROM, AQUASHIELD

LEGENDZ NAME: ORCA
USER: GOH TOKUDAIJI

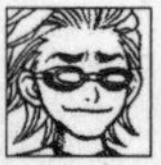

THE KING OF THE OCEAN DWELLERS. HAS UNMATCHED POWER IN WATER BATTLES. GOH HAS CUSTOMIZED IT FOR BATTLES IN THE KOKURYU ELEMENTARY POOL.

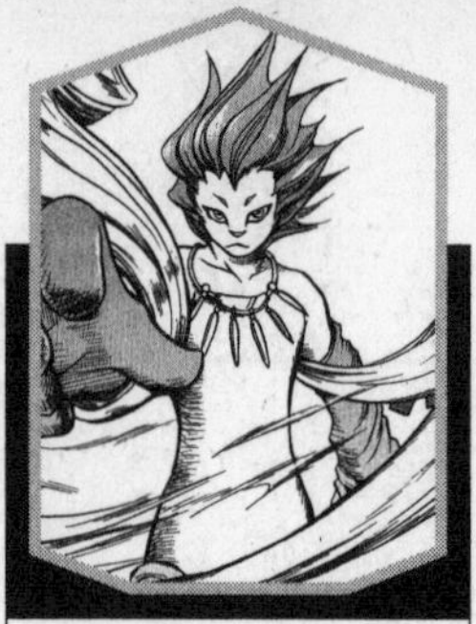

ELEMENT: WIND (TORNADO)
TYPE: CLOUD GIANT
HIT POINTS: 500
FAVORITE ATTACK: THUNDER BLISTER, CLOUDINESS

LEGENDZ NAME: SOFIA
USER: MITSURU AOI

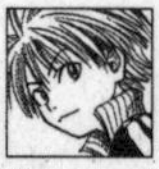

A GIANT OF THE CLOUDS AND WINDS. PEACEFUL FOR A GIANT, BUT VERY POWERFUL. THE PERFECT COMBO WITH MITSURU BECAUSE THEY EXPLOIT THEIR ENEMIES' WEAKNESSES.

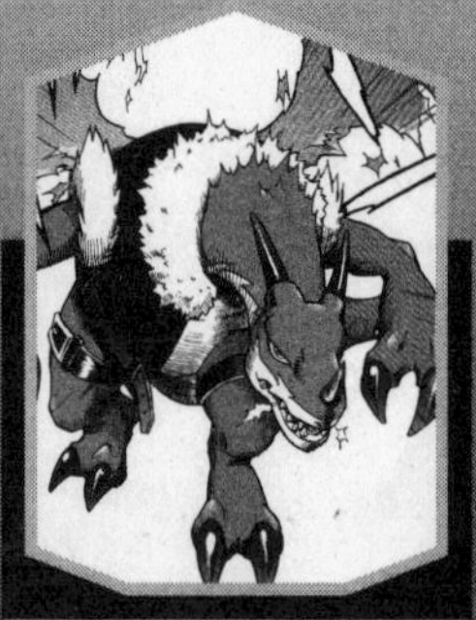

ELEMENT: FIRE (VOLCANO)
TYPE: BLAZEDRAGON
HIT POINTS: 1400
FAVORITE ATTACK: DARKBURN FLAME, FINAL BURNING

LEGENDZ NAME: GREEDO
USER: LEO ENGOKUIN

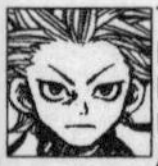

THE MOST POWERFUL LEGENDZ OF THE FIRE ELEMENTS. HAS GREAT DESTRUCTIVE POWER AND IS VERY AGGRESSIVE. LEO HAS RAISED IT THROUGH COUNTLESS BATTLES TO BE EVEN MORE POWERFUL.

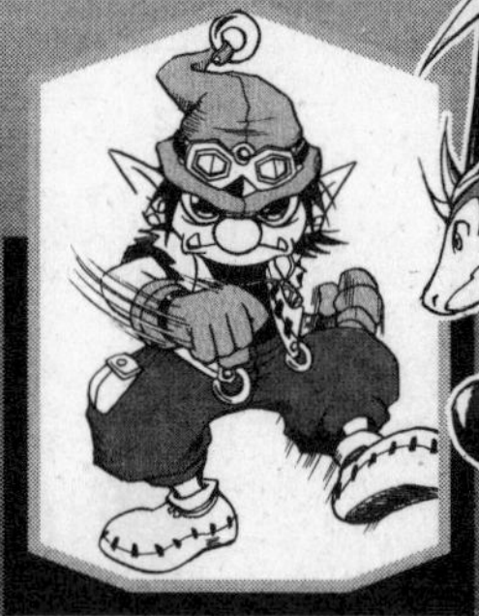

ELEMENT: EARTH (EARTHQUAKE)
TYPE: GOBLIN
HIT POINTS: 300
FAVORITE ATTACK: GOBLIN STEAL, HAMMER BLOW

LEGENDZ NAME: GIRORAMO
USER: SHIZUNA MITA

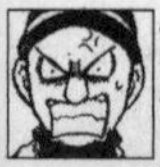

A SMALL OGRE FROM REMOTE FORESTS AND MOUNTAINS. IT'S LITTLE BUT POWERFUL AND WIELDS A LARGE HAMMER. LIKES TO USE COMBINATION ATTACKS.

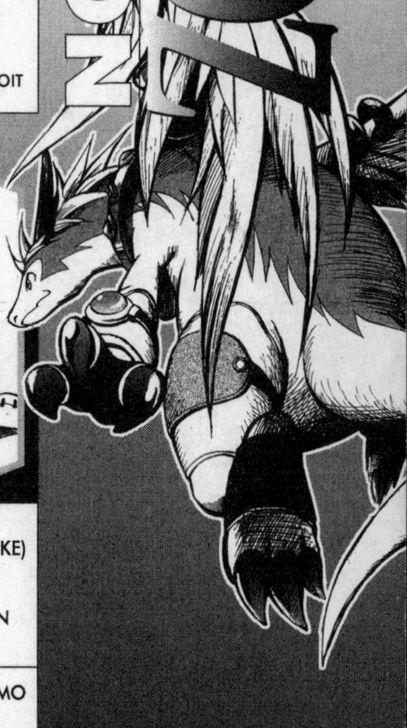

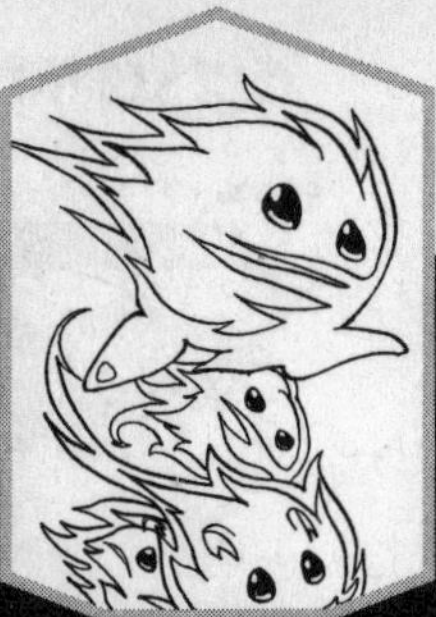

ELEMENT: FIRE (VOLCANO)
TYPE: WILLOWISP
HIT POINTS: 220
FAVORITE ATTACK: FLAME RAMBLING, MAZE FOG

LEGENDZ NAME: NONE
USER: NONE

A MISCHIEVOUS SPIRIT THAT LIKES TO LEAD TRAVELERS ASTRAY. USUALLY JUST WANDERS, BUT WILL CALL FOR ALLIES AND FLY EN MASSE TO ATTACK THE ENEMY.

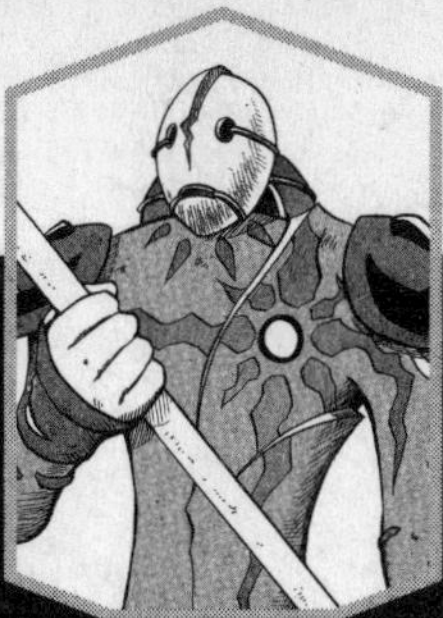

ELEMENT: EARTH (EARTHQUAKE)
TYPE: GOLEM
HIT POINTS: 640
FAVORITE ATTACK: MILLION SPIKE, MALICIOUS IVY

LEGENDZ NAME: BJORK
USER: KAORUKO GOSHIKA

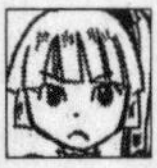

A MAGICAL BEING CREATED FROM THE EARTH. CAN USE MAGIC AND CONTROL PLANTS. KAORUKO HAS RAISED IT TO BECOME A VERY BALANCED FIGHTER.

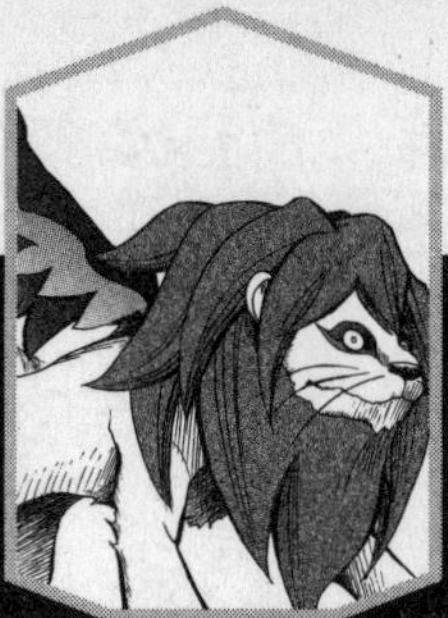

ELEMENT: WIND (TORNADO)
TYPE: MANTICORE
HIT POINTS: 580
FAVORITE ATTACK: WIND DASH, FANGBRIST

LEGENDZ NAME: DARSY
USER: SAKI MA'HA

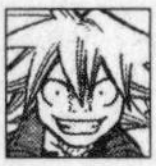

A MAGICAL WINGED BEAST WITH A LION'S HEAD AND SNAKE'S TAIL. NATURALLY FIERCE AND HAS BEEN RAISED TO BE EVEN MORE AGGRESSIVE.

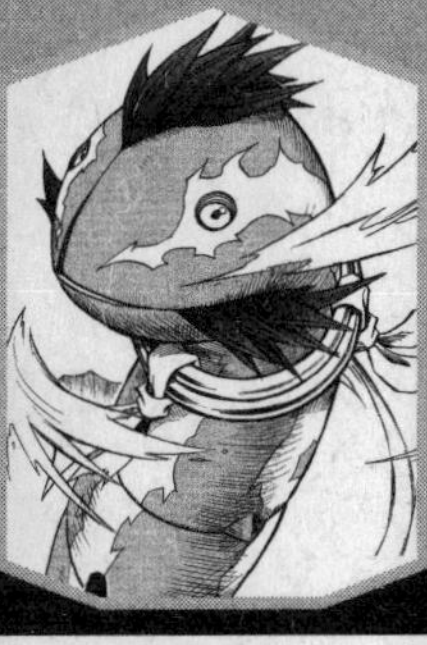

ELEMENT: WATER (STORM)
TYPE: STORM WORM
HIT POINTS: 450
FAVORITE ATTACK: CURE, AQUASPHERE

LEGENDZ NAME: KUPA
USER: NONE

A HUGE WORM. HAS A BIG APPETITE AND REQUIRES LARGE AMOUNTS OF FOOD. DEFEATS ENEMIES WITH A GIANT BLAST OF WATER FROM ITS MOUTH.

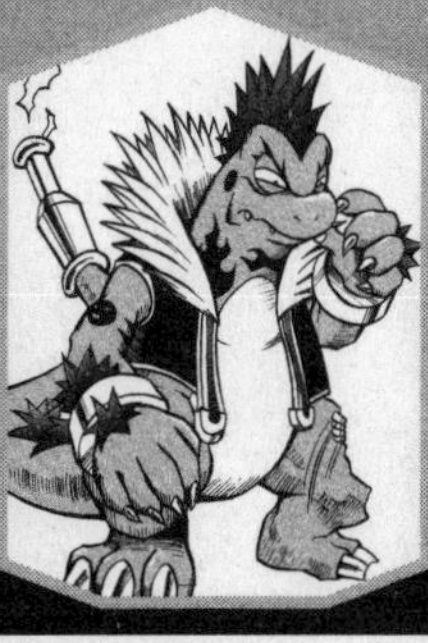

ELEMENT: FIRE (VOLCANO)
TYPE: SALAMANDER
HIT POINTS: 280
FAVORITE ATTACK: IGNITION, SALAMANDER STRIKE

LEGENDZ NAME: FIRE
USER: YOTA NAGISA

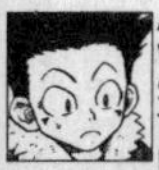

A FIRE SPIRIT. IT WIELDS A FLAME THAT SHOOTS FROM ITS TAIL. CAN ALSO SET FIRE TO ANYTHING IT TOUCHES. ITS HIGH ATTACK POWER IS ITS MAIN STRENGTH.

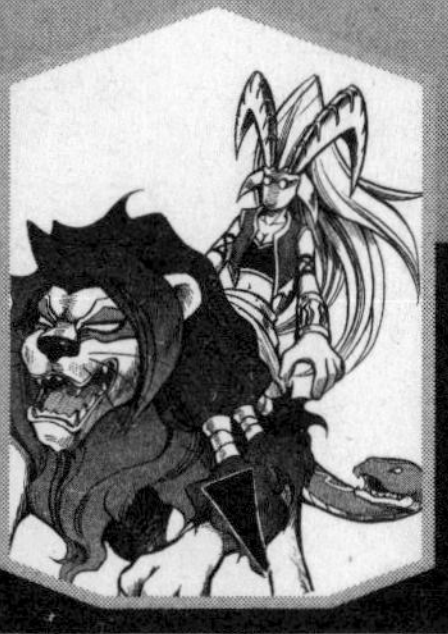

ELEMENT: FIRE (VOLCANO)
TYPE: CHIMERA
HIT POINTS: 720
FAVORITE ATTACK: FOUR FRAME, BONE PULVERIZING FLAME

LEGENDZ NAME: EMINEMA
USER: NONE

A HYBRID BEAST COMPOSED OF A CHIMERA, SNAKE AND FALCON. OVERWHELMS THE ENEMY WITH ITS POWER AND SPEED. DOES NOT ALLOW FOR A COUNTERATTACK.

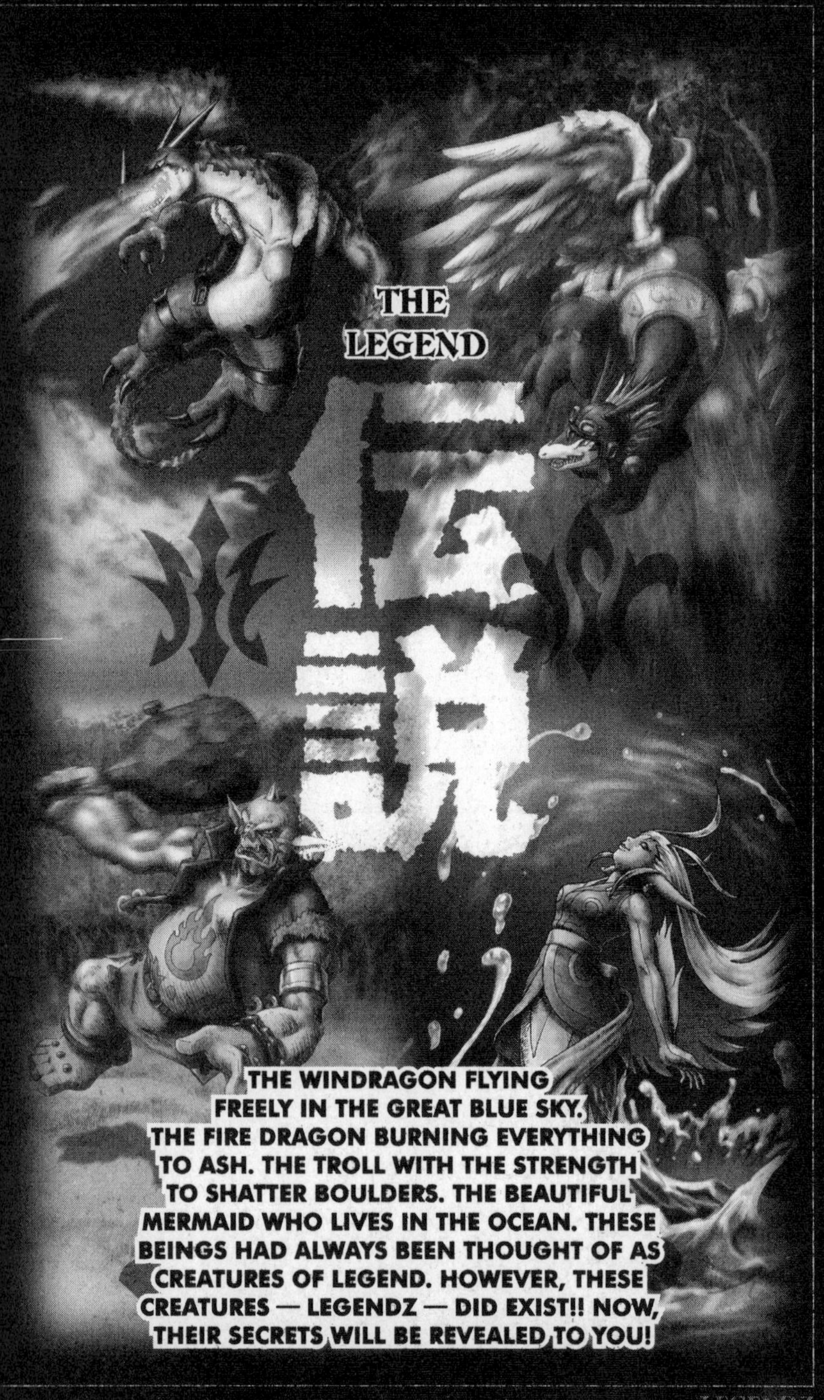
THE LEGEND
伝説
THE WINDRAGON FLYING FREELY IN THE GREAT BLUE SKY. THE FIRE DRAGON BURNING EVERYTHING TO ASH. THE TROLL WITH THE STRENGTH TO SHATTER BOULDERS. THE BEAUTIFUL MERMAID WHO LIVES IN THE OCEAN. THESE BEINGS HAD ALWAYS BEEN THOUGHT OF AS CREATURES OF LEGEND. HOWEVER, THESE CREATURES — LEGENDZ — DID EXIST!! NOW, THEIR SECRETS WILL BE REVEALED TO YOU!

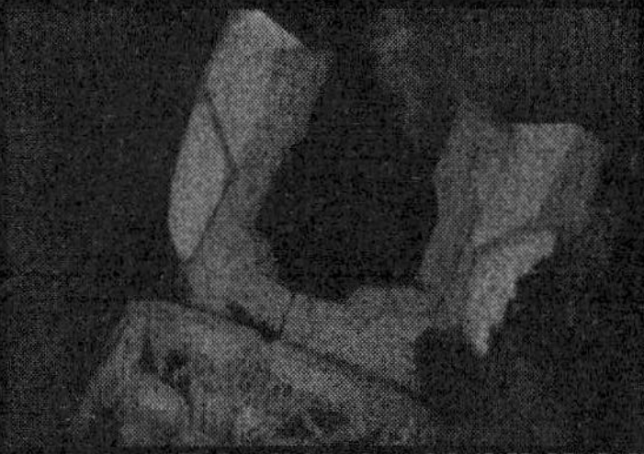

THE EXCAVATED TALISPOD. IT WAS BURIED BENEATH SOME BOULDERS.

IN THE YEAR 200X, THE LEGENDZ WERE DISCOVERED.

DUE TO A CERTAIN ACCIDENT, A DWC ACADEMIC RESEARCH TEAM DISCOVERED AN ANCIENT RELIC. THIS RELIC WAS A MINIATURE TOWER MADE OF STONE. IN IT WAS A CRYSTAL CARVED IN A MONSTER'S LIKENESS. THESE BECAME THE MODEL FOR THE TALISPOD AND THE SOUL FIGURE.

THE "LEGENDZ" WORLD AS REVEALED BY THE DARK WIZ COMPANY (DWC)

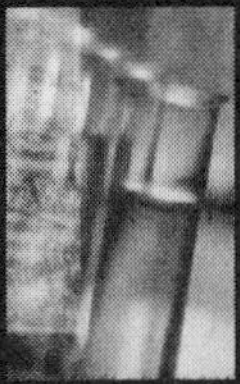

■RESEARCH

RESEARCH PROVED THAT THERE REALLY ARE LEGENDARY CREATURES SEALED WITHIN A SOUL FIGURE.

THE RESEARCH TO RESURRECT THE LEGENDARY CREATURES CONTINUED.

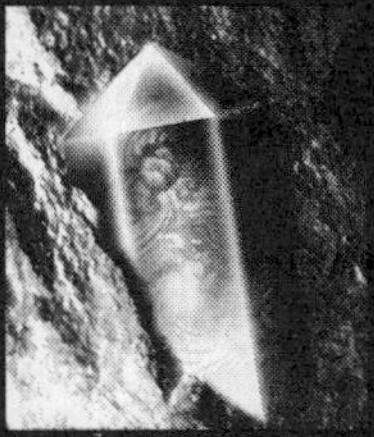

88 SOUL FIGURES WERE DISCOVERED ALL AT ONCE!

◆THE CREATURES THAT WERE SEALED WITHIN.

ON THE SURFACE OF THE CRYSTALS WERE THE CARVINGS OF LEGENDARY CREATURES, ALMOST AS IF THEY WERE SEALED WITHIN...

THE LEGENDARY CONTINENT: ANCIENT ELDANIA.

ELDANIA IS THE LOST CONTINENT WHERE THE LEGENDARY CREATURES ONCE ROAMED. THE FINDINGS OF THE LEGENDZ RESEARCH HAVE ALLOWED A MAP TO BE CONSTRUCTED, WHICH CAN BE SEEN ON THE NEXT PAGE.

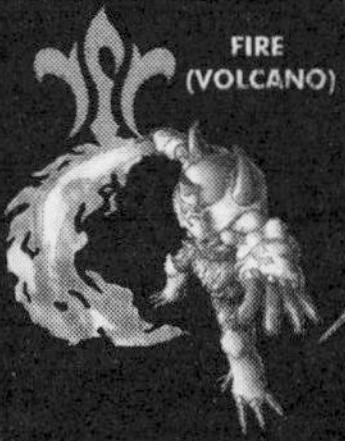

FIRE (VOLCANO)

FIRE GIANT: A GIANT LEGENDZ CREATED MAGICALLY FROM LAVA.

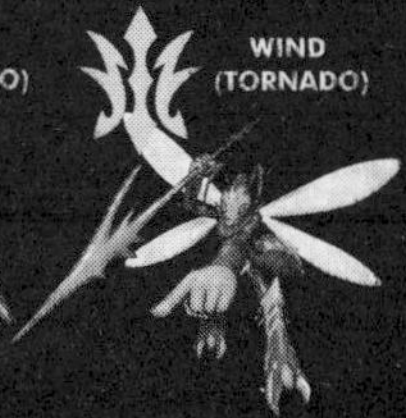

WIND (TORNADO)

ASSASSIN BUG: A FLYING, BEE-LIKE LEGENDZ WITH A POISON STINGER.

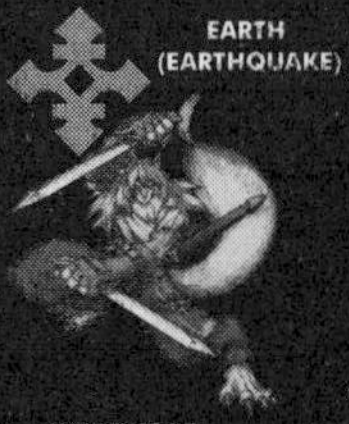

EARTH (EARTHQUAKE)

WEREWOLF: A LEGENDZ WITH THE SPEED OF A HURRICANE.

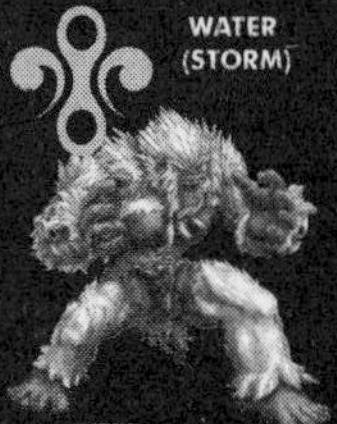

WATER (STORM)

YETI: A GIANT LEGENDZ THAT CAN CONTROL SNOW AND ICE.

WIND (TORNADO), FIRE (VOLCANO), WATER (STORM), EARTH (EARTHQUAKE): THE FOUR ELEMENTS

IT WAS DISCOVERED THAT THE LEGENDARY CREATURES ARE REBORN WITH THE HELP OF THE TALISPOD. THEN IT WAS FOUND THAT THESE CREATURES COULD BE GROUPED INTO FOUR ELEMENTS.

THE DWC CONDUCTS THE MOST CUTTING-EDGE LEGENDZ RESEARCH. WE WILL NOW REVEAL THE RESULTS OF THIS RESEARCH!

■SAGAS: IN ANCIENT TIMES, THOSE WHO HAD THE POWER TO SUMMON THE LEGENDZ FROM THE SOUL FIGURE WERE CALLED "SAGAS." TODAY, THE TERM REFERS TO ANYONE WHO USES A TALISPOD TO PLAY THE LEGENDZ GAME.

■ELEMENTS: LEGENDZ CAN BE DIVIDED INTO THE FOUR ELEMENTS: WIND (TORNADO), FIRE (VOLCANO), WATER (STORM) AND EARTH (EARTHQUAKE). EACH LEGENDZ'S ELEMENT IS EXPRESSED IN ITS HABITAT AND ABILITIES. ACCORDING TO THE LATEST RESEARCH, MORE ELEMENT TYPES EXIST.

■DWC: A MULTINATIONAL CORPORATION THAT SELLS CARD GAMES, COMPUTER GAMES, ACTION FIGURES AND OTHER TOYS. IT EXCAVATED THE LEGENDZ, CONDUCTED RESEARCH AND CREATED THE LEGENDZ GAME. ITS INNER WORKINGS ARE SHROUDED IN MYSTERY.

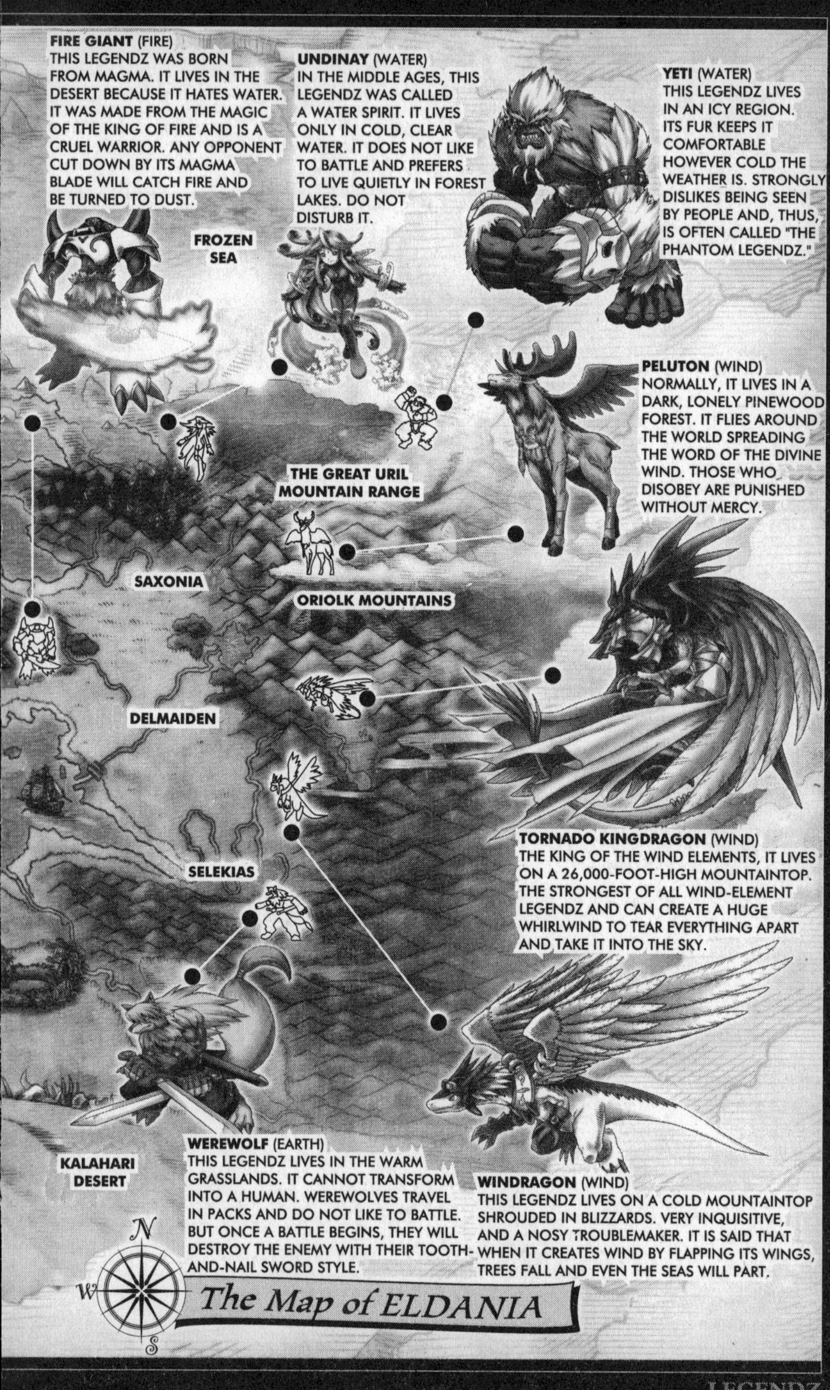
FIRE GIANT (FIRE)
THIS LEGENDZ WAS BORN FROM MAGMA. IT LIVES IN THE DESERT BECAUSE IT HATES WATER. IT WAS MADE FROM THE MAGIC OF THE KING OF FIRE AND IS A CRUEL WARRIOR. ANY OPPONENT CUT DOWN BY ITS MAGMA BLADE WILL CATCH FIRE AND BE TURNED TO DUST.
UNDINAY (WATER)
IN THE MIDDLE AGES, THIS LEGENDZ WAS CALLED A WATER SPIRIT. IT LIVES ONLY IN COLD, CLEAR WATER. IT DOES NOT LIKE TO BATTLE AND PREFERS TO LIVE QUIETLY IN FOREST LAKES. DO NOT DISTURB IT.
YETI (WATER)
THIS LEGENDZ LIVES IN AN ICY REGION. ITS FUR KEEPS IT COMFORTABLE HOWEVER COLD THE WEATHER IS. STRONGLY DISLIKES BEING SEEN BY PEOPLE AND, THUS, IS OFTEN CALLED "THE PHANTOM LEGENDZ."
FROZEN SEA
PELUTON (WIND)
NORMALLY, IT LIVES IN A DARK, LONELY PINEWOOD FOREST. IT FLIES AROUND THE WORLD SPREADING THE WORD OF THE DIVINE WIND. THOSE WHO DISOBEY ARE PUNISHED WITHOUT MERCY.
THE GREAT URIL MOUNTAIN RANGE
SAXONIA
ORIOLK MOUNTAINS
DELMAIDEN
TORNADO KINGDRAGON (WIND)
THE KING OF THE WIND ELEMENTS, IT LIVES ON A 26,000-FOOT-HIGH MOUNTAINTOP. THE STRONGEST OF ALL WIND-ELEMENT LEGENDZ AND CAN CREATE A HUGE WHIRLWIND TO TEAR EVERYTHING APART AND TAKE IT INTO THE SKY.
SELEKIAS
KALAHARI DESERT
WEREWOLF (EARTH)
THIS LEGENDZ LIVES IN THE WARM GRASSLANDS. IT CANNOT TRANSFORM INTO A HUMAN. WEREWOLVES TRAVEL IN PACKS AND DO NOT LIKE TO BATTLE. BUT ONCE A BATTLE BEGINS, THEY WILL DESTROY THE ENEMY WITH THEIR TOOTH-AND-NAIL SWORD STYLE.
WINDRAGON (WIND)
THIS LEGENDZ LIVES ON A COLD MOUNTAINTOP SHROUDED IN BLIZZARDS. VERY INQUISITIVE, AND A NOSY TROUBLEMAKER. IT IS SAID THAT WHEN IT CREATES WIND BY FLAPPING ITS WINGS, TREES FALL AND EVEN THE SEAS WILL PART.
N
W
S
The Map of ELDANIA

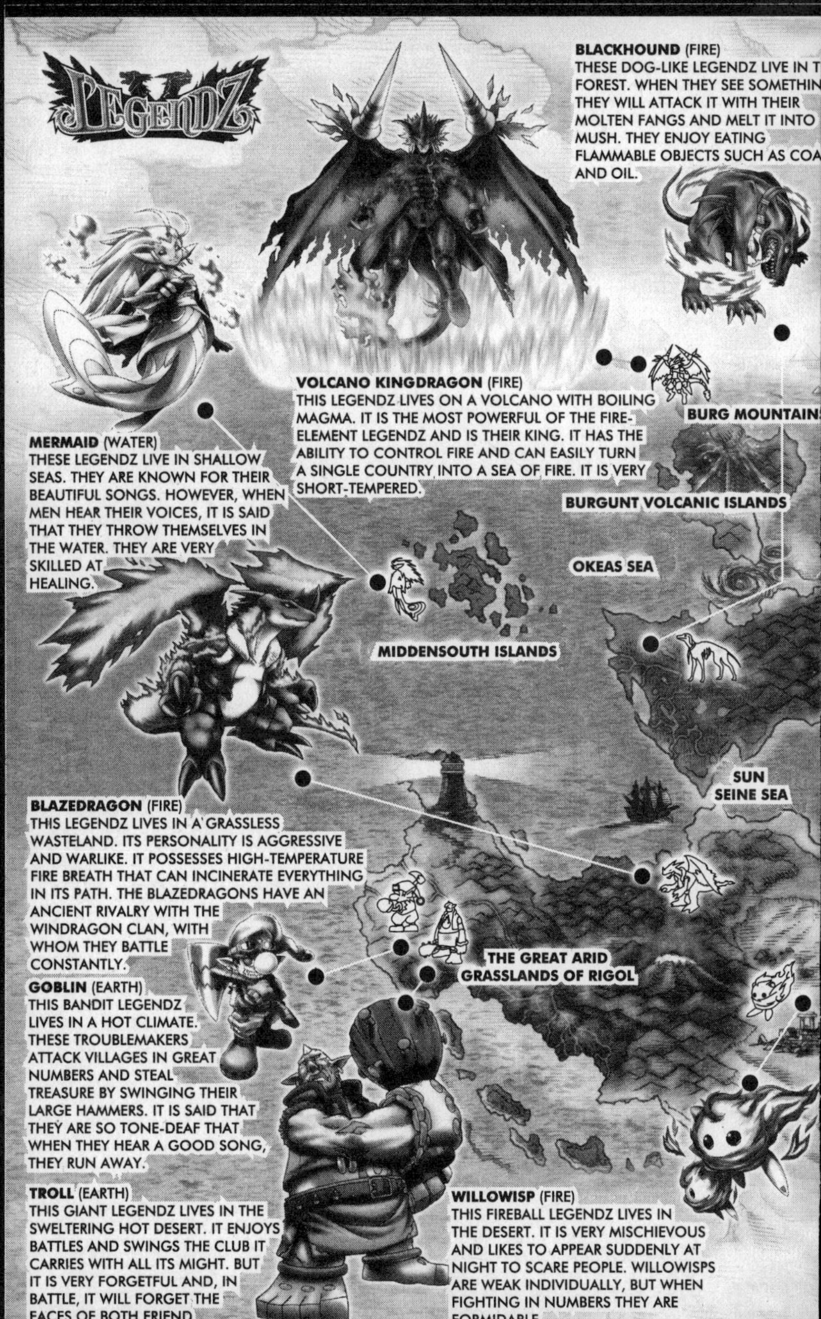
LEGENDZ
BLACKHOUND (FIRE)
THESE DOG-LIKE LEGENDZ LIVE IN T
FOREST. WHEN THEY SEE SOMETHIN
THEY WILL ATTACK IT WITH THEIR
MOLTEN FANGS AND MELT IT INTO
MUSH. THEY ENJOY EATING
FLAMMABLE OBJECTS SUCH AS COA
AND OIL.
VOLCANO KINGDRAGON (FIRE)
THIS LEGENDZ LIVES ON A VOLCANO WITH BOILING MAGMA. IT IS THE MOST POWERFUL OF THE FIRE-ELEMENT LEGENDZ AND IS THEIR KING. IT HAS THE ABILITY TO CONTROL FIRE AND CAN EASILY TURN A SINGLE COUNTRY INTO A SEA OF FIRE. IT IS VERY SHORT-TEMPERED.
BURG MOUNTAIN
MERMAID (WATER)
THESE LEGENDZ LIVE IN SHALLOW SEAS. THEY ARE KNOWN FOR THEIR BEAUTIFUL SONGS. HOWEVER, WHEN MEN HEAR THEIR VOICES, IT IS SAID THAT THEY THROW THEMSELVES IN THE WATER. THEY ARE VERY SKILLED AT HEALING.
BURGUNT VOLCANIC ISLANDS
OKEAS SEA
MIDDENSOUTH ISLANDS
SUN SEINE SEA
BLAZEDRAGON (FIRE)
THIS LEGENDZ LIVES IN A GRASSLESS WASTELAND. ITS PERSONALITY IS AGGRESSIVE AND WARLIKE. IT POSSESSES HIGH-TEMPERATURE FIRE BREATH THAT CAN INCINERATE EVERYTHING IN ITS PATH. THE BLAZEDRAGONS HAVE AN ANCIENT RIVALRY WITH THE WINDRAGON CLAN, WITH WHOM THEY BATTLE CONSTANTLY.
THE GREAT ARID GRASSLANDS OF RIGOL
GOBLIN (EARTH)
THIS BANDIT LEGENDZ LIVES IN A HOT CLIMATE. THESE TROUBLEMAKERS ATTACK VILLAGES IN GREAT NUMBERS AND STEAL TREASURE BY SWINGING THEIR LARGE HAMMERS. IT IS SAID THAT THEY ARE SO TONE-DEAF THAT WHEN THEY HEAR A GOOD SONG, THEY RUN AWAY.
TROLL (EARTH)
THIS GIANT LEGENDZ LIVES IN THE SWELTERING HOT DESERT. IT ENJOYS BATTLES AND SWINGS THE CLUB IT CARRIES WITH ALL ITS MIGHT. BUT IT IS VERY FORGETFUL AND, IN BATTLE, IT WILL FORGET THE FACES OF BOTH FRIEND AND FOE.
WILLOWISP (FIRE)
THIS FIREBALL LEGENDZ LIVES IN THE DESERT. IT IS VERY MISCHIEVOUS AND LIKES TO APPEAR SUDDENLY AT NIGHT TO SCARE PEOPLE. WILLOWISPS ARE WEAK INDIVIDUALLY, BUT WHEN FIGHTING IN NUMBERS THEY ARE FORMIDABLE.

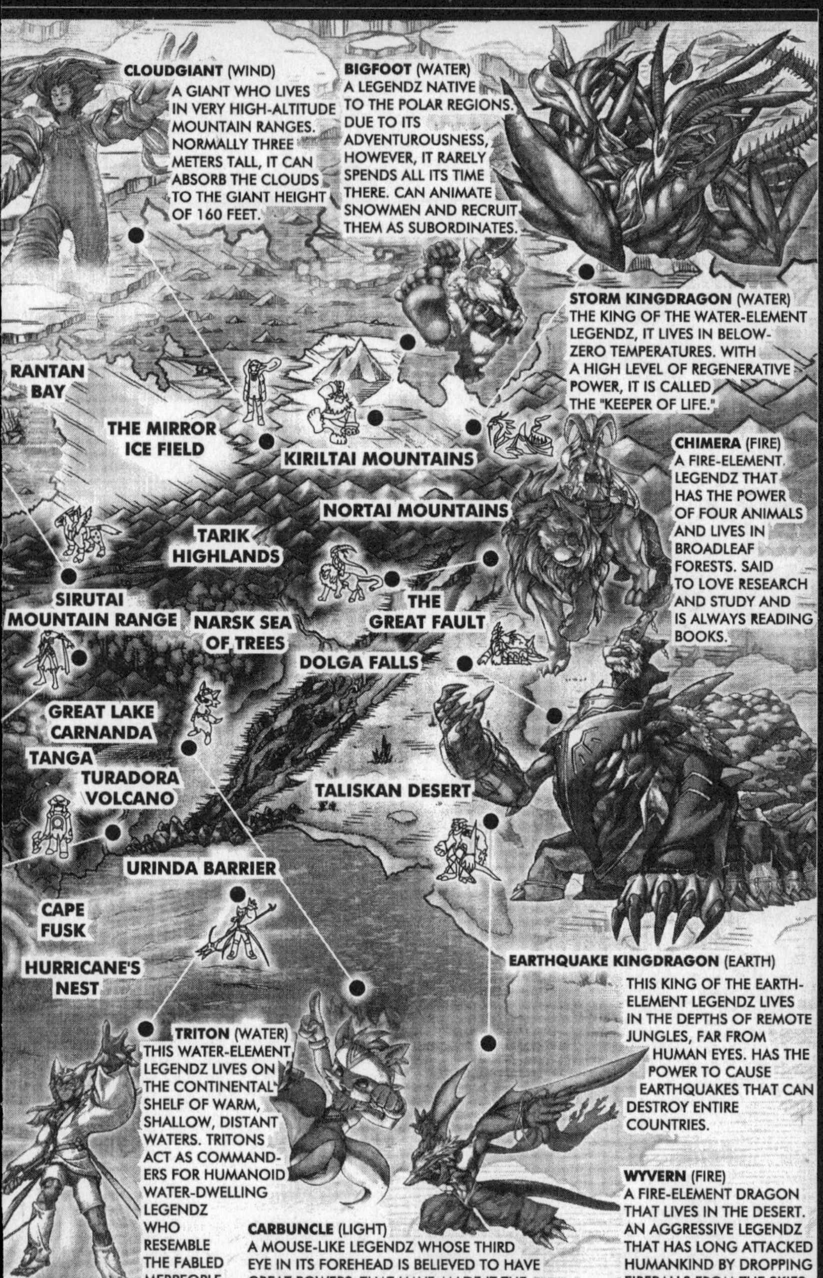
CLOUDGIANT (WIND)
A GIANT WHO LIVES IN VERY HIGH-ALTITUDE MOUNTAIN RANGES. NORMALLY THREE METERS TALL, IT CAN ABSORB THE CLOUDS TO THE GIANT HEIGHT OF 160 FEET.
BIGFOOT (WATER)
A LEGENDZ NATIVE TO THE POLAR REGIONS. DUE TO ITS ADVENTUROUSNESS, HOWEVER, IT RARELY SPENDS ALL ITS TIME THERE. CAN ANIMATE SNOWMEN AND RECRUIT THEM AS SUBORDINATES.
STORM KINGDRAGON (WATER)
THE KING OF THE WATER-ELEMENT LEGENDZ, IT LIVES IN BELOW-ZERO TEMPERATURES. WITH A HIGH LEVEL OF REGENERATIVE POWER, IT IS CALLED THE "KEEPER OF LIFE."
RANTAN BAY
THE MIRROR ICE FIELD
KIRILTAI MOUNTAINS
CHIMERA (FIRE)
A FIRE-ELEMENT LEGENDZ THAT HAS THE POWER OF FOUR ANIMALS AND LIVES IN BROADLEAF FORESTS. SAID TO LOVE RESEARCH AND STUDY AND IS ALWAYS READING BOOKS.
NORTAI MOUNTAINS
TARIK HIGHLANDS
THE GREAT FAULT
SIRUTAI MOUNTAIN RANGE
NARSK SEA OF TREES
DOLGA FALLS
GREAT LAKE CARNANDA
TANGA
TURADORA VOLCANO
TALISKAN DESERT
URINDA BARRIER
CAPE FUSK
HURRICANE'S NEST
EARTHQUAKE KINGDRAGON (EARTH)
THIS KING OF THE EARTH-ELEMENT LEGENDZ LIVES IN THE DEPTHS OF REMOTE JUNGLES, FAR FROM HUMAN EYES. HAS THE POWER TO CAUSE EARTHQUAKES THAT CAN DESTROY ENTIRE COUNTRIES.
TRITON (WATER)
THIS WATER-ELEMENT LEGENDZ LIVES ON THE CONTINENTAL SHELF OF WARM, SHALLOW, DISTANT WATERS. TRITONS ACT AS COMMANDERS FOR HUMANOID WATER-DWELLING LEGENDZ WHO RESEMBLE THE FABLED MERPEOPLE.
WYVERN (FIRE)
A FIRE-ELEMENT DRAGON THAT LIVES IN THE DESERT. AN AGGRESSIVE LEGENDZ THAT HAS LONG ATTACKED HUMANKIND BY DROPPING FIREBALLS FROM THE SKIES. AS SUCH, IT HAS BEEN FEARED SINCE THE START OF HUMAN HISTORY.
CARBUNCLE (LIGHT)
A MOUSE-LIKE LEGENDZ WHOSE THIRD EYE IN ITS FOREHEAD IS BELIEVED TO HAVE GREAT POWERS THAT HAVE MADE IT THE TARGET OF HUNTERS FOR MANY YEARS PAST. RUMORED TO RESIDE QUIETLY IN TROPICAL JUNGLES.

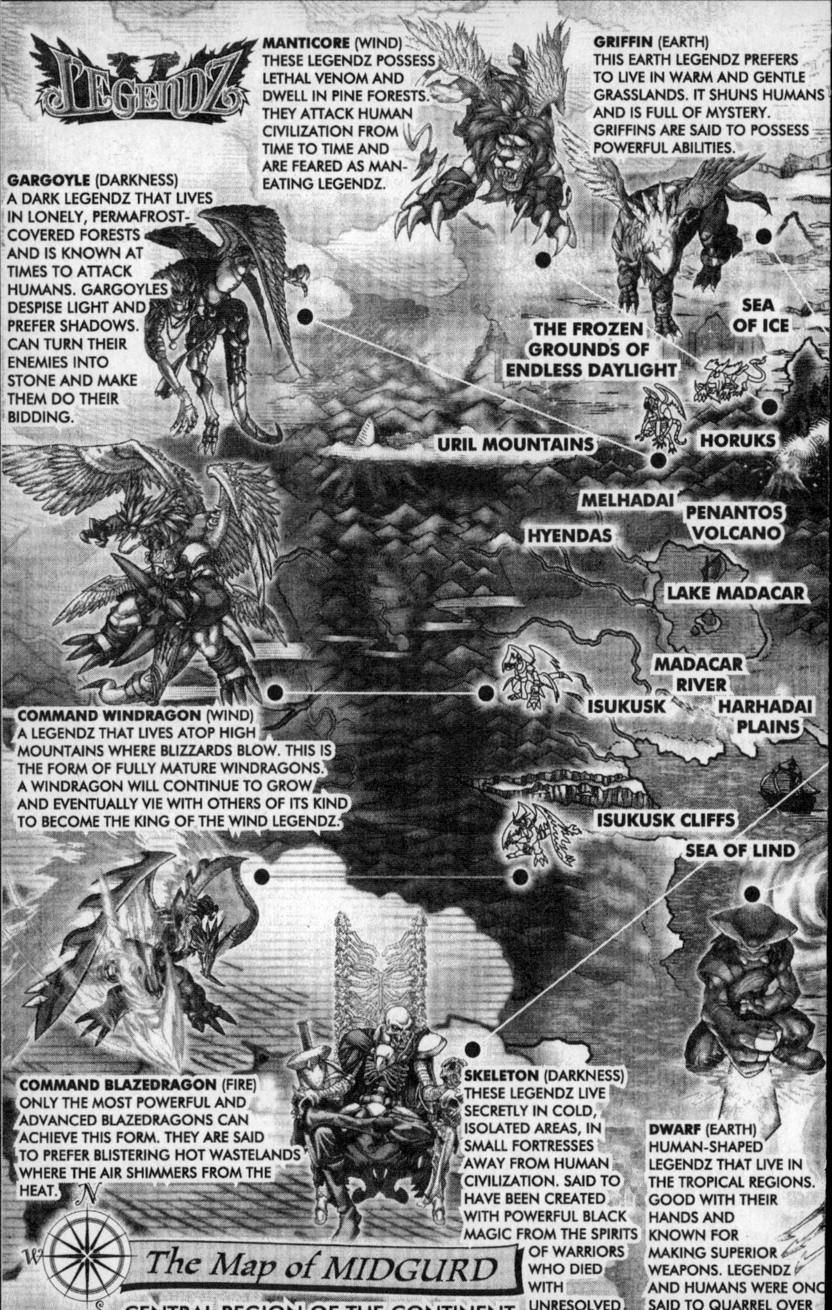
LEGENDZ
MANTICORE (WIND)
THESE LEGENDZ POSSESS LETHAL VENOM AND DWELL IN PINE FORESTS. THEY ATTACK HUMAN CIVILIZATION FROM TIME TO TIME AND ARE FEARED AS MAN-EATING LEGENDZ.
GRIFFIN (EARTH)
THIS EARTH LEGENDZ PREFERS TO LIVE IN WARM AND GENTLE GRASSLANDS. IT SHUNS HUMANS AND IS FULL OF MYSTERY. GRIFFINS ARE SAID TO POSSESS POWERFUL ABILITIES.
GARGOYLE (DARKNESS)
A DARK LEGENDZ THAT LIVES IN LONELY, PERMAFROST-COVERED FORESTS AND IS KNOWN AT TIMES TO ATTACK HUMANS. GARGOYLES DESPISE LIGHT AND PREFER SHADOWS. CAN TURN THEIR ENEMIES INTO STONE AND MAKE THEM DO THEIR BIDDING.
SEA OF ICE
THE FROZEN GROUNDS OF ENDLESS DAYLIGHT
URIL MOUNTAINS
HORUKS
MELHADAI
PENANTOS VOLCANO
HYENDAS
LAKE MADACAR
MADACAR RIVER
ISUKUSK
HARHADAI PLAINS
COMMAND WINDRAGON (WIND)
A LEGENDZ THAT LIVES ATOP HIGH MOUNTAINS WHERE BLIZZARDS BLOW. THIS IS THE FORM OF FULLY MATURE WINDRAGONS. A WINDRAGON WILL CONTINUE TO GROW AND EVENTUALLY VIE WITH OTHERS OF ITS KIND TO BECOME THE KING OF THE WIND LEGENDZ.
ISUKUSK CLIFFS
SEA OF LIND
COMMAND BLAZEDRAGON (FIRE)
ONLY THE MOST POWERFUL AND ADVANCED BLAZEDRAGONS CAN ACHIEVE THIS FORM. THEY ARE SAID TO PREFER BLISTERING HOT WASTELANDS WHERE THE AIR SHIMMERS FROM THE HEAT.
SKELETON (DARKNESS)
THESE LEGENDZ LIVE SECRETLY IN COLD, ISOLATED AREAS, IN SMALL FORTRESSES AWAY FROM HUMAN CIVILIZATION. SAID TO HAVE BEEN CREATED WITH POWERFUL BLACK MAGIC FROM THE SPIRITS OF WARRIORS WHO DIED WITH UNRESOLVED HATRED.
DWARF (EARTH)
HUMAN-SHAPED LEGENDZ THAT LIVE IN THE TROPICAL REGIONS. GOOD WITH THEIR HANDS AND KNOWN FOR MAKING SUPERIOR WEAPONS. LEGENDZ AND HUMANS WERE ONC SAID TO QUARREL OVER DWARF-MADE WEAPONS.
N
W
S
The Map of MIDGURD
CENTRAL REGION OF THE CONTINENT

HOBBY "LEGENDZ" ARE BORN

THE VIDEO GAME "LEGENDZ" WAS CREATED FROM THE RESEARCH OF THE EXCAVATED TALISPOD AND SOUL FIGURES. THE PLAYER, OR SAGA, RAISES AND BATTLES THE LEGENDARY CREATURES CONTAINED WITHIN TO CREATE A POWERFUL LEGENDZ.

LEGENDZ DISCOVERY

⇩

LEGENDZ RESEARCH

⇩

LEGENDZ TOY CREATION

← THE RESEARCH INTO THESE LEGENDARY CREATURES HAS DEVELOPED INTO THE ULTIMATE HOBBY.

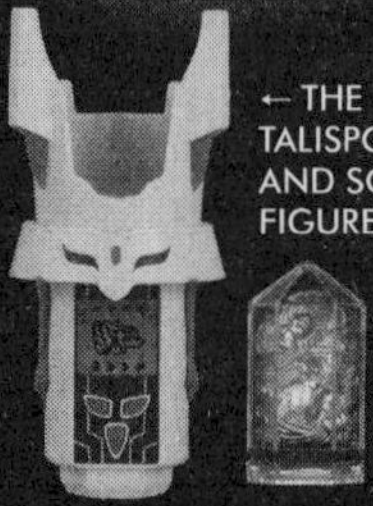

← THE TALISPOD AND SOUL FIGURE

- **LEGENDZ BATTLES GAINING EXPLOSIVE POPULARITY.**

HAVE YOU EXPERIENCED THIS ULTIMATE HOBBY YET? IF YOU HAVEN'T, RUSH TO THE TOY STORE NOW!

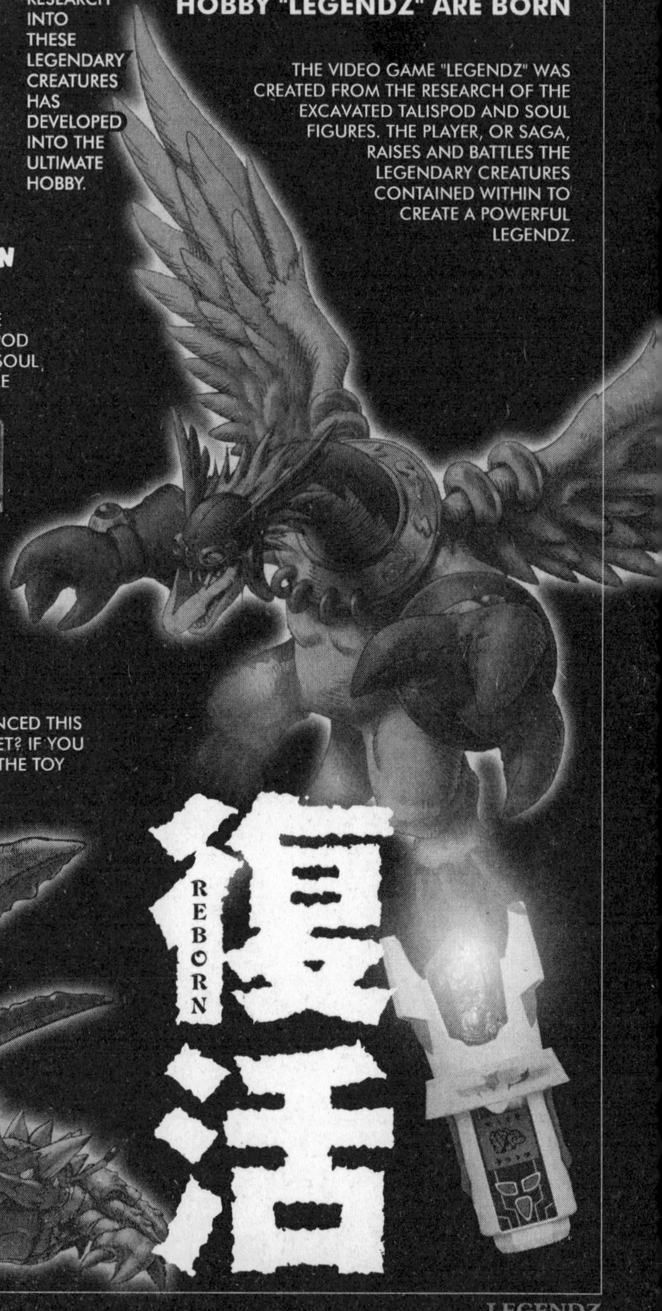
復活
REBORN

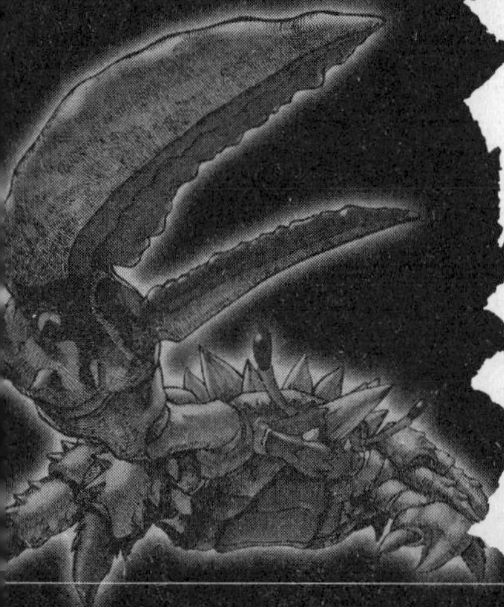

THE LEGEND OF THE SAGAS

WE'VE ASKED THESE SAGAS WHY LEGENDZ BATTLES ARE SO MUCH FUN!

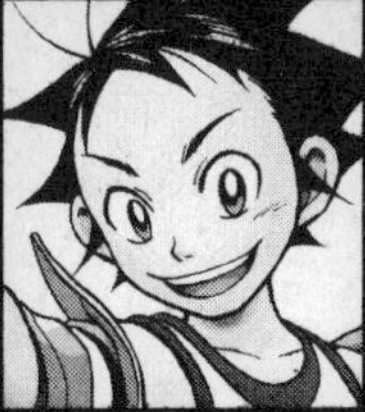

KEN KAZAKI (11 YRS)
FIFTH-GRADER AT
RYUDO ELEMENTARY

PRESENTLY DOING EXTREME BATTLES IN THE MANGA!
BATTLES ARE THE MOST FUN! IT'S EXCITING TO BATTLE STRONG OPPONENTS, AND IT'S NEVER BORING BECAUSE THERE ARE SO MANY TYPES OF LEGENDZ. AFTER THE BATTLE, YOU CAN TALK ABOUT LEGENDZ AND BECOME FRIENDS RIGHT AWAY. ALSO, IF YOU BATTLE AND RAISE YOUR LEGENDZ FOR A LONG TIME, THEY CAN BECOME YOUR REAL PALS, SO IT'S GREAT!!

LEGENDZ CARNIVAL SPONSOR!
THE ULTIMATE HOBBY, HMM? HMPH... IT MUST BE NICE TO BE SO IGNORANT. YOU MUST BE AS STUPID AS ALL THOSE PEOPLE WHO THINK THAT THE LEGENDZ CARNIVAL IS JUST ANOTHER TOURNAMENT. THE ULTIMATE PURPOSE OF LEGENDZ IS A "LEGENDZ WAR." THAT SHOULD BECOME APPARENT VERY SOON. UNTIL THEN, ENJOY YOURSELVES, KIDS.

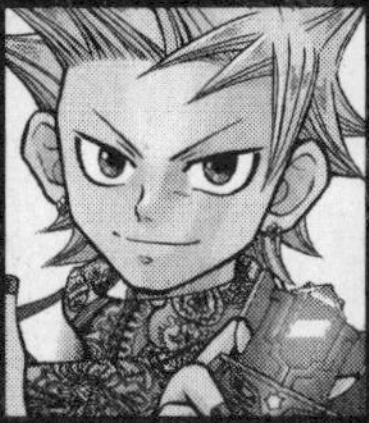

LEO ENGOKUIN
(11 YRS)
DWC HEIR

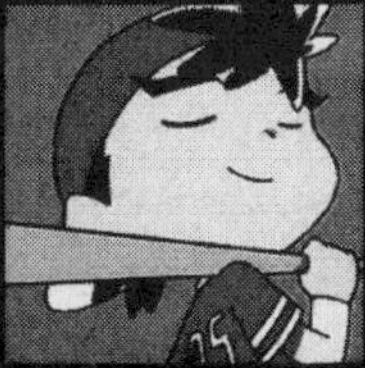

SHUZO MATSUTANI
(11 YRS)
FIFTH-GRADER AT
BROOKLYN 101 ELEMENTARY

BATTLES IN THE ANIME! A WIND SAGA!
LEGENDZ? I'M MORE INTO BASEBALL. THE GIRLS REALLY LIKE ME, TOO. THAT NEZU IS ALWAYS BUGGING ME, BUT SOMETIMES I'LL HANG OUT WITH THE LADY FROM THE DWC. BUT MAN, THAT ANNA WAS CUTE. IT'D BE GREAT IF ALL THE LEGENDZ WERE LIKE HER, BUT THEY'RE MOSTLY SCARY-LOOKING

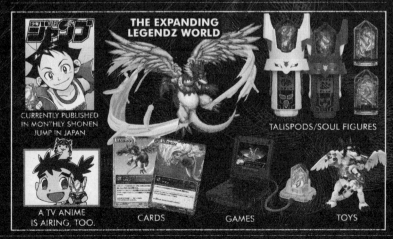

THE EXPANDING LEGENDZ WORLD

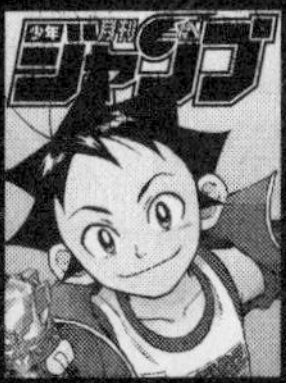

CURRENTLY PUBLISHED IN MONTHLY SHONEN JUMP IN JAPAN.

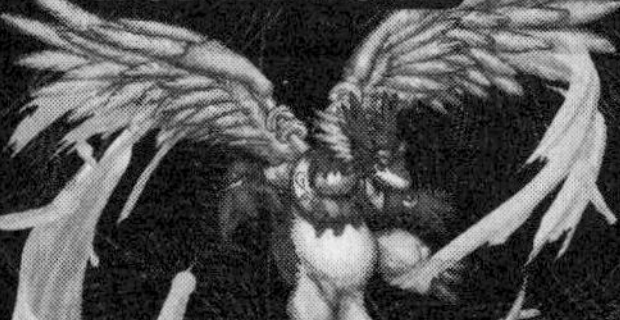

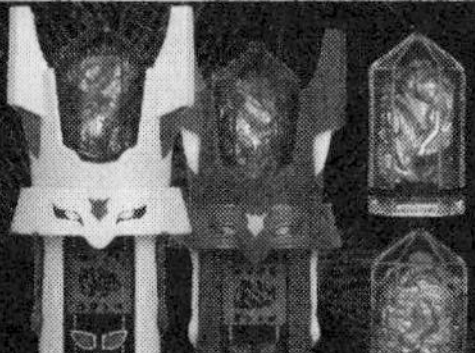

TALISPODS/SOUL FIGURES

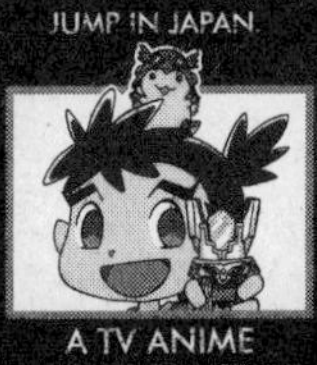

A TV ANIME IS AIRING, TOO.

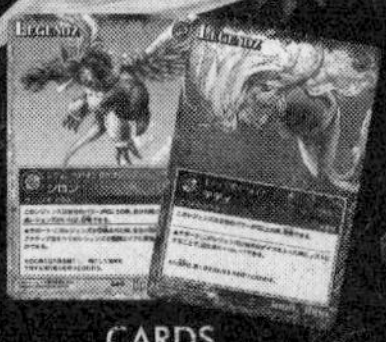

CARDS

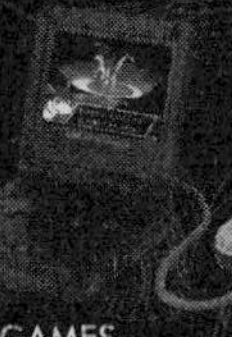

GAMES

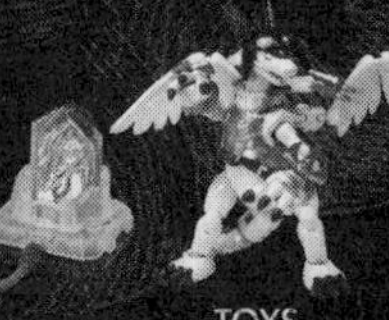

TOYS

In The Next Volume...

Ken and Kaoruko may have recovered the mysterious crystal, but it's only a matter of time before the ruthless Leo catches up to them. Driven by his own personal demons, Leo will stop at nothing to possess the crystal. But he isn't the only one—the agents of darkness are bent on claiming it for their own sinister ends!

Coming in November 2005!

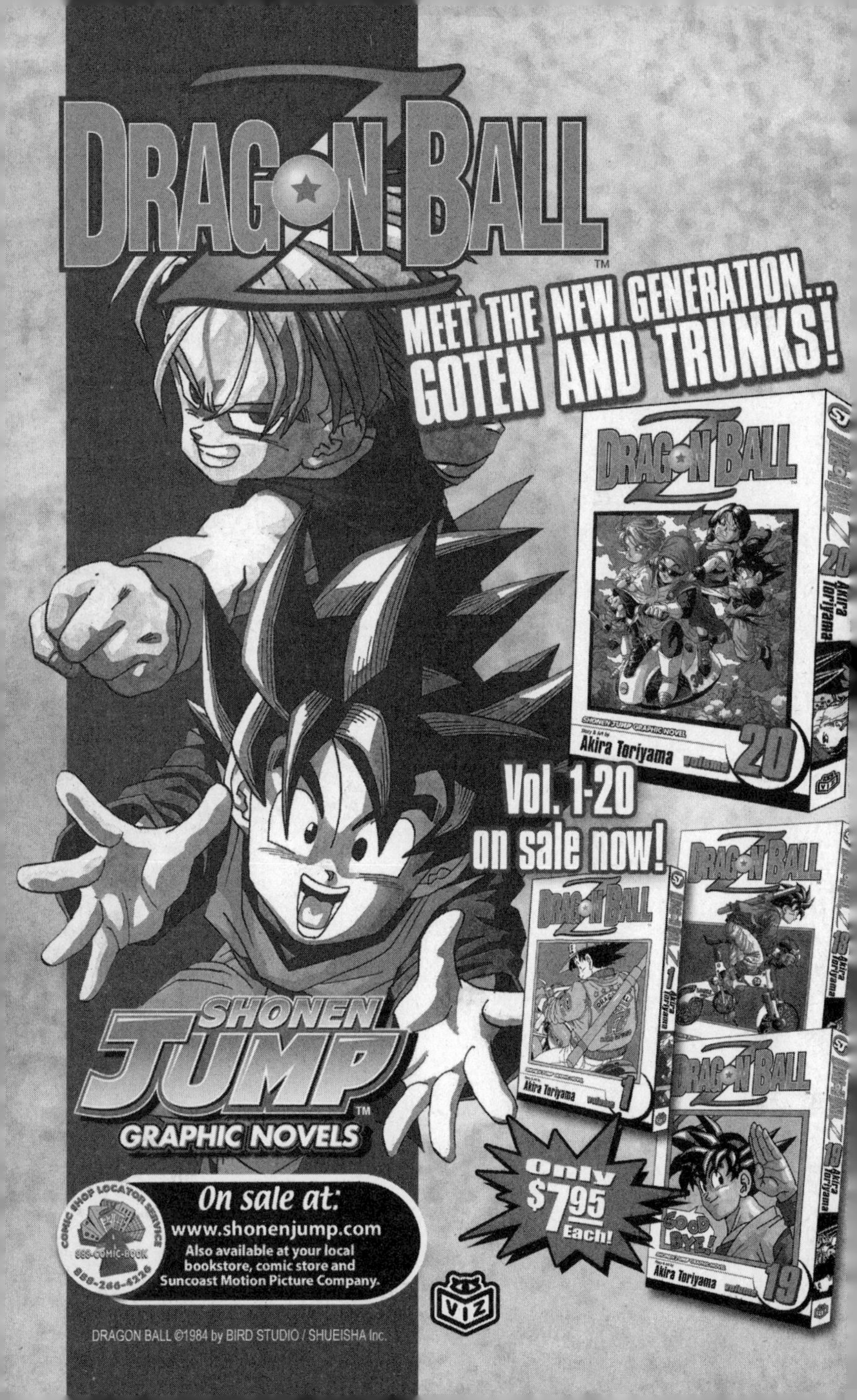
DRAGON BALL Z
MEET THE NEW GENERATION...
GOTEN AND TRUNKS!
Akira Toriyama
Vol. 1-20
on sale now!
Only
$7.95
Each!
SHONEN JUMP
GRAPHIC NOVELS
On sale at:
www.shonenjump.com
Also available at your local
bookstore, comic store and
Suncoast Motion Picture Company.
COMIC SHOP LOCATOR SERVICE
888-COMIC-BOOK
888-266-4226
VIZ
DRAGON BALL ©1984 by BIRD STUDIO / SHUEISHA Inc.

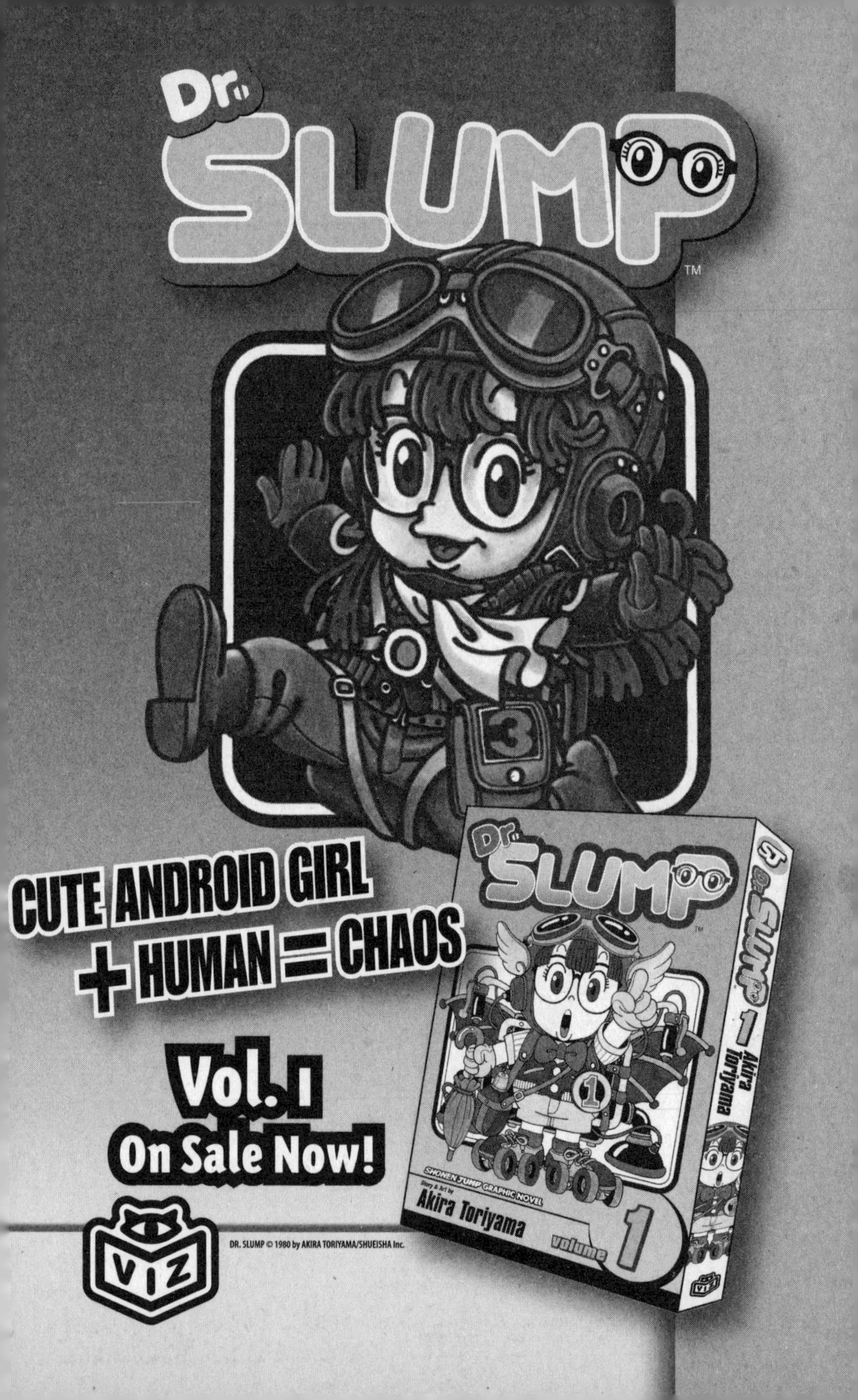
Dr. SLUMP
CUTE ANDROID GIRL + HUMAN = CHAOS
Vol. 1
On Sale Now!
Dr. SLUMP
SHONEN JUMP GRAPHIC NOVEL
Story & Art by
Akira Toriyama
volume 1
Dr. SLUMP 1 Akira Toriyama
VIZ
DR. SLUMP © 1980 by AKIRA TORIYAMA/SHUEISHA Inc.

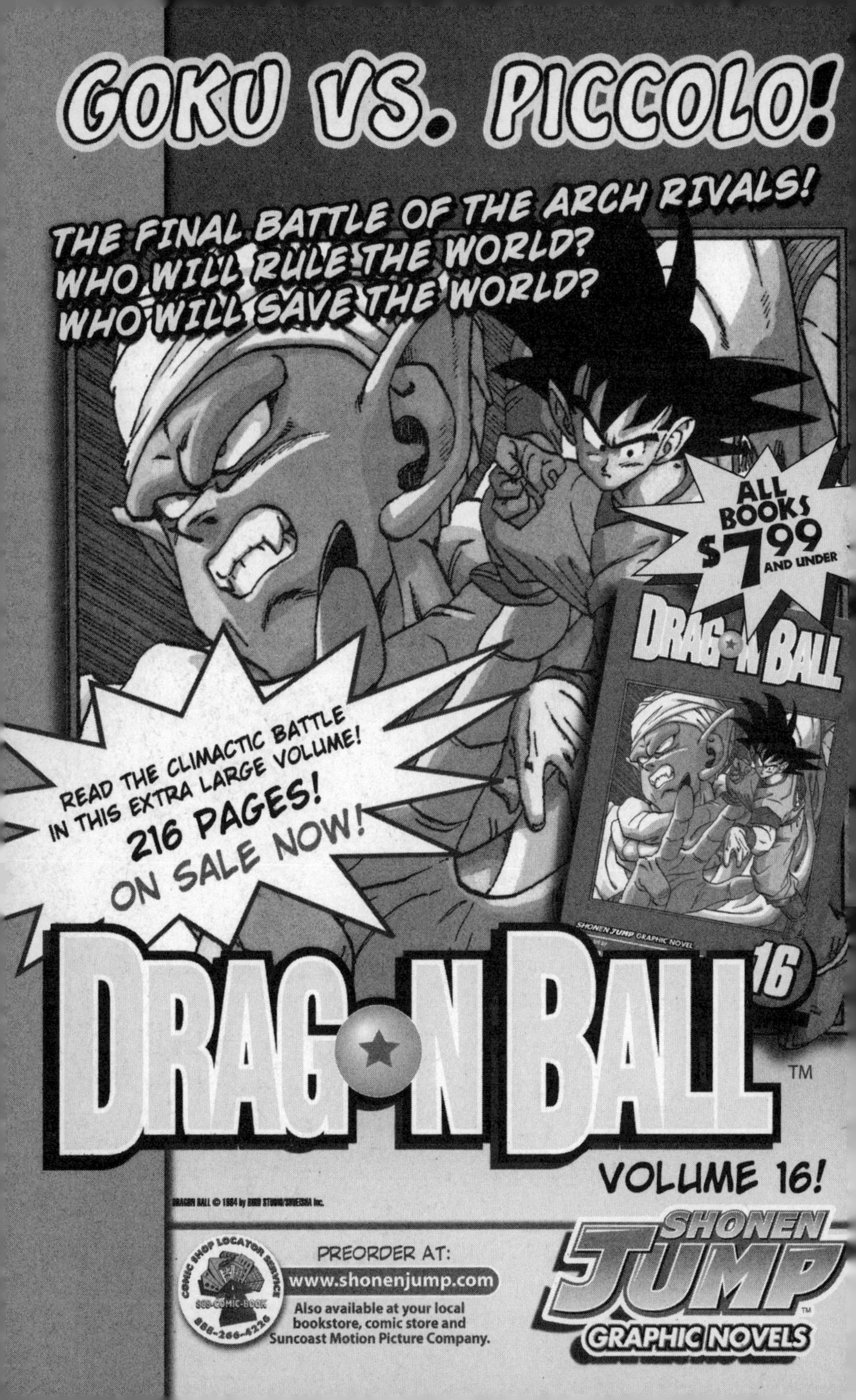
GOKU VS. PICCOLO!
THE FINAL BATTLE OF THE ARCH RIVALS!
WHO WILL RULE THE WORLD?
WHO WILL SAVE THE WORLD?
ALL BOOKS $7.99 AND UNDER
READ THE CLIMACTIC BATTLE IN THIS EXTRA LARGE VOLUME!
216 PAGES!
ON SALE NOW!
DRAGON BALL 16
VOLUME 16!
DRAGON BALL © 1984 by BIRD STUDIO/SHUEISHA Inc.
COMIC SHOP LOCATOR SERVICE
888-COMIC-BOOK
888-266-4226
PREORDER AT:
www.shonenjump.com
Also available at your local bookstore, comic store and Suncoast Motion Picture Company.
SHONEN JUMP GRAPHIC NOVELS

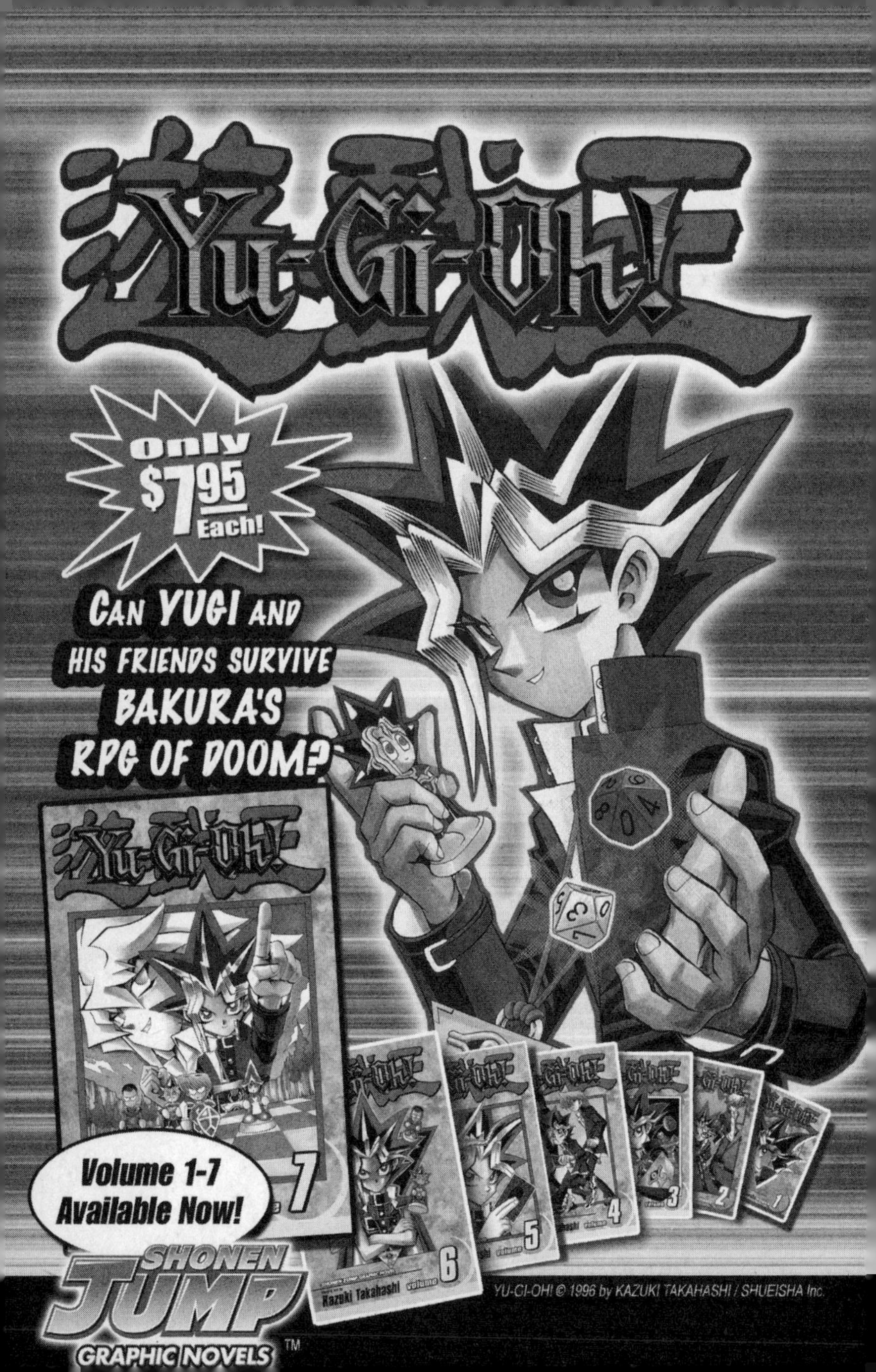

YU-GI-OH!
Only $7.95 Each!
CAN YUGI AND HIS FRIENDS SURVIVE BAKURA'S RPG OF DOOM?
Volume 1-7 Available Now!
SHONEN JUMP GRAPHIC NOVELS
YU-GI-OH! © 1996 by KAZUKI TAKAHASHI / SHUEISHA Inc.

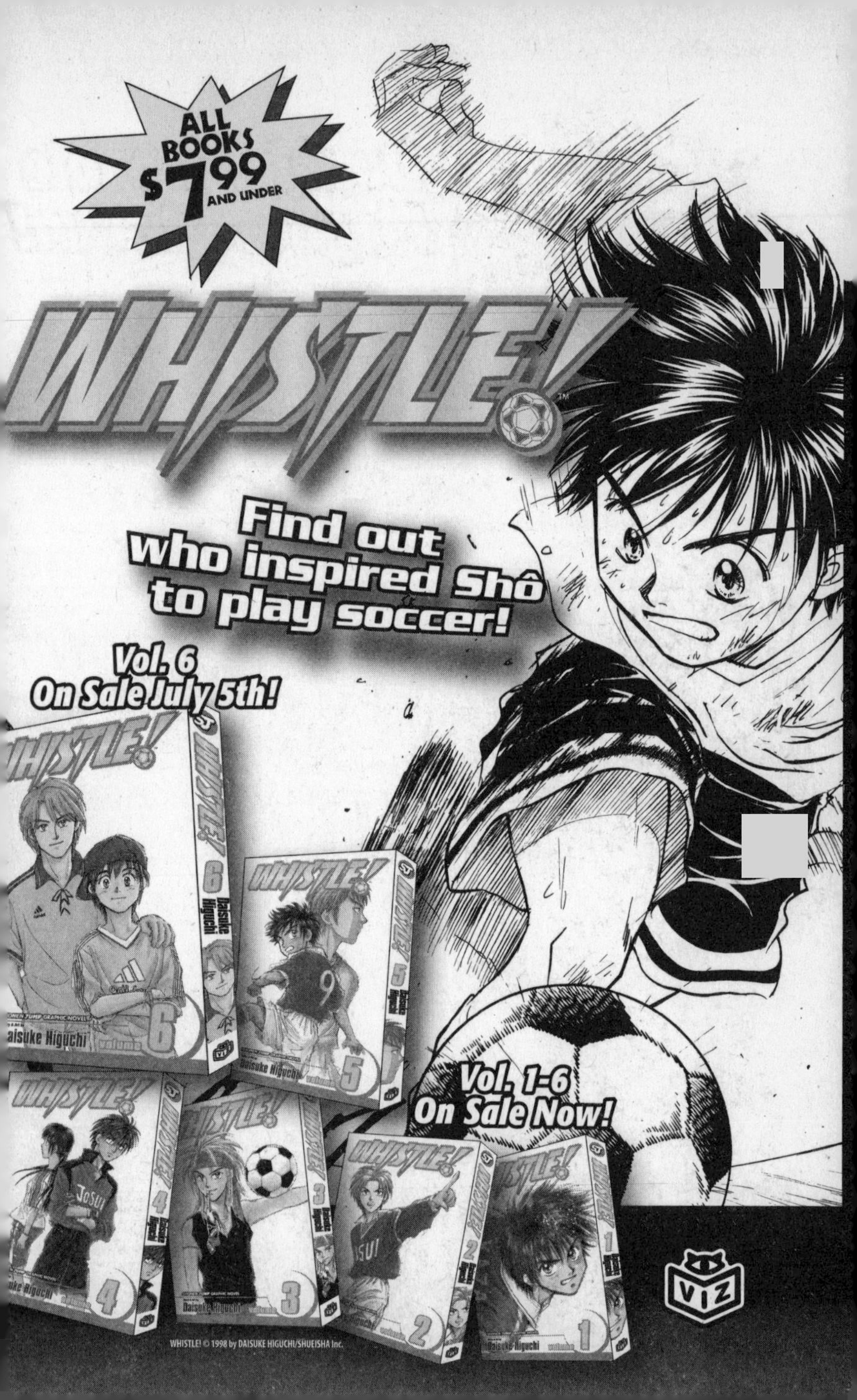
ALL BOOKS $7.99 AND UNDER
WHISTLE!
Find out who inspired Shô to play soccer!
Vol. 6 On Sale July 5th!
Vol. 1-6 On Sale Now!
VIZ
WHISTLE! © 1998 by DAISUKE HIGUCHI/SHUEISHA Inc.

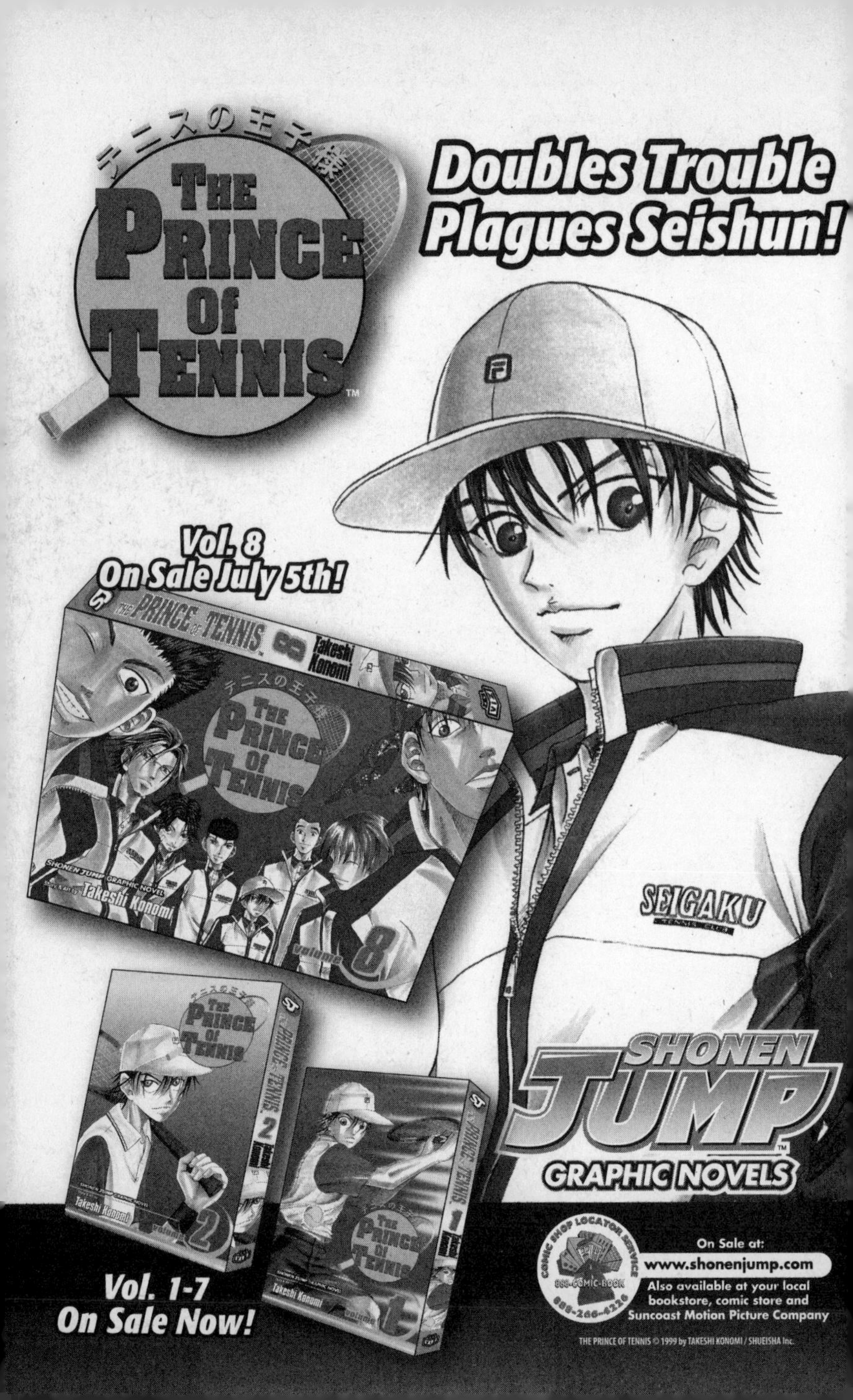

テニスの王子様
THE PRINCE OF TENNIS™
Doubles Trouble Plagues Seishun!
Vol. 8 On Sale July 5th!
SHONEN JUMP GRAPHIC NOVELS
Vol. 1-7 On Sale Now!
On Sale at:
www.shonenjump.com
Also available at your local bookstore, comic store and Suncoast Motion Picture Company
COMIC SHOP LOCATOR SERVICE 888-COMIC-BOOK 888-266-4226
THE PRINCE OF TENNIS © 1999 by TAKESHI KONOMI / SHUEISHA Inc.

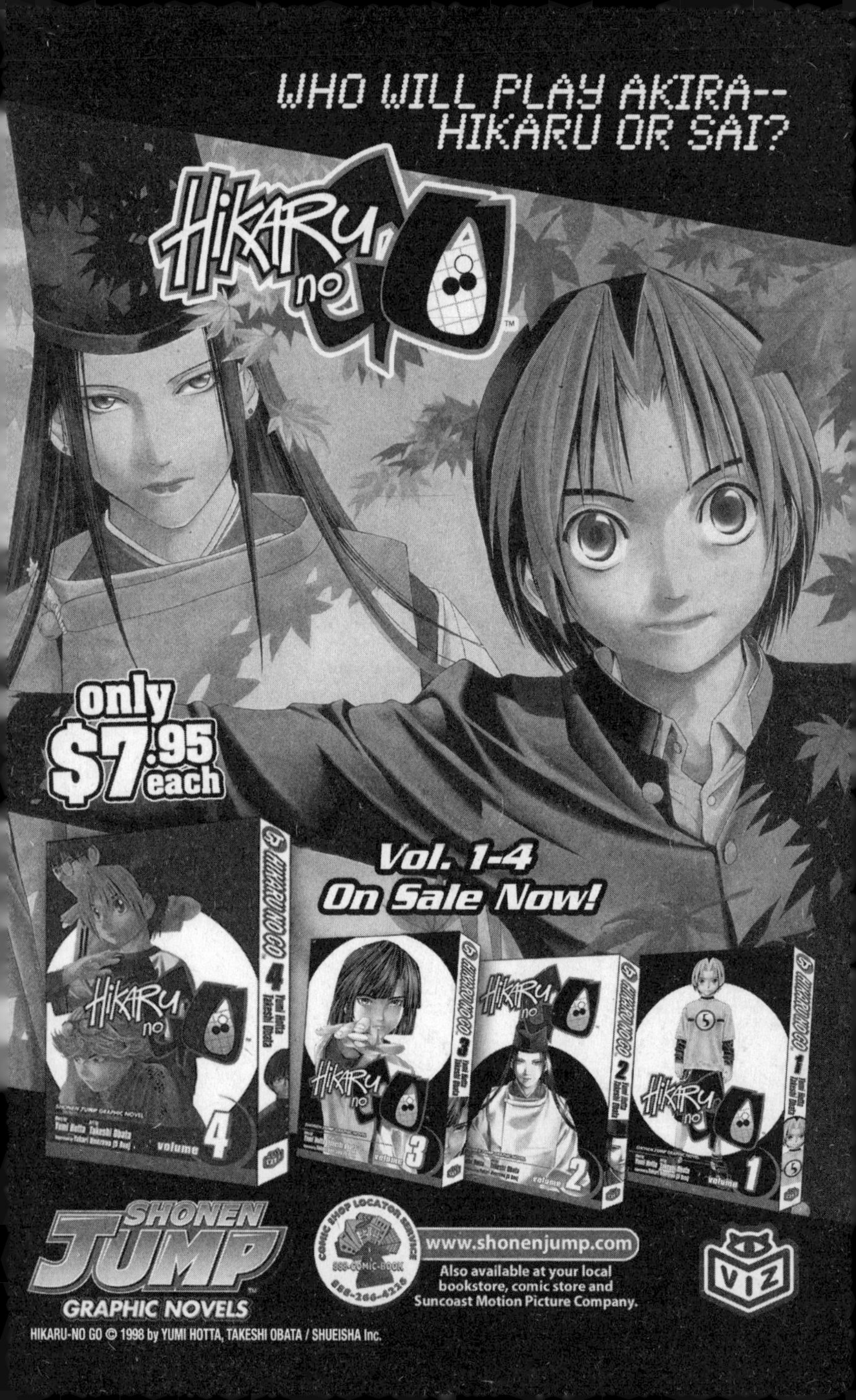
WHO WILL PLAY AKIRA--
HIKARU OR SAI?
Hikaru no Go™
only $7.95 each
Vol. 1-4
On Sale Now!
SHONEN JUMP
GRAPHIC NOVELS
COMIC SHOP LOCATOR SERVICE
888-COMIC-BOOK
888-266-4226
www.shonenjump.com
Also available at your local
bookstore, comic store and
Suncoast Motion Picture Company.
VIZ
HIKARU-NO GO © 1998 by YUMI HOTTA, TAKESHI OBATA / SHUEISHA Inc.

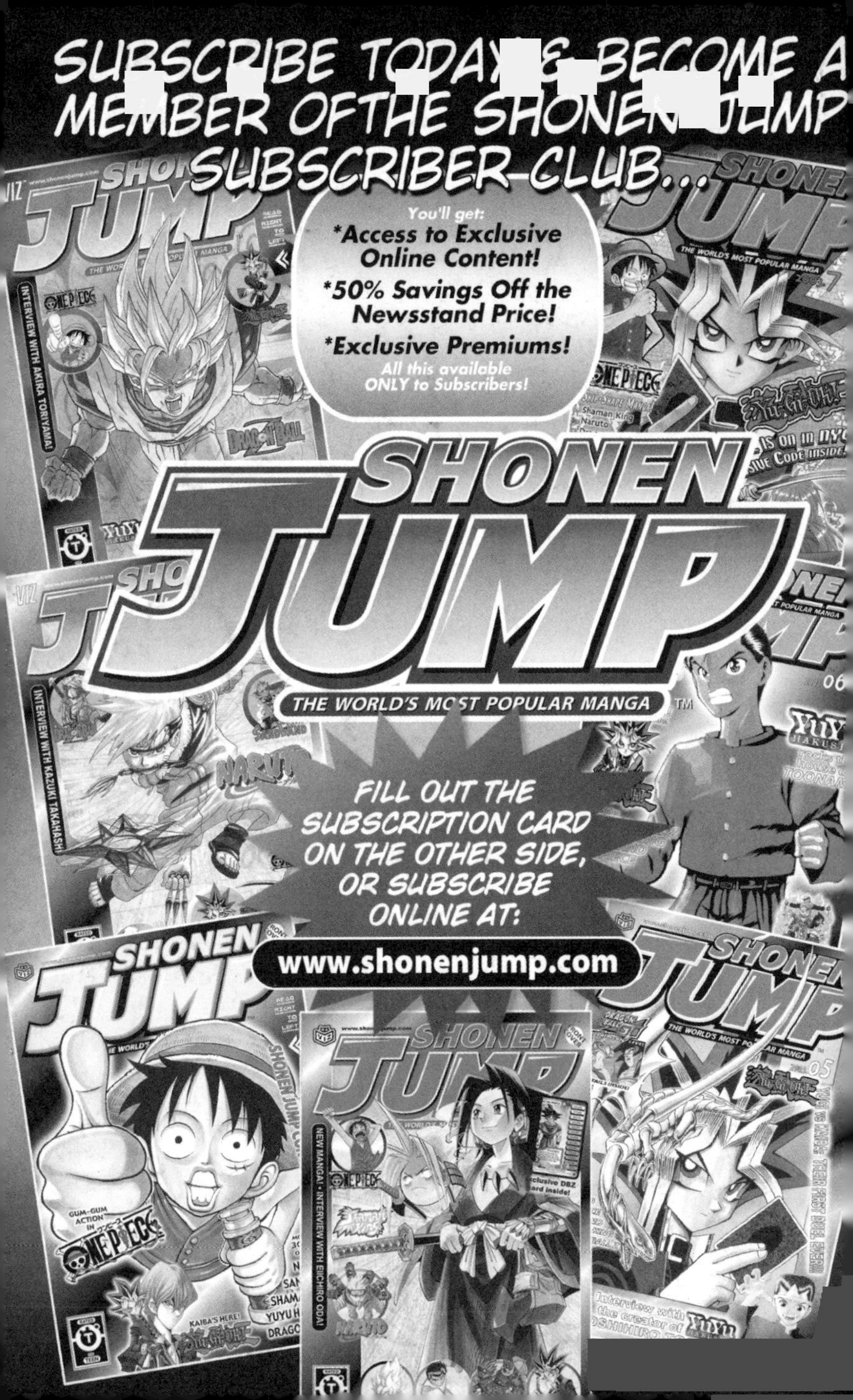

SUBSCRIBE TODAY & BECOME A MEMBER OF THE SHONEN JUMP SUBSCRIBER CLUB...
You'll get:
*Access to Exclusive Online Content!
*50% Savings Off the Newsstand Price!
*Exclusive Premiums!
All this available ONLY to Subscribers!
SHONEN JUMP
THE WORLD'S MOST POPULAR MANGA
FILL OUT THE SUBSCRIPTION CARD ON THE OTHER SIDE, OR SUBSCRIBE ONLINE AT:
www.shonenjump.com